Why I Believed

Why I Believed

Reflections of a Former Missionary

Kenneth W. Daniels

Duncanville, Texas

Kenneth W. Daniels (1968–), former evangelical missionary with Wycliffe Bible Translators, received his BS in computer science and engineering from LeTourneau University, Longview, Texas, and a one-year certificate in biblical studies from Columbia Biblical Seminary (now Columbia International University), Columbia, SC. He currently resides with his wife and three children in suburban Dallas, TX, where he works as a software developer.

PUBLISHED BY
Kenneth W. Daniels
Duncanville, TX 75137, USA
believed@kwdaniels.com
www.kwdaniels.com

Chapter 2 contains a revised version of the electronically published "From Missionary Bible Translator to Agnostic" (Daniels 2003), reprinted with the permission of the editor of *The Secular Web*.

ISBN-13: 978-0-578-00388-7

Contents

Foreword

Kenneth W. Daniels has produced a powerful work that will give Christian readers much to think about. *Why I Believed: Reflections of a Former Missionary* is an important book that should be widely read. The author's approach is gentle and honest while still managing to be unflinching and thorough. As a former fundamentalist Christian missionary who devoted far more time and energy than most to serving that religion, he obviously remembers what it feels like to be fully immersed in belief. Fortunately, Daniels has retained plenty of sympathy for those who cannot yet see that the supernatural claims of Christianity cannot stand up to honest scrutiny.

This brilliant book is not a vicious attack on Christians. It is a strong but polite plea for them to see and hear new ideas, to consider the possibility that their belief system might be a mistake. Daniels maintains a humble tone throughout the book. He does not blast believers with arrogant claims of intellectual superiority on the question of faith. He simply shares thoughts and questions about his journey through Christianity and escape from it. This is a powerful story and Daniels has many piercing ideas that are likely to carry considerable weight with believers because of his difficult work as a missionary in Africa. Daniels earned his stripes as a committed Christian. He went way beyond the easy life of a casual Christian sitting in a pew on Sunday mornings. He lived his Christianity; he made serious commitments and followed through with sacrifices for his religion. For someone like him to walk away from it, with great reluctance, humility, and no rage says a lot. It gives Daniels tremendous credibility.

Daniels is well read and obviously knowledgeable about Christianity. Most importantly, however, he has retained a sense of respect and compassion for believers. Yes, he thinks they are wrong about their religious claims, but he has not turned his back on them as fellow humans. It is likely that many Christians will struggle to reconcile the wisdom and challenges found within *Why I Believed* with their own beliefs. The author's impressive logic and intelligence, combined with a sensitive approach and his top-notch credentials as a Christian missionary, make it impossible for anyone to dismiss him as an angry crank or an irrelevant outsider. Daniels walked the walk, believing and serving with far more sincerity and dedication than most believers do. He writes:

> I invite Christian readers to consider the possibility that my apostasy is a result not of divine or diabolical deception but of a simple weighing of the evidence. . . . It might be that I am wrong. It might be that I have not sought God sufficiently or studied the Bible thoroughly enough or listened carefully enough to the many Christians who have admonished me. . . . Maybe. But the knowledge that billions of seekers have lived and died, calling out to God for some definitive revelation without ever receiving it, or receiving revelation that conflicts with the revelation others have found, contributes to my suspicion that there is no personal God who reveals himself to anyone.

This is a book I will give to Christians because it is forceful and devastating to their irrational beliefs without belittling or mocking them. That Daniels is able to make such a powerful case against Christianity is impressive enough; that he is able to do it without drifting into attacks and name-calling makes *Why I Believed* an important book that should be read and discussed by both believers and nonbelievers.

Wisdom and compassion shine through on many pages of this book. The author clearly wants nothing more than a more rational and peaceful world. He does not seem interested in battering believers with a heavy club of merciless skepticism. Daniels writes:

> Most believers are not prepared to travel as far as I have from my former position as a fundamentalist believer. I implore such readers to consider a middle ground, one that acknowledges both the virtues and vices of the scriptures, as millions of moderate and liberal believers already do. While it is unrealistic to expect a large percentage of Muslims to abandon their faith, most of us can agree that the world would be a better place if Muslim fundamentalists moderated their rigid commitment to every precept of the Qur'an as the divine word of Allah, especially those that call for the destruction of infidels and apostates. Likewise, the world would be a better place if fundamentalist Christians could frankly acknowledge the good, the bad, and the ugly in their own scriptural tradition, whether or not they end up abandoning their faith outright.

I love the honesty of *Why I Believed*. Daniels does not cherry pick by pointing out everything silly and negative about Christianity. In fact, he admits to missing some things about his days as a believer:

> I regret the loss of the almost automatic acceptance I enjoyed on the part of those who belonged with me to the same community of faith, the same church, the same missionary society. . . . There is no sugarcoating the reality that secularists in general do not enjoy the same benefits of a warm community that committed believers typically do. . . . I see the safety net and

fellowship of the church, coupled with the lack thereof outside the church, as one of the most important impediments to the growth of free thought.

Yes, Christians are likely to struggle with this book and find their beliefs on shaky ground, for it packs a mighty combination punch of honesty, reason, and kindness.

Guy P. Harrison
Author of *50 Reasons People Give for Believing in a God.*

Preface

What would you do if you had a sneaking suspicion, and then a growing fear, that your most cherished beliefs about God and the universe were built on sinking sand? What would you do if you wanted to know the truth about something but were devastated by what you learned upon further investigation—that, for example, your spouse was cheating on you, that your son was committing sex crimes, or that your trusted business partner was stealing from you? What if you came to realize that everything you sincerely believed and wanted to be true was false? What would you do?

This book is the story of what happened as the foundation of my faith turned to quicksand beneath my feet.

In this volume I present in some detail the problems I encountered with the claims of Christianity while serving as an evangelical missionary in Africa. Attention to detail makes the difference between a safe plane flight and a crash, between successful surgery and disaster, between engineering an electronic instrument that works and one that doesn't, or between writing a robust computer program or one that fizzles. "The devil is in the details." This is the story of how I studied the details of Christianity and found it wanting.

I am well aware of the risks of undertaking this project. It might lead to alienation from friends, family, and coworkers. But, for reasons I explain later, it is a risk I must take. I mean no ill will against anyone who reads this book and disagrees with my conclusions. I struggled throughout to maintain a balance between respecting my readers and calling a spade a spade. It is not my intent to offend.

This book is not a treatise on the factors that have contributed to the rise of religion in human history, nor is it an attempt to explain why religion retains its appeal for the majority of humanity today. These broader questions are explored in works such as *Breaking the Spell: Religion as a Natural Phenomenon* (Dennett 2006) and the ambitiously titled "The Big Religion Questions Finally Solved" (Paul 2008). My effort is a more limited retrospective on the reasons for my particular brand of Christian belief, as best as I can recall them.

A note on style: I hope to speak both to friends and family and to the Christian community at large. One reviewer considered the style overly formal and wordy for friends and family. Another reviewer insisted I keep it the way it is in order to convey fully the breadth and depth of my reasons for leaving the faith. For now, I have retained a somewhat formal approach, but I may consider an abbreviated, informal and lighter version in the future.

Whether or not you agree with my conclusions, I trust we as a society can ultimately succeed in carrying out a civil discourse among those who see the world in very different ways. I certainly do not expect most of you to be swayed by reading a single book (unless you are already entertaining doubts), but for those of you who do begin a journey away from faith, I trust it will be for you an adventure full of pleasant surprises, even when mixed with inevitable conflict and pain.

I wish to thank the many freethinkers and heretics who have gone before me, some of whom risked or lost their lives as a result of their break with the prevailing religious establishment. Many writers, both historical and modern, have contributed to my thinking, but I especially wish to acknowledge the influence of Thomas Paine, Robert Ingersoll, and Robert M. Price at critical junctures in my journey.

I also wish to thank a closet deist missionary physician who reviewed the manuscript and provided many helpful corrections and suggestions. In addition, I am grateful for the detailed feedback Norman E. Anderson provided on four key chapters. That said, all views expressed in this manuscript are my own, and I take responsibility for any errors.

Finally, I wish to thank my wife Charlene, who has faithfully loved me and stayed by my side despite our differences, and who (for the most part!) patiently put up with my many hours in front of the computer screen while I worked on this project.

Part I

Foundations

Chapter 1

Motives and Method

"It's so sad." This is the most common response I have heard from family, friends, and other interested believers upon learning of my loss of faith on the mission field.

I have been told that if I had embraced a slightly different brand of Christianity, I could have avoided coming down this path. It was because I believed incorrectly, or because I wasn't truly a believer in the first place, or because I did not seek God earnestly enough, or because I did not submit to his sovereignty, that I ended up abandoning the faith. At times I have explained to others my reasons for doubting, only to have these reasons dismissed with the question, "So what's the *real* reason you left God?" I often sense a conviction on their part that my disbelief must stem from an inward moral flaw.

It is not only Christians who wonder why I have left the faith—I, too, have been puzzled by these questions: Why me? Why not Joe? Why not Sally? What is it about my nature that has led me down this road, while the vast majority of believers never take this turn, even though at times they are troubled by doubt? Yet at some point it occurred to me that I had been looking at my experience from the wrong perspective. If I was justified in jumping ship, then a more appropriate question to ask was why I ever believed in the first place. And why did I remain a believer for as long as I did?

Like many believers, I was aware of puzzles in the Christian faith even in my youth. Most of us, whether or not we remain in the fold, have wondered about God's commands to the Israelite soldiers to kill men, women, boys and infants (keeping the virgins for themselves); his endorsement of slavery; the harshness of eternal hell; the apparent discrepancies between parallel passages in the Bible; the hit-and-miss nature of prayer; the mystery of so much human and animal suffering; the silence and hiddenness of God; the kindness and moral uprightness of so many nonbelievers; and the apparent conflict between science and the Bible. Given all these difficulties and many more, why did I not leave the faith earlier in my youth when I first became aware of these issues?

Many recognize problems and unanswered questions in their faith yet persist in believing as I did for years. This is no doubt due to overriding considerations that make belief appear attractive or true despite its difficulties. Throughout this book I will critically explore some of the most important reasons I delayed my exit from the faith. Many evangelicals cite these same factors as anchors for their faith. In short, I will use for my starting point not the problems and contradictions of Christianity per se, but the reasons most commonly advanced for believing. In so doing, I will also take the opportunity to demonstrate that many of these arguments turn out to be liabilities rather than assets for faith.

MY PURPOSE FOR WRITING

I am not naive enough to expect that most who read this book will abandon the faith they hold dear, but I do hope to convince my readers that many of us who walk away have not done so out of a rebellious, juvenile whim, but rather out of a careful weighing of the reasons for and against our former faith. Our decision, far from being "sad," as many of my friends and family perceive it, represents a move from unquestioning acceptance of tradition to a spirit of openness and adventure that pursues the evidence wherever it leads. We left in pursuit of truth.

Many books have been written along these lines, a number of which contributed to my own journey away from faith. So do I have something significant to add to what these books have already offered? My desire is to present the seldom-heard perspective of one whose life was formerly defined *for decades* by his commitment to Jesus and who continues to live successfully with family and friends who retain that commitment. This book brings together in one place the most important factors contributing to my particular journey away from faith.

My reasons for taking up this cause are quite personal. The great majority of my family members, both immediate and extended, are committed evangelical Christians, and I have no desire to sever my family ties over our religious differences. This puts me in a bind: the very ones I love most are praying for me, convinced I am the traitor and that the motives for my decision are suspect. If I could patch things up by forcing myself to believe again, I would do so in a heartbeat. Unfortunately I have tried that several times, only to be besieged again by doubt, and have come to the conclusion that attempting to will myself to believe that which in my heart I do not believe is futile. In this struggle I am not alone; *millions* of others have passed through the valley of the shadow of doubt, finding themselves unable to return to the pastures of faith, despite repeated appeals to God to restore their faith. We have prayed more times than we can count, "I do believe; help me overcome my unbelief!" (Mark 9:24)[1]

So my options are limited: (a) abandon my family; (b) live with them in an uneasy, suspicious truce; (c) somehow will myself to believe again, even if Christianity appears untrue; or (d) attempt to instill in others an appreciation for, if not full acceptance of, the reasons for my unbelief. This book is my effort to undertake option (d), the others having proven unviable or unsatisfactory.

Though my primary audience is my family and friends, I am also concerned to convey my experience to the wider world, especially to those in the evangelical and fundamentalist Christian communities. I appreciate my parents and my evangelical heritage for inculcating in me a deep respect for truth. It is my conviction that only good can come from knowing the truth, even if it seems at first glance too stark, too cold, too inhumane to bear. Nineteenth-century agnostic Thomas Huxley put it this way:

> Sit down before fact as a little child, be prepared to give up every preconceived notion, follow humbly wherever and to whatever abysses nature leads, or you shall learn nothing. I have only begun to learn content and peace of mind since I have resolved at all risks to do this (Huxley and Huxley 1901, 235).

Why should I be concerned with what other people believe, as long as they aren't causing any harm, or as long as their beliefs lead to admirable acts of charity? I have heard this objection from a number of Christians, an objection I find surprising in light of the Apostle Paul's view:

> And if Christ has not been raised, our preaching is useless and so is your faith. More than that, we are then found to be false witnesses about God, for we have testified about God that he raised Christ from the dead. But he did not raise him if in fact the dead are not raised. For if the dead are not raised, then Christ has not been raised either. And if Christ has not been raised, your faith is futile; you are still in your sins. Then those also who have fallen

---

[1] All scripture references are taken from the New International Version (1984 revision) unless otherwise stated.

asleep in Christ are lost. If only for this life we have hope in Christ, we are to be pitied more than all men (1 Corinthians 15:14–18).

Paul goes on to assert that Jesus did in fact rise from the dead, but if his assertion is mistaken, then *according to these verses*, my intention to bring that to light should be seen as a noble endeavor. I don't quite concur with Paul that Christians are to be pitied more than all men if their faith is baseless. After all, knowing the truth is not a precondition for happiness; there are happy and unhappy members of every religion. But Paul does make a valid point: devoting our life to an illusion is not the best use of the only life we have.

One of my primary reasons for writing this book is self-serving: I do not relish knowing that others consider me to be on the road to eternal damnation if I don't repent, and I want to do what I can to change their perception of those of us who do not share their faith. Yet is this self-serving endeavor reckless? If I believed it would worsen the lives of all those who read this book, then yes, it would be reckless. But I am convinced that life can actually *improve* for those who come to understand that our earthly existence is not simply a stage, a cosmic morality play, a precursor to an eternity to come. This life is the real (and only) deal.

I am not out for blood. I love and respect many believers, some of whom are no doubt better people because of their faith (whatever their religion may be). If you are convinced your faith is the only thing keeping you from a life of profligacy, murder, rape, and pillaging, then please read no further; the world already has enough of that to go around. Studies have shown that Christians are on average more generous than non-Christians; for example, religious people are 57 percent more likely than secularists to help a homeless person at least once a month (Brooks 2006, 39). I confess I have reservations about some of the nihilistic, libertine, and disrespectful tendencies I have observed in some freethinking circles. I often find myself more comfortable socially around evangelicals than around many nonbelievers, due no doubt in part to the habits instilled in me through my conservative upbringing.

So am I double-minded, concerned only about truth for its own sake, while acknowledging that Christianity provides a noble way of life, even if untrue? The answer cannot be a simple "Yes" or "No," because there is a great variety of Christianities on the market, and the answer depends on which brand is in view. I have no interest in undermining any form of religion grounded on passages like these:

> He has showed you, O man, what is good. And what does the LORD require of you? To act justly and to love mercy and to walk humbly with your God (Micah 6:8).

> Make it your ambition to lead a quiet life, to mind your own business and to work with your hands, just as we told you, so that your daily life may win the respect of outsiders and so that you will not be dependent on anybody (1 Thessalonians 4:11, 12).

> Religion that God our Father accepts as pure and faultless is this: to look after orphans and widows in their distress and to keep oneself from being polluted by the world (James 1:27).

However, many within fundamentalist and conservative evangelical circles are not content to limit their faith to such expressions. Their views concerning the authority of the Bible, Christian tradition, science, and hell can lead to forms of divisiveness, exclusivity, and insularity that threaten societal cohesion and progress.

I am concerned about the common assumption that unbelievers are on the whole immoral, rebellious, arrogant, or otherwise distasteful individuals whose unbelief stems from their twisted desires or other personal failings.

I am concerned by the marginalizing of unbelievers from public and social life. Both of my sons are involved in Boy Scouts, a nonsectarian organization that requires its members and leaders to believe in God. As long as you believe in Shiva, Zeus, Allah, Yahweh, or Jesus, you're in; but if you cannot declare your allegiance to any member of such a pantheon, you're out. For this reason I am ineligible for official participation in our troop, even though my moral character has not been questioned. A 2006 University of Minnesota survey found that Americans are more likely to vote for members of other races, recent immigrants, homosexuals, and Muslims than to vote for atheists (Edgell 2006). It is next to impossible to be a respected public skeptic of religion in the United States. Even in higher academia, thought by many to be a bastion of unbelief, only 23.4% of American college and university professors are atheists or agnostics (Gross and Simmons 2006, 4).

I am concerned also about the scarring mental torment unwittingly served up to children who are taught that the majority of the world is destined to everlasting hellfire. I want to see children grow up chasing butterflies, catching tadpoles, and reading good books—not agonizing over the possibility that their unsaved friends might suffer eternally. It is one thing for adults to hold to unsubstantiated beliefs, and I respect their right to do so, but it is another matter altogether for adults to press these beliefs on vulnerable children who have not yet developed the cognitive faculties needed to weigh the evidence for and against what they are being taught.

I am concerned about religiously inspired idealism and rigidity that can lead to political initiatives based not so much on their real-world consequences but on their conformity to sacred tradition or divine imperative.

I am concerned that we in the West are headed for catastrophic confrontations with uncompromising factions of Islam and that our failure to heed the call of reason to moderate or abandon our unsupported ideologies will deprive us of any mandate to call Muslims to do the same.

I am concerned about the relative decline in scientific education and research in the United States, fueled in part by religious suspicion of the scientific establishment's naturalistic outlook, and also by an unwillingness to tamper with sacred objects like embryos and genomes.

It grieves me to witness bright, promising young men and women distracted by the study of fundamentalist theology, or by the prospect of traveling the world to convert people from one empirically unverifiable form of supernaturalism to another. I regret having used up the best years of my youth pursuing religious goals. In retrospect I would have preferred a career seeking a vaccination for malaria, which kills one person every 30 seconds in sub-Saharan Africa alone.

I am concerned by the enormous diversion of time, energy and financial resources used to maintain and propagate religion. These activities too often take priority over believers' concrete charitable contributions to society.

I am concerned by the lack of care for the future of our planet on the part of many of the millions of believers who expect Jesus' imminent return:

> Pastor Heneghan of Gospel Community Church sees the issue of population growth in more biblical terms, specifically those taken from Genesis and Revelation. "Some people think that what I'm doing—having 11 children—is wrong. I don't really get into that much. The Bible says "be fruitful and multiply." That's my belief system. They don't believe in God, so they think we have to conserve what we have. But in my belief system, He's going to give us a new earth." Overpopulation isn't a problem in a universe where God promises a clean global slate (Joyce 2006).

Because I am convinced that the world will ultimately be a better place the closer our ideas approach reality, I feel compelled to do my part to uphold free inquiry as a virtue rather than a vice.

As a former Christian I am cognizant of the counterconcerns of believers. What will happen to society if we all abandon our faith? Will we not forsake our moral compass, leading to the collapse of our country, which, according to the Christian Right, was founded on Christian principles? I will address these concerns in due course.

I claim no special expertise in any field but my own experience. Though I grew up as the son of missionary parents, attended a mission boarding school, spent four years at a Christian university, and completed a one-year graduate certificate of biblical studies at an evangelical seminary, I have not yet acquired an advanced degree. Those looking for a scholarly treatise will be disappointed. Indeed, some have raised my lack of knowledge to caution me against judging the Christian faith. The implication is that as long as I am less knowledgeable than others who embrace Christianity, I am not qualified to critique it.

However, most believers consider it a virtue to instill the Christian faith in their children, even before the children have had an opportunity to study the alternatives in depth. Well-intentioned friends and family have reminded me that I need only accept Christ with the faith of a little child. It is as though the Christian faith enjoys a special status not shared by other perspectives: to reject Christianity, we must obtain a doctorate in theology and prove beyond a shadow of a doubt it is untrue, but to accept Christianity, all we need is the faith of a little child, with no prior sympathetic or systematic study of other religious and nonreligious alternatives.

I recognize that many Christians—some of whom I know personally—are far more intelligent and educated than I am. And so are many individuals from other faiths and nonfaiths. It is an enduring mystery to me that bright scholars can hold such widely divergent views. But I am not responsible for believing what others espouse simply because they happen to be intelligent; I can only believe whatever appears to me to hold up best after weighing the various alternatives.

I must emphasize again I have no ax to grind against Christians as people, even if I do not accept their beliefs. The most wonderful people I know are Christians.[2] I have often heard believers assert that ex-Christians leave the faith primarily because of disappointments with the Christian community and not because of any deficiency in the gospel itself. Precisely the opposite was true for me: my desire to stay in fellowship with believers long served as an obstacle to my decision to leave the faith.

---

[2] Most of my acquaintances are Christians, a fact which no doubt contributes to this judgment.

MY APPROACH TO MY READERS

When addressing Christian beliefs throughout this book, I know I will not always accurately portray what you believe, especially if you are not a fundamentalist or conservative evangelical. If this is the case, I trust you will ignore my comments and not take offense, knowing they are being addressed to others for whom the shoe fits.

Among freethinkers there is a tension between those on the one hand who take a hard-line, disparaging view of religion and those on the other hand who take a more sensitive approach. The first group includes the likes of zoologist Richard Dawkins and author Sam Harris, who unapologetically use ridicule and sharp wit to expose the fallacies of those who hold to religion of any sort. Representatives of the second group include the late science popularizer Carl Sagan and his heir apparent Neil de Grasse Tyson.

I have alternatively found myself in both of these camps, but I aspire to the gentler approach, without however hesitating to say "spade" when I see a spade.[3] Individuals respond differently to different tacks. I was influenced in part by the forceful wit and uncompromising confrontations of Thomas Paine, Robert Ingersoll, and Robert Price in my move toward skepticism, so I cannot discount the effectiveness of Dawkins and Harris' approach, which stems from deep-rooted conviction and frustration with the persistence of religion in modern society.

Carl Sagan's perspective on the tension between a hard-line and a gentle approach bears quoting at length:

> Have I ever heard a skeptic wax superior and contemptuous? Certainly. I've even sometimes heard, to my retrospective dismay, that unpleasant tone in my own voice. There are human imperfections on both sides of this issue. Even when it's applied sensitively, scientific skepticism may come across as arrogant, dogmatic, heartless, and dismissive of the feelings and deeply held beliefs of others. And it must be said, some scientists and dedicated skeptics apply this tool as a blunt instrument, with little finesse. Sometimes it looks as if the skeptical conclusion came first, that contentions were dismissed before, not after, the evidence was examined. All of us cherish our beliefs. They are, to a degree, self-defining. When someone comes along who challenges our belief system as insufficiently well based—or who, like Socrates, merely asks embarrassing questions that we haven't thought of, or demonstrates that we've swept key underlying assumptions under the rug—it becomes much more than a search for knowledge. It feels like a personal assault. . . .

---

[3] The closest I come to abandoning the gentle approach is in my chapter on hell.

If we offer too much silent assent about mysticism[4] and superstition—even when it seems to be doing a little good—we abet a general climate in which skepticism is considered impolite, science tiresome, and rigorous thinking somehow stuffy and inappropriate. Figuring out a prudent balance takes wisdom (Sagan 1996, 298–299).

Indeed, the quest for wisdom to strike the right balance in my approach is perhaps the single greatest challenge I face as I write. I have been guilty of crossing the line into a mean-spirited confrontation with certain believing friends. My sincere apologies go out again to the victims of my contempt. On the other hand, some Christians have indicated to me they prefer a direct attack like Dawkins' to an indirect one like Sagan's, since at least one always knows where Dawkins stands.

Unfortunately for Dawkins, many believers who might otherwise give his arguments a fair hearing cannot get past his manner. In its review of Dawkins' and Harris' recent books, *Christianity Today* magazine editorializes:

> You can also tell that atheism is in trouble because it is becoming increasingly intolerant. In the past, atheists (or secular humanists or freethinkers) were often condescendingly tolerant of their less-enlightened fellow citizens. While they disdained religion, they treated their religious neighbors as good-hearted, if misguided. . . . This newly aggressive mood is in danger of undermining civil society. . . . Aikman evoked images of Mao's China and Stalin's Russia as the future of America—if liberals ever abandon true liberalism. Make no mistake; it is that potential abandonment of liberalism that Harris and Dawkins are calling for. . . . The antitheistic rhetoric that erodes the ethos of respect is a clear and present danger. . . . The new atheistic rhetoric betrays panic, another sign of weakness. Atheism knows that it is losing both arguments and the global tide[5] (*Christianity Today* 2007).

After reading this article in *Christianity Today*, how likely would most believers be to pick up Dawkins' *The God Delusion*, even if it contained arguments worth considering? The article discusses very little of the contents of the book. It doesn't need to, because its audience most certainly does not wish do go down the path of Mao's China or Stalin's Russia.

---

[4] While Sagan refers to mysticism in a general sense (as opposed to a hard rationalism), it is likely he also meant to refer to particular religions like Christianity.

[5] Both fundamentalism and atheism are growing in the United States as a percentage of its population, so any talk of atheism's being in trouble is premature.

Does Dawkins liberally employ wit, irony and ridicule? Certainly. But the Bible does the same against its ideological competitors, for example, in this deliciously biting polemic against idol makers:

> He cut down cedars, or perhaps took a cypress or oak. He let it grow among the trees of the forest, or planted a pine, and the rain made it grow. It is man's fuel for burning; some of it he takes and warms himself, he kindles a fire and bakes bread. But he also fashions a god and worships it; he makes an idol and bows down to it. Half of the wood he burns in the fire; over it he prepares his meal, he roasts his meat and eats his fill. He also warms himself and says, "Ah! I am warm; I see the fire." From the rest he makes a god, his idol; he bows down to it and worships. He prays to it and says, "Save me; you are my god." They know nothing, they understand nothing; their eyes are plastered over so they cannot see, and their minds closed so they cannot understand. No one stops to think, no one has the knowledge or understanding to say, "Half of it I used for fuel; I even baked bread over its coals, I roasted meat and I ate. Shall I make a detestable thing from what is left? Shall I bow down to a block of wood?" He feeds on ashes, a *deluded* heart misleads him; he cannot save himself, or say, "Is not this thing in my right hand a lie?" (Isaiah 44:14–20)[6]

I doubt the arch-skeptic Dawkins himself could have matched the poignancy of the above passage. It is one of the finest specimens in all the annals of skeptical literature. It resonates with all nonidolaters. Yet when Dawkins dares to aim similar guns against the foundations of Christianity and theism, he is berated—not so much for his content, but for his approach—as a "fundamentalist atheist," intolerant and antiliberal. If Dawkins considers all religion to be evidentially on a par with idol worship, Christians who embrace Isaiah 44 must grant him the right to engage in the same kinds of rhetoric as does the author of the Isaiah passage. It is irrelevant whether Christians think their faith has greater warrant than that of the idolaters; the point is that Dawkins does not believe so, and he is merely exercising his freedom to say why.

Those who decry the style of Dawkins and his ilk (for example, Bertrand Russell, Madalyn Murray O'Hair, Christopher Hitchens, Daniel Dennett, or Sam Harris) ought also to denounce the style of many of the scriptural authors who took the same—and sometimes a more extreme—approach. Those who will not do so have little ground for complaint against Dawkins' style.

We commonly hear politicians attacking their opponents' ill-founded positions. Political dissent is generally a sign of a healthy democracy,

---

[6] Emphasis (italics) in all scripture quotations throughout the book is mine.

leading to the correction of abuses that often occur in more autocratic societies like monarchies or dictatorships. The engine that drives political dissent is the hope or expectation of positive *change*. But when it comes to worldviews, too often the assumption is that what we believe is who we are and that we cannot change who we are, any more than we can change the color of our skin or our physical height.

This being the case, it is sometimes considered just as insulting to criticize the religious beliefs of others as it is to criticize their race or gender. But I would argue that just as it is possible to change our mind about a political policy, so it is possible (even if difficult) for us to change our mind concerning our religious beliefs. So if we allow for political dissent, we must also allow for religious dissent without crying "Foul!" whenever our beliefs are vigorously challenged. Resistance to criticism and curtailing of free expression ought everywhere to be discouraged, whether on an individual, corporate, or government level. Progress flourishes only where free inquiry and the right to criticize are unhindered; this is as true whether communist governments persecute Christians or Muslim governments curtail the free expression of atheists.

All this to say that, whether I take a gentle or harsh approach, I am sure to elicit criticism. The very act of confronting deeply cherished religious convictions is unforgivable to some, regardless of my tactics.

Nevertheless, my aim is to ask my readers to reconsider at least a few of their convictions, and I cannot do so without inflicting some degree of what may be perceived as insensitivity. Know that any such insensitivity is not deliberate, however uncomfortable my calls for you to reconsider your views may be. Having lived most of my life in the Christian fold, I recognize I cannot ask you simply to jettison your faith as if it were a common pair of dirty trousers. My own transition was long and painful, rather more like ripping off my very skin than shedding my trousers.

TWO KINDS OF BELIEVERS

Though many books have been written in an attempt to discredit religion, there are few signs of its slipping away. Most of you did not come to faith by carefully considering intellectual arguments for the reasonableness of Christianity, nor are you likely to leave the faith by reading counter arguments. My own journey away from Christianity began within as I reflected on the contradictory elements in the Bible, on the conflict between fundamentalist Christianity, and on my observations of the real world. It was only after my doubts began that I undertook to read materials written from a skeptical perspective, and I quickly became struck by the magnitude of the evidence corroborating my initial doubts. Doubt cannot be imposed from the outside; it must begin from within.

Believers generally fall into one of two broad categories: those who are confident they cannot be mistaken regarding their fundamental beliefs and those who entertain doubts to one extent or another. If you are as certain of the veracity of your faith as the Muslim hijackers of September 11, 2001, were certain of theirs, then it is unlikely that anything I have to say will sway you from your current position.

I recall a discussion with a Christian friend who expressed his doubt that I was ever a true believer to begin with. Though it was apparent neither to me nor to my family, friends, church, or mission organization, it is in theory possible that I was never a true believer. But if that was the case for me, how can anyone have assurance of being a true believer in the present? Might you not consider yourself to be a believer and to have a dynamic relationship with God, only to find yourself years later leaving the faith and being told you were never a believer in the first place? When I raised this question to my friend, he looked me in the eye, pointed his finger firmly at me, and stated unequivocally, "I will *never* leave Jesus."

We continued conversing about the merits of our different perspectives, but it occurred to me later that further discussion of these matters was pointless. Those who cannot allow their views to be subject to revision by data or arguments they may not have yet considered live in a separate world from mine. I cannot imagine stating that I will never again become a Christian, even if I consider it from my present vantage point highly unlikely. If you think it impossible that you should ever change your mind, I implore you to reconsider your certainty, just as you would ask firmly believing Muslims to reconsider theirs.

Shortly after my deconversion I began corresponding with a scholar who sought to lead me back to the Christian faith. In response to some of my objections, he wrote the following eloquent appeal:

> All of us have to come down somewhere in the course of life, because of its intrinsic demands. We can't wait forever. So we go with what we have, open to further correction along the way. . . . Why? Because [we] would rather live with the tension of some unanswered objections than live with another tension—the tension of casting doubt on Jesus. And why, in turn, do [we] choose to live with that tension rather than the other? Because the Holy Spirit has made Jesus real to [our] hearts. Again, this is not irrational or subrational but suprarational. It makes sense. It lies within the scope of responsible cognition. But it comes from a source beyond human observation or verification, and it comes with its own self-authenticating finality. And a thoughtful Christian simply cannot deny this Jesus that has confronted him.

So he sees all the problems. And a mature Christian will respect the problems and will let the problems humble him, reminding him of how little he really knows about reality. But none of the problems is of such intrinsic magnitude as to demand a denial of Jesus, and all of them can be comprehended within a universe ruled by someone as complex and majestic as this Jesus.

So the thoughtful Christian lives with the tensions. He does not torment himself endlessly about "all these objections to faith," as if they all had to be met and demolished before Christian commitment could be accepted as possible. There they stand. And some of them are not inconsiderable in their strength. But then, there He stands! And he himself is compelling far more than all these "issues." I know this will not answer you or satisfy you. I don't expect it to. Consider it just an explanation as to why someone could exercise all due personal responsibility in wrestling with the problems of life and still be a Christian without the slightest hesitation but rather with great gladness. And God wants to give this to you, Ken. He does not despise you. He loves you. Maybe that is what you are finding out—how much more he loves you, how much bigger he is, than you ever thought before. May it be.

Reading this message still tugs at my heartstrings today, and it no doubt resonates deeply with most of my readers. This is the essence of what I am up against. Please read on.

A LOOK AHEAD

Part I (chapters 1–5) of this book sets the stage for the detailed critique of my reasons for believing in Part II. In chapter 2 I include an updated version of my electronically published journey entitled "From Missionary Bible Translator to Agnostic" (Daniels 2003). In chapter 3 I recount, from the perspective of the formerly believing Ken Daniels, my recollection of a number of the reasons I chose to remain in the fold. In chapter 4 I present from my postdeconversion perspective a number of obstacles that prevented me from questioning my faith for many years. I then examine critically in Part II my reasons for persevering as a believer for more than a decade after my first crisis of faith. I devote a chapter to each of these commonly cited reasons for belief.

Chapter 2

Journey from Missionary Bible Translator to Humanist

INTRODUCTION TO MY STORY

In recounting my journey in this chapter, I hope to open a window to my life as both a Christian and an apostate, allowing my readers to evaluate the authenticity of my former faith and the motivations for my doubts. To that end, I have liberally sprinkled my story with personal prayers, correspondence, and reflection.

This chapter is based more on personal narrative and experience than on objective arguments. I include my story because of the flesh-and-blood context it provides for the central thesis of this book. Consider the reflections of a Christian friend in response to our dialogues:

> The topics we cover in our discussions sometimes make me question my faith. But what has a greater impact on it and brings deeper questions and pain to my heart is when I hear you say that you have sought God with all your heart, soul, and mind, and not found Him.[7]

I'll take the opportunity up front to clear up any uncertainty as to my present position. I have donned in succession various labels since my deconversion: deist, agnostic, and atheist-leaning agnostic (meaning that I suspect there is no god, while leaving open the possibility that God does exist). For all practical purposes, however, I am an atheist, though I prefer

---

[7] It could be argued that no one, including myself, has ever sought God with all his heart. Not even Martin Luther, about whom it is said he prayed six hours a day, fits the bill. My friend may have (generously) misinterpreted my descriptions of the earnestness with which I sought God.

the more positive terms *naturalist* or *humanist*: I consider it likely that nature is all that exists, and I believe that the most important aspect of our lives is how we relate to other humans in an effort to make society a better place.

LIFE AS AN EVANGELICAL CHRISTIAN

Early years: Unquestioned faith

I was born in Ethiopia in 1968 to evangelical missionary parents. My mother's father was a very warm and kind independent fundamental Baptist pastor. When she was nine, my mother vowed to devote her life to God as a missionary and to abstain from alcohol and movie-going. She kept these vows until her death from cancer in 1998 at the age of 63. I have never met a more selfless individual, and I will always respect the life she lived. She began her missionary career in 1960 as a single nurse in the mountains of Ethiopia, traveling by mule to treat those in need of medical care.

My father's family belonged to the Conservative Baptist denomination, which was somewhat less fundamentalist than my mother's church, but was very evangelical nonetheless.[8] My father built a house on his own at the age of 16, sold it and gave the profits to missionary causes. Having grown up in the Depression, he learned to be industrious, hard working and devoted to the causes he believed in. He joined Sudan Interior Mission (now simply SIM) and traveled to Ethiopia in 1960 as a building construction engineer, overseeing projects such as Bible schools, hospitals, bridges, missionary housing, and seminaries. He met my mother in 1965 and married in 1967.

One of my earliest memories is of a frightening nighttime thunderstorm when I was four while on furlough in California. I called to my mother, who came and comforted me, assured me Jesus would protect us, and invited me to ask Jesus into my heart. Trustingly, I prayed a prayer to accept Jesus as my personal savior. I don't know how much this decision affected my life at such an early age—I couldn't claim a dramatic conversion from a profligate life, though I did understand I was a sinner and needed to accept Jesus' sacrifice to take away my sins so I could be with God. Over the ensuing years I became more committed to the faith I

---

[8] For those unsure of the difference between the terms *fundamentalist* and *evangelical*, the following tongue-in-cheek definition may be helpful: "An evangelical is a fundamentalist who'll let you go to the movies" (Price 2006, 45).

had been taught, even reading the New Testament and nearly half the Old Testament when I was ten years old.

But I was a typical kid, squabbling with my younger sisters while growing up in Ethiopia, California, Arkansas, Liberia, Oregon, and Nigeria. When I was a young teen at a mission boarding school in Nigeria, one teacher in particular impressed me with his sincerity and love. Mr. Crouch lived a disciplined life, running with his dog in the countryside for half an hour each day and spending a great deal of time with his wife. He often emphasized to his students the need for us to talk with God and to relate to him even more personally than with our closest friends. (I was deeply saddened to hear of his death due to cancer in 2008.)

I can remember distinctly the first time I took his advice to heart. I was lying on my bed trying to get to sleep and started pouring out my heart to God, telling him my feelings, praying for all my friends, and letting him know how much I appreciated him until two in the morning. The joy I experienced in knowing I was communicating with the very maker of the entire universe was exhilarating. I continued for many years maintaining an almost daily time of prayer and Bible reading. I sought to please God in my thoughts, actions and words, and even my sisters noticed a significant turnaround in my life as I promoted peace instead of dissension in the family. However, I understood from Paul's epistles that God's acceptance of me was based entirely on his love for me, his sacrifice on my behalf, and not at all on any of my personal accomplishments or righteousness.

After watching the missionary movie *Peace Child* (Forsberg 1972) during my ninth grade year, I became convinced God wanted me to bring the gospel to those who had never heard of Jesus. I particularly sensed God's call to translate the Bible into one of over 3,000 languages in the world in which it was not available.

High school was a difficult but character-forming time of life. I have very fond memories of the tight-knit group of Christian classmates at the missionary boarding school I attended through ninth grade. My sisters did not share my enthusiasm for the rigors of the school, but my awakening to the place God had for me in his world, along with the fellowship of like-minded friends, made the strict regulations of the school and the absence of my parents more tolerable. For my tenth grade year I moved to another Christian missionary school in Nigeria, this time a relatively large day school near our home with a greater mix of religious backgrounds among the students. I missed the cocoon of the boarding school, but I continued to grow in my knowledge of God and the Bible. I read a good deal on young-earth creationism and later wrote a private manuscript defending creationism against evolution.

When I was 16 our family moved to Arkansas, where I attended a public high school for my junior year. I felt like a fish out of water, holing myself up in my room many evenings, listening to songs on the local Christian radio station, and weeping myself to sleep. During my whole year there I knew no one who shared my zeal for God.

Our next move was to Longview in East Texas, where my father became involved in a USA-based technical support mission organization. For my senior year I attended a public high school again, but my experience this time was considerably more positive. Having already adjusted somewhat to American culture, I was able to make more friends and was known as one of the most devout believers in my class. Following my parents' example, I refrained from attending movie theaters, though I did break with them in listening to Christian rock music. As another example of my rigidity, I still recall with pain the evening I invited a less legalistic evangelical Christian girl to the annual high school coronation dance. I was convinced that dancing was not appropriate for serious Christians (I refused to listen to secular music because of its immoral messages, let alone dance to it), so I sat at the dinner table while my date danced with others. A teacher in attendance asked me why I wasn't dancing, and when I explained my reasons, she said she could understand why I might abstain from alcohol, but not dancing.

One of my best friends that year was a Mormon, so I read extensively on Mormonism from an evangelical perspective, finding numerous faults in the Latter Day Saints' scriptures and discussing them with my friend into the wee hours of the morning. After I pointed out a number of historical and theological flaws in Mormonism, he confided in me, "Religion is a bitch." I responded that no, it was clear the universe was created by a personal being, and so it was a no-brainer that we needed to give him our allegiance. I never did convince him to leave his faith, but I became more confident in the moorings of my own faith. I did agree to read an apologetic book he gave me entitled *A Marvelous Work and a Wonder* (Richards 1950) and was able to find enough faults in its reasoning to dismiss it quite readily. It did not occur to me to apply the same level of criticism to Josh McDowell's *Evidence that Demands a Verdict* (McDowell 1979), a popular evangelical apologetic work I read during that same year.

Though we were not Southern Baptists, our family attended a local Southern Baptist church during our time in East Texas. I invited to the church at least one high school student who subsequently accepted Jesus as his savior. (It was awkward at my twenty-year high school reunion in 2006 to encounter this friend and hear him thank me for my role in leading him to Christ, who in his view had helped him through some very difficult situations in subsequent years.) The summer after high school graduation, I went with a couple of friends to share our faith with people in parks and door-to-door, inviting them to believe in Jesus and attend church. In doing so, I felt we were in the center of God's will and experienced a sense of euphoria as a result. I carried out this kind of direct evangelism a few other times, but I was never a regular at it.

Although our family was wary of charismatic and Pentecostal experiences, I sought the baptism of the Holy Spirit during a Christian music festival put on by Last Days Ministries, founded by the late singer-songwriter Keith Green. I experienced a flood of emotion but did not supernaturally "speak in tongues." Thereafter I remained open to the charismatic branch of the evangelical faith but never considered myself to be part of that camp. Theologically I became inclined to call myself an "evangelical ecumenicist," focusing on what united the evangelical faith and not taking strong stands on points of disagreement. I continued to distrust non-Protestant and liberal faiths, but I did consider myself to be a little more ecumenical than my parents.

I chose to attend LeTourneau University, a nondenominational evangelical Christian college in Longview, Texas. I was still interested in Bible translation, but having written to Wycliffe Bible Translators (the organization I was later to join) concerning my dual interest in computer science and biblical studies, they recommended I pursue a degree in computer science, as these skills could be useful not only in Bible translation but in a number of other endeavors. So I studied computer science and engineering at LeTourneau, while taking at least one Bible course per year. I enjoyed my experience there, though my social skills were probably stunted by my obsession with my studies and by the paucity of females on campus.

During spring break of my sophomore year, I sensed a dryness in my relationship with God and found it difficult to keep focused on him while praying. I decided to begin typing my prayers daily on the computer, enabling me to gather my thoughts and avoid daydreaming. My relationship with God was revitalized as a result, and I kept up this practice off and on until I left the faith.

Crisis #1

It was during my junior year of college that I began paying attention to difficult passages in the Old Testament in my personal readings, some that troubled me for ethical reasons, and others that seemed to be internally contradictory. For a while I disregarded them, thinking there must be a good explanation, and who was I anyway to question God (or was it really God)? But enough of these difficulties built up in my mind that I decided to face them head-on, so I began in Genesis, listening to the Bible on cassette while reading the text, writing down any passage that troubled me or appeared contradictory. During spring break, however, after I had reached the book of Jeremiah (over halfway through the Bible), I met an attractive young lady at a Bible college I was visiting. We struck up a long-distance relationship, which, looking back now, helped take my mind off my doubts and likely provided a good incentive to dismiss them. Whatever the explanation, I was able to regain what I considered to be a full-fledged, robust biblical faith. Though we dated for ten months, we never kissed, wanting to reserve that privilege for marriage!

During my college years I became an avid reader of the evangelical news and opinion magazine *Christianity Today*. It helped broaden my perspective and provided a global context for my personal faith. In contrast to my earlier young-earth creationist stance, the magazine staff accepted the earth's great antiquity while rejecting evolution. In my senior year I wrote a paper on the age of the earth for my Pentateuch Bible class, adopting the Day-Age Theory to square the Genesis account with an old earth. It was the book *Christianity and the Age of the Earth* (Young 1988), by Christian geologist and old earth creationist Davis Young, that had convinced me I had been wrong about the age of the earth and that my reasons for believing in a young earth had been merely illusory. However, I never entertained the thought that evolution as an overarching concept could be true, considering it to be simply preposterous, not to mention unbiblical. I now feel that this transition to old earth creationism was significant in that it introduced a tendency on my part to rely on physical and historical evidence to interpret the Bible rather than strictly the other way around.

Out of a desire to serve God and to break out of my social shell, I chose to become the director of student ministries for the college student body during my senior year. It was a stretching experience as I helped organize teams to restore run-down houses in town, plan student mission trips to Mexico, and conduct worship meetings. Despite the pace of my activities, I remained consistent in praying, seeking God and reading the Bible on a daily basis.

Crisis #2

My second crisis of faith began later in my senior year, shortly after I broke up with my girlfriend. My personal study of the Bible again led me to the conclusion that it contained errors and was probably not divinely inspired. However, I had already signed up for a one-year certificate program at Columbia Biblical Seminary (now Columbia International University), a conservative, missions-oriented school in Columbia, South Carolina. Though I wanted my faith to be restored, I was not sure whether I would be able to attend, given the seminary's policy that graduates must assent to the inerrancy of the Bible.

The following summer, after graduating from college, I visited a Unitarian Universalist church in Charlotte, North Carolina, as a seeker. I asked one of the leaders whether he believed God listens to prayer. He said he'd like to think God is out there somewhere listening when we pray, but he wasn't sure. That was profoundly disappointing to me—I wanted the assurance of a personal god[9] who could hear us and orchestrate events for ultimate good—so I never returned to that church. During this time, in August 1990, I wrote the following summary of my ideas about God, ideas I naively believed to be self-evident without scriptural revelation:

> God is that Being than which none greater or equal can possibly exist.
>
> God has made all that ever has existed or that ever will exist.
>
> Man, whom God loves intimately, is the center of and purpose for God's creation.
>
> God possesses all good qualities to an infinite extent and manifests them to the degree that will bring about the least possible conflict among the differing good qualities, which include:
>
> > love, justice, mercy, grace, purity, compassion, humor, aesthetic appeal, creativity, fairness, faithfulness, longsuffering, gentleness, power, free will, knowledge, wisdom, serenity, generosity, self-existence, indivisibility, immortality, joy, sympathy, and comfort.
>
> God created man for the purpose of pleasing himself.

---

[9] To avoid sectarian favoritism, I adopt the practice of capitalizing the word *God* when it is used as an unqualified title ("does God exist?"), while using lowercase when it is qualified by an article or adjective ("a god", "the god", "the gods", "my god," "the Hindu god Ganesh," or "the Hebrew god Yahweh."). This is analogous to the usual convention for familial words like *dad* ("What did Dad do?" versus "What did his dad do?").

God created man with the will to choose whether or not to fulfill that purpose.

God's allowance for man to choose required the creation of options which please God and options which do not please him.

The options which do not please God constitute that which is known as evil.

God has allowed enough evil, suffering, injustice, ambiguity, and pleasure to exist in the cosmos so that the choice between pleasing God and not pleasing God is a choice that requires consideration, for only choices that require consideration are meaningful to God.

No human has without fail chosen to please God.

For man to please God requires that man make the choice to do so, but beyond that man can fulfill no other requirements. All other requirements are fulfilled only through God's enabling.

These requirements include:

> praising God for who he is; thanking him for his favor in all its manifestations; confessing choices made that do not please him; confiding in him the most intimate aspects of one's soul and experience; asking him to reveal the truth in every significant matter; asking him to meet the needs of others; asking him to meet one's own needs; treating others in the same way that one would wish to be treated; and acting upon the directives which God implants in one's conscience after one has honestly and humbly sought God with all his heart.

God, being just, will in some way reward those who choose to please him and will in some way punish those who choose to displease him.

God, being merciful, will in some way temper his justice for those who acknowledge wrong choices and who choose to make God's pleasure their ongoing aim.

God has created man with an immortal soul.

God is free to direct his creation as he chooses, so supernatural events (miracles) are possible.

Just as the universe had a beginning in time, so it will have an end in time.

In sum, I was convinced of God's existence, power and goodness. I earnestly desired to live my life to please him, but my misgivings about the Bible led me to question the Christian faith.

At one point I shared some of my struggles with my father, who had himself experienced at least one crisis of faith as a young man. He listened to my reasons for doubting but chastised me for my disrespect for God's word. I was somewhat hurt by his response at the time, but I understood where he was coming from and did not harbor ill will against him.

I did not relish the inner turmoil I was experiencing, and I truly did want to believe, so I wrote to the seminary I had applied to and explained my situation. When they at last responded a couple of weeks before the start of the school year, they invited me to attend despite my doubts.

Accepting the invitation of the seminary, I found myself a skeptic among a sea of believers. The atmosphere was electric—filled with people who loved God with a passion and degree of sincerity I had rarely witnessed elsewhere. About three months into my seminary studies, after having talked with some understanding professors and friends and having read the no-nonsense nineteenth-century apologetic work *An Examination of the Alleged Discrepancies of the Bible* (Haley 1876), my confidence in the reliability of the Bible was restored.

Because Old Testament ethics had contributed significantly to my doubts, I elected to write a paper entitled "The Morality of the Old Testament God" as part of a Christian apologetics class. Following are its concluding paragraphs:

> Integrity mandates the admission that God's reference to slaves as property poses not a little difficulty. And so it goes for the seeming lesser value attributed to females than to males in Leviticus 27:1–8. Some of the wartime acts of the Israelites carried out with God's sanction stir the soul to revulsion. Not all questions lend themselves to answers that can be detailed in an undertaking of this proportion, and some may not lend themselves to satisfactory solutions in any treatise on the subject. Yet it is not the nature of the transcendent, sovereign God to reveal every matter to finite minds:
>
> > Let a man solve the grand problem of the ages; let him tell us why an infinitely wise, powerful, and benevolent Creator allowed evil to enter at all his universe—let him explain this contradiction, and we may safely engage to explain those which occur in the Bible. For none of them—not all together—are so dark, unfathomable, and appalling as this one grand, ultimate Discrepancy (Haley 1876, 34).
>
> Yes, let a man devise a worldview that eliminates every difficulty, answers every question, and empties life of every challenge. Such a man ceases to bear any relation to the world of all human experience. Rather, let a man diligently and humbly seek to adopt that system which offers the most coherent framework for reconciling the greatest number of conflicts and which provides the greatest unity among the disciplines of science, history, theology, and reason. Then let him not allow that framework to fall on account of a limited selection of mysteries which remain unsolved.

Here is my brief account of that doubting experience from my perspective as a believer two years later:

> First I had to understand that neither life nor the Bible always lends itself to complete understanding by the human mind. God provides for us a firm-enough basis to believe with our minds and desires our trust in the remaining matters of faith that are not self-evident. I believe God has made Himself more real to me through that testing, and I look forward to the ways He will use me because of it.

Marriage and missions

Following my year of seminary I moved back to my parents' house near Charlotte, North Carolina. It was there that I met my beautiful wife Charlene Newton. The day before meeting her, I had asked God to let me meet my wife the next day at church. The very day we met on June 30, 1991, I was impressed enough to think of her as my future wife.

We began a wonderful romance, helped by the Sunday school superintendent who asked us to teach the junior high Sunday school class together. We married in June 1992 and lived in northern Minnesota for a year together before joining Wycliffe Bible Translators (hereafter referred to as Wycliffe). We look back at our time in Minnesota with fond memories of our friends and the Bible Church we attended. I taught the high school Sunday school class, and Charlene and I together helped with junior high AWANA, a Bible memory club for children.

Our next-door neighbor was the only avowed atheist with whom I conversed at length until well after my deconversion. My immediate reaction when he told me of his atheism was to say, "You mean you believe in *evolution?*" From my perspective the theory of slime-to-man evolution was the most preposterous idea imaginable. I could not understand how my friend could wear his badge of evolution and materialistic philosophy so proudly. The night before our departure from Minnesota, I stayed up talking with him until four o'clock in the morning, patiently trying to persuade him that, even if evolution were possible, it could not account for the origin of matter and natural laws. We parted ways respectfully, neither of us having been swayed, but I do recall thinking that atheism could indeed solve a number of difficult questions about the nature of reality. I did not give these thoughts any lasting consideration, however, because I was not able to accept that the universe could have arisen through impersonal, blind forces.

The ensuing years involved in retrospect an almost insane flurry of activity. By 1999, seven years into our marriage, we had lived in 18 places for one month or longer in six different countries. In our first eleven years of marriage, the longest we lived in one residence was 18 months.

On the basis of Paul's theology, we believed that those who die without hearing and responding to the gospel will not be saved:

> "Everyone who calls on the name of the Lord will be saved." How, then, can they call on the one they have not believed in? And how can they believe in the one of whom they have not heard? And how can they hear without someone preaching to them? And how can they preach unless they are sent? As it is written, "How beautiful are the feet of those who bring good news!" (Romans 10:13–15)

> It has always been my ambition to preach the gospel where Christ was not known. (Romans 15:20a).

Taking Paul's example, we chose to minister among the Daza people of Niger on the edge of the Sahara desert. There were no known Christian believers in this ethnic group of 500,000 souls; we felt that by reaching them, we would be helping to speed the day of Christ's return, a day when there would be "a great multitude that no one could count, from every nation, tribe, people and language, standing before the throne and in front of the Lamb" (Revelation 7:9).

Before setting foot among the Daza, however, we were required to take graduate linguistic courses at the University of North Dakota and at a linguistic institute affiliated with Wycliffe in Dallas. Funding for our future ministry required that we raise regular financial support commitments from churches and friends; as a "faith" mission, Wycliffe did not directly provide for our salary or expenses. This support raising involved much travel in the USA and Canada, including two trips of over 10,000 miles each. Difficult pregnancies and infants and toddlers made these journeys quite a challenge, but the hardships were offset by meaningful contacts with friends and churches.

Our first overseas stop was Belgium, where we studied French for a year (1995–96), since the official language of Niger is French (though only a tenth of the populace speaks it). Pregnancy interrupted our plans to go to Africa, so we spent two months at a linguistic school in France, where our second son was born. From there we went to a beautiful Bible school in Switzerland to continue practicing our conversational French for three months before moving on to a three-month orientation to African living in the country of Cameroon. The highlight of our time there was our three-week stay in the village home of a Cameroonian family with our two diaper-clad boys. (Space precludes mention of a great many interesting details in all these travels, but you can imagine how it might have been for us.)

In 1997 we finally arrived in Niamey, Niger, one of the hottest capital cities in the world. Before moving to the Daza area, we spent a year in the capital doing "group service," which for me involved computer support for the over 30 Wycliffe missionaries in the country. We did make a one-month trip to the Daza area, a three-day, 900-mile trip from our center of operations in Niamey. It was during that trip that Charlene became pregnant for the third time. Morning sickness and a five-hour delay due to sand on the road etched the return trip forever in our memories. Because of the pregnancy and because my mother was in the final stages of her sixteen-year battle with cancer, we shortened our four-year overseas term by one year and returned to the USA for furlough in 1998. My mother passed away at the age of 63 while we were en route. The pain of her loss was tempered by the knowledge that her suffering was over and that she was in the presence of her creator. I do not recall being angry at God, nor did I question his sovereignty at that point, even though I missed her greatly.

Crisis #3

For most of our yearlong furlough we pursued further linguistic training in North Dakota and Dallas. From the time of my 1991 crisis, I had managed to avoid serious doubt and remained confident in the truth of the gospel. However, my faith was again shaken in the spring of 1999 during a linguistics course taught by a Wycliffe member. One assignment was to read George Lakoff's *Women, Fire and Dangerous Things* (Lakoff 1990), primarily a treatise on linguistic categories. Somewhat tangentially, Lakoff mentioned so-called "ring species" as an example of the difficulty of making objective linguistic references to reality. For example, several varieties of *Ensatina* salamanders surround the San Joaquin Valley of the U.S. Pacific coast. Traditionally a species is defined as a population that can interbreed and produce healthy, fertile offspring. In the case of this salamander, however, it is difficult to determine the species boundaries. If there are ten varieties surrounding the valley, variety one can interbreed with neighboring variety two, and two with three, and so forth, but where the circle is completed with variety one adjacent to variety ten, the two do not interbreed successfully.

This called to mind a problem that Bible translators face when attempting to determine what constitutes a language. In a prior language survey class, I had learned of dialect chains where speakers of dialect A could understand speakers of neighboring dialect B; dialect B was mutually intelligible with dialect C; C with D; and so forth to F; but speakers of A could not understand speakers of F. So how many languages are there, and which dialect should be the target of a new Bible translation? I had no trouble believing that language dialects evolved from a parent stock, so it seemed that something comparable could have happened with biological species, which disturbed my notion of the fixity of species. I realize that many creationists accept limited evolution even outside the species level, but for some reason I was shaken by the parallels between linguistic and biological evolution, to the point that I began to suspect evolution might be true.

Almost out of the blue, I began to doubt the very existence of God. I recall attending a triumphal Easter service while weeping internally at my inability to connect with the enthusiasm of the believers surrounding me. Wishing to resolve my doubts, I wrote a letter explaining my thoughts to the professor of my linguistics class. When I subsequently met with him, he helped me see that a number of my difficulties stemmed from an overly rigid conception of inerrancy and a limited human view of God's purposes. One rhetorical question he posed stuck with me and helped me see the narrowness of my thinking: "Why is it that just Westerners doubt God's existence?" Quite quickly my doubts were put to rest. This bout with doubt ended after only a month.

Just three months later we were back for our second term in Niger. In July 1999 we moved to our allocation in N'Guigmi, a town of about 10,000 on the edge of the Sahara. We had three children in cloth diapers at the same time, and running water was unavailable during the daytime. However, the perseverance of our closest colleagues and their six children, not to mention the hardships of the people of Niger, helped keep our situation in perspective. One of our most persistent challenges was to discern who was truly in need and how to meet those needs.

Our initial task in N'Guigmi was to learn Dazaga, the language of the Daza people. Though some previous linguistic work had been done in the language, there was no standardized writing system. During the year we were involved in the Dazaga project, we hired a language associate to help us learn some of the basics of the language. We used French as a common language to discuss Dazaga and elicit recordings. It was gratifying to play a role, along with several Dazaga speakers and another missionary, in developing a government-recognized orthography (standard writing system) for Dazaga.

While in N'Guigmi there was plenty of time to read in the evenings. I was greatly encouraged to read *Darwin's Black Box* by biochemist Michael

Behe, who offered extraordinary and seemingly undeniable proof of the irreducible complexity of nature's wonders at the microscopic level. Any lingering doubts about God's role in creation were swept away. This portion of my prayer from January 23, 2000, captures my mood at the time:

> Father God, thank you for continuing to reveal yourself to me and for reaffirming my confidence that you indeed designed all of creation. How could I ever have doubted a year ago that you exist? What got into me? How did I presume to account for the existence of matter and all the interacting physical laws without recourse to Someone outside of matter, time and the physical laws? Given that I can be assured of your existence and interest in my life, why do I ever go through a day without giving you my best, without praising you with all my soul, without confiding in you all my dreams and fears, without invoking your aid on behalf of family, friends, and those who are serving you around the world?

Crisis #4: Return from the mission field

In March 2000 we traveled to the neighboring country of Burkina Faso to attend a phonology workshop. It was during our month there that my doubts again came to a head, setting in motion our return from the mission field. Charlene and I had decided in January to read through a chronological one-year Bible together. As we read through the Pentateuch, I began recalling all the reasons for my earlier doubts. Again, many of my concerns were related to ethics, though I also noted what seemed to be pagan understandings of God and culturally conditioned modes of worship, as well as a few anachronisms that pointed to post-Mosaic authorship of the Pentateuch.

Often when I had been tempted to doubt earlier, I would remind myself of the many fulfilled prophecies of the Bible outlined in *Evidence that Demands a Verdict* (McDowell 1979) and other apologetic works. But I was confused as to why on the one hand the Old Testament seemed so ugly while at the same time it seemed to have amazing predictive ability. The prophecy of the 70 weeks of Daniel particularly impressed me because of its accuracy in predicting the time of the messiah's coming. Subsequently I found arguments on both sides of the issue on the Internet, but the skeptical explanations began to look increasingly plausible.

Not wanting to give up the faith that had been so dear to me for so long, I searched the Internet for some helpful apologetic articles. I had heard that Clark Pinnock was an apologist of a more scholarly caliber than Josh McDowell, so I searched for his name. Instead of finding anything written by Pinnock, I found an online book referencing him entitled *Beyond Born Again* by Robert M. Price (Price 1993). Price spent his youth as a fundamentalist, attended Gordon-Conwell Theological Seminary as an evangelical, transitioned to liberal Christianity, then went on to earn two doctorates in New Testament studies. He was still a liberal believer when he wrote this book, but he later became a humanist after some 20 years as a liberal Christian. In any case, his was the first book I had read specifically attacking evangelicalism, and it was compelling, throwing my already fragile faith into a tailspin. I don't believe I would have been willing to listen to anything he had to say had it not been for my prior misgivings about the Old Testament. Having devoted my life to the calling of Bible translation, it was devastating to realize that the Bible probably is not God's word after all. You can only imagine the knot in my stomach and the beating of my heart with every new discovery I made confirming my suspicions that the Bible is man-made from start to finish.

Following is a prayer from April 7, 2000, shortly after our return to the mission center in Niamey, Niger:

> Father God, God of all creation, the one who made me, the one who loves me more than anyone else, the one who desires my well-being, I come to you today with a very heavy heart. Or more precisely, a knot in my stomach. Once again, it appears to me that all I have been taught about the inspiration of the Bible is false. Deep down inside me, I have a very, very strong suspicion that the Bible is human and not divine through and through. You know the passages I struggle with. I can't seem to reconcile my conception of your nature with the way your character is portrayed in the Bible, particularly in the Old Testament. Where do I get this sense of moral injustice when I read about how a master is not to be punished for beating his slave as long as the slave doesn't die, because the slave is his property [Exodus 21:20]? There seems to be within me a moral law that stands in judgment of the Bible. Is this internal moral law a product of my culture that is to be submitted to the higher moral law of the Bible, or vice versa?
>
> Why does the Old Testament incessantly violate my idea of right and wrong? Why does it regard women in such a poor light? Why are the people of Yahweh supposed to wipe out men, women and children but are allowed to take the virgins for themselves [Deuteronomy 21:10–14; Numbers 31:17–18]? Why are the sacrifices offered in the tabernacle called food for Yahweh [Leviticus 21:21–23]? Why does Yahweh need sacrifices anyway? Can't he simply forgive those who ask for his forgiveness, just as we humans forgive each other? Why do some people get zapped instantly for touching the ark inadvertently [2 Samuel 6:1–8] while Aaron, Moses' brother, gets off scot-free after making a golden calf for the people to worship [Exodus 32], and then he becomes the leader of the priesthood and the recipient of the best of all the offerings of the people? Why do women suspected of adultery have to go through some bizarre ordeal of drinking bitter water and seeing their

womb swell and thigh waste away, while no provision is made for women to test their husbands for the same offense [Numbers 5:11–31]?

God, the weight of all these troublesome passages, and many more, add up in my mind to foolishness. Or at least an attribution of ancient cultural ideas on the God of all creation. The list goes on: the Bible's endorsement of polygamy[10] [2 Samuel 12:8], the magic of the striped sticks causing sheep's offspring to be striped [Genesis 30:31–43], the assertion that camels don't have split hooves [Leviticus 11:1–4],[11] the mixed use of round numbers and exact numbers in Numbers [3:39–51] to justify paying redemption money to Aaron's family, Yahweh's command to hamstring the horses [Joshua 11:6], the barbaric brutality of the Israelites in their holy wars, the contradictory teachings on divorce [Deuteronomy 22:19, 29; Ezra 10:2–3; Malachi 2:16; Mark 10:11–12], the many little historical contradictions, the attempt to explain language diversification through a "how-the-leopard-got-its-spots" Tower of Babel story [Genesis 11:1–9], the conception of a young earth which is clearly unattested to by the facts [Genesis 1–11], the inability of Christians to agree on so many doctrines while reading the same Bible that seems to say one thing in one place and another in another place, the long process of canonizing the Bible, the vengeful attitudes ascribed to Yahweh when his wayward people are attacked by their enemies, the sacrifices in Ezekiel's temple that has yet to be built [Ezekiel 40],[12] the vengeance Samson took on his betrayers under the influence of the Spirit of Yahweh [Judges 14:19], the exclusively physical punishments and rewards promised for the Israelites [Deuteronomy 28] with no mention of heaven until late in the writing of the Old Testament, and on and on and on.

---

[10] I use the term *polygamy* in its most common sense as a synonym of *polygyny* (one man, multiple wives), as opposed to *polyandry* (one woman, multiple husbands). At the time I wrote this prayer, I was troubled by the disconnect between Western evangelicals' general disapproval of polygamy and the apparent biblical endorsement of the same. Polygamy is a complex issue (I see it as sometimes but not always a curse, depending on how it is practiced), and the Bible's approval of polygamy is not necessarily a strike against Christianity, but it is a strike against the prevailing Western evangelical notion that God condemns polygamy.

[11] This was not a major sticking point for me; after all, Middle Eastern animal herders had to be keenly aware that camels have split hooves. As I read later in *The Word Biblical Commentary*, "Although the camel has a split hoof, its sole is thick and cushiony so that the split does not appear" (Hartley 1992, 157). However, see Answering Christianity (Abdallah n.d.) for photos of clearly split-hoofed camels.

[12] What troubled me about this passage is that it seemed to be predicting the building of a temple with specific dimensions that has never been built. I understood this to mean that the temple has yet to be built in the future and that it will include divinely instituted animal sacrifices. But according to Hebrews, no more sacrifices are needed in addition to that of Jesus himself.

How much of this am I expected to absorb and put into the filing cabinet labeled "troublesome, contradictory or unjust but accept it by faith anyway"? How much tension can a soul take? Why does it seem like I'm just about the only one in my circle of friends that struggles with these issues as deeply as I do? Am I warped, proud, or rebellious? Are you blinding my eyes because I haven't spent enough time with you in prayer lately? Or are the things I'm beginning to suspect—that the Bible is not divinely inspired—true after all? This is not just an academic exercise. The direction of the rest of my life, if not eternity, depends on it. I know that even if the Bible is true, you don't mind my bringing these questions before you, since the Psalms record similarly piercing doubts that David experienced.

Father God, take me in your arms just as I would take [our children] in my arms in a time of trouble, and comfort me with words of assurance and love and healing. I know you are my creator. I know beyond a shadow of a doubt that you made me and love me. I ask you to have compassion on me and lead me to the truth. I ask you to search my heart and reveal to me anything that displeases you and that stands in the way of my finding the truth about the Bible. Open up my eyes so I can see my sin as you see it, and give me the courage and strength to put it away. I confess that I have been detached from you and my family and friends. I have been living in a world of my own mind, excluding those who are dearest to me. I have been objecting to the inequality of men and women expressed in the Bible, yet I've effectively been reinforcing it in my own marriage by leaving Charlene to do all the household work. Forgive me, I pray, and help me to get back on the right footing.

Father, if I could only sit before you and talk with you as a man talks with another man, if only I could ask you what you had in mind when you made humanity and allowed so many different religions to take root and lead to so many confusing, contradictory and sometimes harmful paths. Why are people so gullible to believe so many contradictory things? Muslims believe what they do because they've been exposed to Islamic teachings and social influences, and it seems no different from why Christians are Christians. If no one major religion is the truth, then what is? Do I have to make up a minor religion to get at the truth? Heaven forbid! In my opinion there are already too many religions. Oh, Father, I don't want to be impertinent. I don't want to reject Jesus as the Son of God if he really is the Son of God or equivalent to God. But if he isn't the Son of God, then I don't want to spend my life in Africa proclaiming he is. What do I do, Lord, what do I do? Comfort my soul, Father. Thank you. Thank you for coming over me with your presence and that indescribable peace that assures me of your care for me. You have answered my prayer to take me in your arms and comfort me. I love you, I love you, I love you.

Thank you for my loving wife with whom I can discuss freely so many things. Thank you, thank you, thank you that I didn't marry [my former girlfriend]. There's no way I could have discussed any of this with her without being stonewalled. I believe you truly did bring us together, that you meant for me to have her and vice versa. Thank you for our three precious little children. How they bring joy to my life! You are truly an incredible genius to have conceived of the idea of babies and little children. Thank you for keeping them alive and in relatively good health to this point. Even if you decide someday to take them away, I pray that I would be able to join with Job in saying, "The Lord gives and takes away; blessed be the name of the Lord." [. . .]

I love you Father, even though I'm confused. If my unbelief is unsubstantiated, help me in my unbelief, and may I be convinced that the Bible is indeed your word. If my unbelief is merited, I pray you'll help me know how to proceed from here. In either case, I pray you'll take away the blinders from my eyes that stem from my self, my sin, my culture, my religion or Satan, whatever the case may be. It seems that there are very few who manage to rise above the beliefs of their own culture. It's usually the intellectuals. I have a hard time believing that you would set things up in such a way that only intellectuals find the truth. But I see how grotesque the fruits of anti-intellectualism have been in so many societies, and I don't want to have part in that either. How do I find truth, Father? I pray as I come to you in prayer during this special time of seeking that you will reveal yourself to me in such a way that I can be assured of the truth. I certainly can't find it out on my own or exclusively through intellectual evaluation. I want to seek truth in the way that you want me to go about it, whether it means accepting the Bible by faith, reading philosophy, praying until you reveal yourself to me, going to seminary, meditating, reflecting, talking with others, or any combination of the above. My problem is that I really don't know how to go about it. I need your hand to guide me.

At this point I contacted an old friend from seminary who was also working in Niger. He was understanding and reasonable and was able to help somewhat by reading Robert Price and pointing out some inconsistencies, even while acknowledging that Price's chapter on Jesus' resurrection was "devastating" (Price 1993, ch. 6). He did not take the same approach as some other well-meaning evangelicals with whom I shared my struggles. Many reminded me we were in a spiritual battle and the enemy was trying to get the best of me because he didn't want me translating the scriptures for an unreached people. (I grant that this is probably the case if the Bible really is true, but not so if it is not.) Others surmised my disbelief was due to some sin in my life. Still others suggested it didn't matter how many logical arguments could be brought to bear against the Bible; I just needed to accept it by faith. Another took the arguments seriously but interpreted the Bible in such a literal way (advocating a young earth, head coverings for women, and rigid submission of women to men) as to make it hard for me to listen to much else of what he said. I appreciate my friend from seminary for being a friend and honestly helping me confront some of the arguments without judging me. I considered that if I were ever to come back to the faith, it would be through his kind of approach.

Life had been very busy for us with a lot of moving around, and I had not been especially consistent in daily setting aside time alone for personal prayer for some time, apart from my daily devotional Bible reading and prayer with Charlene. I suppose some could argue that my struggle was a result of this lapse (though the first time I had doubts 12 years earlier was during a period in which my devotional life was very consistent and meaningful). I talked to our Niger mission director about my problems and obtained permission for a two-week vacation, during which time I prayed and read intensively, seeking God and worshiping him more earnestly than I had done in months. I found in the mission library Helmut Thielicke's *How the World Began* (Thielicke 1961), a series of sermons on the book of Genesis. Here was a German scholar of the first order, who, though not perhaps an evangelical by the American definition (and certainly not a young-earth creationist or inerrantist), believed that Jesus Christ was the Son of God who bodily rose from the dead. Somehow I had failed to realize that there really are serious scholars who believe the essential message of the Bible. I also perused Arie Noordtzij's commentary on Leviticus (Noordtzij 1982) and Numbers (Noordtzij 1983). Though an evangelical, he recognized many of the problems I had noticed in the Pentateuch without facilely brushing them aside. I appreciated his forthrightness in contrast to those who glibly offered strained harmonizations of difficult problems.

In reflecting on Thielicke's book during a prayer time one morning, I broke down and confessed my unbelief in Jesus as God's son, and I felt a warm presence that convinced me I was back onto the right track. I was still not persuaded that the Bible was without discrepancies, but soon it occurred to me that, just as God creates handicapped people with defects or blemishes (Lev. 26:16) that I would hesitate to call errors, so the Bible could contain "blemishes" that I would not call errors. This allowed me to consider myself a Biblical inerrantist in conformity with the Wycliffe doctrinal standard while still honestly acknowledging that it contains discrepancies. This breakthrough occurred in Niamey in April, about a month after reading Robert Price.

We were now free to go back to our assigned location to continue language learning. Meanwhile, I had ordered from Amazon.com a number of books on the Christian faith, both pro and con, and they were waiting for me upon our return to N'Guigmi. Titles included Alvin Plantinga's *Warranted Christian Belief*, Thomas Morris' *Philosophy and the Christian Faith*, Kelly James Clark's *When Faith is not Enough*, C. Stephen Evans' *Philosophy of Religion*, Donald Bloesh's *Holy Scripture*, Larry Richards' *735 Baffling Bible Questions Answered*, Helmut Thielicke's *The Evangelical Faith*, Waldemar Janzen's *Old Testament Ethics*, John Barton's *Ethics and the Old Testament*, Willard Swartley's *Slavery, Sabbath, War & Women*, and Cyrus Gordon and Gary Rendsburg's *The Bible and the Ancient Near East*. I spent every moment I could spare devouring these books, feeling an insatiable hunger to know the truth. It was particularly *The Bible and the Ancient Near East* (Gordon and Rendsburg 1997) that plunged me back into a state of doubt from which I could see little hope of escape. Though these authors are certainly not the most liberal in their field, they made it clear to me that the Bible contains errors and that not all the Old Testament stories are historical. Here is but one example of many troubling observations I came across in the book:

> The Goliath episode, which is part of David's history in the mind of posterity, may well have been attached to him wrongly. The Bible gives us contradictory evidence concerning it. According to the main narrative, David killed Goliath. But this account occasions quite a bit of difficulty in that after the reputed episode is over, Saul and Abner forget completely who David is, whereas he is supposed to have been on the court staff for quite some time. Aside from this and other contradictions, the Bible itself contains a more plausible variant tradition: In 2 Samuel 21:19 it is the hero Elhanan who slays Goliath at the town of Gob. Furthermore, the name of Elhanan's father is obviously connected with the weapon used (the weaver's beam), whereas the latter is inappropriate in the case of the account whereby David is credited with the slaying of Goliath. The author of the Books of Chronicles had before him the Books of Samuel with both variants, which he tried to harmonize. Thus 1 Chronicles 20:5 makes Elhanan the killer of Goliath's brother. Since it is much more natural for a heroic event to be transferred from a minor personage to a great hero, than vice versa, the situation may be summed up as follows: Elhanan slew Goliath but the victory was popularly transferred to David. Both the true and the transformed versions appear in Samuel. The Chronicler, seeing the discrepancy, tried to harmonize them (Gordon and Rendsburg 1997, 186–87).

I could not adopt the position of these authors and remain in good standing with Wycliffe, since all its members are required to assent to biblical inerrancy. Following is the prayer I typed on June 15, 2000, in N'Guigmi, Niger:

> Father God, Creator of all things, lover of my soul, have mercy on me, a sinner. How I learn more and more each day of my inadequacy to discern truth by myself! I don't know whether it's because of pride or because for some other reason you've chosen not to reveal yourself to me, at least to the extent I would like. All I know is that I do not have full assurance of the truth, and I submit myself before you now, asking that you will somehow reveal the truth to me and give me confidence that it is indeed the truth.

> The Bible seems so conditioned by the ideas of the times in which it was written and to me bears no evidence of divine authorship. Must I be eternally damned because I can't believe that Samson, under the influence of your Spirit, avenged himself on his personal enemies by killing 1,000 of them with the jawbone of a donkey? Or because I see inconsistencies in the accounts and viewpoints of the biblical authors, such as whether Jehu was justified in killing the household of Ahab (Kings) or not (Hosea)? Or because I see many of the ethics of the Bible (for example, polygamy, taking virgins as war captives and slaughtering the rest, and slavery) as objectionable? Or because I see innumerable parallels between the myths of the Ancient Near East and those of the Bible, leading me to believe that they are in fact mere myths? Or that I can't see why you couldn't just forgive truly penitent people for their sins without requiring a blood sacrifice, just as humans forgive each other? Or that I can't see any fundamental reason to choose Christianity over Islam except for evangelical Christianity's emphasis on a personal relationship with you (but there are sects within Islam and other religions that do emphasize such a relationship)?

> In short, it seems quite clear to me that Christianity is just another religion like the others, perhaps a little more advanced than others, but a human creation nonetheless. Would it be wrong for me to seek the illumination of your Spirit and ask you to reveal to me the essentials of belief and practice so that I can live a life that pleases you? If that should entail leading me back to the Christian faith, then so be it! In fact, I would love to remain a part of the fold. But at this point it all seems so misguided. If I am being led to the truth in leaving Christianity and accepting a simple theism, then it cannot certainly be because I am a person who is more pleasing in your sight than all other Christians who failed to grasp the insights you've given me. That would certainly be delusional. I am a selfish, lazy, proud and unloving person who finds it hard to improve. Perhaps it is precisely because of these faults and sins of mine that I am being prevented from seeing the truth of Christianity. But why am I so rare among Christians? Very few seem to struggle with their faith to the extent that I do, and yet it doesn't seem (though I could be deluded) that I am among the most sinful of Christians, if there even exists a

scale of sinfulness among believers. Perhaps you see my pride as more evil than the adultery committed by Christians who seem to have no trouble believing despite their ongoing sin.[13] Perhaps it's as a result of this pride that you are deliberately giving me over to doubts that to me seem well founded, but which would not be so if I were given the enlightening of the Holy Spirit. If so, then it is my pride that needs to be dealt with. God of all creation, who has the power to call the worlds into existence, I entreat you to use your power to excise my pride and to reveal to me my utter dependence on you. I cannot plumb the depths of the motivations, desires and interests of my soul. It's so easy to deceive myself. Reveal to me where I err and spur me on to repentance and good deeds and right belief.

Father, I do know two commandments that I have no inclination to question: love the Lord your God with all your heart, soul, mind and strength; and love your neighbor as yourself. And I can agree with Micah, who enjoins us to do justly, to love mercy, and to walk humbly with our God. Perhaps my job description at the moment should be to implement these in my own life, rather than trying to determine metaphysical truth through an intellectual pursuit. It is only those who obey who can believe, and those who believe obey. Help me to obey the light you have given me and to wait on you to reveal the truth to me. You have showered my life with such privilege and opportunity, and I have been so miserly with it, keeping most of it to myself. I am not an island; there are people around me with needs, even my own wife. May I not spend my time selfishly but seek to love, to pour out myself, to get up and do what I should do, even when I'd rather remain in bed. I have to face it, Lord: I'm lazy. Continue to reveal that to me until I've dealt with it sufficiently in my life. I love you and am hopeful you'll lead me where you want me to go.

I felt I could not in good conscience continue actively serving with Wycliffe while entertaining these persistent doubts about the Bible, so I wrote to our mission director in Niamey, and he suggested returning to the USA for counseling. During the week we were awaiting our airline tickets, I recorded my doubts in a document so my designated counselor would know the background of my struggles. I wrote the following on July 1, 2000, in an e-mail message to many of our financial supporters and friends explaining our situation:

Dear Friends,

---

[13] Perhaps I had in mind the memory of a married missionary man who had an affair with a married missionary woman at the missionary compound where I had lived in Liberia as a youth. The two later divorced their spouses and married each other yet remained in the church.

Most of you have received our April newsletter in which we mentioned that it was a difficult one to write. Unfortunately, this one is even more difficult. Though for a few weeks I had dealt with my doubts so that I could believe the Bible again after questioning its inspiration, I find myself doubting the Bible now more than ever. I cannot begin to communicate the inward struggle I feel. But we are encouraged by the many of you who have written saying you are praying for us. And I am comforted in my prayer times by God's presence. My greatest prayer is that He will lead me to the truth and to a life that pleases Him.

Two weeks ago in N'Guigmi we decided we could not continue business as usual. Everyone we contacted agreed it would be best to return to Dallas for counseling with a seasoned, well-respected leader in Wycliffe. [. . .] During this past week I have written a 25-page document explaining my doubts in order to provide points of discussion in my counseling sessions. If you are interested in reading the document and offering feedback, I would be glad to send it to you. . . . (Keep in mind that it does not reflect Wycliffe doctrine, just my musings as a troubled seeker.) [. . .]

Our future is uncertain to us at the moment. We have not sold our belongings and hope to come back in a few months if my doubts can be resolved. Charlene is taking it as well as can be expected, though of course it is not easy for her. Our marriage remains strong. We continue to depend on your prayers.

We welcome your feedback, but do not be concerned if we do not respond to you until after we've settled in Dallas. It's a busy, difficult time.

With heavy hearts,

Ken (& Charlene) Daniels

Over thirty individuals requested to read my document, entitled "Why I doubt the Bible." At the time I wrote it, I did not doubt God's existence but felt that he had simply not revealed himself through any particular religion. "Simple theist" is the label I would have given myself.

The responses to my announcement and the document were mixed. A number of people assured us of their understanding and prayers, as in the following message:

Dear Ken (and Char,)

I am responding to your letter. First of all, let me say that I am so grateful for your honesty and your willingness to express how you truly feel. It gives me confidence and hope for us all if there are those among us who are willing to face the truth about ourselves squarely and then let God move. After we rec'd word about your struggles in this area, I was profoundly touched and was praying and after I prayed, I looked in the Bible and believe God led me to a verse that I want to share with you.

> Some of the wise will stumble, so that they may be refined, purified and made spotless until the time of the end, for it will still come at the appointed time. Daniel 11:35

I remember a similar struggle I had about the Holy Spirit and how we actually are indwelt with the Holy Spirit. It was a horrendous time, but God brought me through that valley teaching me more about myself than answering my questions. This [was] his method with Job as well. We are praying for you and are confident that it is a very good thing that you are going through and are pulling for you not to despair, but know that He is big enough to resolve all doubts and loving enough to do it. I hope that your counselor is a good one and not going to try to argue you into faith. But we will pray that God leads in all this even to whom you speak and how those conversations go.

Others, like the following correspondent, took more of a hard-line approach.

> Just one overall comment before I make individual comments, page by page. As I started out, I thought I would be able to comment on specific points fairly adequately. As I got further on and especially near the end, I grew more and more frustrated. At the end I didn't know whether you needed more love and sympathy and patience and a "handle with care" approach, or whether you needed a good kick in the pants!

> Cyrus Gordon: Just what kind of outstanding evangelical was he? What was his theological outlook and his set of biases?

> p.19 end: HUH? Are YOU telling God what he can and cannot say thru his prophets? Really, just who do you think you are, telling God how to run his business? [As you can tell, by now I am getting frustrated.]

> p.21 Price: and just who is this guy, writing not in any formal publication? And what are his biases? Man, in this day and age, if you are looking for any sort of trash of any kind to feed your mind, you'll find it on the internet. I don't determine my theology by looking at the internet. This has become absolutely ridiculous. Frankly, Ken, at this point you don't deserve loving help if this is where you are going to go to determine your outlook on Scripture. I mean it.

> So I say here, all right, if you want to sit in judgment on Scripture and listen to all the critics uncritically, instead of letting the record and its defenders speak, go ahead and do so, at your eternal risk. But I ask, is this a wise course? Again, read Proverbs 1–7.

A brief recovery of faith

After returning to Dallas, I began meeting with my designated counselor. He was wise, charitable, gentle, and willing to listen. He admitted he did not have answers to all my concerns. Though I was ready to leave the mission, Wycliffe decided to grant me a three-month probationary period during which I was to limit myself exclusively to the reading of Christian books. At first I chafed at the thought, but I realized it would not be prudent to give up so quickly seven years of training and service with the mission, not to mention a lifetime of devotion to Christ, so I agreed to the conditions. During the ensuing three months I read a number of apologetics books by authors like C. S. Lewis, Lee Strobel, and Greg Boyd. By two months into this period, I felt my faith had been substantially restored and was able to write the following to our supporters on September 11, 2000:

Dear Friends,

Thanks so much for your continued messages of encouragement and for your prayers. I've answered a number of your messages but am still working on the rest. Your prayers have indeed been effective as I have traveled through the long, dark tunnel of deep doubt. Though many questions remain, I made the decision about three weeks ago to continue in the faith. I am thankful to God for his grace in restoring my confidence in the reasonableness of the Christian faith and in assuring me personally that it is true. The book that helped the most was *Letters from a Skeptic*, by Greg Boyd, who exchanged letters for 3 years with his 70-year-old agnostic father before his father finally believed. I would recommend it highly to anyone going through struggles like mine. His emphasis was on the historical reliability of the Gospel record, focusing on the core of Christianity (that is, Christ). It is Christ who is the center of our faith, and the difficulties of the rest of the Bible are peripheral matters that can be dealt with (or held in suspension) after the central question of faith in Christ is resolved. I've also rediscovered the warmth and genius of C. S. Lewis (*God in the Dock, Surprised by Joy, Mere Christianity*) and am humbled by the depth of his knowledge and insight. I particularly appreciate his approach to the similarities of Ancient Near East myth and the stories in the Bible. He has a way of turning difficulties into an apologetic for the faith. . . .

Many of you expressed that my struggles are part of a spiritual battle.

While I do not understand much about what happens behind the scenes, nor do I have an interest in speculating, I do agree that my mind has been a spiritual battleground. . . .

We plan to meet again with Wycliffe administration in late October to determine our next step. Our desire is to return to Niger, though not before my renewed faith has stood the test of a few months' more time. We also depend on the ongoing input of Wycliffe and our supporters and friends in making this decision. The earliest we might return is January 2001.

Evolution

During this probationary period I happened upon a website by Glenn Morton, a former young-earth creationist. He had ghostwritten a chapter in defense of creationism for Josh McDowell's apologetic book *Reasons Skeptics Should Consider Christianity* (McDowell and Stewart 1986) and had contributed a number of articles to the *Creation Research Society Quarterly*. As an oil-exploring geophysicist, however, his findings in the field over time did not square with the young-earth creationist views he espoused, and he eventually became a theistic evolutionist. Though driven to the brink of atheism, he discovered a way to reconcile naturalistic, unguided evolution with the Genesis account of creation and was able to retain his belief in the inerrancy of the Bible. In reading his reasons for espousing evolution, I became convinced—unhappily at first—that the evidence was strongly in favor of common descent, and that I could not with integrity simply choose to disregard it. His attempt to reconcile evolution with Genesis seemed a little strained, but I felt it opened up the possibility for me to accept both evolution and the Bible. I read more on the subject by other Christian authors, notably Kenneth Miller, a Catholic cell biologist who wrote *Finding Darwin's God* (Miller 1999). I moved from seeing evolution as absurd to acknowledging there was no other way to explain the data.

I will have more to say about my reasons for acknowledging evolution in chapter 6.

Resignation from the mission board

When it came time to report to my counselor at the end of the probationary period, I was able to say that my faith had been substantially restored, but that I was somewhat troubled about the relationship between evolution and Christianity, particularly the evangelical brand of Christianity espoused by Wycliffe Bible Translators. Given that my faith had progressed, however, I expected Wycliffe at least to grant an extension to my probation or suggest a leave of absence, but instead they asked for our resignation. Charlene and I were both taken aback, but it was especially difficult for Charlene, who had grown up and served in the mission all her life. Though it hurt, I was somewhat relieved that I did not have to struggle with the decision any longer, and that I was free to resolve my remaining doubts without the pressure I had been experiencing as a member. In retrospect I believe

Wycliffe's decision was appropriate, and I am grateful for it. Here is the letter we wrote to our friends and supporters in December 2000 informing them of the decision:

> This is not the sort of letter we thought we would have to write at this stage in our lives, but here we are. In August we wrote of our return from Niger due to my doubts about the Christian faith. Through counseling, praying and reading, my faith was substantially restored by the end of August, though some issues continue to trouble me.
>
> On October 26 we met with our personnel administrator, who gently and apologetically recommended that we resign from Wycliffe Bible Translators. Though we knew it was a possibility, hearing those words was a real shock, especially for Charlene. Those in leadership feel that after having been through such a time of deep doubt, I needed a period of restoration without pressure to answer lingering questions, just as Wycliffe would recommend that new Christians not apply to Wycliffe until their faith has matured. They feel it would be best for our sake to put some roots down in a community and a church for several years before making a decision about further service with Wycliffe.
>
> After praying and reflecting on this recommendation, we submitted this letter:
>
>> Dear Wycliffe Bible Translators [. . .]:
>>
>> We, Ken and Charlene Daniels, hereby submit our resignation from Wycliffe Bible Translators [. . .], effective February 1, 2001. Though we are grieved over this departure, we are in full agreement with Wycliffe that this is the right decision in light of my (Ken's) recent and earlier struggles of faith.
>>
>> I concur with the Wycliffe administration that, in order to arrive at and demonstrate a genuine, internal faith that stands the test of time, it is best for me to resign and thereby be free from the external pressure to conform to Wycliffe's doctrinal statement. Though I have recently regained my faith after a period of intense doubt, my longstanding tendency to waver between faith and doubt make ministry as a Wycliffe member inadvisable at this time. We will wait several years before making a decision on whether to return to Wycliffe, and then only after receiving a clear sense of God's call to do so.
>>
>> The seven and a half years we have spent in Wycliffe have been both challenging and gratifying. We are at peace with all members and hold no ill will against anyone in the organization. We will greatly miss our colleagues in Niger and around the world. Despite the pain of this decision, we believe God has used us to accomplish His purposes both in us and

through us during our time as members. Please pray that He will continue to do so as we pursue life outside the organization.

In Christ,

Ken & Charlene Daniels

LIFE AS A NONBELIEVER

Crisis #5: Deism

Following the October 2000 decision I continued reading Christian literature, including the Bible and evangelical commentaries. After a couple of months, however, I began again to wonder whether I was simply propping up my faith by limiting my reading to only one perspective. I reasoned as follows: If Christianity is true, as I believe or hope it to be, then no alternative truth claims can stand up to it, and the gospel will be vindicated against its competitors as I seek God in prayer. Conversely, if Christianity is not true, I must know the truth, no matter the consequences. It is not legitimate for me to determine truth on the basis of its effect on me or on the basis of my personal desires. I simply want to know the truth— what it is that corresponds to reality, regardless of my desires or any other consideration.

It was then that I began reading *The Age of Reason* by Thomas Paine (Paine 1794), a deist[14] who championed human rights, fought slavery, and arguably more than any other individual shaped the colonialists' vision of American independence from England and the nature of the ensuing government. Though he rejected the Bible and Christianity, he was a firm believer in God:

> Do we want to contemplate His power? We see it in the immensity of the creation. Do we want to contemplate His wisdom? We see it in the unchangeable order by which the incomprehensible whole is governed. Do we want to contemplate His munificence? We see it in the abundance with which He fills the earth. Do we want to contemplate His mercy? We see it in His not withholding that abundance even from the unthankful (Paine 1794, 29).

His belief in God made me more open to his writings than to those of most modern atheistic skeptics. Anyone who denied God's existence was, in my opinion, unworthy of attention. Though Paine was not a biblical

---

[14] A deist is one who believes in God as creator but not as the author of any holy books or religions. Deists typically do not believe God intervenes supernaturally in the world.

scholar and some of his assertions were speculative and intemperate, many of his arguments were quite poignant, particularly the following:

> If those accounts be true, [Moses] was the wretch that first began and carried on wars on the score or on the pretence of religion; and under that mask, or that infatuation, committed the most unexampled atrocities that are to be found in the history of any nation. Of which I will state only one instance:
>
> When the Jewish army returned from one of their plundering and murdering excursions, the account goes on as follows (Numbers xxxi, 13 [KJV]):
>
> "And Moses, and Eleazar the priest, and all the princes of the congregation, went forth to meet them without the camp; and Moses was wroth with the officers of the host, with the captains over thousands, and captains over hundreds, which came from the battle; and Moses said unto them, *Have ye saved all the women alive?* behold, these caused the children of Israel, through the counsel of Balaam, to commit trespass against the Lord in the matter of Peor, and there was a plague among the congregation of the Lord. Now therefore, *kill every male among the little ones, and kill every woman that hath known a man by lying with him; but all the women-children that have not known a man by lying with him, keep alive for yourselves.*"
>
> Among the detestable villains that in any period of the world have disgraced the name of man, it is impossible to find a greater than Moses, if this account be true. Here is an order to butcher the boys, to massacre the mothers, and debauch the daughters.
>
> Let any mother put herself in the situation of those mothers, one child murdered, another destined to violation, and herself in the hands of an executioner: let any daughter put herself in the situation of those daughters, destined as a prey to the murderers of a mother and a brother, and what will be their feelings? It is in vain that we attempt to impose upon nature, for nature will have her course, and the religion that tortures all her social ties is a false religion.
>
> After this detestable order, follows an account of the plunder taken, and the manner of dividing it; and here it is that the profaneness of priestly hypocrisy increases the catalogue of crimes. Verse 37, *"And the Lord's tribute* of the sheep was six hundred and threescore and fifteen; and the beeves were thirty and six thousand, of which the Lord's tribute was threescore and twelve; and the asses were thirty thousand, of which the *Lord's tribute* was threescore and one; and the persons were sixteen thousand, of which the Lord's tribute was thirty and two." In short, the matters contained in this chapter, as well as in many other parts of the Bible, are too horrid for humanity to read, or for decency to hear; for it appears, from the 35th verse of this chapter, that the

number of women-children consigned to debauchery[15] by the order of Moses was thirty-two thousand.

People in general know not what wickedness there is in this pretended word of God. Brought up in habits of superstition, they take it for granted that the Bible is true, and that it is good; they permit themselves not to doubt of it, and they carry the ideas they form of the benevolence of the Almighty to the book which they have been taught to believe was written by his authority. Good heavens! It is quite another thing, it is a book of lies, wickedness, and blasphemy; for what can be greater blasphemy, than to ascribe the wickedness of man to the orders of the Almighty! (Paine 1794, 86–88; emphasis in original)

Not only did passages like these challenge my modern ethical sensibilities, but I came to see such commands as standing in contradiction to other biblical teachings like the Golden Rule. I had heard a number of explanations as to why the Old Testament morality differs from the New, but these now began to seem like mere rationalizations. And I confess I became *weary* of the *rationalizations*, concluding there could never be a legitimate explanation for self-serving behavior like the above. Any attempt to explain it away only lowered my respect for the apologists doing the explaining. Why would anyone, particularly mothers who love their daughters and daughters who value their dignity, even *want* to try to defend passages like these? The very inclination to justify such barbarism revealed to me the unyielding grip of an absolute faith upon its adherents. By Christmas of 2000 I found myself once more in the morass of doubt, and I have not considered myself a Christian believer since that time.

In this final crisis it was not only the Old Testament that drove me to doubt, but increasingly the New Testament as well. While the Old Testament can seem cruel in its advocacy of genocide and capital punishment for Sabbath breakers and rebellious sons, all these punishments are limited to the present life. By contrast, the New Testament suggests (at least, as I understood it; evangelical leader John Stott and Seventh-Day Adventists would disagree) that unbelievers will spend an eternity of conscious torment in hell, an infinitely worse proposition than being stoned

---

[15] If we assume that the Israelite soldiers married their captives, perhaps *debauchery* is technically not the most appropriate word here. Still, whether or not marriage was involved, and whether it was permanent or temporary (c.f. Deuteronomy 21:14), taking these virgins for sexual union was likely not a necessity in a culture where there were probably (we cannot know for sure) more women than men due to military losses. Some have posited that marrying these virgins was an act of protection, as these virgins could not have survived on their own. But it was the Israelite soldiers that had put them in this position in the first place, having slaughtered their compatriots.

to death. I could no longer believe that a god who enjoins us to love our enemies and to turn the other cheek could be capable of subjecting his own enemies to endless punishment with no further offer of mercy or reprieve (Hebrews 9:27). Why not simply annihilate his rebellious subjects and put them out of their misery?

Other objections to the New Testament I began to consider at this time were the failure of Jesus to return in the generation of his disciples as promised and the significant discrepancies in the resurrection accounts of the Gospels. I discuss both of these matters in chapters 10 and 11.

Though I wanted a world in which God was active, my personal observations during my relatively well-traveled life had never encountered an unambiguous supernatural event. Experience seemed to be at odds with the belief that God is at work in the world. I will expand on this issue in chapter 13.

In addition to Thomas Paine, I voraciously consumed books from a variety of perspectives, Christian and otherwise, opening up intellectual vistas I had been sheltered from all my life. Instrumental in cementing an empirical worldview were Harvard entomologist E. O. Wilson's *Consilience: The Unity of Knowledge* (Wilson 1998), which painted a neodeistic vision of a universe that follows natural laws from the motion of the planets to the neurons in our brains; Roger Fout's *Next of Kin: My Conversations with Chimpanzees* (Fouts 1997), which surprised me with the many cognitive similarities between chimps and humans; and Ed Babinski's *Leaving the Fold: Testimonies of Former Fundamentalists* (Babinski 1995).

Breaking the news of my relapse to Charlene was difficult, and she was understandably upset, but I could not pretend to believe what I thought to be untrue. Despite the challenges raised by our differences, my love for Charlene has remained steady, and our relationship, while occasionally strained, has stayed strong.

Wycliffe was generous in its severance package, offering continued financial support until February 2001. Though our support had been waning since the time of our return from Niger, we were able to make ends meet until I found a computer programming job in December 2000 at a small software company near Dallas, a job I have held up through the present. I returned to Niger in January 2001 to sell our remaining possessions and to say good-bye to our colleagues and African friends. It was difficult to come to terms with my lost role in God's eternal purpose that had originally led us to Niger. No longer was I a part of that tight-knit group of Christians who stood together through the heat, dust, and material and cultural challenges to bring the gospel to the ends of the earth. These challenges had seemed a small price to pay in return for the fellowship and sense of purpose that came from answering God's call. With all this behind me, I still firmly believed in God and continued to seek him, but I was puzzled by his silence and my inability to discern the purpose of my existence.

To illustrate the extent to which I remained convinced of God's existence, I include here an excerpt from a message I wrote to Robert Price (whose previously mentioned writings had heavily influenced me toward skepticism) in July 2001.

> I've often pondered the long path you've taken from fundamentalism to agnosticism if not atheism. For now I've found a stopping place in deism, having read Thomas Paine and some of the articles in deism.com and deism.org. Along with Einstein, I cannot conceive of how the mechanisms that generated matter, space, time, and the physical laws of the universe came into being naturalistically. I understand that there are naturalistic explanations for how matter and the universe may have come into being, but who/what made the naturalism on which these things were based? No matter how far one goes back in making explanations, there is always a prior something upon which the explanations must be founded. I have always wondered how the original bootstraps got pulled up, and I am compelled to imagine an entity outside the constraints of natural law. Perhaps you could comment on how you have answered that question for yourself. I accept evolution (in fact have spent much time recently debating my Christian friends on the subject), but am drawn to the mystery and wisdom of the intelligence that set the whole process in motion. Further, I do continue to seek God, believing s/he knows my thoughts, cares for me and desires for me to grow morally, even if s/he does not as a matter of principle pull any strings on my behalf in response to my prayers. I confess that this vision of God, the God of deism, raises a number of unanswered questions, but fewer questions than the vision of the God of the Bible.

> However, I have not shut the door on Christianity, perhaps because (a) I'm attracted to the kind of God who would intervene directly and self-sacrificially on behalf of his creation, (b) practically all my friends and family, including my wife, whom I dearly love, are evangelical Christians (not a good reason from an intellectual perspective, but it is a major personal factor) and (c) if Christianity turns out to be true, despite appearances, and I spend my life opposing it, then I'm in eternal trouble with the my Maker and Redeemer. If it were only flat earthers and young-earth creationist types who believed it, I might be able to dismiss it quite readily. But there are some very intelligent, scholarly people who accept it [Christianity] (for example, C. S. Lewis, Kenneth Miller, Alvin Plantinga), and I keep scratching my head, wondering how they, as intelligent and educated as they are, could believe

something that I, as a relative peon, find so incongruous. Even if there's only a 10% chance they're right, I hesitate to reject it completely, knowing the possible consequences. I would not get into an airplane if I knew there was a 10% chance of its crashing. This must appear to you as intellectual cowardice (it does to me too), but as one who is at least in part motivated by self-preservation, I would like to be virtually 100% sure that Christianity is untrue before closing the door on it.

Crisis #6: From deism to agnosticism

Though I never saw theism and naturalistic science as mutually exclusive, the more I reflected on the nature of evolution, the more troubled I became about its theological implications.[16] The problem of suffering and evil is a reality whether or not evolution is true, but evolution brought it into greater focus for me. Bertrand Russell captured my growing uneasiness:

> Since evolution became fashionable, the glorification of Man has taken a new form. We are told that evolution has been guided by one great Purpose: through the millions of years when there were only slime, or trilobites, throughout the ages of dinosaurs and giant ferns, of bees and wild flowers, God was preparing the Great Climax. At last, in the fullness of time, He produced Man, including such specimens as Nero and Caligula, Hitler and Mussolini, whose transcendent glory justified the long painful process. For my part, I find even eternal damnation less incredible, and certainly less ridiculous, than this lame and impotent conclusion which we are asked to admire as the supreme effort of Omnipotence. And if God is indeed omnipotent, why could He not have produced the glorious result without such a long and tedious prologue? (Russell 1950, 72)

---

[16] Though most of my fundamentalist and conservative evangelical readers may (as I did) see evolution as being somewhat at odds with their faith, moderate readers may wonder what all the fuss is about. Here is how my thinking proceeded:

Creationism *may* be true with or without phenomenon x, but without phenomenon x, evolution could *not* have happened. For example, creationism may be true whether the earth is young or old, but without an old earth, large-scale evolution would be impossible. Or creationism may be true if apparent homologies like five-fingered whales and five-fingered land mammals exist, but evolution would be untenable if there were no apparent homologies in nature. When enough of these phenomena built up in my mind, the scales began to tip in favor of evolution. I was especially concerned that to continue clinging to special creation in the face of these phenomena that supported evolution was to attribute deception to God, which I could not entertain. I then applied this same line of reasoning to the truth of Christianity and later to the existence of God. Though theism *may* be true with or without evolution, naturalism *cannot* hold without evolution (or something like it).

As did Richard Dawkins:

> The total amount of suffering per year in the natural world is beyond all decent contemplation. During the minute that it takes me to compose this sentence, thousands of animals are being eaten alive, many others are running for their lives, whimpering with fear, others are slowly being devoured from within by rasping parasites, thousands of all kinds are dying of starvation, thirst, and disease. It must be so. If there ever is a time of plenty, this very fact will automatically lead to an increase in the population until the natural state of starvation and misery is restored. In a universe of electrons and selfish genes, blind physical forces and genetic replication, some people are going to get hurt, other people are going to get lucky, and you won't find any rhyme or reason in it, nor any justice. The universe that we observe has precisely the properties we should expect if there is, at bottom, no design, no purpose, no evil, no good, nothing but pitiless indifference (Dawkins 1995, 85).

I continued reading various perspectives on philosophy and was moved particularly by the criticisms of deism (and other religions) by nineteenth-century agnostic Robert Ingersoll:

> Most people, after arriving at the conclusion that Jehovah is not God, that the Bible is not an inspired book, and that the Christian religion, like other religions, is the creation of man, usually say: "There must be a Supreme Being, but Jehovah is not his name, and the Bible is not his word. There must be somewhere an overruling Providence or Power."

> This position is just as untenable as the other. He who cannot harmonize the cruelties of the Bible with the goodness of Jehovah, cannot harmonize the cruelties of Nature with the goodness and wisdom of a supposed Deity. He will find it impossible to account for pestilence and famine, for earthquake and storm, for slavery, for the triumph of the strong over the weak, for the countless victories of injustice. . . .

> How can the Deist satisfactorily account for the sufferings of women and children? In what way will he justify religious persecution—the flame and sword of religious hatred? Why did his God sit idly on his throne and allow his enemies to wet their swords in the blood of his friends? Why did he not answer the prayers of the imprisoned, of the helpless? And when he heard the lash upon the naked back of the slave, why did he not also hear the prayer of the slave? And when children were sold from the breasts of mothers, why was he deaf to the mother's cry?

> It seems to me that the man who knows the limitations of the mind, who gives the proper value to human testimony, is necessarily an Agnostic. He gives up the hope of ascertaining first or final causes, of comprehending the supernatural, or of conceiving of an infinite personality. From out the words

Creator, Preserver, and Providence, all meaning falls (Ingersoll 1889, 237-38).

Though I followed Ingersoll's reasoning, I found it hard to abandon the conviction that a supreme being had at least set the cosmos in motion. I had earlier come to accept that God's purposes are hidden from us, yet I still gained comfort from the belief that a personal god does in fact exist and that we are here for a reason, even if we are ignorant of that reason. The transition from deism to agnosticism was in some respects as frightening as that from Christianity to deism.

I had nurtured a hope of an afterlife, but that prospect faded the more I considered evolution and the variety of life from protozoa to fish, reptiles, birds, mammals, apes, hominids, and humans. Through which twigs in this great bush of life can we draw a line between creatures that end their lives in the grave and those that continue through eternity? Do the immortals include tapeworms, insects, slugs, lizards, mice, dogs, dolphins, chimpanzees, *Homo erectus*, or just *Homo sapiens*? When defending God's purposes in relation to the natural suffering of animals, C. S. Lewis speculated that they may be given a place in the afterlife (Lewis 1970), yet it would be a stretch to think that all the lower animals could participate.[17] When a chimpanzee dies of hunger or cancer or as a result of blows from fellow chimps, is there any consolation of eternal bliss in the hereafter (and even if chimps go to heaven, of what benefit is their suffering on earth)? What leads us to believe that we, of all creatures, will live in a place where all our tears and pain will be wiped away and where we'll be reunited with our loved ones and our creator? While it was painful to acknowledge the likelihood that nothing lies beyond the grave, I was able to find consolation in the thought that there will indeed be no pain, no tears, no regrets, no bereavement, no disappointment: nothing.

In October 2001 there was an incident reported in the local news that tipped my perspective farther from deism toward an atheistic-leaning agnosticism. A driver struck a pedestrian on a freeway in Fort Worth and

---

[17] Some point to Isaiah 65:25 ("The wolf and the lamb will feed together, and the lion will eat straw like the ox, but dust will be the serpent's food. They will neither harm nor destroy on all my holy mountain") as evidence that animals will participate in the "new heaven and new earth" to come. Yet few Christians would accept the existence of procreation and death in heaven as Isaiah 65:17a, 20 suggests: "Behold, I will create new heavens and a new earth… Never again will there be in it an infant who lives but a few days, or an old man who does not live out his years; he who dies at a hundred will be thought a mere youth; he who fails to reach a hundred will be considered accursed."

continued the journey home, parking in the garage with the victim still on the hood of the car. The victim was conscious and pled for help, but the driver simply left him there for four days until he died, then with the help of a friend, dumped the body in a local park. The universal reaction to this incident was one of shock and outrage. Yet as I considered the millions of children who have died of starvation, wasting disease, and natural disasters, knowing that an omnipotent god could have come to their rescue in response to their pleas but did not, it was difficult not to see a parallel between God and the negligent driver. The more I contemplated the world in which we live, the harder it became to identify any clues that a benevolent, omnipotent Personality intervenes and orchestrates any of the events in our lives.

When responding to difficult questions about God's nature such as his apparent failure to intervene on behalf of suffering children, it is common for Christians to maintain that, like a dog undergoing a painful medical procedure, we cannot understand God's purposes in all that happens; we must simply trust that God knows what he is doing. This may be the case, but if so, how can anyone be held accountable for thinking like the dog, for failing to grasp that the purposes of God, if he exists, are good? We do not blame the dog for its reaction to the medical procedure. If we cannot imagine a good reason for the starvation or slow death of a child or a chimpanzee[18] due to leukemia, and our minds lead us to consider that God is either not good, not omnipotent, not omniscient, or nonexistent, is this grounds for the infinite wrath of God, even if he does in fact exist? Does God give us a mind and prevent us from drawing natural conclusions on pain of eternal punishment? It seems to me that such a stance is driven not by reason, or even by love, but by fear—fear that, whether or not traditional notions make sense, God may indeed turn out to be an infinite, exacting judge to those who question him. Might makes right, if you will.

Other troubling questions came to mind that I had never heard discussed in evangelical circles. These conundrums in themselves did not disprove God's existence, and I did not deny the possibility there might be good answers for them that lay beyond my ability to comprehend. But they illustrated to me that, by invoking the concept of a prime mover (God) to explain the problem of the origin of the universe (setting aside the problem of his origin), a number of other problems arise in its stead, some of them

---

[18] Animal suffering casts doubt on the argument that unexplained trials are intended for the development of people's character as a precursor to dwelling with God for eternity. Even if animals go to heaven, it is difficult to see that their suffering here below prepares them for an afterlife.

no less perplexing than the original problem that led to positing God in the first place.

Here are a few of the many that occurred to me: If God is infinite and the universe is finite, how much relative effort did it take for God to design and create the world? Anything finite compared to infinity is nothing. How much effort does it take him to keep us free from disease or accidents, or to give us a raise on the job or a nice tax refund, or to watch the miracle of a baby developing from conception to adulthood through gene expression and natural development? Did he make himself good, or does he simply happen to be good? If the latter, what choice does he have but to be good, and if he has no choice, can he legitimately be considered a free agent rather than subject to a higher law of goodness outside himself? Is his wisdom a virtue; does he carefully decide between two options and select the best, or does he, being omniscient, automatically know what is best? Is there any virtue in that which requires no effort?

If God is not bound by time, how can he decide to do or create anything? We cannot conceive of the acts of thinking, deciding and creating apart from time. These acts require a progression in time, moving from one state of mind and activity to another. If there was a "time" when there was no time or matter, at what "point" and in what manner, in all the infinite reaches of non-time and nonspace, was it possible for God's mind to transition into a decision to create time, space and matter? Or did he never make a decision, his plans having been an eternal aspect of his nature? If so, of what credit to him are such "plans"?

Some will perceive these as impertinent questions, sophistry on the order of Zeno's paradoxes, but they are honest questions, and suppressing honest questions is no virtue. If God does exist, surely he is big enough to bear them. Or must we make him out to be like a human despot, a king who cannot tolerate any challenge to his authority or existence? I do not know for sure whether God exists—I strongly doubt he does—but I am convinced that if he does exist, he knows my thoughts; I cannot hide them, and he must not mind my expressing them. I have asked him on many occasions to reveal himself to me and to overturn my doubts if they are ill-founded. So far this has not happened, either through a heavenly or a still, small voice; through scripture; or through the admonitions of many concerned believers.

Yet despite these puzzles, the difficulty of imagining naturalistic answers to the big questions like, why is there something rather than nothing? and, where did the natural laws come from? prevented me from diving headlong into atheism. I will discuss such questions in chapter 6.

During my years as a Christian (and even afterward), every now and then I would sense what I thought was God's presence: a warm, beautiful sensation flooding my soul as I talked to God (or sometimes when hearing a patriotic song or stirring classical music, but that's another category, or so I thought). One day in 2002 I prayed, as I had prayed many times before, "God, if Jesus is your Son, I accept his sacrifice for my sins, and I ask you to help me believe." Immediately this same wonderful sensation flooded my soul. I was thrilled. But wanting to know whether this was a unique confirmation of the gospel, I prayed, "God, if you are Allah, and if Mohammed is your prophet, please let me know." And the same sensation came over me! What was I to make of that, if as I had always been taught, Islam and Christianity are incompatible?

I cannot doubt that Mormons and members of other faiths experience this same phenomenon when they talk about a "burning in the bosom" as a way of authenticating their faith. Given this reality, I don't think it's unwarranted to ask for more than a sense of God's presence, a satisfaction with the doctrines of a particular faith, a sense of joy, the fellowship of believers, or a "could be" miracle to authenticate the kinds of claims that are made by many religions. If God truly intervenes in people's hearts, why did he allow this real sense of peace, what seemed like God's presence, to flood my soul in both cases, rather than in just the first case or in neither case? If God, being able to intervene in any way, had prevented any sensation at all, I would have been left much less confused. Though I continued to pray occasionally for God to make himself known to me were he to exist, this experience marked a turning point, a loss of expectation of ever hearing from God after years of seeking him.

On more than one occasion I even uttered desperate prayers such as these: "God, if you exist, and if you are the god of Abraham, Isaac, Jacob and Jesus, please strike me blind, or strike me dead today, leaving me enough chance in the last minute to repent and acknowledge you." Yet here I am, still alive with my vision intact.

Implications of my decision

In discussing my doubts with believers, the most persistent objection I have encountered is that, if Christianity is not true, and if there is no afterlife, and if God either does not exist or does not intervene in the world, then what is the basis for morality and ultimate meaning in life? Should we not simply eat, drink and be merry, for tomorrow we die? I will address these practical concerns in chapters 8 and 9.

For a full four years after my deconversion, I made the choice to continue attending an evangelical church with my wife and children in spite of my new outlook. But in matters of belief, I found I had no choice but to believe what I thought to be true and to disbelieve what I thought to be untrue. I cannot, for example, choose to believe that the earth is flat if I don't really think it is. Admonitions like, "You must choose to believe" are incomprehensible to me. But in matters of practice, I retain the option of choosing my behavior (at least, that is my perception). I continued to attend church for the sake of my wife and for the chance to interact with friends.

Some of my readers might wonder, "Why did he do it? Why did he leave the riches of his faith for the despair and danger of unbelief? It couldn't be that he sincerely believes Christianity to be untrue; there must be some deep underlying issues he's dealing with, some flaw, some hidden agenda, some dashed expectation." I have been asked this question directly, and my response has been this: you can dig as deeply as you like, and when you get to the bottom of it, you'll find I believe what I believe *because I think it's true.* There may indeed be some hidden issues that have driven me to this point, but if so, they are as hidden to me as to anyone else. I have shared freely with others and with God the matters I consider relevant to the question, but nothing definitive has turned up.

What is the source of Christians' reluctance to accept the above simple explanation for my unbelief? I cannot speak for all, but as a former Christian, here is how I might have internally processed a story like mine:

> He appears to be sincere, and he seems to have been a genuine believer, but he has now rejected God, so despite appearances, it may be that he never experienced a true relationship with God. According to Hebrews 10:26–27, the penalty for rejecting Christ after having followed him is divine judgment with no further hope for redemption, so Ken must be in danger of this fate. He claims his motives are pure, and that he truly perceives Christianity to be untrue, but there must be some fundamental flaw in him, something that marks him off from other believers who remain faithful to the faith, or he could not justly be subject to the judgment described in Hebrews 10. I don't know what it is, but I trust God's word over Ken's. His willingness to embrace something as problematic as evolution and to believe that the universe could have formed by chance must indicate an underlying desire to disbelieve despite the evidence for God and the Bible. At times he displays an argumentative, arrogant spirit, which may reveal a willful rebellion against God. Perhaps his motives are not as pure as he claims.

> On the other hand, he does seem to be aware that he's putting the eternal fate of his soul in jeopardy if he turns out to be wrong, so he must have a high degree of confidence in his belief that the gospel is not true. What could possibly have motivated him and driven him to such a degree of certainty that he would be willing to invite the disapproval of his friends, family,

supporters and mission board, to live without the hope of a hereafter, to abandon his calling and sense of purpose, and to risk divine judgment? Perhaps 2 Thessalonians 2:10b-11 pertains to him: "They perish because they refused to love the truth and so be saved. For this reason God sends them a powerful delusion so that they will believe the lie. . . ." This could mean he truly does believe what he says he believes, but God has brought this on him because of his rebellious spirit and his failure to acknowledge God for who he is. Only God knows his heart; it may be that Ken will ultimately recognize his error and return to God, refined by fire and more useful to God than before.

I invite Christian readers to consider the possibility that my apostasy is a result not of divine or diabolical deception but of a simple weighing of the evidence. It would be impossible for me to relate here the volumes of arguments I have considered on both sides of the question. It is my hope that those who are unable or unwilling to read skeptical works extensively will consider the possibility that there might be legitimate reasons for taking the position I have taken, given my willingness to risk my eternal destiny as a result of what I have come to believe.

It might be that I am wrong. It might be that I have not sought God sufficiently or studied the Bible thoroughly enough or listened carefully enough to the many Christians who have admonished me. Maybe if I could just be corrected in this or that point of misunderstanding, or if I could adjust my disposition in one way or another, then the beauty of Christ and the message of the gospel would dawn on me once again. Maybe. But the knowledge that billions of seekers have lived and died, calling out to God for some definitive revelation without ever receiving it, or receiving revelation that conflicts with the revelation others have found, contributes to my suspicion that there is no personal god who reveals himself to anyone.

When my second son was six, he asked my wife, "Mommy, is daddy going to go to hell?" I appreciated her response: "I don't know. Only God knows his heart." I was grieved to think that my own son should be tormented with such thoughts at his tender age. Yet it serves no purpose for me to blame anyone; we all believe what seems true to us, and I must (however reluctantly) respect the right of others to hold views contrary to mine if I am to expect the same from them. It is not always easy to navigate this no-man's land between my Christian loved ones and an unbelieving intellect, but I persist for the love of my family and for the chance to show other doubters that it's possible for life to go on even after breaking with the faith for the sake of intellectual integrity. May I always stay on the journey to truth and remain faithful to my family.

Chapter 3

Why I Remained a Christian: Pre-deconversion Perspective

In this chapter I present my reasons for remaining a Christian as faithfully as I can recall them, resisting any tendency to caricature my former reasons for believing. This approach will help safeguard me from the charge of creating straw men, as I will be discussing what I actually believed and why.

There will no doubt be a tendency for some to identify the Missing Piece or Pieces in my life that would have prevented me from exiting or that would have shown up my former faith as a shadow of the True Faith. This is fair. Perhaps certain readers will be able to uncover and share with me what I missed during my decades as a Christian, and the scales will fall off my eyes and I will embrace the True Faith, this time with all the essential ingredients in place. That is my genuine hope, but only if the Christian faith is true in any sense.

The positive factors I discuss in this chapter contributed to my ongoing commitment to Jesus for many years, even in the face of troubling questions and doubts. These are factors I openly cited to others and to myself as reasons for believing. In chapter 4, by contrast, I will examine what I now consider the more salient negative reasons for my reluctance to leave the faith. In chapters 5 through 14 I will examine critically and in more detail each of my positive reasons for believing. Following all that, in chapter 15 I will revisit in more detail one important negative reason for hesitating to abandon my faith.

THE POSITIVE INFLUENCE OF OTHER BELIEVERS

As previously mentioned, I was (and still am) an avid reader of the news and opinion magazine *Christianity Today*. I found its contributors to be reasonable, even intellectually stimulating. My favorite author was Philip Yancey, whose regular columns and books like *Disappointment with God* (Yancey 1988) probed many of the same aspects of doubt I was struggling with. His honesty concerning his own struggles, along with his willingness to confront the most disturbing aspects of the Christian faith, were like refreshing raindrops in a parched desert. In college I wrote to *Christianity Today* concerning my doubts about the Bible, and they responded with an intelligent letter about the pitfalls of the kind of wooden literalism that contributed to my doubts.

At the Christian university I was attending, I gained strength from deeply committed believers like electrical engineering professor Dr. Graff, who would invite students to his home on Sunday evenings to discuss the teachings of Francis Shaeffer, the twentieth-century apostle to educated skeptics. My later reading of Michael Behe's *Darwin's Black Box* impressed me like no other book—surely no intelligent person could accept Darwinism after such a stinging indictment, and surely there could be no excuse for not acknowledging the wisdom of God as creator.

As I mentioned in chapter 3, my March 2000 crisis of faith began while I was attending a linguistics workshop in the West African country of Burkina Faso. An exceedingly well-qualified PhD linguist from the Netherlands led the workshop, and I kept asking myself, "If Christianity is untrue, as I'm coming to realize, how is it that such an intelligent person accepts it? Am I more intelligent than she? Am I more knowledgeable than she? In short, why does she apparently not struggle to the extent that I do?"

I was also impressed with the intelligence and authority of authors I was reading during this crisis, particularly the German scholar Helmut Thielicke, who, though no fundamentalist "Bible thumper," made no apologies for his acceptance of Jesus' bodily resurrection.

In addition to my respect for intellectual believers, I was also drawn to the gospel through the example of those who had poured out their lives in the service of others. I thrived on missionary stories of savage tribes converting to Christianity and becoming peaceful and productive. Bible smuggler Brother Andrew; humanitarians Mother Teresa and Corrie Ten Boom; the roll call of martyrs throughout Christian history; civil rights activist Martin Luther King, Jr.; missionaries Bruce Olson ("Bruchko"), Don Richardson, Jim Elliot, and our own co-workers the Walters—how could the thinking of all these self-sacrificing individuals be so fundamentally misguided?

I recall as if it were yesterday the conflicting emotions I felt on a March 2000 day when I lay in bed, infected with malaria, struggling with doubt, hearing the joyful voices of my fellow missionaries across the courtyard singing "You came from heaven to earth to show the way," wishing I could have the assurance that I knew the way. Oh, that I could share their unquestioned faith, that I could rejoice as they, unburdened by the shackles of doubt! How could I ever survive if I turned my back on the sustaining fellowship of my co-laborers in Christ, friends who held a shared commitment to a noble, eternal vision?

THE DESIGN OF THE UNIVERSE AND OF LIFE

When I considered the origin of all things, including the very laws of nature I had studied in physics class, my mind was forced to conclude that a supervening intelligent, personal force was behind it all. I studied what William Lane Craig (Craig 1979) and J. P. Moreland (Moreland 1987) referred to as the *kalam* cosmological argument and found it unassailable. The existence of everything, especially the order and complexity of life and consciousness, cries out, "Design!" And where there is design, there is a designer.

During college I taught a Sunday school class in which I laid out the probabilities for all the steps required for the origin of the first living cell. The overall probability was smaller than the inverse of the number of atoms in the entire universe! And that's a probability that had to be overcome before natural selection and evolution could even get started!

In my youth I was consumed with arguments for creationism, reading and listening to Henry Morris, Duane Gish, Harold Slusher, Ken Ham, and others. Even after abandoning young-earth creationism for old earth creationism in college, I found the very idea of evolution laughable. It was just inconceivable to think that the astounding complexity of every life form could have come about through chance.

Reading Michael Behe's *Darwin's Black Box* put to death any doubt about the supernatural origin of living things.

I knew these arguments did not prove Christianity to be true, but they convinced me that God did in fact exist, eliminating atheism as a possibility and narrowing down the field to theistic religions like Judaism, Christianity, and Islam.

THE SUPERIORITY OF CHRISTIANITY OVER OTHER WORLDVIEWS

Though I was long troubled by many aspects of the Bible and the Christian faith, I could not find a more reasonable alternative. Islam, as I perceived it, seemed violent and (apart from Sufism) lacked the Christian emphasis on a relationship of love between God and humanity; Hinduism was polytheistic and far-fetched; Buddhism was distant and culturally alien and lacked the concept of a transcendent god with a will; Mormonism was historically shaky; Jehovah's Witnesses had falsely prophesied Jesus' return in the early twentieth century; deism lacked any anchor or way of knowing God's will; and atheism could not account for the origin of the universe, life, or human consciousness and morality. In short, though Christianity had its difficulties, it was less difficult than the alternatives, all of which were fatally flawed. There was simply nothing better than Christianity.

Prior to my brief return to faith in August 2000, I recall contemplating the attractive aspects of Christianity not shared by other religions. In the Christian worldview in which I was reared, it is God who reaches down to us, not we who reach up to God. God is not a distant creator unable to identify with our struggles and weaknesses; rather, he became a man, underwent temptation and hardships, and poured out his life for us. The Christian Bible emphasizes love as an attribute of God (see 1 John 4:7–21), and I did not observe a similar emphasis upon divine love in other religions.

The alternative worldview that for me came closest to the appeal of Christianity was simple monotheism or deism, a belief in a creator god stripped from all the trappings of scriptures and traditional doctrines. I recognized many of the same foibles in other religions as I did in Christianity, so I was not inclined to take any of them seriously. However, simple theism or deism left me cold; why would God create us and leave us in the dark with regard to his purposes for us? My struggle was between the coldness of deism and the difficulties of biblical Christianity. It was as though I were being forced to choose between the lesser of two evils.

THE FOUNDATIONS OF MORALITY

One of my greatest fears as I stood at the threshold of apostasy was the possibility of drifting morally if I could not rely on the presence of the Holy Spirit or the teachings of the Bible as a foundation for my moral convictions and behavior. I long resisted reading any materials critical of evangelical Christianity, but when I did so, my fears were confirmed. It seemed that most who left the faith for intellectual reasons also adjusted their views on objective morality, and then often ended up taking paths in their personal lives that I considered unfortunate or misguided. In particular, I was disturbed that free thought tended to lead to loose sexual mores.

I did not want to risk lowering my standards on extramarital sex, divorce, homosexuality, and abortion. My standards were high: I had never kissed a girl before meeting my wife, nor had I slept with anyone before marriage, nor had I slept with anyone outside marriage, nor had I been divorced. I had successfully resisted pornography, profanity, lying, stealing, cheating, drunkenness, and cruelty. And I did not want to make any moves that might jeopardize my purity. Knowing the tendencies of most apostates, I considered it a real risk to abandon the certainty of my moral convictions and the supportive structures of the church. (Incidentally, as a good Protestant, I never considered my purity to be a means of salvation, but a response of gratitude to Christ for saving me.)

PURPOSE AND MEANING

Another somewhat subjective motive for my remaining a believer was the dread of losing all ultimate purpose in life. My understanding as a Christian was that I had a reason for being on this earth and that my actions during my brief sojourn here would have a real impact for all eternity, not only on my own life, but also on the lives of all those I influenced. I had a reason for getting up in the morning and a reason for living each day to the end of my life with deliberation and purpose. Without Christ, what anchor would I have? What would my life be *for*? Why continue living? The thought that nothing might lie beyond the grave and that the most I could expect from life was to grab all the gusto I could get was profoundly, shatteringly unappealing, like walking into a long tunnel and seeing no light at the end; indeed, like not knowing whether there even was an opening at the other end.

The despair awaiting those outside the Christian faith is poignantly captured by Michael Ramsden:

> I was recently at a conference and asked all who had read any of the existentialists to raise their hands. A surprising number did. I then asked them to keep their hands in the air if they had ever read a happy one. Two things happened. Everyone put his or her hand down, and everyone laughed. There is no such thing as a happy existentialist novel! Why? For all the existentialists' desire for hope, when their open future was realized, it always disappointed. Indeed, confronted with this void, some (like Camus) concluded that suicide was the "one truly serious philosophical problem." In

this sense, hope becomes wishful thinking when it has no secure future (Ramsden 2001).

FULFILLED PROPHECIES

As a young adult I was captivated by apologetics and read many of the works of C. S. Lewis, Francis Shaeffer, Josh McDowell, and others. The Old Testament prophecies of the coming messiah particularly impressed me. McDowell equated the chances of all these prophecies having been fulfilled naturalistically with the probability of successfully picking up a single premarked silver dollar among others randomly spread two feet deep across the entire state of Texas (McDowell 1979, 167).

When I began contemplating the possibility of leaving Christianity, I recall thinking to myself, "What about Daniel's precise prediction of the time of Jesus' coming and death, issued over five centuries before the fact?" (McDowell 1979, 170–74) and, "What about the uncanny descriptions of Jesus' crucifixion and atonement in Isaiah 53 and Psalm 22?" Though I was troubled by many aspects of the Christian faith, I could not for many years deny the impressive nature of these prophecies.

THE RESURRECTION OF JESUS

Another intellectual support for my continued belief was the difficulty of accounting for the spread of early Christianity and the alleged martyrdom of several of the disciples if Jesus' resurrection had not actually occurred. People do not give up their lives for what they *know* to be untrue, so the martyred disciples must have truly believed that Jesus rose from the dead. And the disciples could not have believed in the resurrection as strongly as they did if a naturalistic alternative had been possible—for example, that the body had been stolen or lost or that Jesus had merely been revived from an almost-dead state.

THE RELIABILITY OF THE BIBLE

While reading through the Pentateuch at the age of ten, I came across a number of passages that disturbed me, but I reasoned as follows: Though the Bible contains many accounts I find difficult, it also contains great moral teachings that have led millions to be better people than they otherwise would have been. How could the scriptural authors, who enjoin us to tell the truth and to live up to high moral standards, themselves be guilty of lying? Surely they could not have been making up all these stories!

C. S. Lewis, an expert in mythological writings, had this to say of the Gospels:

> Now, as a literary historian, I am perfectly convinced that whatever else the Gospels are they are not legends. I have read a great deal of legend and I am quite clear that they are not the same sort of thing. They are not artistic enough to be legends. From an imaginative point of view they are clumsy, they don't work up to things properly. Most of the life of Jesus is totally unknown to us, as is the life of anyone else who lived at that time, and no people building up a legend would allow that to be so (Lewis 1970, 158–59).

Other scholars of the highest caliber, like N. T. Wright and Bruce Metzger, concurred with Lewis' assessment. In the absence of any positive proof to the contrary, why question the integrity of the biblical authors? I tend to give others the benefit of the doubt in what they say, particularly if I consider them trustworthy and do not discern any apparent motives for promulgating falsehoods. The same benefit of the doubt, then, should be accorded to the writers of the Gospels and of the other books of the Bible.

MIRACLES AND ANSWERED PRAYER

From early childhood my faith was bolstered by stories of supernatural events in a Christian context. Several members of an Ethiopian firing squad were dumbfounded when all their guns failed to deploy against a would-be Christian martyr. A surgeon was taken aback to find a pervasive malignancy simply disappearing before his eyes when operating on a cancer patient. A man was found levitating above his bed. An individual with legs of unequal lengths found them equalized in an instant. A woman bound to a wheelchair for years was suddenly able to jump up and walk one day while in the course of praying and listening to inspirational music. Several of these reports came from reputable people, ones I trusted—not hucksters or fame seekers. Surely Christianity had to be true and naturalism or deism false if these reports were credible, and I did not have any compelling reason to doubt them. These were confirmations to me that even if I did not have the privilege of witnessing an astounding miracle myself, God was indeed active in this world and looking out for his children.

As previously related, on a Saturday I prayed to meet my wife at church the next day, and my prayer was answered. That was one of the most exciting and faith-building experiences of my life, a story I proudly shared with anyone who asked how Charlene and I met.

A PERSONAL RELATIONSHIP WITH A LOVING, ALMIGHTY GOD

Though a professing Christian from the age of four, I experienced what I considered to be a profound deepening of my relationship with God at the age of 14. I recall vividly a night when I lay awake until 2:00 a.m., pouring out my gratitude to God for creating such an awe-inspiring universe and for calling me to be a part of his grand plan. I felt as though I was an audience of one before God, telling him my innermost thoughts, fears, and desires, while calling on him to reveal himself in a similar way to all my friends.

This intimate relationship with God, which I believed was possible only through the sacrificial death of Jesus on the cross, grew and matured over the years, though with many peaks and valleys, and remained the most defining aspect of who I was. It was a thought too terrible to entertain that this relationship could have been merely imaginary. I could not accept that I had simply been talking to myself, that the waves of joy and the earnestness with which I believed I had been in touch with the very creator of the universe were no more significant than the Mormons' "burning in the bosom." Nothing meant more to me, so I was in no hurry to give it up, despite the many intellectual challenges to my faith.

When I eventually read for the first time a book challenging evangelical Christianity (Price 1993), it was the chapter entitled "The Personal Savior" that I found hardest to swallow. Much of what the author wrote in the other chapters captured my attention, but his attack on the notion of "a personal relationship with Christ" upset me to the core. If God exists (which I firmly believed at the time), shouldn't it be reasonable to conclude he would want to relate to his creatures? To think that God might have created us and then left us to drift in this difficult world on our own seemed pointless and cruel.

Chapter 4

Why I Hesitated to Examine my Faith Critically

In virtually every domain we are well served to treat unusual or outlandish claims skeptically. If we hear on the radio that a new diet pill will allow us to shed 50 pounds with no effort, we would be remiss not to investigate what studies have been done to test and approve this new miracle drug before pulling out our credit card. It might turn out that the claims are true, but until an independent scientific study has been conducted, we risk losing our money, time, and possibly health in pursuit of an ineffective or harmful product. Likewise, if a used car salesperson offers us a deal that sounds too good to be true, we had best hire an independent mechanic to inspect it before making the purchase.

As an evangelical Christian I was encouraged to think critically about my beliefs and the beliefs of others as long as I restricted my critical thinking to a biblical framework. This spirit of intramural inquiry is exemplified by the Bereans in the early church:

> Now the Bereans were of more noble character than the Thessalonians, for they received the message with great eagerness and examined the Scriptures every day to see if what Paul said was true (Acts 17:11).

It was fair game to examine critically the beliefs of cults and prosperity gospel televangelists using the Bible as the standard, but it was always understood that we were not to examine critically the basis for biblical authority or the gospel itself. Why did I accept the rule that I must not question the foundations of the gospel? That is the subject of this chapter.

Not all believers are equally reluctant to entertain critiques of their faith. If you have read this far, you are no doubt more open to inquiry than I was for most of my Christian life. A Reformed Christian scholar I dialogued with in 2001 chided me upon learning I had never read skeptical materials until shortly before my deconversion. Perhaps I might have been inoculated to critical arguments against Christianity if I had faced them head-on when my faith was more stable.

However, as a member of the evangelical faith, was I to blame for my neglect in this matter? In all my years of faithful church attendance, Bible studies, Christian college, missions training, and seminary, I do not recall one sermon, not one injunction encouraging me to examine my faith critically. Imagine your pastor preaching this from the pulpit next Sunday:

> I believe the Christian faith is true. As such, it can withstand any criticism. I encourage you not to take my word that it is true, nor the Bible's word, nor C. S. Lewis' word, nor anyone else's word. Think for yourself and come to your own conclusions. Probe your faith mercilessly to see whether it can stand the test. Read Thomas Paine, Robert Ingersoll, Bertrand Russell, Richard Dawkins, and Robert M. Price. Read the most appealing texts you can find from other faiths. Get into the minds of these writers, and listen to them sympathetically in an effort to compensate for the years that Christianity has been presented to you in the best possible light.

When I was still a Christian, I was able to provide to others a number of what I considered to be good reasons for my faith. In the chapters to come I will investigate many of these openly held reasons for believing. In the present chapter, however, I will focus on several underlying factors that prevented me from reconsidering my faith for many years, factors I would have been less likely to acknowledge overtly at the time.

I have a puzzle on my hands: how could Christianity *not* be true if so many individuals find it compelling and remain in the faith? What am I missing? Why is my story of apostasy the exception and not the rule? More to the point, I now come to the central question of this chapter and the entire book: *What would it take to ensure that a religion like Christianity thrives even if untrue?*

To answer this question I will look back at my experience and the struggles I faced as I transitioned out of faith. Why was I reluctant to subject my faith to the same scrutiny to which I would naturally subject a used car deal when the price appears too good to be true? I invite you to consider each section in this chapter as an ingredient in a recipe for ensuring the survival of a religious faith, whether or not the faith is true.

THE SUM OF ALL FEARS AND COSTS

This first ingredient is more of a cluster of considerations, a meta-obstacle if you will, than it is a specific impediment to reconsidering my commitments. It is the sum of all the fears and costs, real or imagined, that I believed I would incur were I to leave the fold.

I recall the dread that came over me in Burkina Faso when I first began to think that I had been misguided all my life. My mind raced with dire imaginings about how all my friends and family would react to my change of heart. What could I say to my wife upon suspecting my faith was ill-founded? To my family? To our financial and prayer supporters and churches who had sacrificed to make it possible for us to come to Africa to lead the unreached peoples to the Light? To our fellow missionaries and to our mission organization of which we had been members for seven years? I did not know of anyone else who had done such a thing as I was contemplating—a missionary coming out of the closet to declare he no longer had confidence in the very foundation of his faith. I risked becoming a curiosity and a pariah at the same time. In short, I risked losing all that I held dear—friends, family, and faith.

My heart seemed to palpitate out of control and my stomach turned sick. Would I lose the respect of those I held dearest?

What ongoing purpose would my life serve? If God exists, how could I discern his will? And even more frightening, what if I were to find myself alone in an enormous universe that doesn't give me a thought? What if I were to become just another human in a sea of six billion others—*just another human!*—not, as I had previously imagined, a set-apart son of the Most High?

If I moved into uncharted territory away from the moorings of the Christian community, would I be set adrift morally? How could I live without the Christian fellowship I enjoyed in church, Bible studies, missions meetings, and devotional times with my wife?

How could I support my family if I were to leave Wycliffe? Though I had studied computer science in college, it had been over seven years since I had worked in software development, and the fast changing would of computers had become almost unrecognizable to me over the course of those years. My prospects for secular employment were limited.

In the wake of a crime, the judicial system actively seeks out a plausible motive for the deed. As the great Agatha Christie detective Hercule Poirot put it, "I am very old-fashioned in my methods. I follow the old adage, 'Seek whom the crime benefits'" (Christie 1974, 532). Was financial gain, revenge, or the quest for power a factor? Identifying the motives for the crime helps narrow the field of possible perpetrators. In the same way, it can be instructive to ask, when two individuals hold two opposing viewpoints after looking at the same evidence, which of these two has the most to lose by switching sides. Though it does not necessarily follow that the one who has the most to give up is deceived, it can serve as a good starting assumption. In my case the potential costs for leaving my faith served as a powerful disincentive to examining my beliefs clearly and critically.

One cost factor we are all prone to if we have given our allegiance to a cause for a significant period of time is what psychologists call the "sunk cost fallacy." As a software developer I am all too familiar with the argument that says, "We've already spent x number of dollars on this product. We cannot waste that investment, so we must see it through to the bitter end." Rather than simply calculating the cost of starting over and comparing it with the cost of making the existing product viable, we somehow feel it necessary to factor in the already invested cost of prior development (Shermer 2007a). Or if our country has fought a failing war for years with great loss of life, we rationalize the continuation of that war by insisting we must not allow our deceased soldiers to have died in vain.

Likewise, I had invested a great deal of time and energy and dreams to become a Bible translator, and I was finally on the cusp of realizing these dreams. I had spent seven years training with Wycliffe Bible Translators, had taken a year of seminary before that, and had studied four years at a Christian college before that. From the time I was fourteen, my single-minded purpose was to serve God, and every decision I had made was driven by this desire. I had spent no doubt thousands of hours in prayer and Bible study. To concede that I was mistaken all along was to be confronted with the possibility that all of this was in vain. What a bitter pill to swallow!

Anyone who maintains a fundamentally incorrect worldview in the face of sufficient evidence to discount that view is likely motivated by factors other than a pure love of truth and reason. On this many Christians would agree, as evidenced by those who have sought to identify the *real* reasons behind my defection from the faith. Perhaps it was brought on by malaria-induced discouragement as a missionary in Africa. Or maybe it was my lack of steadfastness in resisting the wiles of Satan, or a fatal dose of pride that pitted me against my creator.

The point I am making is that, all else being equal, those who have the most to lose by giving up their beliefs are less likely to apply effective skepticism to their ideas than those who have less to lose. Given this consideration, it is little wonder that my deconversion process was so long, winding, and tumultuous. Imagine what it would cost you to give up your faith tomorrow morning; if it is unbearable even to think of it, then you ought to consider how much the cost of leaving your faith is influencing your ability to judge your faith critically and objectively.

Many of the consequences of deconversion I feared most turned out to be exaggerated. Perhaps if I was mistaken, I thought, God would mess up my life or even bring it to an end. Perhaps I would be shunned and despised by all those I held dear, and I would end up divorced and paying child support. Perhaps I would lose all my friends. Perhaps I would have no means of supporting my family. Perhaps I would feel empty and aimless.

I cannot guarantee you immunity from all these things; they are real fears. But it's unlikely that every one of these things will happen to you or that any of them that do will be as tragic as you might imagine. If they do befall you, you will be surprised how capable you are of weathering your worst fears, provided you face them one day at a time.

The church would like you to believe that life outside its boundaries will be bleaker and more meaningless than the life most apostates actually experience. It serves the purposes of the church quite well if she can succeed in painting the darkest possible picture of what your life will be like if you dare to leave the fold.

If you leave your faith behind, you may no longer feel a sense of supernatural protection from accidents on the road, and you may fear the loss of providence in your health and finances, but at the same time, you'll gain an assurance that no one (whether God, Satan, angels or demons) has a silver bullet with your name on it, as Robert Price likes to put it (Price 2006).

Even though it would be costly for most devout Christians to leave their faith, it does not necessarily follow that Christianity is untrue. After all, in some contexts (for example, in former Soviet Russia and in some Muslim societies), it can be very costly indeed to *become* a Christian believer. However, if my experience has any general applicability, these cost factors contribute significantly to keeping Christians in the faith, at least for a time.

PSYCHOLOGICAL INERTIA

In our grade school science classes we learned the principle of inertia: an object in motion tends to stay in motion unless a force changes its course. A speeding locomotive, for example, cannot readily be put into reverse. The same is true of our core beliefs. If we were to jump rapidly and endlessly from one opposing idea to another, we would be deemed unstable, even psychotic, and would not be able to function in society. If the ideas we have held for many years work for us and we're comfortable with them, we have little motivation to consider seriously any other perspective.

In the apt words of the seventeenth-century pioneering scientist Francis Bacon:

> The human understanding when it has once adopted an opinion . . . draws all things else to support and agree with it. And though there be a greater number and weight of instances to be found on the other side, yet these it either neglects and despises . . . in order that by this great and pernicious predetermination the authority of its former conclusions may remain inviolate (Bacon 1620, sec. 46).

This psychological inertia is common to us all, whatever our worldview. It does not favor Christianity over atheism or any other system of belief. Nevertheless, it long served for me as an important obstacle to considering other points of view.

Accident of Birth, Benefit of Doubt (ABBOD)

Several years ago one of my sisters wondered aloud whether she would have been a Christian if she had grown up in a non-Christian country to non-Christian parents. This question, one that had earlier come to my mind, had occasionally given me pause during my years as a believer.

Looking back now as a nonbeliever, I am not sure why I was only mildly troubled by the likelihood that I was a Christian (rather than, for example, a Muslim or a Hindu) because my family and society had influenced me to accept Christianity (rather than Islam or Hinduism). Over time I began to realize that my tendency to give the benefit of the doubt to the religion of my parents was no different from the tendency of individuals from other lands and other faiths to give the benefit of the doubt to the religion of their parents.

I call this tendency the Accident of Birth, Benefit of Doubt (ABBOD) principle. I will have more to say concerning this factor in chapter 5. For now I note that I consider this to be one of the most important ingredients for maintaining a religion, whether or not the religion is true.

The Virtue of Faith

If God is infinite and we are his finite creation, as I firmly believed until well after my departure from Christianity was complete, we should expect to have difficulties understanding God and his ways. Just as ants cannot understand the ways of humans, I reasoned, we cannot comprehend the designs of God. It should be no more disconcerting that the Bible contains difficulties than that God creates babies with deformities or allows seemingly innocent suffering in the world.

Since I had no doubt of God's existence until well after my deconversion, I had to acknowledge the following as stated from God's perspective: "As the heavens are higher than the earth, so are my ways higher than your ways and my thoughts than your thoughts" (Isaiah 55:9).

From childhood it was instilled in me that faith is a virtue. Just as it is a virtue to trust those we love, even when we don't understand certain actions of theirs, we must trust the wise and good creator of the universe, even when his actions appear mysterious to us. I was reminded that, if Christianity were plain and obvious, there would be no merit in believing it, much as there is no merit in our believing that the earth is round in the wake of ample evidence that it is indeed round. God provides sufficient reasons for accepting his way to those who desire to follow him but leaves enough ambiguity and doubt to allow for self-justification on the part of those who prefer to go their own way.

A verse I had memorized in fourth grade was my constant companion during times of doubt: "And without faith it is impossible to please God, because anyone who comes to him must believe that he exists and that he rewards those who earnestly seek him" (Hebrews 11:6).

There are two common meanings of the word *faith*: (a) trusting a person who has not let us down in the past, and (b) believing a set of propositions in the absence of empirical evidence. It is this latter sense of *faith*, the one set forth in Hebrews 11:1, that is the object of my discussion in this section: "Now faith is being sure of what we hope for and certain of what we do not see."

The virtue of faith is common to most successful religions; this is why we call them "faiths." But can it be only a coincidence that the most successful religions happen to be those that value faith, or is it rather that this value permits them to survive in the face of all criticism? The skeptic's version of Hebrews 11:6 might read, "And without faith it is impossible to maintain a religion grounded upon insufficient evidence."

Of all the requirements for a religion to thrive without being true, the virtue of faith stands out as the most transparent. If I had a dollar for every time I've heard, "Sure, Christianity may have difficulties, but God's ways are higher than our ways," I believe I might be quite wealthy by now.

It may well be true that God exists, that he inspired the Bible, and that his ways are incomprehensible to us. But if this is *not* the case, how could we ever hope to find that out?

I was able for several years to fall back on faith in the face of many troubling questions about the Bible and the Christian faith. However, the time eventually came when I began to consider the possibility that this escape hatch could also be used to prevent members of other religions from leaving *their* faith, just as I was using it to justify staying in *my* faith. I perceived many other religions to be more problematic than Christianity, but what if their gods' ways were even higher (that is, beyond human understanding) than the Christian god's ways?

As mentioned earlier, I have often been confronted with the assertion that God doesn't want the truth to be too obvious; otherwise, it would be a no-brainer for everyone to believe, and that would undercut our free will, making us into robots. (Those who use this argument have tended to be quite persistent, even when I do my best to explain why I find it unsatisfactory.) Francis Collins, director emeritus of the Human Genome Project, puts it this way:

> If the case in favor of belief in God were utterly airtight, then the world would be full of confident practitioners of a single faith. But imagine such a world, where the opportunity to make a free choice about belief was taken away by the certainty of the evidence. How interesting would that be? (Collins 2006, 33–34)

Perhaps the world would indeed be a less interesting place if everyone held the same religious beliefs by force of evidence. But consider what a price we must pay merely for the sake of a little more spice: wars without end; animosity between family members who practice different faiths; bickering among coreligionists over the proper interpretation of their holy books; and in the life to come, eternal banishment and torture of the majority of earth's population.[19] If God merely wanted to make life interesting, why punish eternally those who aren't able (through accident of birth or intellectual objections) to piece together the many ambiguous clues to come to the correct and safe conclusion?

Why is the idea that pleasing God requires faith so seldom challenged? For those of us with children, must we make our existence uncertain to them in order to give them an opportunity to make free choices? No, if our children are normal, they routinely manage to get themselves into trouble

---

[19] To be fair, Collins does not seem to take a firm stand on hell, but this same argument is employed by many who do take hell seriously.

in full view of us, knowing we exist, and knowing we have explicitly forbidden such behavior, and knowing they will be punished for it. If this is the case, then why must God hide himself or his will to test us? Is it not more likely that God simply does not exist, or at least that he does not hold individuals eternally accountable for their decision to believe one way or another, than that he deliberately obfuscates the evidence for his existence and will?

SANCTIFIED EXCEPTIONALISM

Along with many evangelicals (especially in the Reformed tradition), I tended to distrust human reason—particularly unregenerate human reason. As a result of the original sin of Adam and Eve, all humans since the beginning have been cursed with a totally depraved nature, affecting not only our actions but also our will and intellect. We are thus powerless to arrive at the truth through our own ponderings; we are doomed to failure even before we start. The only hope we have of escaping this fate is to receive the atonement of the Second Adam, that is, Jesus Christ. By this atonement we are regenerated and sanctified so our intellect is freed to perceive the glorious truth of the gospel that was not apparent to us in our depraved state. John Calvin insisted we are incapable of knowing truth without Christ:

> As soon as ever we depart from Christ, there is nothing, be it ever so gross or insignificant in itself, respecting which we are not necessarily deceived (Calvin 1578, "The Argument," 25).

It was not often as a Christian that I studied the writings of non-Christian philosophers, but whenever I ran across a confident nonbeliever, I was able to dismiss his confidence as the ill-begotten fruit of an unregenerate mind.

Eventually I came to see this position as circular: we cannot hope to know the truth unless we are sanctified, but we cannot be sanctified unless we know the truth. Before questioning this tenet, I was generally impervious to arguments unbelievers might lay at the feet of my faith, knowing that these skeptics were by definition depraved, even at the level of the intellect. Later I came to see that this axiom provided a too-convenient escape from having to examine my views as critically as I would expect others to examine theirs. Initially I was convinced I had received the gospel through the influence of the Holy Spirit and believed that the creator of the universe dwelled within me, so I did not have to do the hard intellectual work of determining whether my faith was true. I sensed the presence of the Holy Spirit in my life and believed that apart from that presence, my intellect was bankrupt. There was therefore no point in applying my mind to uncover the demerits of Christianity or the merits of other competing worldviews.

The message from the Bible is clear: human reason, unsupported by a commitment to God, is worse than useless; it is irredeemably deceptive.

> Trust in the LORD with all your heart and lean not on your own understanding (Proverbs 3:5).

> See to it that no one takes you captive through hollow and deceptive philosophy, which depends on human tradition and the basic principles of this world rather than on Christ (Colossians 2:8).

Lest any evidence against the gospel come to light on the part of the intellectually minded, Paul locks the exit door by casting aspersions on those who would investigate using human reason. I came to realize that this renders the Christian faith a self-supporting fortress, true by definition, and impervious to any external criticism. This is a very shrewd tactic, whether or not the Christian faith is true, but is especially effective if Paul's claims cannot withstand intellectual scrutiny. Before my deconversion I heard many a sermon based on passages like this:

> Do not deceive yourselves. If any one of you thinks he is wise by the standards of this age, he should become a "fool" so that he may become wise. For the wisdom of this world is foolishness in God's sight. As it is written: "He catches the wise in their craftiness"; and again, "The Lord knows that the thoughts of the wise are futile" (1 Corinthians 3:18–20).

Later I came to understand the need for a level playing field, absent the (sometimes self-righteous) assumption that the presence of the Holy Spirit endowed me with a certain degree of immunity from error, an immunity that unbelievers do not enjoy. Granted, if the Holy Spirit does in fact exist and he dwelled within me, it goes without saying that I had a decided edge over those not making such claim. But to assume without firm evidence that this is the case begs the question. What is the basis for claiming that the Holy Spirit lives within Jesus' followers? Is it because the Bible tells us so? This is a circular argument, for the authority of the Bible is the very question at stake. Unless we can prove the Bible to be true, we cannot legitimately use it to prove that the Holy Spirit lives within us, granting us privileged insight and wisdom not available to those outside the faith. And unless we can support the claim that God lives in us, we cannot use that claim to support the Bible.

If our conviction that the Holy Spirit takes residence in us is based on a personal feeling, how do we answer Mormons or Sufi Muslims[20] or Buddhists who claim similar experiences? Has the Holy Spirit given us an objective basis for making his presence known? Did he, for example, speak to some of my readers verbally five years ago and inform them that on today's date, they would find themselves reading a discussion of the Holy Spirit written by Ken Daniels, and did they record this revelation in writing and provide it to others in advance of their reading this? If he has done anything that specific to confirm his presence, then I would be the first to want to know of it; my eternal destiny might hang on being made aware of such a marvel. But if our assurance of his indwelling is merely subjective and personal, then I trust I will be forgiven for not lending any more credence to such claims than I now give to my own sense of God's presence as a former believer or to the claim of the "burning in the bosom" of the Latter Day Saints (Mormons) or to the "inner light" of the Quakers.

The Bible does not have a monopoly on the observation that "the heart is deceitful above all things" (Jeremiah 17:9). Whether or not the basis for his reasoning is sound, cognitive scientist and atheist Steven Pinker sides with the pessimists of human nature:

> And by showing that self-deception is likely to evolve (because the best liar is the one who believes his own lies), sociobiology encourages self-scrutiny and helps undermine hypocrisy and corruption (Pinker 2002, 111).

We are all liable to self-deception when it suits our interests; for this reason we must maintain a constant state of vigilance against it. For most of my believing life, the conviction that God was on my side and that my mind had been regenerated through the sanctifying action of the Holy Spirit effectively prevented me from understanding or acknowledging that my own tendency toward self-deception was no less debilitating than for outsiders. Until I fully accepted I had no edge over unbelievers in discerning truth, I remained in effect at greater risk for self-deception than those making no such claim.

As long as I believed my faith in Jesus secured my redemption and that unbelievers' persistent lack of faith secured their damnation, it was impossible to respect the arguments of skeptics. Even though I appealed to the self-effacing doctrines of grace, unmerited favor, and election, it was

---

[20] See *The Conference of the Birds* (Attar 1177) for a Sufi work with an evangelical flavor.

difficult to suppress a sense of divinely conferred righteousness that barred consideration of outsiders' views.

In an interview following the publication of her book *Mistakes Were Made (But Not by Me): Why We Justify Foolish Beliefs, Bad Decisions, and Hurtful Acts*, Carol Tavris explains the mechanisms by which we justify our own behavior and beliefs (Tavris 2007). Almost without exception, we inwardly tend to think of ourselves as good people,[21] and good people cannot be fundamentally mistaken. For example, prosecuting attorneys will often develop elaborate face-saving techniques in the wake of DNA-based exoneration of criminals they had previously helped to convict. These include, "The guy may not have done it, but he was a menace to society; he had been convicted of previous crimes and needed to be off the streets and behind bars anyway," or "Someone in the DNA lab must have made a mistake; the guy is guilty—I just *know* it." These prosecutors, often hard-working, respectable members of their community, nonetheless fail to recognize their ability to err. The lesson to be learned is that goodness in no way guarantees correct belief. Before the advent of science there were countless good individuals who believed the sun revolves around the earth, but they were mistaken nonetheless.

It is not a sin to be mistaken; it happens to all of us. The noblest and most sincere people on earth could be mistaken in some of their core beliefs. If it happens to good Mormons, good Muslims, good Hindus and good atheists, why not also to good Christians? I had to ask myself, "Is there something special about me that exempts me from being mistaken?" As C. S. Lewis wrote of Bishop John Fisher (it could well be true of most if not all of us), "His sincerity is undoubted; but while his heart is in earnest, his intellect is perhaps not so hard at work as he supposes" (Lewis 1954, 162).

If, according to Tavris, we are all vulnerable to thinking of ourselves as good people, and hence unlikely to be mistaken in fundamental moral or spiritual matters (even if we are in fact mistaken), how can any of us hope to escape this trap and see reality for what it is, rather than what we mistakenly think or hope it to be? How can we take to heart physicist Richard Feynman's injunction, "The first principle is that you must not fool yourself, and you are the easiest person to fool" (Feynman 2000, 212)? There is no sure solution, but if we really do wish to have a shot at exposing our blind spots, we must make an effort to expose ourselves to

---

[21] This is known as the "Lake Wobegon Effect," where all the children are "above average." Polls show that interviewees consistently rate themselves as being more friendly, honest or intelligent than average.

others with whom we disagree. If I'm a Democratic politician, I must associate with and *listen to* my Republican colleagues. If I'm an atheist, I must go out of my way to associate with and *listen to* Christians, Muslims and Jehovah's Witnesses. If I'm a white person and can't understand the complaints of African Americans, I must go out of my way to establish friendships with African Americans—or, as John Howard Griffin did, turn my skin black and see how others treat me (Griffin 1961).

The spirit of sanctified exceptionalism driven by the belief that God lived in me—the notion that I was divinely exempted from having to vet my faith through the same critical evaluation I required of others—calls to mind the despots in George Orwell's allegory of Communism, *Animal Farm*. The animals started out their experiment by sharing all possessions in common, with equality held up as the greatest of virtues. It was not long, however, before the pigs began appropriating more than their fair share of the provisions for themselves. Their response when confronted with the ensuing inequality: "All animals are equal, but some animals are more equal than others" (Orwell 1946, 133).

Chaz Bufe describes this spirit on an edgier note in *The American Heretic's Dictionary*:

> **ATHEIST**, n. A person to be pitied in that he is unable to believe in things for which there is no evidence, and who has thus deprived himself of a convenient means of feeling superior to others (Bierce and Bufe 2004, 68).[22]

GOOD AND BAD

It had been drilled into my thinking that the only or best sanctuary of bona fide goodness is within the Christian faith, and that only sin, depravity and despair lie outside of it. A simple equation was burned almost irrevocably into my mind: *Christian = good; Unchristian = bad*. Within Christianity dwell chastity, sobriety, wisdom, peace, love, humility and every other virtue. Outside of it lie fornication, licentiousness, drunkenness, pride, deceit, anger, violence, arrogance, and every other vice.

It is little wonder, then, that I was hesitant to examine my faith critically. No skeptical arguments, no matter how valid, could hold a candle to these two dictums: "It works for me," and, "He changed my life." I was convinced that if I were to abandon my faith, it would amount to aiding and

---

[22] In all fairness, atheists can be just as prone to an air of superiority as their believing counterparts. Yet there remains this important distinction: the believer will often appeal to the Almighty Moral Arbiter in the Sky to put adversaries in their place, while the atheist is by definition bereft of any such weapon.

abetting the "bad guys," leading to personal and cultural ruin. I will have more to say concerning this in chapter 8, but for now I simply ask rhetorically, Why? Why should I have felt that abandoning my faith would *necessarily* entail moral decline? If I considered Christian virtues to be good while still a believer, why should they all suddenly cease to be good after leaving the faith? I was misguided to think that adultery, for example, might suddenly become more attractive if I were to lose my accountability to the god of the Bible.

It cannot be a coincidence that all successful religions promote various virtues. Empirically unverifiable religions cannot hope to gain a foothold without some form of enticement, much like the sweet fruit that entices animals and humans to ingest and disseminate the seeds of fruit-bearing trees through excretion. One particularly sweet fruit of Christianity is its ability to promote personal and societal goodness. Even if its track record is mixed, there is no denying its power to motivate many of its adherents to live decent, even exemplary, self-sacrificial lives.

FOCUS ON THE FLAWS OF THE FOES OF THE FAITH

Closely related to the exceptionalism engendered by a sense of the Holy Spirit's presence in my life and the conviction that goodness comes from a commitment to Christ was my fear that listening to the opposition might aid and abet the "bad guys."

It was convenient for me as a believer to exploit the moral failings of my ideological opponents since it eased the burden of having to respond adequately to their philosophical or scientific objections. The only open atheist with whom I engaged in any meaningful conversation before my deconversion was a bachelor who lived next door to me during my time in Minnesota. His girlfriend would often come from out of town to spend the night with him. This was clear evidence to me at the time that his atheism and loose sexual mores went hand in hand.

In his book *Intellectuals,* conservative Catholic historian Paul Johnson exposes the personal quirks and failings of many of the liberal Enlightenment thinkers in an attempt to discredit their ideas through the back door of their personal lives (Johnson 1988). His approach was undermined when his mistress of 11 years revealed his philandering and predilection for erotic "spankings" (Carville 2003, 288).

Rick Warren, author of the best-selling book *The Purpose Driven Life,* asserted in a *Newsweek*-hosted discussion with atheist Sam Harris, "You just don't want a boss. You don't want a God who tells you what to do" (Meacham 2007).

Perhaps many unbelievers, though certainly not all, are bent on living their own lives the way they wish. But this does not invalidate their unbelief, nor does it follow that unbelief necessarily leads to immorality.

In his forward to Geoffrey Simmons' book, *What Darwin Didn't Know: A Doctor Dissects the Theory of Evolution*, Intelligent Design leading light William Dembski asks,

> Why, then, does Darwinism continue to garner such a huge following, especially among the intellectual elites? . . . It provides a materialistic creation story that dispenses with any need for design or God (this is very convenient for those who want to escape the demands of religion, morality, and conscience) (Dembski 2004, 12).

Dembski's parenthetical statement is representative of much anti-evolutionary sentiment; how else can an anti-evolutionist explain why so many intelligent individuals accept such a preposterous theory with little or no real evidence? Dembski suggests that evolutionary scientists and laypersons are simply looking for a way to get God off their backs, *willfully* denying the evidence against evolution. Yet how could anyone in her right mind (or anyone with any level of self-interest) think like this? If at the bottom of our heart we know God exists and holds us eternally accountable, then saddling up to evolution will do nothing to change that fact; such a decision is far from being in our best interest. (I do not deny that we all make shortsighted choices. But my goodness! An eternity of torment is infinitely graver than the possibility of suffering from smoking-related lung cancer!) What would Dembski say of committed evangelical Christians like geneticist Francis Collins and geologist Keith B. Miller who unapologetically adopt evolution but who in no way wish to escape the demands of religion, morality, and conscience?

I too held Dembski's perspective as a believer, as shown by this excerpt from an unpublished, uncompleted manuscript entitled "For Skeptics Only," which I wrote at the age of 16:

> To reject religion is to reject a supreme being, and to reject the latter is to be forced to explain the origin of the universe and of life by chance. Therefore, the theory of evolution was contrived, [becoming] the most widely accepted explanation for the spontaneous origin of life. Along with the rejection of the belief in a supreme being comes freedom from responsibility. Therefore the atheist is free to act according to what he or she believes is right in a particular situation.

So we have seen a tendency on the part of some believers, including me, to highlight the dissolute and immoral lives of certain skeptics. Their alienation from God is attributed at least in part to their flaws, thus providing ample justification for their miserable fate in the hereafter. But what of the skeptic who apparently leads a moral life? It is naturally more uncomfortable for believers to envisage the eternal doom of a decent unbeliever than that of a perverted one. Accordingly, believers may conclude that the decent skeptic has some hidden, perhaps spiritual flaw not shared by the believer; otherwise, the believer and the unbeliever would share the same views and participate in the same salvation through faith in Christ. In short, there must be a legitimate reason (unless you're a strict Calvinist) for God to damn particular individuals to hell for eternity and not others. So if the unbeliever's flaws are not apparent on the surface, they must lie within.

I have encountered this outlook subtly in many forms. It most often takes the form, "Ken, it's a matter of your *will*." It doesn't matter how difficult it might be for me to believe certain biblical propositions; I must simply swallow my pride (the same pride that ultimately underlies all sin and which led Satan to rebel), repent, and will myself to believe.

In addition to associating unbelief and immoral living, it is common for believers to conflate skepticism itself with an offense against the Almighty. If the Bible is God's very Word, any challenge to it is seen as an affront against God himself. This outlook discouraged me from taking a step back and asking myself the question, "What if I'm wrong? What if the Bible is not God's word? Then those who critically examine the Bible, rather than offending God, might actually be ferreting out the truth." These are elementary questions I should have been free to ask myself all along. However, as long as the possibility remained that questioning the Bible— even though written by men—was tantamount to judging the creator of the universe, it was safest to keep my distance from the views of biblical critics.

In the end I realized it is human judgment alone that comes to the conclusion that the Bible is God-breathed. When skeptics challenge the Christian faith, they are merely pitting one fallible human perspective against another. There is no more to it than that. Did God tap ever me on the shoulder to tell me he wrote the Bible? No, and even if he had, how would I have known it was God? Ultimately I had to fall back on human judgment to make that determination. This debate is not one between skeptics and God; it is one between fallible skeptics and fallible believers. When my high school Mormon friend learned of my deconversion, he admonished me not to lean on "the arm of flesh" (Book of Mormon, 2 Nephi 4:34) or human reason, but to listen to God. Yet we must all use our human reason or intuition or tradition to decide where we think God's voice can be found (if it is to be found at all), whether in the Jewish scriptures, in the Protestant Bible, in the Catholic Bible, in the Koran, in the Upanishads, in the Book of Mormon, in other sacred texts, in nature, or in our own heads. There is no way out of this bootstrapping problem other than to make a human judgment at some level.

It is common for Christians who firmly believe in the existence of the god of the Bible to consider that unbelievers also must secretly believe, but that they are bitter against God or God's people and are merely taking out their frustration by denying God. This outlook surfaces in comments such as the following by creationist Jonathan Sarfati, addressed to agnostic Ed Babinski:

> I hope you will understand that we can't possibly respond to all claims disseminated by every God-hater inhabiting the darker hovels of the Internet (Babinski 2005a).

Though Babinski claims no belief in God, Sarfati insinuates that Babinski retains a level of belief sufficient to hate God. But by definition only believers in God can hate him. I do not hate God, nor does Babinski. There are certainly many irrational half-believers, half-unbelievers who alternate between hating God and not believing in the existence of any god that could serve as the object of their hate. But to assert that all unbelievers hate God is puerile slander. I, and most other skeptics, do indeed hate teachings like hell that were invented by men, and we do chafe against the reproach we often endure on the part of those who believe they speak on behalf of God or the mere men who wrote the Bible. But this reaction of ours against men and their teachings must not be mistaken for any sort of animosity toward God. If God exists, what possible good would it do to hate him? And if he does not exist, there is no such being to hate.

I have observed time and again a tendency on the part of believers to find one or a few real or imagined flaws in a skeptical book and then use their findings to justify dismissing the entire book, many of whose other arguments may be legitimate. This tendency prevails even though skeptical authors make no claim to infallibility. For example, I belonged to a discussion group of agnostics and Christians for over four years. Though we certainly had our disagreements, it was for the most part an enjoyable and (I think) profitable time for the exchange of differing ideas. There were already signs of deterioration in our ability to get along, but when one of the participants accused Israeli archaeologists Finkelstein and Silberman of bald-faced lying about one of their claims, not only were all the good arguments of the book *The Bible Unearthed* ruined, but so was our discussion group, to my great disappointment. (I do acknowledge and regret my role in the mutual intransigence that led to the demise of our group.)

The most common character flaws I have heard attributed to skeptics are pride and arrogance, or the more culturally refined term *hubris*. Following a debate between Robert Price and Greg Boyd entitled "Jesus: Legend, Teacher, Critic, or Son of God," a questioner directed these comments to Price:

> For those of you who may be seduced or disconcerted by his analysis, there's a very healthy antidote in the form of C. S. Lewis' *Abolition of Man*, in which he describes the human hubris to deconstruct, which eventually ends up in rejecting objective reality. I think if you read that particular slim volume by C. S. Lewis, I think you'll be strengthened in your notion that Dr. Robert Price's analysis is mere deconstruction and reflects a human hubris (Boyd and Price 2003, starting at 1:22).

Price wisely said nothing in response to this comment in the debate. There is no way to defend oneself against the charge of hubris; any defensive response would be taken as further evidence of arrogance. This brings to mind the experience of Martin Luther, whose Catholic interrogators interpreted his challenge of Catholic dogma and practice as high-minded, prideful treason. Likewise, both Catholic and Protestant leaders decried the arrogance of Copernicus and Galileo in daring to overturn the long-held belief that the sun orbits the earth.

In short, the charge of arrogance is a handy, powerful and often-used weapon employed against those who challenge any orthodox position (whether in religion, politics or science), thereby increasing the odds that the faithful will pay no mind to their opponents. It generally requires courage and independence of mind to stand up against established ideals, and only a fine line divides these attributes from true arrogance.

There is no denying that many freethinkers cross the line from healthy, independent thought to arrogance or disdain for their ideological opponents, and I readily confess I have all too often crossed that line myself.

Consider the perspective of Christian philosopher Alvin Plantinga, who believes in an old earth but not in Darwinian evolution:

> In this connection, consider the despised creationists, who believe that the world is only ten thousand years old: they are ignorant, pitifully ignorant about when God created the world. From the point of view of the model, this ignorance pales into utter insignificance compared with that of many of their cultured detractors, who foolishly believe that there is no God and thus (naturally enough) are ignorant of the vastly more important fact that the world was, indeed, created by God (Plantinga 2000, 217).

The first part of this quote is sure to raise the hackles of young-earth creationists and to earn for Plantinga a reputation of arrogance among them. And the second part is likely to earn him the same reputation among atheists. For those who agree with him, he is not arrogant but simply right.

One tactic I deplore on both sides of the divide is the use of *ad hominem,* attacking one's opponents rather than their arguments. For example, though Robert Price is an insightful nontheist scholar whose influence on my views has been considerable, and though I share his frustration with slick apologists, I cringed when I read his tirade against Christian apologist William Lane Craig in his essay, "By This Time He Stinketh: The Attempts of William Lane Craig to Exhume Jesus" (Price and Lowder 2005). Similarly, popular Internet apologist James Patrick Holding makes little effort to withhold his contempt for counter-apologists, and former missionary-turned-atheist Farrell Till is only too eager to respond in kind. This kind of behavior does little to advance the debate.

The bottom line is this: those whose beliefs are nonnegotiable will do whatever it takes to discredit those who challenge the Christian faith. *Whatever it takes.* Often the easiest way to do this is to impugn their character—they are arrogant, self-absorbed, immoral, willfully self-deceived, or unscrupulous. Focusing on the character of one's opponents is especially effective for those whose theology holds that God will eternally judge nonbelievers.

As an illustration of the "whatever it takes to impugn the nonbeliever" tendency, I mentioned to a pastor with whom I was dialoguing in 2001 that my morals had not changed since I had left the faith. His response was to chastise me for relying on my own works and on my own goodness rather than on Christ. Yet it was far from my intention to justify myself before God, whom in any case I did not believe would judge anyone in the hereafter. My only purpose for having mentioned anything about my character was to head off the commonly held prejudice that the primary reason apostates leave the fold is so they can pursue their own lives without regard for a heavenly boss or for Christian moral standards. This incident shows how we unbelievers are "damned if we do, damned if we don't." If we proceed to live immoral lives (at least by Christian standards), it is a sure indication we left the faith to get God off our backs and live as we please; but if we retain our moral standards, we are relying on our works for self-justification, which makes us equally culpable in God's sight.

Who can insist that the universe should yield its secrets only to those who meet the qualifications set by the gatekeepers of a particular creed? If Albert Einstein's freethinking and philandering tendencies did not prevent him from cracking the mystery of relativity, then we should pause before asserting that an individual's personal life, character or disposition necessarily bears on her ability to arrive at the truth in any domain. It is quite beside the point how good we are, how pious we are, how sincere we are, how humble we are: we can still be mistaken about any number of matters about which an evil baby torturer knows the truth.

In this section I hope I have been able to head off the following thoughts on the part of at least some of my readers: "On the one hand, I've got my faith that provides meaning, hope, joy and a relationship with my loving creator. On the other hand, I've got this skeptic Ken who wants me to believe his honest search for truth has led him to reject that faith. I must choose between Ken's thinking and my faith. It's a no-brainer: Ken's claim to an honest search for truth has to go. He *must* not be as honest as he claims."

INSULATION

If my experience as a former evangelical is in any way representative of the movement as a whole, most believers receive very little sustained exposure to serious arguments against their faith. I was fed a steady diet of pro-Christian teaching in Sunday school, worship services, Bible memory programs, Wednesday evening prayer meetings, missionary grade school, Christian university, seminary, conferences, music, books, television, movies, and radio.

I recall a number of occasions during my youth when pastors and Christian teachers warned us not to expose ourselves to the ideas of the enemy. After all, bank tellers learn to distinguish real dollar bills from counterfeit ones by repeatedly handling legitimate bills, not by studying fake ones. Then when they encounter a fake, they are able to detect the difference and know it's counterfeit. Likewise, in order to distinguish between true and false religion, we must immerse ourselves in the (evangelical) Christian faith (which we know to be true) rather than studying other faiths and worldviews (which we know to be counterfeit).

Even when I did attend a public high school and took a biology class, evolution was never discussed. In 2006 my son mentioned to me that his sixth grade science teacher was promoting young-earth creationism in his public school, even though the textbook made no reference to evolution. (The teacher graciously agreed to desist when I presented her with material summarizing various court rulings against the promotion of creationism in public schools.)

I have heard Christian leaders complain that our children are exposed to secularism eight hours a day, five days a week in the public schools (and even more on television), and that an hour or two of Sunday school or church a week is not enough to set them straight. This understanding has helped fuel the burgeoning homeschooling movement, which seeks to extricate all vestiges of secular thinking.[23]

The homeschooling movement is one aspect of a broader trend that includes maximal procreation (exemplified by the "Quiverfull movement," from Psalm 127) and insulation from others outside the family unit, even from church youth groups. When we lived in Minnesota, my wife and I befriended a family with twelve children (they now have sixteen). Though we initially attended the same church together, they later joined several other large homeschooling families to form the Family Fundamental Church. We have other similarly oriented friends in Texas who have formed a home church of three or four large families. They take turns meeting for Sunday services in each other's homes, the father of the host home providing the sermon and leading the children in song and Bible memorization.

An important objective of this movement is not only to keep the children in the fold but also to swell the ranks of believers through procreative multiplication. For insight into the basis for this growing phenomenon, see Mary Pride's influential book *The Way Home: Beyond Feminism, Back to Reality* (Pride 1985).

From my perspective these families are exemplary in their cohesiveness, discipline and warmth. I have nothing but praise for many of their values (apart from the patriarchal outlook and contribution to planetary population pressures, which they typically deny is a problem). Yet if the foundation on which this movement is built—fundamentalist Protestant, young earth, biblical inerrantist religion—is demonstrably untrue, how will these uninformed children ever hope to come to that realization? Instead, they will most likely propagate the same outlook to their children, who will retain the same sense of privileged righteousness and the "us-versus-them" outlook of their parents.

As I discussed in the section on psychological inertia, it is human nature to seek out confirmation for one's preexisting beliefs. I freely confess I now read more materials from a skeptical perspective than from a

---

[23] Ironically, the movement is strongest in the South and Midwest of the USA, in regions where evolution and secularism are least likely to be promoted in the schools, since many if not most of the teachers themselves are conservative Christians.

Christian perspective, yet I generally make a good faith effort to read books Christians offer me. There are exceptions when I feel a book is not worth my time, particularly if it's from a young-earth creationist perspective (having already read my fair share). I wonder how many of those who offer me such materials have taken the time to read as much from a non-Christian viewpoint as I have read from a Christian outlook. After one individual handed me a creationist journal, I offered to provide her some materials from an evolutionary standpoint. When she mentioned she would have to get approval from her husband first, I backed down, knowing it would be fruitless to insist.

I will have more to say concerning evolution in chapter 6, but the point I am trying to make here is that the average evangelical believer is not inclined to give alternative views the time of day, having been shielded from the opposition, whether through a deliberate personal decision or through the insulation of one's family or religious community. I do not intend to convey that all believers refuse to expose themselves to the outside world. Many apologists do study secular scholarship, if for nothing else but to know the enemy and to pick out flaws, presenting those flaws for the benefit of the faithful who dare not venture into enemy territory themselves.

Proverbs 18:17 summarizes perfectly the downside of insulation: "The first to present his case seems right, till another comes forward and questions him."

THE BIG STICK

Though as a believer I did not consider the hope of heaven and the threat of hell to be legitimate reasons in themselves for subscribing to one belief or another, there remained a nagging "what if?" in the back of my mind during the course of my struggle with doubt. As expressed by Pascal's famous Wager (Pascal 1670, sec. 233), if I was somehow mistaken about my growing doubt, and if I persisted in my doubt, I not only risked losing the things I held dear in this life, but I also subjected myself to the possibility of endless torment in the hereafter without possibility of reprieve. But if I persisted in my faith, and it turned out to be untrue, what was there to lose? And if it turned out to be true, I would gain everything! From a pure profit-loss standpoint, it made sense to stick with the status quo.

I will have a good deal more to say about hell in chapter 15. I mention this subject now because of the role it played in discouraging me from taking the final plunge away from faith, even as my suspicion mounted that I had been on the wrong path all my life.

My reluctance to examine my faith critically stemmed in part from the antipathy of the Bible itself toward any skeptical evaluation of its claims:

> If your very own brother, or your son or daughter, or the wife you love, or your closest friend secretly entices you, saying, "Let us go and worship other gods" (gods that neither you nor your fathers have known, gods of the peoples around you, whether near or far, from one end of the land to the other), do not yield to him or listen to him. Show him no pity. Do not spare him or shield him. You must certainly put him to death. Your hand must be the first in putting him to death, and then the hands of all the people. Stone him to death, because he tried to turn you away from the LORD your God, who brought you out of Egypt, out of the land of slavery. Then all Israel will hear and be afraid, and no one among you will do such an evil thing again (Deuteronomy 13:6–11).[24]

As I began considering the need to examine my faith critically in March 2000, I had to settle in my mind the purpose of such an investigation. If it was merely to check off an item from a to-do list so I could get on with the business of living my faith, then the exercise would have been pointless. If, on the other hand, my purpose was to know the truth, then I had to be prepared to follow the results of my investigation wherever it might lead. (Incidentally, if I had been living in a less enlightened time when injunctions such as that in Deuteronomy 13 above were still practiced, the fate awaiting me should my investigation lead to apostasy would have been death by stoning at the hands of those I loved most dearly. It goes without saying that this would have left precious little incentive for free inquiry.)

The New Testament is no less ambiguous on the perils of critically investigating our faith. Paul had no patience for those who entertained any teaching contrary to his own:

> But even if we or an angel from heaven should preach a gospel other than the one we preached to you, let him be eternally condemned! As we have already

---

[24] Islam makes similar demands: "O you who believe! Choose not your fathers nor your brethren for friends if they take pleasure in disbelief rather than faith. Whoso of you takes them for friends, such are wrong-doers" (Surah IX.23). "If anyone desires a religion other than Islam (submission to Allah), never will it be accepted of him; and in the Hereafter He will be in the ranks of those who have lost (all spiritual good)" (Surah III.85). "When the sacred months have passed, slay the idolaters wherever you find them" (Surah IX.5).

said, so now I say again: If anybody is preaching to you a gospel other than what you accepted, let him be eternally condemned (Galatians 1:8–9)!

As for those agitators, I wish they would go the whole way and emasculate [that is, castrate] themselves! (Galatians 5:12)

After my deconversion a couple of friends warned me darkly that it is one thing to reject the Christian faith myself; it is far more serious matter to lead my children astray:

But if anyone causes one of these little ones who believe in me to sin, it would be better for him to have a large millstone hung around his neck and to be drowned in the depths of the sea (Matthew 18:6).

THE EASE AND SECURITY OF A PACKAGE

My wife does the majority of our grocery shopping, but when I have occasion to shop for fresh fruit, I find it much easier and cheaper to grab a prepackaged bag of mediocre apples than to make a careful selection of the best from various piles of freestanding fruit. This reduces my decision-making requirements in that there is generally only a very limited choice of bagged apples at the store, and I do not have to select each apple based on its quality. Similarly, when approaching a tollbooth on the road, if I observe two lanes with a long line of vehicles and another with none, I instinctively tend to "go with the herd" and assume they know best; there must be some good reason they're not taking the shortest line. But perhaps they're simply lining up behind the other cars for the same reason. It's hard to tell. In any case, it feels more secure to wait in line than to take the risk of going for the empty lane and then finding I have to back out against the traffic.

Decision-making is not something most of us relish. It's easier and less risky just to follow what seems to be working for others, to accept tradition, to follow its prepackaged answers and solutions. But what if everyone is lining up behind the others for the same reason? What if there's an open lane, a road less traveled, a new way of thinking that bypasses the long, unnecessary queue? How would we know unless we bravely ventured from the pack and actually gave it a try? And if we're courageous enough to take the road less traveled, should we be deterred by the finger-wagging of those still in the pack, trying to discourage us from what they think is a foolish venture? No! Should we be discouraged by Proverbs 14:2, "There is a way that seems right to a man, but in the end it leads to death"? It depends. If good evidence can be shown that it leads to death, then it would be suicide to flaunt it. Otherwise, it simply doesn't apply; it serves merely as a mechanism for preserving the status quo.

Where did I come from? Where am I going? How should I live? Should women work outside the home? Is abortion acceptable under any circumstances? How should I spend my money? Should we go to war? What political party should we support? What and how should we teach our children? How do I rid myself of the guilt I feel? Answers to these and many other life questions are more readily available for those who subscribe to a package, the bag of apples provided by a religious framework. Even if the Bible doesn't directly address certain of these questions, one can always count on James Dobson, Rick Warren, Chuck Swindoll, John Eldredge, Bill Gothard, Dave Ramsey, or a local pastor to serve up their solutions based on their interpretation of the Bible. Often it is far easier for evangelicals to adopt this package with its stock answers on family, politics, money, education, and morality than to think outside the box.

Evangelical author John Eldredge's popular book *Wild at Heart* (Eldredge 2001) encourages men to break out of the pack, to take risks, to be manly—in short, to be wild! What better expression of this injunction could there be than to begin the hard work of thinking for ourselves, of refusing to accept uncritically the traditional answers to life's questions handed to us on a platter, of sorting out the good apples from the bad, even if they're part of what most around us claim is a perfect package? There is no place for conformity to unsubstantiated tradition for those who choose to be wild at heart. Is it easy to go against the grain in this way? I will be the first to say No! But it's an adventure like no other to investigate, to sift ideas and to stand tall against the wind after concluding, to the best of our knowledge, that this is the way forward.

A SET-APART IDENTITY

As a believer I subscribed to the evangelical persecution complex, counting myself a member of the true household of faith, a minority movement in a complacent, godless society. While this situation was something we evangelicals outwardly lamented, we also tended to take pride in our uniqueness, our set-apart status. We were going against the grain, and we believed we were right in doing so.

It is a paradox of human nature, including my own nature, that we tend to value both group solidarity and individualistic bravado. We seek to enjoy the benefits of both tendencies simultaneously by rising above average and gaining status within the group whose package of ideals we have adopted or inherited. In evangelical circles an effective way of establishing respect is to be spiritual: to be "on fire for God," to pray without ceasing, to know and understand the Word of God, and to have a passion for "winning the lost." These were ideals to which I strove and for which I was recognized in my high school and college years. I will be honest: I enjoyed the respect I received from being seen as a spiritual young man.

In addition to standing out within our own group, we also gain solidarity by recognizing the minority or persecuted status of our community, differentiating ourselves from the "others," the "uncommitted Christians," the "liberals," or the "lost."

While in college I considered the lives of those who graduated and went on to live a comfortable, boring work-a-day life and settle down in a house with a white picket fence in suburbia, and I wanted nothing of it. I wanted my life to count for God; if the gospel is true, I reasoned, then Jesus is worthy of all my devotion. A few years ago a friend recounted how God had led him to launch a new ministry venture: "I was serving God, doing OK, but I didn't want to be content with an 'A minus'; I wanted to strive for an 'A plus.'" I admire him for his zeal; he is living consistently with his beliefs, as I was when I made the decision to become a missionary.

As social primates, the drive to seek status and approval in our social group is indelibly stamped in our nature, whatever our worldview, and in spite of any conscious attempts to be humble and self-effacing. Political leaders do not generally seek office merely to serve their constituents as they claim; they are driven also, and often primarily, by their inborn desire for social status. If they are honest, church pastors, missionaries, and other Christian leaders are not immune from similar motives, nor am I. The same is true of those who distinguish themselves in more mundane ways—for example, through volunteering at a homeless shelter, leading Bible studies, or staying late to clean up after a church social event.

As I discussed in the section on costs, once my identity and status were established within my Christian community, the very thought of abandoning it all served as a powerful impediment against critically examining the faith underpinning that community. To abandon Jesus was going to entail either trying to maintain ties with the same community but with a complete loss of my former status or starting all over again at zero in an unbelieving, foreign, and despised community.

I am still very much prone to this same human desire for influence and status. Ironically, I have now carried the persecution complex with me; as an unbeliever, I am in an even smaller minority than I was as an evangelical. This provides the potential to differentiate myself from those around me, especially in the predominantly Christian Dallas, Texas suburb I now call home. I must guard against this tendency to cherish the persecution complex or to consider myself a cut above those who have not "seen the light."

In sum, we must all give thought to the extent to which our identity and status within our like-minded community, along with our pride in belonging to a group set apart from the wider world, prevent us from reexamining our current position, whatever that position may be.

MODERATION INOCULATION

In high school I recall coming down on the "liberal" side of two burning issues: whether it is appropriate to use anything other than the King James Version of the Bible (for example, the New International Version, or even the Living Bible) and whether God approves of Christian rock music. Later in college I came to accept that the universe and the earth are billions of years old, all the while maintaining my opposition to evolution. Though I continued to accept the doctrine of inerrancy, I came to recognize that God did not dictate the Bible to men who merely fulfilled the secretarial task of writing down the words, but rather that men penned the scriptures in their own style under the inspiration of the Holy Spirit. The text could not be interpreted using an inflexible, wooden approach. My favorite author, Philip Yancey, challenged many of the legalistic and literalistic views that were significant veins of thought throughout much of American evangelicalism. I was inspired by the social gospel of Tony Campolo, based on the anti-wealth teachings of Jesus in Luke and other books of the New Testament. I also came to deplore the tactics of those who would bomb abortion clinics or hold up placards saying, "God Hates Fags."

These minor concessions gave me a sense that I had hammered out what I believed personally, rather than blindly inheriting what others had taught me. I did not have to be a snake handler, Bible thumper, in-your-face screamer, King-James-only advocate, young-earth creationist, or biblical literalist to have the dynamic faith I witnessed in many of the moderate Christians from whom I drew inspiration. Then when the outside world challenged the Christian faith, I could respond, "No, you're attacking a particular extreme version of Christianity I don't espouse." This served for me as an effective antidote against external attacks for a decade.

Even the most conservative Christians in America today are generally more liberal and tolerant than many of their spiritual forebears. As we will see in later chapters, for example, the great Protestant reformers Luther and Calvin considered heresy to be a crime punishable by death. Theologian Jonathan Edwards claimed the redeemed would look from heaven on the fate of the damned—even their own family members—and give praise to God:

> The sight of hell torments will exalt the happiness of the saints forever. . . . It will really make their happiness the greater, as it will make them more sensible of their own happiness (Edwards 1739, 276).

> Can the believing husband in Heaven be happy with his unbelieving wife in Hell? Can the believing father in Heaven be happy with his unbelieving children in Hell? Can the loving wife in Heaven be happy with her unbelieving husband in Hell? I tell you, yea! Such will be their sense of justice that it will increase rather than diminish their bliss (Edwards 1738).

If a religion is not divinely inspired, we would expect its initial teachings and claims to reflect the ideals and knowledge of humans living in the time and place of its origin. If new discoveries are made in later generations that call into question an earlier understanding of the world, or if cultural ideals change over time and make the original ideals no longer tenable, then the religion must either adapt or fail to survive.

During my years in the Christian faith, I recognized that the Christianity I practiced was not exactly the same as that of the first Apostles, but I believed the differences were mostly cultural and were relatively insignificant; on the fundamentals, my faith was the same as that of the biblical authors. There were certain biblical teachings that seemed difficult to discern—for example, whether a Christian once saved could lose his salvation. Yet this was the exception rather than the rule. I believed that my adherence to a strong view of biblical authority and inerrancy and a daily study of God's Word, coupled with input from others who had systematically studied the scriptures themselves, ensured that my beliefs paralleled those of the earliest Christians.

It was easy during those years to see how other religions had adapted to new realities in order to survive. The example I was most familiar with was the repeal of polygamy by the Church of Jesus Christ of Latter Day Saints. Though Joseph Smith advocated polygamy in section 132 of the *Doctrine and Covenants,* Mormon Church President Wilford Woodruff issued a manifesto in 1890 urging Mormons no longer to practice it following its prohibition by the United States government. It is difficult to see how Mormonism could have grown into the mainstream religion it is today had Woodruff not made this decision.

In time I began to wonder how close *any* present-day denomination or movement conforms to the teachings and practices of the early church. Given that the followers of so many divergent sects believe themselves to be closer to the apostolic ideal than others, I began to suspect that chances were slim that my particular brand of Christianity hit the mark.

How could I be sure that I had not adopted a smoothed-over version of Christianity that would have been unrecognizable to Jesus and to the original apostles? How could I be sure that Paul really didn't accept the legitimacy of baptism for the dead? What if Luke really did think baptism was necessary for salvation, contrary to the teachings of most Protestant denominations today? Did the biblical authors really believe slavery was inherently evil? Did they really not consider the earth to be flat like a disk, supported below by pillars and covered above by a dome-like firmament to which were affixed the celestial bodies? Did Jesus and the New Testament authors think the second coming could occur at any other time than in their generation? I was supposed to accept the evangelical party line on these questions, but the texts made me wonder what the biblical authors really thought. Was I accepting an evolved interpretation of these texts rather than the authors' original intentions? If so, was that adaptation a key to the ability of twenty-first-century Christians like me to think of Christianity as a coherent, viable worldview in our day, just as the Mormon repudiation of polygamy enabled that church to thrive in the face of anti-polygamist sentiment?

It is comforting to be able to look upon others more conservative or fanatical than we are and to believe our religion—or our particular version of it—to be more urbane and less prone to excess. Thus, the killing of infidels is now seen primarily as a Muslim practice, even though in times past it was a Catholic, Protestant and Jewish practice also, supported by various biblical texts. Racism and slavery are now widely regarded as evil within the Christian and Jewish communities, even though pro-slavery Southern pastors once routinely quoted the Bible to justify their position. In an e-mail exchange a few years ago, an Intelligent Design proponent friend of mine took delight in castigating young-earth creationism and some of its attendant absurdities like a worldwide Noachian flood. Though a Bible-believing evangelical, he strove to make it clear his ideas were not to be confused with those of his farther-right-wing coreligionists.

Indeed, it is quite common for semi-conservative or moderate believers to pooh-pooh or to distance themselves from their more ignorant or hard-line brethren. While I understand the motivation for doing so, I wonder how such moderates view Jesus' teaching that the Holy Spirit "will guide you [believers] into all truth" (John 16:12). What is the reason for the differences between moderate believers and fundamentalists who cite chapter and verse in support of their positions? Are moderates smarter than fundamentalists, or did the Holy Spirit choose to reveal the light to less rigid believers than to their more conservative brethren? If so, why did he not choose to reveal the same things to the latter, especially if they are as earnest as moderates are in their love for God and in their desire to know the truth? For my part, I now see every attempt of moderates to distance themselves from conservatives and vice versa as a strike against the unity of the church Jesus promised through the power of the Holy Spirit. It looks for all the world as though each believer or congregation or denomination is simply using human reason to come to whatever conclusions they come to, the Holy Spirit playing no role in the process.

In his interview with secular humanist D. J. Grothe (Collins 2007), geneticist Francis Collins complains that Richard Dawkins attacks a form of Christianity that Collins does not recognize. This is a case that Dawkins simply cannot win. If he targets the traditional beliefs and practices of the majority of evangelicals (who, unlike Collins, generally reject evolution), then Collins is allowed to say, "I don't recognize that form of Christianity," thus immunizing himself from Dawkins' arguments, many of which do in fact directly address Collins' core beliefs.

Since 2006 I have been corresponding with a missionary physician who has transitioned to deism while remaining in the closet, so to speak. After recently reading a pro-evolution article in *Christianity Today* (Giberson 2008), he described the process of deconversion as follows:

> I see Christianity as a square peg and reality a round hole. The square peg doesn't fit in the round hole, so we start whittling and sandpapering the corners, trying to make it fit. The tools we use for whittling and sandpapering are collectively known as "Bible commentary." We find, for example, that the earth is very ancient, not a few thousand years old, that there are biological bases for illnesses like schizophrenia, not merely demon possession, that the Bible had a lot of editing as it was put together and doesn't appear error free. We incorporate these and other items into our Christian worldview, slowly sandpapering the edges and modifying our Christianity. When we finally get our Christianity smoothed down so that it can fit into the round hole of reality, we are relieved—until we realize that what we are looking at is no longer a square peg but a round one, no different from the round peg of Naturalism that fits into reality. Can what we have left of the peg, now completely rounded, still be labeled Christianity? No, it is Naturalism (or at best, Deism). Hence the loss of faith.

> I think this process (for me at least) describes what I see as Christians concede first one thing and then another to science. I see this in the

publications of *Christianity Today*—ceding more and more with the passage of time.

Despite my criticisms, I do commend moderates for their ability to reject some of the more anti-intellectual, divisive teachings of their conservative counterparts. I would much prefer that the world be filled with moderate believers than with fundamentalists. But "moderate" is a relative term. Many who consider themselves moderate continue to believe in hell, a belief so extreme that it in my view invalidates every other laudable step toward moderation. If you have set aside belief in this doctrine, then I can truly appreciate your claim to have moderated your faith, and I consider you to be in a fundamentally different camp from those who have not taken this step.

A moderate movement that has gained some currency in the United States is the Emergent Church, which considers itself at least quasi-evangelical but which downplays the importance of doctrine in favor of practice. The movement does not take a strong stand on divisive issues like biological evolution and eternal damnation for those belonging to other religious traditions. Whether or not their faith is biblically or logically defensible, I am encouraged to witness the direction they are taking toward a respect for the conclusions of science and away from the divisiveness of the traditional evangelical church that gave them birth.

On August 17, 2007, I watched Bill Moyer interview liberal University of Chicago theologian Martin Marty on PBS Television. What a gentle, gracious, humble man! I do not see eye to eye with him on many matters, but if every believer were like this man, what a wonderful world it would be!

I recognize that many moderate and liberal believers have thoughtfully considered the foundations of their views, in many cases more thoughtfully than fundamentalists and atheists have done. I do not doubt the sophistication, sincerity, and earnestness with which moderates forge a worldview that meets their spiritual needs, but in my own journey I have come to view moderation more as a means of holding onto as much as possible of what is *hoped* to be true than as a raw reckoning with what *is* true.

BUT WHAT ABOUT YOU NOW, KEN?

While reading this chapter you may have thought to yourself, "Well, Ken, you're insisting we all need to spare our faith no mercy, but do you now heed your own injunctions? Have you looked at your skepticism skeptically? Are you sure you have not exchanged your allegedly problematic worldview for an even more improbable one?"

These are fair questions. Quitting our faith because of its perceived or real difficulties does not guarantee we'll end up with a superior alternative, any more than leaving an incompatible spouse necessarily leads us to a happier subsequent marriage.

No doubt a concerned Christian could undertake to write a book similar in approach to mine, probing the psychological, social and personal reasons why skeptics like me reject Christianity. In this vein C. S. Lewis' allegorical vision of the afterlife, *The Great Divorce,* constructs a discussion between two apostates, one who repents before leaving earth and the other who persists in his unbelief. In neutral territory between heaven and hell, the repentant Spirit addresses the unrepentant Ghost as follows:

> Let us be frank. Our opinions were not honestly come by. We simply found ourselves in contact with a certain current of ideas and plunged into it because it seemed modern and successful. At College, you know we just started automatically writing the kind of essays that got good marks and saying the kind of things that won applause. When, in our whole lives, did we honestly face, in solitude, the one question on which all turned: whether after all the Supernatural might not in fact occur? When did we put up one moment's real resistance to the loss of our faith?

> We didn't *want* the other to be true. We were afraid of crude Salvationism, afraid of a breach with the spirit of the age, afraid of ridicule, afraid (above all) of real spiritual fears and hopes.

> Having allowed oneself to drift, unresisting, unpraying, accepting every half-conscious solicitation from our desires, we reached a point where we no longer believed the Faith. Just in the same way, a jealous man, drifting and unresisting, reaches a point at which he believes lies about his best friend: a drunkard reaches a point at which (for the moment) he actually believes that another glass will do him no harm. The beliefs are sincere in the sense that they do occur as psychological events in the man's mind. If that's what you mean by sincerity they are sincere, and so were ours. But errors which are sincere in that sense are not innocent (Lewis 1946, 41–42).

As the two proceed in their discussion, the unrepentant Ghost continues offering excuse after excuse as to why he will still not join the repentant Spirit to meet God: "I should want a guarantee that you are taking me to a place where I shall find a wider sphere of usefulness . . . and an atmosphere of free inquiry." The Spirit responds, "You have experienced truth only with the abstract intellect. I will bring you where you can taste it like honey and be embraced by it as by a bridegroom. Your thirst shall be quenched." The Ghost rejects the offer: "I am not aware of a thirst for some ready-made truth which puts an end to intellectual activity in the way you seem to be describing. Will it leave me the free play of Mind, Dick? I must insist on that, you know" (Lewis 1946, 43–44).

In contrast to the experience of the Ghost, my own departure from Christianity was slow and painful. I was far from eager to give it up, praying and seeking reading material to convince myself it had to be true, even as it was occurring to me it was probably untrue. I *knew* atheism was untrue and remained rigidly critical of it for over a year into my post-Christian experience. At the beginning of this time, my mission board counselor warned me that most who leave Christianity in my frame of mind eventually stop believing in God. I resisted the thought and stated that rejecting God would be the worst fate I could imagine for myself. (Incidentally, arguing for atheism is not the focus of this book. If I can convince some of my readers to relax their hold on fundamentalist Christianity in favor of some form of simple theism, deism or agnosticism, or even a more moderate form of Christianity, I will not consider my effort to be in vain.)

The notion that a skeptical stance against religion requires as much skepticism as religion itself brings us to the burden of proof question. Do some claims by their very nature require more evidence than others? Yes. If a television infomercial claims we can take a new drug and quickly lose 50 pounds, easily keeping off the weight, does the burden of proof rest with the skeptics or with the believers? The onus remains on the believers until conclusive scientific evidence of its effectiveness has been established. Without evidence, the proper starting position or the null hypothesis is that the pill does not live up to its claims.

No one denies that biblical Christianity makes extraordinary claims: a talking serpent, a talking donkey, rods that turn into serpents and swallow other serpents-from-rods, resurrections, and blood sacrifices (of goats, bulls, and man—the man Jesus) for the forgiveness of sins. Clearly these ideas, and many others, bear the burden of proof, just as the claims of the diet pill bear the burden of proof. I am not stating these things are impossible, given the existence of the god of the Bible; I am simply insisting we should not give them the benefit of the doubt without *very* good reasons for doing so.

Many of the ancients, when pondering the mystery of how the earth is held up, were not content to let it remain a mystery, even though they lacked the tools and evidence to crack the mystery. By analogy with everything on earth that requires a support, the earth itself must have been held up by pillars or elephants. In hindsight, we can appreciate that their haste to solve an unknown by inventing an explanation out of thin air stood little chance of arriving at the nature of reality. Today there remain many genuine unsolved mysteries about the nature and origin of the universe and of life. Christianity and other religions are eager to fill our thirst for a certain answer to these questions. These religious systems exploit our desire to explain what we do not know. In doing so, they illegitimately shift the burden of proof to the skeptic to answer questions that religion pretends to address, but whose answers are no more empirically grounded than the proposition that pillars bear the weight of the earth.

The lesson to be learned is that the burden of proof rests on those who make empirically unsupported claims. It is the partisans of such claims that are obligated to make their case, not the skeptics of those claims. "I don't know" is a proper response to questions we do not have the tools to answer.

I continue to read books written in support of Christianity, even if not at the same pace as I once did. I have recommended to deconverting Christians that they should read books on both sides of the divide to avoid being hoodwinked by either party. My children know where I stand, but I always insist that they postpone any decision about what to believe until they reach an age when they can carefully and deliberately consider the arguments for themselves. Many if not most evangelical parents would never address their children in this way. They are enjoined by the Bible to impress their faith on their children at every turn:

> These commandments that I give you today are to be upon your hearts. Impress them on your children. Talk about them when you sit at home and when you walk along the road, when you lie down and when you get up. Tie them as symbols on your hands and bind them on your foreheads. Write them on the doorframes of your houses and on your gates (Deuteronomy 6:6–9).

I will be the first to admit I am far from objective in my pursuit of truth. I am fallible like everyone else. That is why I value free inquiry and a wide exposure to the ideas of others, believers and unbelievers alike. It is in my interest to know the truth, because if I am mistaken, the consequences could be eternally grave. Yet despite this threat, and against familial, social, and personal interests, I have accepted the inconvenient truth that my former faith was a mistake.

Part II

My Reasons for Believing:
A Critique

Chapter 5

The Positive Influence of Other Believers

EXEMPLARY BELIEVERS

The faith of many Christians throughout church history and into today has led to many noble, brave, and charitable deeds. St. Francis of Assisi, William Wilberforce, Albert Schweitzer, Florence Nightengale, Dietrich Bonhoeffer, Martin Luther King Jr., and my mother come to mind among many others. It is understandable that millions of believers should see the fruit of these saints as a vindication of the faith that inspired them. Christian apologist J. F. Baldwin recognizes the importance of heroic, Spirit-filled living as the most powerful argument beckoning nonbelievers to the faith:

> We may certainly teach people about God's grace by telling them the story of *Pilgrim's Progress*; we teach it better when we tell them the true story of John Newton [former slave trader who authored the song *Amazing Grace*]; and we teach it best when we demonstrate it with our lives. Our actions matter more than any words. . . .

> In order to be best used by the Holy Spirit, you must model truth for the rest of the world. Only when non-Christians see Christ manifest in His Body will they, like Dr. Jekyll, see "the veil of self-indulgence . . . rent from head to foot." You (and I) must exemplify the fact that Christ changes lives—and this means leading heroic lives (Baldwin 1998, 242–43).

Baldwin's exhortation to acts of heroic, selfless service is commendable, as are similar exhortations throughout the Bible. He openly acknowledges that Christians have often failed to live up to the ideals of the Christian faith:

Why don't I shine brighter in a dark world? I don't need non-Christians to tell me that Christians can be hypocritical—I see it in the mirror every day. The failures of Christians are painfully obvious both in the world and in my life (Baldwin 1998, 238).

My very devout mother complained that often the most committed Christians can be the most overbearing, nit-picky, and generally undesirable neighbors. But I will indulge Baldwin and refrain here from reminding my readers of all the ways Christians have failed morally throughout history. Baldwin and many other believers lament this state of affairs, calling followers of Jesus to live more like their Master in order to make the gospel more attractive to outsiders.

Nevertheless, inasmuch as believers heed these calls to perform good deeds, we must ask ourselves who is actually carrying them out. Is it the Holy Spirit who enables Jesus' followers to serve others, or is it humans who do so by their own efforts? Are nonbelievers (who presumably are not filled with the same Spirit as Christians) incapable of performing the same good deeds to which Christians aspire? By what power was Mahatma Ghandi able to spawn peaceful liberation movements throughout the world? Does the Holy Spirit inspire and strengthen Muslims serving with the Red Crescent to give charitably to those in need? If the Holy Spirit is indeed active in the lives of true Christians, why must apologists like Baldwin even have to exhort them to live according to the precepts of their faith? If believers have to be told to behave in order to attract nonbelievers to the faith, could it not be that the source of their eventual good deeds is not the Holy Spirit but rather the motivating desire to draw non-Christians to God?

If Christians lead exemplary lives out of a desire to lead others to the gospel, I cannot complain; the world will be a better place as a result, as long as they are not sowing unnecessary division in their proselytizing efforts. Yet it is not obvious to me that their good deeds necessarily spring from a supernatural source.

Often those who use the example of saintly or heroic believers as an argument in favor of Christian faith are unwilling to use the example of obnoxious, divisive and hateful believers as an argument against their worldview. God is always to be credited for Christians' good works but cannot be blamed for their failures. Heads I win, tails I don't lose.

I will have a good deal more to say about morality in chapter 8. For now I acknowledge the good deeds of many believers, but it is unwarranted to leap to the conclusion that such individuals prove the gospel to be true.

THE MYTH OF INDIVIDUAL FAITH

As a believer I was reluctant to admit that my decision to follow Christ was anyone's but my own. While studying French in Belgium prior to our mission work in Africa, I chafed at my French teacher's suggestion that Charlene and I were merely following in our parents' footsteps in choosing the evangelical Christian faith and becoming missionaries. After all, had I not survived two earlier crises of faith in my college years? I had for a time abandoned the faith of my parents, returning to Christ only after weighing the options and concluding (after much agonizing thought and prayer) that he is the Way, the Truth and the Life. I had established the right to call my faith my own, or so I thought.

The evangelical emphasis on appropriating one's faith as one's own, rather than as an inheritance from one's family, is reflected in the saying, "God doesn't have any grandchildren." This emphasis is maintained despite certain scriptural passages suggesting the unit of salvation to be the household rather than the individual. For example, my children participated in an AWANA Bible memory club at the church they attend with my wife. I noticed that the last four words of the following verse were excluded from their Bible memory handbook, presumably not because it rendered the verse too lengthy to memorize, but more likely because it conflicted with the doctrine of individual salvation:

> Believe in the Lord Jesus, and you will be saved—*you and your household* (Acts 16:31).

Paul maintained that it is possible for an unbelieving husband (like me) to be sanctified through the faith of his wife:

> To the rest I say this (I, not the Lord): If any brother has a wife who is not a believer and she is willing to live with him, he must not divorce her. And if a woman has a husband who is not a believer and he is willing to live with her, she must not divorce him. For the unbelieving husband has been sanctified through his wife, and the unbelieving wife has been sanctified through her believing husband. Otherwise your children would be unclean, but as it is, they are holy (1 Corinthians 7:12–14).

What is the reason for this modern evangelical valuation of individual choice? My recollection as a part of this movement was that it was based on the need to counter any suspicion that our faith was merely a cultural inheritance. Perhaps this emphasis gained currency in the aftermath of the Enlightenment and during the Great Awakenings when rationalists challenged the Christian faith as culturally determined. Many believers are consciously or subconsciously aware that if they were to admit their faith is largely determined by the cultural influences to which they are exposed, it would be tantamount to acknowledging that their beliefs are based less on the inherent merits of Christianity than on accidents of birth and culture.

To be fair, most skeptics and freethinkers, including me, are also heavily influenced by the ideas of others. I doubt I would have had the courage to break with the faith of my youth had I lived five hundred years ago, before enough brave souls had risked their lives challenging the reigning dogmas of the day and ushering in the Enlightenment. It is difficult enough for me today to give up the trust and in some cases the friendship of my peers in taking the stand I have made. I could not imagine facing the possibility of the torture or death that many of the early freethinking heretics endured. For example, unitarian Michael Servetus was executed at the behest of Protestant reformer John Calvin (Willis 1877, 281–86, 304–13, 498–508). Calvin's severe outlook concerning heretics is representative of the repression that reigned before the Enlightenment and Western liberalism paved the way for freedom of speech and religion:[25]

> Whoever shall now contend that it is unjust to put heretics and blasphemers to death will knowingly and willingly incur their very guilt. This is not laid down on human authority; it is God who speaks and prescribes a perpetual rule for his Church. It is not in vain that he banishes all those human affections which soften our hearts; that he commands paternal love and all the benevolent feelings between brothers, relations, and friends to cease; in a word, that he almost deprives men of their nature in order that nothing may hinder their holy zeal. Why is so implacable a severity exacted but that we may know that God is defrauded of his honor, unless the piety that is due to him be preferred to all human duties, and that when his glory is to be asserted, humanity must be almost obliterated from our memories? (Schaff 1892, sec. 157, 791).

ACCIDENT OF BIRTH, BENEFIT OF DOUBT (ABBOD REPRISE)

As I noted in my ABBOD section in chapter 4, I am convinced that the influence of other believers is likely the primary reason for which most Christians are Christians, as opposed to Hindus or Buddhists or Muslims. Most children grow up accepting the dominant worldview of their family or culture, quite apart from any intellectual merits of their particular faith. In other words, the chances are that if you are a Christian, it is because

---

[25] I am not unaware of the excesses of the repressive radical Enlightenment, especially in France, but that does not invalidate the contribution of the Enlightenment to the ideals of liberty in the American constitution, for example.

someone influential in your life—whether parents or peers—introduced you to the gospel. The same goes for most members of all religions.

If the human mind had no tendency to reinforce its established ideas and interests, the average soccer mom would acknowledge that bad referee calls in favor of her child's team are as common as bad calls against her child's team. Children of a politician would be no more likely to favor their parent's candidacy than that of the opposition.

Alas, the human mind is not an objective machine, and I was and am fully prone to its many weaknesses. As a Christian my loyalty to kith and kin particularly clouded my ability to see clearly the faults of my group's beliefs, stifling any appreciation for the ideas of those on the outside.

A conversation in 2006 with an evangelical friend of mine illustrates this principle well. In response to some of my objections to the Bible, he implored, "You're just not giving the Bible the benefit of the doubt." I countered, "Would you have given the Qur'an the benefit of the doubt if you had grown up in a Muslim country like Afghanistan?" His response: "I would have given it the benefit of the doubt until I discovered it was untrue." I replied that this was precisely what I had done; I had ceased giving the Bible the benefit of the doubt after discovering it was not true.

In retrospect, though, it may have been more to the point to ask him whether he, growing up in a Muslim country, would have had the disposition, will, or fortitude to find and pronounce Islam untrue. If he is disinclined to look at the Bible critically within a Christian milieu, would he have fared better than the vast majority of Afghanis at critically examining and rejecting the Qur'an if he had been taught all his life to revere it?

How can we determine whether a holy book is untrue if we are to give it the benefit of the doubt? To which text do we owe the benefit of the doubt? To the particular set of scriptures to which our culture subscribes? This is a recipe for guaranteeing that all Muslims will remain Muslims, all Mormons Mormons, all Protestants Protestants, and so on. Should we not rather make every effort to divest our minds of all vestiges of the ABBOD effect if our goal is genuinely to seek the truth? Even if it entails the risk that we might have to say good-bye to the faith of our family and friends whom we cherish and respect, thus incurring upon us all manner of suspicion and ill will on the part of those we love most?

Could I deny that I would have been a follower of Zeus had I lived in Greece in the fifth century BCE, or a believer in astrological signs if I had lived at the same time in Babylon, or a subscriber to animistic practices if I had lived in the heart of pre-colonial Africa?

On the other hand, just because most people who accept the faith of their culture are mistaken does not mean they must all be wrong. One worldview is likely closer to reality than the others; if so, individuals abandon it to their own detriment. The question is, how could I know whether I was a part of the fortunate minority that happens to have the truth if I was unwilling to examine critically the group to which I belonged? Could I be sure that mine was the only group exempt from doing the hard work of investigating our faith without reservation, of subjecting ourselves to the possibility that our investigation might lead us in an undesirable direction, and of making a monumental change of course should that turn out to be the case?

Regardless of which worldview most closely represents reality, it still stands that we are more likely to be mistaken than not if we give the benefit of the doubt to the prevailing beliefs of our culture or family, since there are many competing worldviews and no one worldview is in the majority. While at the threshold of deconversion, I reasoned as follows: If the dominant faith of my culture happens to be true, then I should not shy away from applying the scalpel to it, for it can withstand any critical scrutiny. If I refuse to apply the scalpel, or if I resist those who attempt to apply it on my behalf, I might never know whether Christianity can withstand the refining fire, and I will always be beset by a still, small voice asking whether the critics were right after all.

I, like many evangelicals, was eager to examine critically the origins and history of Mormonism, and rightly so. But it was not enough to apply the scalpel of critique to others; I had to apply it to myself. And it would not do to apply the scalpel in a token or mediocre fashion; I had to apply it as mercilessly as I expected non-Christians to apply it to themselves. I will go further: given the near-universality and effectiveness of the ABBOD principle for making us prisoners of our beliefs, I had to be willing to subject my views to a stronger dose of skepticism than the skepticism I tended to apply to other points of view, or I could never hope to compensate for the illegitimate tendency to give my own worldview the benefit of the doubt. I reflected on the extent to which Muslims must apply the scalpel in order to see the error of their ways and leave their faith; that is how assiduously I had to apply the scalpel to my beliefs, my scriptures, my Jesus, the miracles of my religious tradition, my answered prayers, my favorite apologetic proofs, and my god.

If I was unwilling to subject my beliefs to this kind of criticism while expecting Muslims in Niger to take this yoke upon themselves, I had to admit to myself I was operating under a double standard. There were two possible ways out of this bind: (a) abandon any expectation or desire for

Muslims or anyone else to convert to my faith, or (b) accept the need to investigate my worldview critically and mercilessly. For a short time I adopted option (a), embracing a form of liberal, universalist Christianity. I later came to think I might be kidding myself; what assurance did I have that liberal Christianity had any basis in reality? If it wasn't true, how could I know? It was only then that realized I could not escape alternative (b).

Surely an impartial Martian observer would be struck by the nearly universal applicability of the ABBOD principle in generating conformity of belief across generations of believers belonging to communities of faith. Surely these humans cannot be impartial, or there would not be such a tendency for belief to be clustered geographically and culturally. I can only conclude that we as humans are inherently susceptible to the suggestions of our culture and that we are in most cases virtually powerless—yes, powerless—to recognize this susceptibility in ourselves, but we are more than eager to identify it in others.

But why is this so? Why do we tend to be prisoners of what we have been taught, rather than forming our beliefs independently? Richard Dawkins offers a compelling explanation: A child's very survival depends on unquestioning adherence to the dictates of those in authority. Don't touch—it's hot! Don't get near the edge of that cliff! Don't move; there's a snake! Believe as I say, or hellfire will await you! The mind of a youngster is like a sponge, soaking up cultural and linguistic norms that allow it to survive in an often harsh world. It is not generally constituted in such a way that its survival can be bettered by skepticism. The ability of the brain to learn from others who have learned the hard way is an indispensable human asset, but it is this same ability that contributes to our reluctance to question authority or to cast doubt on the unsupported claims of our forebears (Dawkins 2006, 174).

Some may object that we are all prisoners of the ABBOD principle, believers and unbelievers alike. Children of atheist parents are as likely to become atheists as children of Christian parents are to become Christians. Let us grant this for the sake of argument. In this case, any one worldview is as likely to be mistaken as any other, and we can have little confidence that the views we have inherited from our parents or our culture are superior to any other point of view. Yet we are supposed to accept, from a fundamentalist Christian or Islamic standpoint, that those who reject the correct faith are destined to an eternity of suffering. There is a disconnect between maintaining on the one hand that nonbelievers are as vulnerable as believers to the ABBOD principle, while on the other hand holding unbelievers eternally accountable for said vulnerability. Those who insist that we unbelievers are guilty for our choice, then, should not blame ABBOD for it; rather, they ought to be bold and make us personally responsible for our unenviable fate. Skeptics, unlike conservative believers, make no threats concerning the eternal destiny of those with whom they disagree. Only from this nonthreatening perspective can one legitimately appreciate the full weight of ABBOD, acknowledging that the majority of humankind adopts *with all sincerity and good will* the beliefs—whether true or false—of family or culture.

What are we to make of a world in which different people come to sincere but different conclusions on so many matters, based in large part on the culture to which they belong? These differences are as culturally conditioned in mundane matters like the shape of the earth as they are in matters of great importance such as the ultimate purpose of life. Where these views are opposed to each other, either they are all mistaken or only one is true. It could be that we are all fundamentally mistaken in our views about ultimate reality, or it could be that Christians are correct, or Muslims or atheists, but not all at the same time. Now, if God exists and desires the allegiance of all his creatures,[26] it seems odd he would allow a state of affairs to exist in which equally sincere people come to diametrically opposed views on the nature or existence of God, in the same way that they have historically come to different views on the shape and age of the earth, the origin of disease, the appropriateness of dancing, or the relative merits of Macintosh versus Windows computers. The same psychology, the same defensiveness, the same argumentative spirit surfaced when geocentrists long ago sparred with heliocentrists as when Christians now spar with Muslims or atheists. But if there is no personal god, then this situation—the confusion and conflict that reign from the mundane to the critical, from the dawn of man up to the present—is *precisely* what we would expect in a world in which there is no personal creator who reveals himself to his children.

In summary, ABBOD offers a potent answer to one of the central questions of this book, *What would it take to ensure that a religion like Christianity thrives even if untrue?* ABBOD does not explain how an untrue idea might have gotten off the ground in the first place, but it does account in large part for how an established belief can maintain an unyielding hold over the generations. If a religion can co-opt the natural

---

[26] This is an assumption shared by many, though not all, believers. In particular, some Calvinists might maintain that God in his sovereignty has simply decided he does not wish to have a relationship with certain of his human creations as vessels prepared for destruction (see Romans 9).

trust we place in our family and culture, so much the better for the survival of the religion, be it true or false.

TRADITION AND AUTHORITY

The weight of tradition is a close cousin of the ABBOD principle, though with more of an emphasis on how long a set of beliefs has been held by how many followers.

My study of church history in college gave me a sense of the rich tradition that upholds the Christian faith. There have been in the history of Christianity a great number of brilliant theologians and courageous martyrs: the Apostle Paul, Polycarp of Smyrna, Irenaeus, St. Augustine of Hippo, St. Thomas of Aquinas, St. Francis of Assisi, St. Anselm, St. Joan of Arc, Martin Luther, John Calvin, and Jonathan Edwards, to name but a few. However, I only later reckoned that this did not mean their understanding of reality was more informed or correct than ours. The possession of intelligence or bravery does not guarantee the possession of truth. To illustrate, after centuries of scientific progress, the average schoolchild knows more today about the nature of the cosmos than the majority of these luminaries, through no fault of their own.

One of the songs I heard as a Christian proclaimed, "Two thousand years of followers can't be wrong." By that logic, we should still believe the earth is flat and is the center of the universe, for these are beliefs that were widely held far longer than two millennia.[27]

If only one or two individuals hold to a strange idea—for example, that the Virgin Mary never died but ascended directly to heaven, or that a wafer turns into flesh, or that a donkey spoke to a man (Numbers 22)—it is easy to ridicule and dismiss their claims. But if thousands, millions, or billions embrace such ideas, they are more readily considered worthy of respect, not because the ideas are inherently more reasonable, but simply because many have held them for so long.

It should go without saying that the number of adherents to any belief in no way guarantees its truth or reasonableness. It simply means the idea succeeded in getting off the ground long ago and propagating itself over many generations, growing ever more respectable with age. If you've ever

---

[27] I do not subscribe to the myth that most medieval Europeans believed in a flat earth or that Columbus' sailors feared falling off the edge of the earth. Nevertheless, there was a time, at least prior to the Greek Classical period, when the majority of humanity believed in a flat earth—from India to China to the Middle East and Europe.

received Internet chain letters recounting fabulous stories that turn out to be urban legends, you know how easy it is for such tales to get around. As long as there are enough individuals not sufficiently conscientious to verify the stories before passing them on, such messages may be propagated and believed by millions.

For many years I inwardly wondered about the reasonableness of certain teachings of the Bible and the church, but I could not bring myself to abandon my faith, in large part because of the many intelligent and authoritative individuals who embraced it over the centuries and in my generation. I eventually came to the conclusion that I had to think for myself, knowing how easy it is for various traditions around the world to have led their followers astray, and knowing it was very possible I belonged to one such tradition.

FEAR OF OTHERS' REACTIONS

For many fundamentalists and evangelicals, nothing is more important in life than their faith. Expressing doubt or criticism against any dearly held religious belief can be considered impolite or offensive. It cuts to the core of who the other person is and can be felt as a personal attack.

I have learned that one of the most offensive things I can do is to question the legitimacy of what someone considers to be a miracle. An acquaintance once told me of a faith healer who visited her church and was able to pronounce something about her that could not have been known by anyone else. What she apparently wanted me to say in response was, "Wow, that sounds miraculous." Instead, I started to say, "Well, . . .", to which her response was, "You always say, 'Well, . . .' Can't you just accept it's from God?" I will have more to say concerning this in chapter 13.

Most of us—regardless of our worldview—generally do not relish confrontation and wish to avoid offense. By asking too many questions, by digging too deep, it is difficult not to manifest a distrust in what our friends, family, and acquaintances trust, thus potentially calling their judgment or integrity into question.

In response to my online story "From Missionary Bible Translator to Agnostic" (Daniels 2003), I have received a number of e-mails from individuals who quietly doubt or reject their faith but who continue going through the motions of their religion for fear of offending their parents or other relatives and friends. Better to wait until Mom and Dad or Grandma and Grandpa have passed on than to break the awful truth to them.

The result is that untold thousands, perhaps millions, of churchgoers, some sitting in a pew next to you, silently reject what they are told, but their lips remain sealed out of deference to their loved ones. This compounds the difficulty of "coming out," since the silent ones believe they are the only ones struggling. If more doubters had the courage and integrity to make their positions known—however difficult, and however offensive to their family and friends—then other doubters would come to realize they are not alone, and they too could muster the courage to come clean.

In the end, this would help promote a true dialogue between competing worldviews, permitting healthy skepticism to be brought head to head with the reigning forms of supernatural belief.

If you are even remotely reconsidering your commitment to your faith, chances are that one of the greatest fears you face is the wall that might be erected between you and those you love. I wish I could say from my experience that this fear is unfounded and that you will encounter only a minor bump in the road. This will not be the case if your relatives or friends take their faith seriously. They will analyze you to figure out what went wrong; they will chalk it up to the wiles of Satan; they will blame it on some negative experience you had with the church; they will tell you they are praying for you; they will say your situation is sad; they will blame you for being the one who moved from the original position; they will assert you were never truly saved to begin with; they will blame it on your misunderstanding of the True Christian Faith; they will seek you out not for who you are as a friend but for the opportunity to set you straight; they will question your integrity—in short, they will look for any explanation that exonerates their faith and places the blame on anything but the deficiencies of the Christian faith itself. You may be thankful you do not live prior to the Enlightenment when heresy was rewarded by torture or death, but you *will* have to live with the suspicion of those you love most.

To illustrate the resistance you will encounter on the part of some (certainly not all!) of your friends, family and acquaintances, I will include parts of an online discussion initiated by a college friend on "The Fighting Fundamental Forums" website after he received my letter from Africa expressing my struggles with doubt (Hyles 2005a):

> Back in 2000 I received a disturbing email from a missionary supported by my church. I had hosted this missionary in my home just a few months earlier and I followed his work closely. His name was Ken Daniels, and he was a Bible translation missionary to Niger, West Africa, with Wycliffe Bible Translators.

I first met Ken when we were both students at LeTourneau University in Longview, Texas. He was a visible, well-respected spiritual leader in the school and even served as the student chaplain for student government. Ken graduated and then pursued a master's degree.[28] Believing he was called by God, he applied to and was accepted by Wycliffe as a linguist and translator. He deployed to Niger where he worked among a people with no written language, no grammar, and no concept of God beyond oral tradition.[29] When he came to our church in 2000, I gave him a generous offering to help with the purchase of a jeep. He seemed to be smack in the middle of God's will.

I cannot fully express the shock, dismay, horror, and grief that overcame me when I received the following email July 1, 2000. . . .

Some time later, after my friend read the story of my deconversion process, he posted an excerpt of it and received the following responses (Hyles 2005b); (Hyles 2005c):

[A respondent] People turn from the faith all the time. The Bible talks about them many times and in many ways. Here are just a few. . . .

2Pe 2:1 But there were false prophets also among the people, even as there shall be false teachers among you, who privily shall bring in damnable heresies, even denying the Lord that bought them, and bring upon themselves swift destruction.

2Ti 3:5–9 Having a form of godliness, but denying the power thereof: from such turn away. For of this sort are they which creep into houses, and lead captive silly women laden with sins, led away with divers lusts, Ever learning, and never able to come to the knowledge of the truth. Now as Jannes and Jambres withstood Moses, so do these also resist the truth: men of corrupt minds, reprobate concerning the faith. But they shall proceed no further: for their folly shall be manifest unto all men, as theirs also was.

1Jo 2:19 They went out from us, but they were not of us: for if they had been of us, they would no doubt have continued with us: but they went out, that they might be made manifest that they were not all of us.

[My friend] I find it compelling because he was a personal friend and acquaintance. He was highly regarded and considered by many to be one of the best Christian men they had ever known. He certainly had me fooled. After the initial shock, our thoughts turned more towards his wife and kids when this all happened.

---

[28] Actually, I was in graduate school but was not pursuing a master's degree.

[29] In fact, there were many educated Daza individuals who could read the Qur'an in Arabic and so learned about Allah in writing.

[A respondent] I am truly sorry to hear about your friend. Regardless of how seemingly fine a Christian fella he was, it is sad to know people reject Christ, particularly that once professed Him. . . . We have a situation on this forum of that same nature and it breaks my heart for the family and kids.

People pose as believers all the time, many will proclaim they have cast out demons, preached and predicted, and done many mighty Univeralist [*sic*] works, but He says that their righteousness is as filthy rags.

[My friend] I find Ken's assertion that the OT has sub-standard ethics to be almost laughable. I won't resort to an ad hominem argument, but I just have to ask, what kind of ethical standard allows a man to seek employment and financial support in Bible translation if he doesn't believe the Bible.[30] That's a sub-standard ethic itself and could be a starting point for demonstrating that Ken is not qualified to judge the ethical standards of the OT.

[A respondent] Nothing like the "I'm better equipped to judge than God" types. The "fundamentalists" are the ones who usually have to have every question answered to absolute dogmatic certainty.

[My friend] God has the entire universe set up so that he gets the glory for everything good. Ken Daniels' slowly unveiling arrogance is incompatible with and diametrically opposed to a God that refuses to be controlled, handled, understood, broken, or otherwise trained to obediently serve his creation. . . . Ken has replaced God with Ken. You'll see this more and more as I post further into his writings.

[A respondent] I told you that before you ever posted part 2 or any of the rest.... "Ever learning but never coming to truth."

[A respondent] I don't know whether or not this would apply to your friend, but I found this quote to be very enlightening.

It is by Augustine, and Ruth Bell Graham includes it in her book "Prodigals and Those Who Love Them" (which book, BTW, has recently been a wonderful blessing to me).

The quote:

"The loss of faith always occurs when the senses first awaken. At this critical moment, when nature claims us for her service, the consciousness of spiritual things is, in most cases, either eclipsed or totally destroyed. It is not reason which turns the young man from God; it is the flesh. Scepticism but provides him with the excuses for the new life he is leading."

---

[30] My friend is mistaken: I did believe the Bible when I joined Wycliffe Bible Translators. It was only later that I abandoned my faith.

[Another respondent] Sad, sad, sad. Seems this man is looking to everyone except the Author of mankind, faith and the Book for the answers.

My friend's final online comment holds back nothing (Hyles 2005d):

ICHABOD. After reading this I felt strongly compelled to mail Ken a loaded gun and a note with instructions on how to more completely realize the ramifications of his arrogant, meaningless worldview. Here is the last installment of his drivel. Five years have passed and he has gone from Wycliffe Bible Translator to celebrated deconverted Atheist.[31] Atheistic drivel begins here. [Followed by an excerpt of my writings.]

But do not despair. I am only preparing you for the worst, which may not last indefinitely. It is possible that some or all of your relatives will come around to your new point of view, or at least come to accept, however reluctantly, that you have turned a corner and may never return. The beginning stages will be the most difficult: some of what is said to and about you will create a tight knot in your stomach. Over time, however, the confrontations will decrease in frequency and intensity, and you will be able to get on with life in a more or less stable relationship with your family and friends, provided you don't live up to their expectations of an apostate and become a jaded, angry, licentious fool.

I feel fortunate that I have not been hounded any more than I have. Most Christians who learn that you have left the faith for intellectual reasons (as opposed to a desire to sow your wild oats) will tend to avoid getting into confrontational conversations with you, except for those who are steeped in Christian apologetics. Thankfully, these are in the minority of those whom I hold dear.

CHRISTIAN FELLOWSHIP

I confess I still miss the camaraderie of fellow believers joined in a cause greater than ourselves. I look back longingly at the hymns and choruses we sang together and the fellowship we enjoyed in sharing our prayer requests and in praying for each other. I regret the loss of the almost automatic acceptance I enjoyed on the part of those who belonged with me to the same community of faith, the same church, the same missionary society. I still catch myself wanting to say to others in difficult circumstances, "I'll pray for you."

---

[31] While I am flattered by my friend's assessment of my notoriety, I am not exactly a household name in the skeptical movement.

There is no sugarcoating the reality that secularists in general do not enjoy the same benefits of a warm community that committed believers typically do. In many regions there are few others of like mind with whom unbelievers can open up and share their deepest personal struggles. This is due not only to the dearth of freethinkers, but also to our relative independence (we probably would not be freethinkers in the first place if we were not independent in mind and spirit!). To be sure, there exist some "communities of nonfaith," but such congregations are few and far between, and they often tend to focus more on reminding themselves why they are not religious than on providing a warm community of encouragement for those who have left the church.

I see the safety net and fellowship of the church, coupled with the lack thereof outside the church, as one of the most important impediments to the growth of free thought. In order for it to grow and flourish, there needs to be a community of support, but as long as local freethinking communities are rare, few Christians will be willing to abandon the nurturing environment they currently enjoy in the church. It's a catch-22 that is likely to exist until those who harbor doubts about their faith begin to show a willingness to raise their hands and collectively find other hand-raisers with whom to journey in a world suspicious of and antagonistic toward their stand. On the bright side, the Internet now provides a wealth of resources and online communities for those who would otherwise have remained completely cut off.

Chapter 6

The Design of the Universe and of Life

The problem of explaining the complexity and beauty of nature without appealing to a superhuman intellect was the final barrier to my loss of faith. My confidence in the doctrines of Christianity had eroded well before I abandoned my belief in God.

Now that I have set aside supernatural explanations for origins, I have found that the focus of my conversations with intellectually minded believers quickly turns to the question of cosmic and biological design. They seem to be convinced that if I could come to accept the evidence for God's existence, then it would be only a small step for me to go all the way and accept biblical Christianity.

As I mentioned earlier, my focus in writing this book is not to convince my readers to become atheists. Though I presently do not believe the evidence warrants belief in God, I am far more open to the possibility of God's existence than I am to the idea that the Almighty inspired the collection of books known as the Bible or that God displaced his wrath for us by sovereignly orchestrating the murder of his god-man son Jesus. It is not simply a small step between accepting God's existence and embracing the tenets of a conservative Christian faith; a gaping canyon remains between the two.

Though I will not seek to make an extensive case against God's existence, as a nontheist I feel an obligation to present at least an outline of a response to those who demand to know how I might account for the universe and life without God. Keep in mind that if my case remains unsatisfactory to my readers, this provides no particular warrant for the truth of Christianity or for any of the thousands of other supernatural worldviews on the market.

I must make a point of saying that no one—neither atheistic scientists nor creationists—has any conclusive evidence concerning how the universe and the first life form began. This being the case, we must hold lightly to our theistic or naturalistic hypotheses for these questions. I will present some of the naturalistic hypotheses currently in the playing field, but I am not lending my unequivocal "you'll-be-damned-if-you-don't believe" support to them. This is not to say we can know nothing about the past, however. The evidence *does* unambiguously show, for example, that the earth is several billion years old and that life on earth has changed significantly from simpler forms over the course of its existence. Our understanding of many of the details and mechanisms accounting for those changes is incomplete, but the big picture is well established by a wealth of interlocking evidence.

In my years as a Christian I was fully convinced that the origin of the universe and of life demanded a supernatural explanation, and I was not shy about presenting the case for design. I recall the great passion with which I researched and taught a young adult Sunday school miniseries in North Carolina on the wonders of the simplest life forms and the impossibility of their having arisen by chance. In retrospect, perhaps my conviction was driven in part by deeper factors (for example, the meaning and moral framework that theistic belief confers) than the desire to align my beliefs with reality. As a result, I was simply unwilling to consider any perspective that challenged what I knew in my heart had to be true. This is in keeping with the findings of a survey conducted by Michael Shermer and Frank Sulloway:

> Psychologist Frank J. Sulloway of the University of California at Berkeley and I made a similar discovery of an attribution bias in a study we conducted on why people say they believe in God and why they think other people do so. In general, most individuals attribute their own faith to such intellectual reasons as the good design and complexity of the world, whereas they attribute others' belief in God to such emotional reasons as that it is comforting, that it gives meaning and that it is how they were raised (Shermer 2004, 46).

SUSPICION OF THE SCIENTIFIC ESTABLISHMENT

Though I as an evangelical generally appreciated the successes of the scientific method (at least those of the experimental sciences and their technological offerings), I was suspicious of the motives and methods of scientists whose findings are at odds with traditional interpretations of biblical texts and conservative theology.

If I had been asked as a white evangelical Christian whether O. J. Simpson murdered his wife, I would have answered unequivocally in the affirmative on the basis of the circumstantial, forensic, and DNA evidence. But if I had been asked whether common DNA markers in chimpanzees and humans (including inactivated genes that are active in more distant species) imply any real relatedness based on common descent, I would have demurred: "Science can only take us so far—it cannot establish anything with certainty, it makes assumptions that cannot be taken for granted, and it succumbs to fatal biases."

This distrust of science—particularly the evolutionary, geological and cosmological sciences—is inculcated early in the education of most children in fundamentalist households like mine. In the face of facts that challenged my perspective, I naturally gravitated to religious authorities and materials that reinforced the failings of evolutionary and geological scientists (remember Piltdown Man?) and comforted myself with the knowledge that it was the scientists (not I) who were deceived.

The tendency to favor traditional or biblical understandings of the world over those of the scientific establishment is not new. Christian historian Philip Schaff relates the perspectives of the Protestant Reformers on Copernican astronomy in his *History of the Christian Church:*

> But in this matter Calvin was no more in advance of his age than any other divine. He believed that "the whole heaven moves around the earth," and declared it preposterous to set the conjecture of a man against the authority of God, who in the first chapter of Genesis had pointed out the relation of the sun and moon to the earth. Luther speaks with contempt of that upstart astronomer who wishes to reverse the entire science of astronomy and the sacred Scripture, which tells us that Joshua commanded the sun to stand still, and not the earth. Melanchthon condemned the system in his treatise on the "Elements of Physics," published six years after the death of Copernicus, and cited against it the witness of the eyes, which inform us that the heavens revolve in the space of twenty-four hours; and passages from the Psalms and Ecclesiastes, which assert that the earth stands fast and that the sun moves around it. He suggests severe measures to restrain such impious teaching as that of Copernicus (Schaff 1892, sec. 135, 678–79).

As an adult who rejected evolution, I had never been exposed to any compelling evidence in its favor until I was well into my deconversion process. Sure, I had seen PBS nature shows in which evolution is taken for granted, but I had never closely studied the evidence that drove Darwin to his conclusions or the evidence that had come to light since the time of Darwin that had forged a consensus among earth and life scientists. I had never read books critiquing the creationists' critiques of evolution; I was thus under the impression that my favorite creationist and Intelligent Design (ID) arguments had gone unanswered or were unanswerable. I had never been challenged in my views, since I had read and absorbed materials written only from an ID or creationist perspective. It was simply more comfortable that way.

For those who distrust the scientific establishment because of its many failings, I offer the perspective of Daniel Dennett:

> Through a microscope, the cutting edge of a beautifully sharpened ax looks like the Rocky Mountains, all jagged and irregular, but it is the dull heft of the steel behind the edge that gives the ax its power. Similarly, the cutting edge of science seen up close looks ragged and chaotic, a bunch of big egos engaging in shouting matches, their judgment distorted by jealousy, ambition and greed, but behind them, agreed upon by all the disputants, is the massive routine weight of accumulated results, the facts that give science its power. Not surprisingly, those who want to puncture the reputation of science and drain off its immense prestige and influence tend to ignore the wide-angle perspective and concentrate on the clashes of schools and their not-so-hidden agendas. But ironically, when they set out to make their case for the prosecution (using all the finely polished tools of logic and statistics), all their good evidence of the failings and biases of science comes from science's own highly vigorous exercises in self-policing and self-correction. The critics have no choice: There is no better source of truth on any topic than well-conducted science, and they know it (Dennett 2006, 372).[32]

To sum up Dennett's point, science is far from perfect—we know this to be true after hearing conflicting statements on whether butter or margarine is better for our health—but it's the best tool we have for understanding nature, just as democracy, imperfect as it is, serves us better than any other political system. As Winston Churchill put it:

> Many forms of government have been tried, and will be tried in this world of sin and woe. No one pretends that democracy is perfect or all wise. Indeed, it has been said that democracy is the worst form of government except all those other forms that have been tried from time to time (Churchill 1947, 43).

EXCURSUS: THE AGE OF THE EARTH

As recounted in chapter 2, I embraced old earth creationism for the final decade of my life as a Christian. As an unbeliever I still do not consider

---

[32] I take this not to mean that science can answer all questions we might have, but that no other source of knowledge has proven more reliable or productive.

Christianity to be incompatible with an old earth. Though Western Christianity largely came to terms with the antiquity of the earth in the nineteenth century, a revival of young-earth creationism (YEC) and Flood geology starting in the mid-twentieth century has resulted in its becoming the majority view of American evangelicals today. Were it not for the continued widespread embrace of this belief, I would ignore it in favor of more important concerns. Those who already accept the great antiquity of the earth are encouraged to skip on to the next section.

Many (though not all) proponents of YEC have not thoroughly investigated the reasons why almost every geologist—Christian or otherwise—accepts that the earth is several billion years old. Sometimes there is a perception that this is a question of fidelity to God and the Bible, so anyone who presents evidence seeking to disconfirm YEC is motivated by rebellion against God. In effect, no amount of physical evidence against YEC can sway those who adopt this stance.

At the same time, many Christian leaders and evangelical colleges remain open to old earth creationism (OEC). I ask my YEC readers to consider whether all the following well-known evangelicals who accept an old earth are fundamentally unfaithful to God:

> John Ankerberg, Gleason Archer, John Battle, Michael Behe, William Jennings Bryan, Walter Bradley, Jack Collins, Chuck Colson, Paul Copan, William Lane Craig, Norman Geisler, Robert Godfrey, Guillermo Gonzales, Hank Hannegraff, Jack Hayford, Fred Heeren, Charles Hodge, Walter Kaiser, Greg Koukl, C. S. Lewis, Paul Little, Patricia Mondore, J. P. Moreland, Robert Newman, Greg Neyman, Mark Noll, Nancy Pearcey, Perry Phillips, William Phillips, Mike Poole, Bernard Ramm, Jay Richards, Hugh Ross, Fritz Schaefer, Francis Schaeffer, C. I. Scofield, Chuck Smith Jr., David Snoke, Lee Strobel, Ken Taylor, B. B. Warfield (Coffee 2008).

To the above list I might add James Dobson (Hamliton, Dobson, Gish, and Ross 1992) , Billy Graham (Frost and Graham 1997, 72), the late linguist Kenneth Pike, and the majority of the members of the Intelligent Design movement. Most nationally known America Christian colleges and universities have no problem with OEC: Biola, Calvin, John Brown, Gordon, Taylor, and Wheaton, among many others.

If YEC is untenable, as virtually all geologists and many prominent evangelicals apparently believe, then those who insist the earth is only a few thousand years old run the danger of hitching their wagon to a sinking ship (to mix metaphors), thereby undermining their credibility in other matters. Just as I would be hesitant to seek treatment from a doctor who believes in the efficacy of homeopathy or who denies the germ theory of disease (no matter how sincere and personable he might be), I (along with virtually the entire unbelieving world) find it very difficult to take seriously the metaphysical assertions of anyone who maintains the earth is young. The earth is *not* young, a fact that was established by Christian geologists in the eighteenth and nineteenth centuries, well before the advent of radiometric dating, and even before the time of Darwin. As St. Augustine of Hippo famously wrote more than a dozen centuries before the advent of modern geology:

> Usually, even a non-Christian knows something about the earth, the heavens, and the other elements of this world, about the motion and orbit of the stars and even their size and relative positions, about the predictable eclipses of the sun and moon, the cycles of the years and the seasons, about the kinds of animals, shrubs, stones, and so forth, and this knowledge he holds to as being certain from reason and experience. Now, it is a disgraceful and dangerous thing for an infidel to hear a Christian, presumably giving the meaning of Holy Scripture, talking nonsense on these topics; and we should take all means to prevent such an embarrassing situation, in which people show up vast ignorance in a Christian and laugh it to scorn. The shame is not so much that an ignorant individual is derided, but that people outside the household of faith think our sacred writers held such opinions, and, to the great loss of those for whose salvation we toil, the writers of our Scripture are criticized and rejected as unlearned men.
>
> If they find a Christian mistaken in a field which they themselves know well and hear him maintaining his foolish opinions about our books, how are they going to believe those books in matters concerning the resurrection of the dead, the hope of eternal life, and the kingdom of heaven, when they think their pages are full of falsehoods and on facts which they themselves have learnt from experience and the light of reason? Reckless and incompetent expounders of Holy Scripture bring untold trouble and sorrow on their wiser brethren when they are caught in one of their mischievous false opinions and are taken to task by those who are not bound by the authority of our sacred books. For then, to defend their utterly foolish and obviously untrue statements, they will try to call upon Holy Scripture for proof and even recite from memory many passages which they think support their position, although they understand neither what they say nor the things about which they make assertion (Augustine 408, sec 39, 42–43).

Though there is a large, interlocking web of evidence pointing to an old earth (about 4.5 billion years old) and an old universe (about 13.7 billion years old), I won't burden my readers with more than a couple of phenomena that show the earth and the universe to be over 10,000 years old. I am aware of the oft-repeated argument that God created the universe with the appearance of age, so I have selected evidence for which that argument is problematic: Greenland ice cores and distant supernova explosions.

According to Bo Møllesøe Vinther's dissertation at the University of Copenhagen, scientists have extracted cores from at least 20 different locations in the vast Greenland ice sheet, up to 3 kilometers deep (Vinther 2006, 12). The focus of Vinther's dissertation is on the past 12,000 annual layers of a 120,000-year ice core record based on four key core samples from different regions in Greenland.

While the counting of the annual layers is not always straightforward and carries some assumptions about the regularity of cold versus warm seasonal weather patterns, these basic assumptions are independently confirmed by cross-comparison with major volcanic eruption events in history. For example, we know from historical records that Vesuvius blew its top in 79 CE, and all four of the core samples show a greatly increased level of sulphuric acid in that year and for other years with known major volcanic events (Vinther 2006, 54). The same correlation has been done by studying tree rings from very old trees that are still alive from the time of Vesuvius and by employing Carbon-14 and Beryllium-10 radiometric dating. The conclusion is that the possible margin of error for the ice core dating is 0.25% going back 4000 years, 0.5% going back 7000 years, 2% going back 10000 years, and 0.67% going back 12,000 years (the latter being based on radiometric cross-confirmations) (Vinther 2006, 43). These basic assumptions have also been borne out through analysis of Antarctic ice cores.

There is no evidence to suggest that the lower layers (for a total of 120,000 layers) do not follow a similar pattern of one year per layer. From a YEC/Flood geology perspective (Whitcomb and Morris 1961), the ice sheets could not have originated before the Flood, since the earth was supposed to have been warm prior to that event. What is more, any pre-Flood glaciers would have been melted by a global inundation lasting an entire year.

The most common YEC response to these data is to question the assumption that the layers are annual—perhaps multiple cooling and warming cycles and storms led to multiple layers per year (Oard 2001). This is an ad hoc explanation for which no evidence is forthcoming. We have seen that the annual-layer assumption is independently corroborated through historical volcanic events and tree ring analysis. The onus is thus on the YEC to produce evidence for a precipitous departure from this annual pattern deeper in the ice core layers.

The other line of evidence for an old universe I explore here concerns the light from distant supernova explosions. I can understand that God might have wanted Adam to see starlight from distant stars the day he was created, so he might have created the universe in such a way that the light from stars thousands of light years away had already reached the earth at the beginning. It becomes more problematic to think of supernova explosions billions of light years away. If we assume that the speed of light has always remained more or less what it is today, then the light our telescopes capture when we witness one of these events has either been in transit for billions of years, in which case the universe really is old, or the light did not come from these actual supernovas but was divinely fabricated to seem as though it did. But if we allow for divine fabrication, then we have to ask whether this would be in some sense deceitful on God's part— it means we think we're following the physical evidence, but God has deliberately made it so the evidence can't be followed, and then he blames us for following it. It is not only skeptics that find this problematic; YEC astronomer Danny Faulkner expresses the same concern:

> Most creationists have adopted the concept of a fully functioning universe as the best explanation for the light travel time problem. In the garden Adam would have been a particularly healthy male. If we could go back in a time machine and examine him we might have concluded that he was 20 to 30 years old. Of course we would have been wrong, because Adam was created only a few days before. In other words, creation implies some sort of apparent history. It is argued that in like fashion, for the stars to serve their intended purpose (for the marking of time and seasons) their light must have reached earth in time for Adam to see them two days later. Thus God must have created the light in transit. But did Adam bear the scars of past history, such as injuries that never happened? When the fossilized remains of large extinct and previously unknown creatures were unearthed over a century ago, some Christians responded that the fossils were created in the rocks and that the creatures never existed; they just appeared to have existed. Most people would reject this as absurd. Yet the creation of starlight in transit raises a similar philosophical point. In the spring of 1987 a superdeca was observed in a nearby galaxy called the Large Magellanic Cloud. Since that time the progress of the explosion and its aftermath have been carefully observed. We have been able to piece together many fine details of what happened. But if the notion of light created in transit is correct, then none of the observed events happened. How is this different from God creating fossils in the ground? (Faulkner 1998)

Faulkner rejects the idea that the speed of light has changed significantly since creation (think of how Einstein's famous equation $E=mc^2$ would affect the universe if c, the speed of light, were significantly greater!) and also rejects Humphreys' "white hole cosmology" hypothesis as an attempt to solve the light-in-transit problem from a YEC perspective.

Faulkner's forthrightness on the problem of starlight from distant stars is refreshing. He admits there is a genuine puzzle without making up a nonempirically based work-around as Oard appears to have done in an attempt to dismiss the Greenland ice core problem.

To be frank, I have become increasingly closed to engaging in dialogue about religion with YEC believers. If one's preconceived notions about the physical world cannot be amended by the clear evidence of the rocks and stars, then neither will one's religious or spiritual views be subject to any argument or critique that challenge's one's faith. I therefore request that any who wish to dialogue with me first read *The Bible, Rocks and Time: Geological Evidence for the Age of the Earth* by evangelical Calvin College professors Davis Young and Ralph Stearley (Young and Stearley 2008). I see no point in dialoguing about faith with anyone who remains unconvinced of the evidence for the antiquity of the earth presented in that volume, which was written by geologists who accept the inerrancy of the Bible.

EVOLUTION

Though the popularity of an idea does not establish its truth, those who oppose evolution ought at least to reflect on the reasons for which the vast majority of earth and life scientists accept it. I had earlier rejected evolution because I thought I was sufficiently qualified to dismiss it as ludicrous, much in the way medieval commoners and theologians felt qualified to judge the absurd notion that the earth is spinning on its axis at the rate of 1,000 miles per hour while hurtling around the sun at 67,000 miles per hour.

Instead of regularly developing *testable* hypotheses for peer review and scientific publication (whether in friendly creationist journals or in mainstream evolutionary journals), creationists often tend instead to write books or present conferences directly to the majority of the populace that already rejects the shared ancestry of humans and apes. I am disturbed by the flippant disregard and disdain on the part of many creationists for the patient investigation and analysis that have led most scientists in the past century to accept evolution. While a lay creationist, I refused to consider that scientists might know a little more about the facts bearing on origins than I did. Instead, I felt that scientists were simply blinded by their impulse to reject God or to meet with the approval of their peers, thereby increasing their chances of securing tenure in universities or obtaining research grants. After reading the evidence for evolution presented by scientists who believe in God, I could no longer in good conscience retain this position.

This is not the place for a detailed defense of evolution, but I will briefly mention a bit of the evidence that changed my mind. Particularly convincing for me was an article entitled *Plagiarized Errors and Molecular Genetics* (Max 1986–2003), which establishes common descent as firmly as any forensically solved crime. It is fairly technical but directly addresses those who rely on the oft-heard "similarity among species does not entail common ancestry but common design" defense.

Among the extensive body of genetic evidence for common descent, one straightforward argument is that all mammals, with the exception of guinea pigs, apes, and the monkeys that are most closely related to apes, are able to fabricate their own vitamin C. Guinea pigs and jungle-dwelling primates have a diet rich in vitamin C, so the loss of this capability would not have been harmful to them. Humans, too, as primates, lack this capability. That in itself would be food for thought, but even more startling is that we, along with certain monkeys (like macaques) and apes, possess an inactive gene corresponding to the gene for vitamin C production in other mammals. To top it off, the stop codons responsible for inactivating that gene are found in the same position on the same gene for both humans and other primates. This can be readily accounted for if humans and apes share a common ancestor, a primate that long ago lost its ability to generate its own vitamin C while obtaining its necessary supply from the readily available fruit on which it fed. From a creationist standpoint, however, there is no a priori reason to suppose that if certain monkeys have a broken gene for vitamin C production, then humans and apes should also carry such a broken gene, let alone that it should be broken in precisely the same location.

In the ongoing debate between creationism and evolution, there is one crucial matter creationists seldom address. While responding point by point to the commonly presented forest of evidence for evolution, attempting to explain away and knock down one tree at a time, they rarely stop to ask the question, "Why would God allow so much *apparent* evidence for evolution to exist in the first place? Did he plant this evidence as a means of giving unbelievers a ready excuse for rejecting God? Is God deceitful, or is there in fact not even any *apparent* evidence for evolution?" If indeed evolution did not happen, there are countless ways God could have prevented it from even getting off the ground as a scientific theory.

For instance, if he had created the universe without the appearance of great age, evolution simply would not have had the necessary time to do its work.[33] When astronomers witness a supernova explosion in a galaxy nine billion light years away, this suggests at least an *appearance* that the universe is old, since (apparently) it would take billions of years for the light from that event to reach earth. The point is not whether there might be some alternative explanation (for example, Humphrey's thoroughly discredited "Starlight and Time" hypothesis (Ross and Conner 1999)) to defend a young earth. The point is that this appearance of age does in fact exist, an appearance that God could have preempted in any number of ways—for example, by making the visible universe smaller or the speed of light much greater.

Another showstopper for evolution might have been for God to have made no animals at all, or at least to have left much larger gaps between species, both living and extinct. If dogs had been the closest animals to humans, for example, Darwin would never have been able to propose his theory. As it is, we share some 95% of our genome with chimpanzees and 99.4% of our known functional genes (Wildman et al. 2003). There exist a number of fossil skulls intermediate in size and form between apes and humans; creationist leaders disagree over which ones are apes and which are humans (Miller 2008, 95).[34] Like chimpanzees and other mammals, we have miniscule muscles that make our body hair stand on end when we're frightened or cold. For mammals with fur, this serves to make their body appear larger and intimidate predators or prey (cats not only stick out their fur but also arch their backs), or to enhance the insulation effect of the fur when cold. But for those of us with insignificant body hair, these functions are correspondingly insignificant and suggest the *appearance* of descent from mammals in which the function was significant. Again, the point is not whether an alternative explanation can be imagined for these

---

[33] After Darwin proposed his theory of evolution, Lord Kelvin calculated the maximum age of the sun to be 100 million years, based on the assumption that it burns chemical fuel. As this was considered insufficient time for the evolution of modern life forms, Darwin insisted there had to be a mistake, but his vindication came only after his death: Einstein's theory of relativity allowed the sun to have been "burning" for billions of years, thanks to the process of nuclear fusion (Pigliucci 2002, 25).

[34] If there are no real intermediates between apes and humans, and if humans and apes are entirely different "kinds," it is worth pondering why several prominent creationists (Cuozzo, Gish in 1985 and Mehlert) consider *Homo ergaster* specimen ER 3733 to be an ape, while others (Bowden, Menton, Gish in 1979, Taylor, and Lubenow) consider the same specimen to be fully human.

phenomena, but why God did not act to prevent the *appearance* of our descent from furry mammals when it was in his power to do so.

Additionally, God could have nipped the idea of evolution in the bud by arranging the fossil record in any of a virtually limitless number of possible ways other than the way in which it is in fact arranged, with only simple organisms in the deepest (oldest) strata and more complex ones appearing in higher (younger) strata. Ad-hoc creationist explanations for this ordering, such as the tendency of more advanced animals to seek higher ground during Noah's flood (and thus to be buried in higher strata than the simpler animals) (Morris 1974, 118-20), serve only to acknowledge but not solve the problem. This explanation is untenable because relatively advanced plants like grass and flowering plants (which cannot flee the oncoming flood) appear only in the higher strata. In response to friends who have asked me what it would take for me to believe in God again, I have laid it on the line: find me a trilobite fossil in the same layer as a mammal fossil (whether marine, like a dolphin, or terrestrial, like a rodent), and I will abandon my belief in evolution. I have not heard back from my friends, nor do I ever expect to. Do you know why? Because evolution did in fact happen.

Creationists are continually being forced to change the goalposts concerning their predictions that certain transitional forms will never be found. No sooner is a new specimen unearthed (for example, morphological intermediates between land mammals and whales such as *Ambulocetus, Rodhocetus*, and *Dorudon*; or morphological intermediates between fish and tetrapods, like *Tiktaalik roseae*; or the Cambrian fossil *Orthrozanclus,* which bridges the "unbridgeable" gap between three top-level phyla: mollusks, annelids, and brachiopods) than creationists begin publishing explanations for why these are not or cannot be transitional forms after all. The elephant in the room, the question I never hear them address is, "Why, in the first place, should there exist fossils whose appearance as intermediates requires explaining away?" Again, whether or not such explanations are legitimate, it is clear that many of these fossils do manifest features to some degree intermediate in form between two groups for which creationists earlier predicted no intermediates would be found. It is irrelevant whether the intermediates precisely bisect the previous gap, whether the intermediates are of the expected size, and whether parts of the skeleton are incomplete. What matters for the credibility of the creation model is that there exist intermediate features that creationists had earlier predicted not to exist, and that these erroneous predictions require explaining away. This is not to deny that significant gaps do still exist, but it does not change the reality that many previously unknown, morphologically intermediate forms have been found since the time Darwin advanced his theory.

Despite the oft-heard assertion that no true intermediate forms exist in the fossil record, young-earth creationist paleontologist Kurt Wise acknowledges both their existence and their importance:

> Of Darwinism's four stratomorphic intermediate expectations, that of the commonness of inter-specific stratomorphic intermediates has been the most disappointing for classical Darwinists. The current lack of any certain inter-specific stratomorphic intermediates has, of course, led to the development and increased acceptance of punctuated equilibrium theory. Evidences for Darwin's second expectation—of stratomorphic intermediate species—include such species as *Baragwanathia* (between rhyniophytes and lycopods), *Pikaia* (between echinoderms and chordates), *Purgatorius* (between the tree shrews and the primates), and *Proconsul* (between the nonhominoid primates and the hominoids). Darwin's third expectation—of higher-taxon stratomorphic intermediates—has been confirmed by such examples as the mammal-like reptile groups between the reptiles and the mammals, and the phenacdontids between the horses and their presumed ancestors. Darwin's fourth expectation—of stratomorphic series—has been confirmed by such examples as the early bird series, the tetrapod series, the whale series, the various mammal series of the Cenozoic (for example, the horse series, the camel series, the elephant series, the pig series, the titanothere series, etc.), the *Cantius* and *Plesiadapus* primate series, and the hominid series. Evidence for not just one but for all three of the species level and above types of stratomorphic intermediates expected by macroevolutionary theory is surely strong evidence for macroevolutionary theory. Creationists therefore need to accept this fact. It certainly CANNOT be said that traditional creation theory expected (predicted) any of these fossil finds (Wise 1995, 218–19; emphasis in original).

To be fair, Wise does go on to explain how the existence of these morphologically intermediate fossils is not a problem for his creation model. The point to be made, however, is that it is not only evolutionary biologists and paleontologists who assert the existence of such forms; competent and devoted creationists also freely acknowledge them.

Here are a few other questions that come to mind: Why, in keeping with the expectations of evolution, has there been a relentless struggle to survive, along with diseases, parasites, vines, thorns, poison, shells, predation, camouflage, and starvation, going back for eons? Why have so many species gone extinct, and why are the creatures that succeeded them in the fossil record similar to the ones they replaced? Why are certain animal groups (for example, marsupials) bound to particular geographical regions? Why do our genes show a seeming common history with those of the apes, including certain neutral or even harmful genes? Why can mutant chickens grow alligator-like teeth (Biello 2006)? Why do some whales and anteaters sprout teeth in the womb and lose them before birth? Why do certain fossil whales have hind legs (Sutera 2001)? Why do some modern-day humpback whale specimens sport external legs while most members of their same species do not (Theobald 2007a, part 1, sec. 4)? Why don't whales have gills? Why do dolphins have all the same arm and finger bones (for five fingers) as other mammals while sharks have only cartilage for the same function? Why do bats have what appear to be five long webbed fingers for their wings? Why can HIV adapt quickly to synthetic drugs? Why have certain microbes adapted to consume and metabolize artificial nylon by-products (Miller 2008, 80–83)? Why can mosquitoes come to resist pesticides? Why have carnivorous lizards released from one small island to another developed a special intestinal valve to facilitate digestion of plant material after only three decades (Herrel et al. 2008)?[35] I'm only scratching the surface.

Creationists may choose to think nothing of these phenomena, or to poke holes in the logic of those who present them as evidence for evolution, or to find an alternative grid by which to interpret them, or to emphasize only the unsolved puzzles of evolution, yet I see a pattern suggesting the *appearance* of evolution, something an omnipotent, undeceiving god could easily have preempted in any number of ways if evolution had not in fact happened. Note that, contra the protests of Intelligent Design authors like Cornelius Hunter (Hunter 2002), I am not here assuming anything about the nature of the designer—what I think God would or would not do—other than that he is not deceptive and that he would not create in such a way as to suggest the strong *appearance* of evolution, if indeed he did not use evolution to create the diversity of life on earth today.

There is no shortage of books, magazines, radio shows, and websites devoted to highlighting unsolved mysteries and anomalies in evolutionary theory in an attempt to prove that not all species (especially apes and humans) are descended from a common ancestor. No one denies the existence of puzzles; how could they be absent in a historically contingent process spanning a four billion year period? The same is true of all the

---

[35] This finding prompted a response entitled "Life: Designed by God to Adapt" by creationist organization Answers in Genesis (Lightner 2008). In view of such explanations, there is simply no evidence that could falsify the creationist contention that evolution fails as an over-arching theory.

historical sciences. For example, no one today denies languages have evolved over the centuries; modern French, Italian, Spanish, Portuguese, and Romansh are all traceable back to Latin. Yet historical linguists dispute many of the details of this evolutionary process as they seek to piece together how exactly it all came about. But the mysteries surrounding the development of the Latin-based languages pale in comparison to those of other language families like Japanese[36] or Uralic/Finnish. See the article "Uralists Against History" (de Smit 2001) for a taste of how contentious historical linguistics can be. The article presents a potential goldmine of quotes and facts for anyone interested in undermining the methodology and results of this field.

Yet for all these disagreements, no serious linguist doubts for a moment that modern languages have evolved significantly over time. They simply disagree on the details of that process. Why is there such a widespread effort in the United States to discredit evolutionary theory but not historical linguistics? Is it because the details of linguistic evolution are any less thorny than those of biological evolution? Is it not rather more likely that the backlash against evolution is due, like the backlash against Copernican astronomy, to its theological implications? To its undermining of a belief in a benign creator and our central place in the universe? If we are basically just apes, does that not make our existence pointless and call into question our basis for morality?

Fair enough, some would say—perhaps there is sufficient evidence to establish common ancestry among the species, as even some Intelligent Design advocates like Michael Behe acknowledge.[37] But surely it is not possible for all the complexity of living things to have arisen naturalistically through Darwinian random mutation and natural selection! There had to be a guiding force, a supervening intelligence behind the process. We are driven to this conclusion because of the arrangement of irreducibly complex machines within our bodies and cells that could not have arisen in a step-by-step fashion with functional intermediates between each stage (Behe 1996). As a creationist, I was fully satisfied that natural processes could not account for the development of say, a bird from a lizard; what, after all, would be the use of half a wing? If the wings were

---

[36] There is no consensus on the origin of Japanese, which seems to bear virtually no resemblance to other languages in the region.

[37] William Dembski also came out in favor of common descent in the May 9, 2005 episode of ABC News' *Nightline*, but has subsequently distanced himself from it in his book *Design of Life* (Dembski and Wells 2007).

not fully functional from the outset, surely they would be a detriment to the lizard's ability to flee from predators. And it would be far too much to ask of mere chance to provide fully developed wings in one stroke. The same could be said of many finely tuned organs and body parts like eyes: until they are fully functional, their precursors can only be impediments destined for elimination by natural selection. Case closed.

Then I began considering examples of functionally intermediate organs and structures scattered throughout the present-day natural world. There are flying squirrels with flaps of skin between their limbs that allow them to glide from tree to tree. Not as elegant as bird wings, to be sure, but useful nonetheless when it comes to escaping predators. As soon as my curiosity was aroused, such intermediates came to my attention everywhere: "flying" snakes with flattened bodies to permit gliding; "flying" frogs with giant webbed feet; bacterial poison pumps whose parts correspond to those of the bacterial flagellum in other bacteria; and every imaginable form of vision from the light-sensitive spots of microbes, to the slightly cupped light detectors of starfish, to the black-and-white eyesight of most mammals, to the exquisite color vision of birds and primates. What good is half an eye? As the saying goes, "In the land of the blind, the one-eyed man is king." It matters little that your vision is imperfect; if it is ever so slightly superior to that of your competitors, you have an advantage that, in a cutthroat environment, will make your genes more likely to become part of the wider gene pool, all else being equal.

Michael Behe recognizes the concept of functional intermediates at the macroscopic level, but in his bestselling book *Darwin's Black Box,* he turns our attention to the dizzying and less studied world of microscopic cellular machinery. At the microscopic level, all the parts of a functional unit (for example, the bacterial flagellum) must be in place and in sync at once, or they are useless. Any lay reader of Behe's book is likely to be impressed with the astounding complexity of cellular mechanisms working in concert (they are indeed *extremely* complex), to the point of considering naturalistic explanations for such structures to be patently absurd. I was no exception when I read the book in 2000.

While it is true that fewer scientific articles have been published on the evolutionary origin of these cellular nanomachines than on the origin of macro structures, productive research is in fact being conducted and published, contrary to the ongoing claims of Behe. In the famous 2005 "Dover Intelligent Design" trial, he was presented with a stack of 58 publications addressing the origin of the immune system alone (Bottaro, Inlay, and Matzke 2006). Of course neither he nor any committed proponent of Intelligent Design or creationism will find them satisfactory, but molecular precursors and genetic fossils of intermediate functions for many of the components said to constitute irreducibly complex machinery are being discovered at a rapid pace, demonstrating that these mechanisms are not in fact irreducibly complex as claimed. For a detailed treatment of functional molecular precursors to the bacterial flagellum, the flagship of irreducible complexity, see N. Matzke's "Evolution in (Brownian) space: a model for the origin of the bacterial flagellum" (Matzke 2003). For a succinct refutation of the argument from irreducible complexity, see Douglas Theobald's "The Mullerian Two-Step: Add a part, make it necessary" (Theobald 2007b).

In his second book, *The Edge of Evolution,* Behe probes more deeply into what he considers to be the limits of unguided evolution, while fully embracing and defending the idea that all species, including humans and apes, share a common ancestor.

> When two lineages share what appears to be an arbitrary genetic accident, the case for common descent becomes compelling, just as the case for plagiarism becomes overpowering when one writer makes the same unusual misspellings of another, within a copy of the same words. . . . More compelling evidence for shared ancestry of humans and other primates comes from their hemoglobin—not just their working hemoglobin, but a broken hemoglobin gene, too. . . . The bottom line is this. Common descent is true; yet the explanation of common descent—even the common descent of humans and chimps—although fascinating, is in a profound sense *trivial.* . . .
>
> More recent work on whole genomes of yeast species further shows the power of the idea of common descent. Even better, this line of analysis has produced some of those eureka moments that make science so exciting— moments when newly accessible data suddenly illuminate a murky landscape like a flare in the night (Behe 2007, 70–73).

Behe's unqualified support for common descent is surprising in light of his previous statements in *Darwin's Black Box,* in which he attacks evolutionary biologist Kenneth Miller for his appeal to the hemoglobin pseudogene as evidence for the common ancestry of humans and apes:

> This argument is unconvincing for three reasons. First, because we have not yet discovered a use for a structure does not mean that no use exists. The tonsils were once considered to be useless organs. . . . The second reason Miller's argument fails to persuade is . . . in order to make even a pseudocopy of a gene, a dozen sophisticated proteins are required. . . . The third reason. . . arises from the confusion of two separate ideas—the theory that life was intelligently designed and the theory that the earth is young (Behe 1996, 226– 227).

Curiously, Behe provides no explanation for his use of arguments he had rejected in his earlier book (Korthof 2007).[38]

If Behe accepts common descent, what mechanism did the designer (God) use to implement his plan to generate complexity and ultimately intelligent human life? Behe provides his view in his final chapter: God is like a master pool player who determines in advance which balls will end up in which pockets following a single shot. In other words, like an über-physicist, he "called" the position of every important particle in the universe at the time of the Big Bang, ensuring that life would ultimately unfold billions of years later according to his plan.

In 2007 as I was reading *The Edge of Evolution*, I explained to my then twelve-year-old son that the author accepts common descent while maintaining that God designed the complex features of life. His response: "That's silly; why would God do it that way if he could just create everything all at once?" If we're honest, I suspect that this untutored, knee-jerk response resonates with most of us. Yet it is also true that if Behe's thesis is correct—that the complexity of life really does require a designer—then we cannot limit the designer's methods by our intuitions concerning how he ought to create.

But is Behe's thesis correct? He admits natural selection can account for certain limited adaptive features of the natural world, for example, drug resistance on the part of HIV and the parasite that causes malaria. But, he says, such adaptations are trivial, involving at most one or two protein substitutions, and as these parasites are so numerous and reproduce so quickly, their inability to evolve extensively allows us to make inferences concerning the limits of random mutation and natural selection. In particular, they have been unable to generate any novel protein-protein bonding sites, a feat which would fall far outside the ability of unguided evolution to orchestrate.

I found myself intrigued by Behe's finely tuned arguments while reading his book, wondering whether he might have a legitimate, even if unconventional, case. Alas, it turns out his central claim that novel protein-protein binding sites have not arisen since the time we began studying the DNA of human parasites is unfounded. For example, the relatively new HIV-1-specific gene VPU has already developed a number of variants involving different protein-protein binding sites to enable the virus to extract itself more readily from infected cells (Smith 2007). Any critical

---

[38] Behe did indicate his provisional assent of common descent in *Darwin's Black Box*, but his rejection of arguments in its favor—arguments he now appears to embrace—leave the reader confused.

peer review of his manuscript should have brought this fact to light prior to publication. As it turns out, he was placed in the awkward position of having to acknowledge this earlier discovery as a counterexample to one of the central theses of his book after its publication (Musgrave 2007).

I have focused primarily in this section on the arguments of Michael Behe, whom I consider to be one of the most gifted and knowledgeable opponents of Darwinian evolution. He, unlike many of his anti-evolution colleagues, at least understands and accepts the evidence for the antiquity of the earth and the shared ancestry of all living species. But it is this concession to mainstream science that will marginalize his reception among more traditional creationists. And his failure to engage the scientific community, to submit his principle claims for scientific peer review and criticism prior to publication, will marginalize him among evolutionary biologists.

Those who continue to hitch their faith to the anti-evolutionary bandwagon would do well to consider the perspective of outspoken evangelical Christian Francis Collins, who headed up the monumental Human Genome Project. The following is an excerpt from his Point of Inquiry podcast interview with D. J. Grothe:

> Intelligent Design, by the way, which is a recent arrival on the scene, I think is headed for collapse in the not-too-distant future. It's based upon a premise which is sort of a god-of-the-gaps idea, that evolution just wasn't quite good enough to come up with all the complex machines we find inside people's cells, and basically, as we learn much more about cell biology, and particularly about the human genome and other genomes, it's pretty clear that that was a naive interpretation—evolution is actually *quite* capable of such complexity because it occurs in a stepwise fashion. I actually am quite heartbroken to see the way in which many churches have embraced Intelligent Design because they felt they had to have *something* to defend against evolutionary atheism, and yet they've attached themselves to a perspective that is headed for trouble, and in the process, I fear that the churches will be demoralized, and faith will be made to look foolish, all of which is totally unnecessary (Collins 2007).

This brings me to the end of the space I have to discuss evolution, but there is a wealth of material available to those who would like to learn more. For those who maintain the earth is only a few thousand years old, see Dave Matson's *How Good Are Those Young-Earth Arguments? A Close Look at Dr. Hovind's List of Young-Earth Arguments and Other Claims* (Matson 2004) or Brent Dalrymple's "How Old is the Earth: A Response to 'Scientific' Creationism" (Dalrymple 2006). For those who are skeptical of evolutionary theory, I recommend Kenneth Miller's *Finding Darwin's God* (Miller 1999) and *Only a Theory* (Miller 2008); Douglas Theobald's "29+ Evidences for Macroevolution" (Theobald 2007a); and the Talk Orgins Archive (Talk Origins Archive 2006) as good introductory material. The Talk Origins Archive maintains a comprehensive "Index to Creationist Claims," answering all the common objections to evolution (Isaak 2006). For ongoing coverage of the evolution-intelligent design debate, see the Panda's Thumb weblog (Panda's Thumb 2009).

NATURALISM VERSUS SUPERNATURALISM

I could say much more about the engaging topic of evolution, but at the heart of the controversy lie far greater stakes than technical discussions of molecules, genes, chance, irreducible complexity, probabilities, protein-protein bindings, functional precursors, and selection. What is at stake is the dominance of opposing visions of the world: one in which God is active, and one in which he relegates his creation to chance and natural selection or is absent altogether. In short, it is a battle between supernaturalism and naturalism.

As a former creationist I know the frustration of watching evolutionists attempt to patch gaping holes in their theory with "just-so" stories. I know the exasperation that says, "Why can't they just come out and acknowledge it's all just a farce? Why do they have to persist so doggedly in their wishful thinking and in the pursuit of contrived naturalistic explanations when an alternate Explanation is available? Why do they define science to exclude supernatural design out of hand? Can't they see how futile it is to continue making stuff up? Isn't it obvious that mere chance cannot account for the dazzling complexity of life? Wake up already!"

Good questions, all of these. Why *do* scientists, after all, keep supernaturalism out of science by definition? Is it an arbitrary choice, driven by a twisted desire to keep God out of the picture, or are there legitimate reasons for doing so? I submit it is for the same reasons that we keep supernaturalism out of forensics and law. If mystical forces can be respected in a court of law (for example, "Your honor, an angel—or was it a demon?—grabbed the knife out of my hand and plunged it into her heart. Honest to God!"), then there is no way of adjudicating the past; there can be no rigor, no accountability, no fruitful investigation—in short, no science. Philosopher of science (and practicing Quaker) Robert Pennock further illustrates this point:

Empirical testing relies fundamentally upon the lawful regularities of nature which science has been able to discover and sometimes codify in natural laws. For example, telescopic observations implicitly depend upon the laws governing optical phenomena. If we could not rely upon these laws—if, for example, even when under the same conditions, telescopes occasionally magnified properly and at other occasions produced various distortions dependent, say, upon the whims of some supernatural entity—we could not trust telescopic observations as evidence (Pennock 1999, 194–95).

Well, perhaps allowing supernatural explanations could make science a little more difficult, but should we exclude them out of hand simply because they happen to get in the way of our scientific method? We don't get to call the shots; if there really is a god who has intervened in the history of the universe, then the most scientific posture is to acknowledge that science has reached the end of its naturalistic explanations and to admit that there may be more to the world than what we can see, feel, hear, smell, or taste.

Let us consider the consequences of abandoning too soon the quest for natural explanations for phenomena we do not understand. From a practical standpoint, it removes incentives for further discovery. For example, after centuries of research, scientists still do not understand what causes lightning. Should we then conclude that, on the basis of this failure, Thor, the Norse god of thunder, is responsible for this phenomenon after all? Or perhaps Baal, the Canaanite god of rain and thunder? Here is the rub: if we cede to supernatural explanations, we are essentially saying, "We don't know the causes, and furthermore we know we *cannot* know; therefore, we conclude that God did it, and by doing so, we're giving up on any fruitful scientific research into the causes." Few modern believers would fault scientists for their ongoing quest to discover the natural causes of lightning, yet many criticize naturalists for their determination to explain the origin and development of life without reference to God. Nothing spells the end of investigation like holding out the possibility that a thorny problem requires a supernatural explanation.

Furthermore, because of our experience with the way the world works, we all subscribe to a naturalistic outlook in our everyday lives. Imagine you park your car at a mall parking lot to do some shopping. A couple of hours later you return to find your car missing. Well, maybe you forgot where you parked it. No, you had noted the parking area—E2—in your notebook, and you returned to the same location, and you remember the same tree with the oddly twisted branches next to it. Perhaps someone stole it. No, you had installed a radio alarm to alert you remotely if anyone bumped it, and you had received no signal. Perhaps the alarm receiver malfunctioned. But why would anyone have been interested in your rusty, dilapidated, decades-old car with an ugly paint job? Perhaps it was a collector's item, unbeknownst to you. Or maybe your spouse needed the car, was in the area, and drove it away using her key.

You get the idea. Notice you start with the most mundane explanations first (for example, you forgot where you had parked it), then you work your way to more unusual possibilities. But however puzzling the situation, a supernatural explanation (for example, that an angel lifted it away) is the very last possibility you would consider, and probably one you would not consider at all. As a rule of thumb, we instinctively (and correctly) follow the perspective of Sherlock Holmes, who reasoned with his partner Watson as follows in attempting to determine how an intruder gained access to a room:

> "How came he, then?" I reiterated. "The door is locked, the window is inaccessible. Was it through the chimney?"

> "The grate is much too small," he answered. "I had already considered that possibility."

> "How then?" I persisted.

> "You will not apply my precept," he said, shaking his head. "How often have I said to you that *when you have eliminated the impossible, whatever remains, **however improbable**, must be the truth?* We know that he did not come through the door, the window, or the chimney. We also know that he could not have been concealed in the room, as there is no concealment possible. Whence, then, did he come?"

> "He came through the hole in the roof," I cried.

> "Of course he did. He must have done so" (Conan Doyle 1890, 93-94; emphasis added).

Consider that if we subscribe to supernaturalism, then nothing is impossible (one could easily substitute the words *miraculous* or *supernatural* for the term *impossible* in this context), and we risk forfeiting the truth if we set aside the improbable in favor of the impossible. This, in a nutshell, is why Sherlock Holmes never considered the possibility of the supernatural (for example, that the intruder passed through the wall) in his investigations, and it is for this same reason that scientists are bent on pursuing a nonsupernatural account for the origin of life and the evolution of the species.

Ironically, many who without hesitation apply Sherlock's Principle when trying to get to the bottom of a mystery in their everyday life proceed to castigate scientists who pursue this course when it comes to historical questions like the origin of the species. When biologists are confronted with a puzzle and fail to find a door, they will seek a window, and if not a window, a chimney, and so on, to explain a biological feature nonmagically. At some point in this process, supernaturalists begin to accuse the biologists of inventing "just-so" stories. Yet it is a double standard to apply Sherlock's Principle regularly in one's quotidian life but to refuse to allow scientists to apply it to a domain such as evolution that threatens one's religious preconceptions regarding origins.

Are all evolutionary hypotheses "just-so" stories? No. Many are attested through multiple, independent lines of evidence. To cite just one example, over a century ago, biologists observed that two jawbones in the fetus of mammals become part of the inner ear during fetal development, while the same bones in reptilian fetuses remain associated with the jaw. This led to the seemingly preposterous hypothesis that the three-bone inner ear of mammals derived historically from the jawbones of our reptilian ancestors. But subsequently paleontologists uncovered an exquisite set of fossils intermediate in form between reptiles and mammals showing just how this transition was accomplished: the two reptilian jawbones migrated in stages to serve simultaneously as part of both the jaw and hearing apparatuses, then later reached their present position in service of the inner ear alone (Theobald 2007a, part 2, sec. 4).

Incidentally, the religious refusal to allow naturalists to apply Sherlock's Principle to the origin of the species is but one manifestation of the same tendency in many other domains. We will see in chapter 11 that apologists have little tolerance for creative naturalistic explanations for Jesus' alleged post-resurrection appearances, preferring instead to invoke the supernatural to explain the data. The same holds true for allegedly fulfilled biblical prophecies and modern reports of miracles. However, when it comes to evaluating unlikely events in other religious traditions, Christians tend to be much more open to nonsupernatural explanations. For instance, how likely was it for an orphan like Muhammad to have initiated a movement that conquered the entire Middle East and beyond in one generation? Muslims highlight the implausibility of this having happened without divine assistance, but few non-Muslims are convinced that this is proof of the supernatural.

In principle, it is possible that the naturalists are wrong and that the complexity of life requires a supernatural explanation. But as long as fruitful avenues for research into the outstanding mysteries of life remain open, scientists must be given leeway to pursue and test every naturalistic alternative until all such possibilities are exhausted (all the while taking care to indicate plainly which hypotheses have empirical backing and which ones remain pure speculation or "just-so" stories). We are a long way from such a state; indeed, exciting discoveries that help fit the pieces together are being made at a rapid pace. Even origin of life research, which remains one of the most intractable problems facing a naturalistic paradigm, is a long way from reaching a brick wall. Certainly the critics are correct to cast doubt on the possibility of functional, coding DNA arising all at once by chance, or even RNA for that matter. Instead, perhaps a simple chemical reaction cycle driven by an external energy source, or what is known as the "metabolism first" world, is one of many possibilities worth exploring (Shapiro 2007, 47–53).

All natural phenomena—rain, lightning, disease, dust devils, crop growth and failure, and so on—have in various cultures been attributed to gods, demons and other spiritual forces. A theologian by the name of Dr. Price living in Massachusetts objected to the use of Benjamin Franklin's lightning rod because it removed lightning as a tool of God's judgment. God was not to be thwarted, however; Dr. Price noted that earthquakes became more frequent in the area as lightning rods became more common (Russell 1950, 74). Protestant Reformer Martin Luther further illustrates this outlook:

> The heathen writes that the Comet may arise from natural causes; but God creates not one that does not foretoken a sure calamity (American Historical Association 1888, 16).

> It was asked, can good Christians and God-fearing people also undergo witchcraft? Luther replied, "Yes, for our bodies are always exposed to attacks of Satan. The maladies I suffer are not natural, but devil's spells (Luther 1541, 252).

> I maintain that Satan produces all the maladies which afflict mankind, for he is the prince of death (Luther 1541, 256).

> Many Demons are in the woods, the waters, in swamps and it deserts, in order to hurt men. Others, in the dense clouds, cause tempests, thunder and hail and infect the atmosphere. But philosophers and scientists ascribe these phenomena to nature and I know not what causes (Luther ca. 1540, 158).

History is full of such interpretations of God's activity in the world. Some modern Christians may think their predecessors' views curious, yet they still fail to learn the lesson of the priority that empiricism enjoys over metaphysical speculation. The great physician Hippocrates (460–377 BCE) got it right:

Men think [a disease] divine merely because they do not understand it. But if they called everything divine which they do not understand, why, there would be no end of divine things (Solomon and Higgins 1996, 30).

History, then, teaches us to avoid any temptation to appeal to divine explanations for unknown phenomena, whether it be the naturalistic origin of the bacterial flagellum, of the first living creature, or of the universe itself.

I have often heard supernaturalists accuse naturalists of "bias against the supernatural." While we certainly do avoid appeals to magic, this stance is rooted in the stunning success of empirically based science; it is no more biased than following what works in any other domain. If stopping at a red traffic light reflects a bias against running red lights, then yes, avoiding the miraculous in science reflects a bias against the supernatural.

The practical track record of naturalistic science is available for all to evaluate, while supernatural science comes up empty handed. Indeed, the enterprise of science is to turn unknowns into knowns, while the business of supernaturalism is to make pronouncements concerning what *cannot* be known and which therefore requires magic. In other words, it is not unfair to accuse supernaturalists of "bias against the natural."

I will close this section by responding to Intelligent Design proponent Stephen Meyer of the Discovery Institute. In his *Darwin vs. Design* lectures he discusses capably the dizzying complexity of the simplest known forms of life. We simply never find technology that is not designed by intelligent agents. In an appeal to geologist Charles Lyell's famous maxim that "the present is the key to the past," Meyer concludes that, based on our observation that intelligence is the key to explaining complex artifacts (such as the faces of the United States presidents at Mount Rushmore) in the present, so a super intelligence is the key to explaining the complexity of living things created in the past.

This analogy has a reasonable air to it, but it fails for the following reason: We have abundant evidence that human intelligence exists and that its workings fall within the purview of naturalism. Our intelligence is dependent on a physical brain and on natural processes that can be tested scientifically. However, we have no reference point for a disembodied, colorless, odorless, invisible, supernatural, hidden intelligence of the sort Meyer proposes. Without direct empirical evidence for it, this sort of intelligence should be considered no more than a human philosophical construct invented to explain the origin of things we do not understand. Thus, the natural human intelligence we observe in the present bears no resemblance to Stephen Meyer's spiritual, brainless[39] intelligence operating in the past, and his appeal to Lyell's uniformitarianism breaks down. Perhaps such an intelligence does exist as a naturally undetectable being, but physical analogies do not serve as a legitimate basis for establishing his, her, or its existence.

Before invoking this empirically unknown intelligence, we must first consider whether there are naturalistic forces, forces that we can investigate empirically, that could explain the complexities of the biological world. This is in keeping with the stunning historical successes of empirical science in naturalistically explaining disease, rain, mountain building, canyon carving, and star and galaxy formation. We have a naturalistic program in operation that simply *works*. Why not press it to its limits in the biological domain and see how far we can get? Is there a nonrandom force in nature that can account for the complexity of the species? Yes, it goes by the name of natural selection. The power of this force, operating ruthlessly and continuously over eons, must never be underestimated. Computer scientists appreciate the power of a successive binary search mechanism to zero in on an element in a very large list of values. I do not claim that the binary search is directly analogous to evolution, but it does suggest how, for example, the optimal length and shape of a dragonfly wing could be arrived at through the continual *nonrandom* selection of slightly better designs, discarding the bulk of the sub-optimal designs along the way. Once a pair of dragonfly wings (or extended gills)[40] confers any survival value at all, this process of selection can begin to shape the wings into what they are today. The first steps may involve nothing more than a gust of wind against the extended gills propelling the dragonfly away from predators (in much the same way fins of flying fish provide a means of escape).[41]

---

[39] Not in the derogatory sense, but in the sense of lacking a physical organ we call the "brain."

[40] The hypothesis that gills served as the precursor to insect wings is not arbitrary but is based on homologies between the genes that code for gills in crustaceans and those that code for wings in insects.

[41] This tendency toward optimization is constrained by many factors, including but not limited to: the level of competition for resources required by other organisms in the same environment; the number of steps required to attain a more efficient adaptation; the degree to which a given adaptation might affect reproductive success rates; and the availability of fortuitous mutations providing the raw material for the adaptation. Thus, under intense competition for resources on the savannah, the expansion of the brain cavity of our hominid ancestors apparently conferred a greater survival advantage than

As previously mentioned, this kind of selection has been proven to allow certain bacteria to develop the ability to metabolize man-made nylon by-products. We are continually challenged to refine our pesticides, herbicides, antibiotics, and antiviral drugs to combat the ever-evolving pests that threaten our well-being. Brainless natural selection never ceases to find ways to counter our most ingenious attempts to eliminate these pests, supporting what is referred to as Orgel's Second Law: "Evolution is smarter than you." Computer simulations of artificial life demonstrate the power of natural selection to develop parasites, counterparasitic mechanisms, super parasites, and super counterparasitic mechanisms from simpler forms that lack such features (Ray 1991; Lenski et al. 2003). We know that natural selection exists, just as we know that humans who can carve the Mount Rushmore profiles exist; why look outside of nature, to something of which we can have no empirical knowledge, to explain the biological species?

In the final analysis this debate comes down to how consistently we should apply Sherlock's Principle. What is the threshold of probability that must be crossed before a supernaturalist will insist that a naturalistic explanation does not suffice? Theists like Martin Luther had a very low threshold, while modern day evangelical theistic evolutionist Francis Collins maintains a relatively high threshold. Believers can be found at virtually every point along the spectrum between the two. Intelligent Design proponent William Dembski believed he had found an objective measure by which to identify the divide between the natural and the supernatural using his specified complexity theorems, but his work has been challenged on multiple counts (Olofsson 2008, 42–45), and he has lately waffled on the value of his own Explanatory Filter (Dembski 2008a and 2008b). Michael Behe attempts to define the line in *The Edge of Evolution,* though many ID proponents would disagree with how far he goes in his acceptance of common descent and natural selection. In the end, there are no universally agreed-upon criteria to determine when to abandon Sherlock's Principle, even within the ID community.

---

did a hypothetical adaptation to rid us of our tendency to develop gallstones, for example. Perhaps this is partly because only a minority of the members of our species develops lethal gallstones, and when we do, we are often advanced enough in years that they do not affect our reproductive success rate significantly—the only thing natural selection really operates on. Thus, if evolution has managed to furnish us with a big brain while failing to rid us of gallstones, it does not negate the general principle that natural selection tends toward optimizations that enhance our survival and reproductive success in the context of our environment.

It requires significantly more effort to explain the rationale for a consistent adherence to Sherlock's Principle than to stand before an audience of ID proponents, as Stephen Meyer has done, and declare that the Darwinists perversely wish to rule ID out of the debate by defining it as nonscientific. Nothing could be farther from the truth. The reluctance to admit supernatural causation into science has far more to do with the impressive success and productivity of naturalistic science compared to the failure of supernaturalism to yield any significant testable claims, let alone any successfully tested claims. It could have been otherwise, but that is not how it has turned out.

THE ORIGIN OF THE UNIVERSE

How did matter, the natural laws, and the Big Bang all originate? How could something have come from nothing?[42] How is it that the physical laws and their constants are all precisely fine-tuned to allow for the existence of life? Scientists do not have a definitive answer to the question of how everything began (if indeed it ever began), nor do I. Some speculate that ours is not the only universe—there may be an infinite number of them—which may help explain why the natural laws in our particular universe happen to be conducive to life, but this simply pushes back the question one step further. How did whatever first began begin? When theists pose this question, atheists typically retort, "Well, how did God begin?" To which theists respond, "God is not a part of the physical world, but stands outside of it by definition, so the question is irrelevant." The arguments can go on and on, but in the end, both positions seem to raise imponderable, insoluble questions. Atheists start with nature, and theists start with God—both accept some sort of foundational reality.

I am, quite frankly, unable to fathom it all. In this respect I am like those of antiquity who pondered the foundation of the earth. The earth is solid; what does it rest on? Rather than admitting and accepting their ignorance, many in premodern times felt compelled to speculate and pass on their speculations through tradition. Thus, some cultures believed the

---

[42] This is quite possibly an illegitimate question. While most Westerners (as opposed to Easterners) almost instinctively feel that nothingness is the most natural state of affairs, we have no way to judge its likelihood. Why should it be any more likely for nothing to exist than for something to exist? In other words, we could turn the question around and ask, Why should there be nothing, as opposed to something? (Grünbaum 2008)

earth rested on elephants or pillars. At least some of the Hebrews apparently favored the pillar hypothesis:

> He raises the poor from the dust, He lifts the needy from the ash heap to make them sit with nobles, and inherit a seat of honor; for the pillars of the earth are the LORD'S, and He set the world on them (1 Samuel 2:8, NASB).

Consider the following fictitious scenario, set in 1000 BCE in southern Asia. Tradition has established that the earth rests on elephants. A boy named Rajah, like all his peers, grows up accepting this view, but as he reaches intellectual maturity, he begins reflecting on the difficulties associated with it: What are the elephants standing on? Where did the elephants come from? What do the elephants eat? Rajah begins posing these questions to some of the community sages, but instead of answering his questions, they accuse him of disloyalty to the sacred traditions and ask, "If the earth is not standing on elephants, what supports it? The earth is firm; it must be supported by something, and if you can't come up with a better solution than elephants, you must accept that elephants indeed support it. Or do you think there is nothing to support the earth? Virtually everyone from every culture accepts that there must be something solid underneath the earth to support it—whether pillars, turtles or elephants. To doubt the existence of these supports is simply ludicrous! You must make a decision one way or another."

Rajah agrees that it seems reasonable for the earth to be supported by something firm, but, in the absence of any evidence as to the nature of that support, thinks it best to withhold judgment as to whether that support consists of elephants, pillars, or turtles, or perhaps something else that no one has yet considered. So despite the threats of the sages, he does what he must do: he professes his ongoing ignorance concerning the nature of the earth's foundations. He remains an agnostic, and in his lifetime he is reviled and fails to be vindicated. It is not until centuries later that science empirically determines the true nature of the earth's support: gravity and centrifugal force, which no one in their wildest dreams could have imagined in Rajah's day.

Given the track record of premodern speculation versus the results of science, it is unwise to commit oneself to ungrounded answers to ultimate questions such as the origin of the universe until or unless empirical evidence can be brought to bear on them or until God reveals himself personally, directly, and unmistakably to us—not to ancient writers whose claims of inspiration cannot be authenticated—but to *us*. However uncomfortable it is for us to accept that there are things we simply do not know, we are on surer ground to admit our ignorance than to fill the vacuum with our imaginings or with tradition; we must not pretend we know that which we do not know. In the words of Thomas Jefferson, "He who knows nothing is closer to the truth than he whose mind is filled with falsehoods and errors" (Curtis 2002, 26). Thus, the Oracle at Delphi said Socrates was the wisest man in the world. He did not know any more than anyone else, but unlike others he was willing to admit his ignorance.

But ignorance is an unsatisfying state of mind, so scientists continue to seek answers to the big questions, and they have floated a number of hypotheses that are not presently subject to testing. It is profoundly ironic to hear theists' most common response to the multiple universe ("multiverse") hypothesis: "There is no proof of such a thing." They may be correct in observing there is no evidence for it, but the same may be said of the god hypothesis. The difference is that most scientists who subscribe to the multiverse option do so only provisionally—at least not with the same air of finality with which most theists hold to the god hypothesis. And they certainly do not threaten with eternal punishment those who do not subscribe to their untested point of view.

A significant obstacle to a nonmiraculous origin of the universe is the so-called fine-tuning problem, which states that the physical constants (for example, the so-called cosmological constant) and laws of the universe are exquisitely and fortuitously calibrated to allow for the existence of life. Apologist Lee Strobel presents this problem in an interview with physicist and theologian Robin Collins:

> When I asked Collins about this, he told me that the unexpected, counterintuitive, and stunningly precise setting of the cosmological constant "is widely regarded as the single greatest problem facing physics and cosmology today."
>
> "How precise is it?" I asked.
>
> Collins rolled his eyes. "Well, there's no way we can really comprehend it," he said. "The fine-tuning has conservatively been estimated to be at least one part in a hundred million billion billion billion billion billion. That would be a ten followed by fifty-three zeroes. That's inconceivably precise" (Strobel 2004, 133).

While many scientists appeal to the concept of a multiverse to circumvent this problem, other scientists maintain that the fine-tuning of even a single universe is not as improbable as has often been claimed. Consider the perspective of physicist Victor Stenger:

> Only four parameters are needed to specify the broad features of the universe as it exists today: the masses of the electron and proton and the current strengths of the electromagnetic and strong interactions. . . . I have studied

how the minimum lifetime of a typical star depends on the first three of these parameters. Varying them randomly in a range of ten orders of magnitude around their present values, I find that over half of the stars will have lifetimes exceeding a billion years. . . . The universe is certainly not fine-tuned for this characteristic.

Physicist Anthony Aguire has independently examined the universes that result when six cosmological parameters are simultaneously varied by orders of magnitude, and found he could construct cosmologies in which "stars, planets, and intelligent life can plausibly arise." Physicist Craig Hogan has done another independent analysis that leads to similar conclusions. And theoretical physicists at Kyoto University in Japan have shown that heavy elements needed for life will be present in even the earliest stars independent of what the exact parameters for star formation may have been.

Roni Harnik, Graham Kribs, and Gilad Perez have constructed a [model of a] universe without any weak nuclear interactions. They find that this universe undergoes big bang nucleosynthesis, matter domination, structure formation, and star formation. Stars burn for billions of years, synthesizing elements up to iron and undergoing supernova explosions, dispersing heavy elements into the interstellar medium. Chemistry and physics are essentially unchanged. (Stenger 2007, 148–49, 164).

Another oft-used weapon against a naturalistic origin of the universe is the *kalam* cosmological argument, popularized by apologist William Lane Craig in the following syllogism (Craig 1979):

1. Whatever begins to exist has a cause.
2. The universe began to exist.
3. Therefore, the universe has a cause.

If the first two premises are valid, then the conclusion (3) follows logically from the premises, though even then, the cause could as well be natural as supernatural. However, modern physics has called the first two common-sense assertions into question. Quantum mechanics tells us that events at the atomic and sub-atomic levels can occur without any prior cause and that particles can come into and out of existence without a cause, thus nullifying premise (1). Premise (2) also fails if we consider physicist Stephen Hawking's no-boundary model of the universe, alluded to in his *A Brief History of Time:*

So long as the universe had a beginning, we could suppose it had a creator. But if the universe is really completely self-contained, having no boundary or edge, it would have neither beginning nor end; it would simply be. What place then for a creator? (Hawking 1998, 146)

Victor Stenger has presented a mathematical scenario based on Hawking's model that allows for our present universe to have "tunneled" its way from a prior universe without a beginning (Stenger 2007, 126). While such scenarios are not rooted in empirical evidence, they suggest that the second premise of the *kalam* cosmological argument cannot necessarily be taken for granted. Neither Stenger's hypothesis nor the assertion that the universe began to exist enjoys conclusive observational support, so neither one must compel our assent.

After all this, we are left with a bewildering assortment of theistic arguments and atheistic counterarguments. The appeal of theistic arguments is their grounding in common sense, which tells us, for example, that whatever begins to exist has a cause. Unfortunately, common sense has also told us that the earth is flat and that the sun goes around the earth, revealing that our intuition can sometimes be an unreliable guide. The appropriate course for us to take in the face of the uncertainty surrounding the origin of the universe, then, is to hold our ideas lightly until they can be tested and confirmed.

THE ORIGIN OF GOD

There comes a time in the life of many inquisitive believers when the question arises, Where did God come from? I posed this question to my father when I was perhaps eight years old, and he offered the standard response, "God has always existed; he was not created." While a little puzzling, I accepted my father's answer at the time and did not seriously revisit the question until well after my deconversion from Christianity.

In my reading on this subject in recent years, I have observed a certain degree of frustration on the part of theists who consider that even raising the question of God's origin is borne out of ignorance, impertinence or both. After all, God *by definition* is eternal, so asking where God came from is a contradiction in terms. End of story.

I do not find this response satisfying. If we can assert that God is eternal *by definition,* why not posit the very same thing concerning the natural universe or universes? Also, in the real world, definitions are intended to correspond to some aspect of reality; we do not create our own reality by appealing to unanchored definitions. To illustrate, outside the world of fiction we cannot assert that a beaver by definition is a dam-building rodent that can speak English. We study beavers, learn their characteristics, and define the word *beaver* according to the features we empirically observe; we do not invent its characteristics through philosophical reflection. Since we cannot study God in this way, we cannot legitimately assert what does or does not define God, if in fact he exists. If a child asks her parents how Santa Claus enters homes without chimneys, and her parents explain that Santa *by definition* is able to squeeze through vents in the roof, it may temporarily satisfy an uncritical child, but it does not guarantee the plausibility of the Santa hypothesis or solve any real problems.

Richard Dawkins (Dawkins 2006) argues at length that any being capable of bringing the universe into existence, fine-tuning all its laws, creating life, and knowing the position of every particle in the universe—past present and future—cannot be a simple being but must be unfathomably complex. This renders the theistic argument from design self-defeating, since the core of the argument is that complexity requires a designer, and if the designer (God) himself is complex, an even more complex superdesigner (Super-God) is required to have designed God, ad infinitum.

After I explained this problem to a Christian friend of mine, he proceeded to reiterate that everything complex he has observed was made by a designer; therefore, the universe and life must require a designer. It was as if my presentation of the problem had fallen on deaf ears, and he did not realize he was reinforcing the very argument I was attempting to make, namely, that requiring a designer to explain every instance of complexity leads to an infinite regress of ever more complex designers to design the prior designers.

The only satisfactory way out of this infinite regress is to accept the possibility of design from the bottom up, rather than from the top down. This is a compelling philosophical argument for naturalism. But is this bottom-up approach merely a philosophical construct, or do we have any corroboration in nature? Interestingly, we do; as mentioned earlier, the lowest and oldest fossil strata contain only simple organisms, with more complex organisms appearing higher (and later) in the strata. We have ample evidence of star formation from interstellar dust, much as rain precipitates from clouds.[43] We can peer back over ten billion light years away (and thus ten billion years in time) and observe a universe in a more

---

[43] In a 1992 *Focus on the Family* radio broadcast, James Dobson sided with old earth creationist apologist Hugh Ross in his debate with young-earth creationist Duane Gish. Ross had this to say concerning star formation: "Duane's right—I do believe that stars are forming today. But I also believe that raindrops form today. In fact raindrop formation is a whole lot easier naturally than star formation... The equations that describe star formation are far simpler than those that describe raindrop formation. You're dealing with a gas" (Hamliton, Dobson, Gish and Ross 1992).

immature state with fewer heavy elements than it contains today. And known processes like natural selection, gravitation, and condensation are available to explain this kind of development.[44]

Christian Philosopher Alvin Plantinga has responded to Dawkins' infinite regress problem by noting that classical Christian theology (for example, that of Thomas Aquinas) has long postulated that God is simple in essence (Plantinga 2007). Here we find a problematic definition. In what possible sense can it be said that a god who counts the hairs on our head is *simpler* than the very hairs he counts?

In conclusion, the question, "Where did God come from?" is not simply the idle, uninformed query of an eight-year-old. Instead, it represents an inversion of the traditional argument from design in favor of God's existence.

---

[44] One reviewer of my pre-publication manuscript pointed out a fact I have openly admitted: I do not have a compelling explanation for the origin of the elements and the laws of chemistry and physics that permit the condensation that leads to star formation. Yet, as I have taken pains to point out, the theistic solution is no more evidentially grounded than that of physicists who postulate various unverifiable hypotheses. In fact, the theist's difficulties are greater in that any designer capable of designing the laws of nature must be more complex than the very laws the designer is supposed to explain. Which is more difficult to account for: the origin of the laws of nature or of the vastly more complex theistic designer?

Chapter 7

The Superiority of Christianity over Other Worldviews

DEFORMED TO FIT

It is often not long into a conversation with believers before I am told of the superiority of Christianity over all the other religions. In a recent dialogue a pastor assured me that after examining the other religions objectively, none of them measure up to the standard of Christianity. During my mini-crisis of faith in 1999, my Christian professor reasoned with me that despite the questions we all have about Christianity, nothing else is adequate—certainly not evolution—and therefore we should embrace Christ by default.

Yet how easy it is to perceive the shortcomings of all but one's own faith! How easy it is for a Christian to dismiss Islam because of its violence and fanaticism, and how easy it is for a Muslim to see the heresy of the Virgin Birth or of polytheism in the Trinity! How easy it is for a Christian to feel contempt for Hindus who allow well-fed cattle to roam their streets while many humans go hungry; and how hard it is for a secularist to comprehend the stance of the conservative Christian who would oppose stem cell research on unfeeling embryos, even if such research might hold out the potential of alleviating suffering for millions of sentient children and adults! [45]

In reading Islamic and Mormon apologists, I am struck by their ability to find flaws in other religions, including evangelical Christianity, and by the parallels in their respective tactics for defending their faith. Consider the classic of Mormon apologetics, *A Marvelous Work and a Wonder* (Richards 1950), which builds a case for Mormonism by pairing up Old Testament prophecies with their fulfillments in the Book of Mormon and in later times. A Mormon reviewer on Amazon.com gushes,

> In general, I will simply state that this book illustrates, in its text, the peerless majesty of the Church of Jesus Christ of Latter Day Saints (hereafter, "this Church"). It demonstrates, among other things, that: a.) this Church strictly upholds the doctrines and liturgical procedures set forth in Scripture, including the Bible; b.) this Church has been the means through which God has restored the precepts and powers previously lost to the world, and c.) all of this comes as the fulfillment of ancient prophecy, including Bible prophecy.
>
> One thing in particular that must be borne in mind, I believe, in reading "A Marvelous Work and a Wonder," is the principle of Prophetic Dualism, spoken of in numerous scholarly writings (in and out of the Mormon Church). This principle reminds us that Scripture might be—and often is—fulfilled more than only once. Of course, the general interpretation and overall meaning of a scriptural passage are the same, always. But, the application can vary.
>
> For example, in referring to Isaiah 6:9–10, Jesus said that this passage was "fulfilled" in the multitude which stood hearing Him upon the sea shore (Matthew 13:14–15). This multitude, naturally, was assembled at a sea side in Palestine. And yet, years later, in Acts 28:25–27, the Apostle Paul applied this exact same prophecy of Isaiah to: a.) the unbelievers at Rome (not Palestine!), and b.) those among whom Isaiah ministered (Paul calls them "our fathers").
>
> So, here we have the same prophecy of scripture fulfilled in three different groups of people. Hence, the doctrine of Prophetic Dualism, which must ever be kept in mind when studying "A Marvelous Work and a Wonder." Otherwise, some might rashly object to Legrand Richards' claims that certain

---

[45] If adult stem cells are equally or (perhaps) better suited than embryonic stem cells for such research, then those who have objected to using embryonic stem cells on purely religious grounds will have dodged a bullet. However, the question must be asked: Would such opponents maintain their position, in principle, if embryonic stem cells were indeed significantly superior?

prophecies are fulfilled in the Mormon Church, blurting such things as, "Heresy! That passage of scripture has been fulfilled, already!" (Taylor 2004)

A non-Mormon reader does not share the same lofty opinion:

The problems began even before the first page.... in the very TITLE itself. "A Marvelous Work and a Wonder," a reference to Isaiah 29:14, is claimed by the author to be a prophecy pointing to Joseph Smith. However, Mat 15:7–8 clearly indicates that this exact same prophecy is specifically fulfilled in Jesus Christ, God in the flesh.

The abominable butchering of God's word continues non-stop throughout the first few chapters, and I'm quite certain it continues on throughout.... If you are going to read this book, make sure to check out every reference and read each one IN FULL CONTEXT. The overwhelming errors will be plainly apparent (McCabe 2003).

Consider this excerpt from the Muslim apologetics site *Answering Christianity:*

Let us see how [the] Bible describes the power of God:

"And the LORD was with Judah; and he drave out the inhabitants of the mountain; but could not drive out the inhabitants of the valley, because they had chariots of iron" (Judges 1:19).

As we told above, the Biblical God cannot fight with chariots of iron but according with [*sic*] Christians God is powerful BUT when he confronts with chariots of iron, he is helpless. How [*sic*] chariots of iron can stop God Almighty to do what he wills? (Eldin n.d.)

How easy it is for a Christian with an inclination to give the Bible the benefit of the doubt not to flinch while skimming past such a passage! And how easy it is for a critical Muslim to ferret out such instances of apparent internal contradiction, given the opposite inclination!

Terry Eagleton made the point succinctly: "Ideology, like halitosis . . . is what the other person has" (Eagleton 1991, 2).

Robert Ingersoll, never one to hide his feelings, expressed his disdain for this human tendency as follows:

The average man believes implicitly in the religion of his country, because he knows nothing of any other and has no desire to know. It fits him because he has been deformed to fit it, and he regards this fact of fit as an evidence of its inspired truth (Ingersoll 1889, 244).

Even for those who have, unlike Ingersoll's "average man," studied other religions, relatively few are converted to another perspective as a result of their studies. Whether a Christian studies Islam or a Muslim studies Christianity, both are likely to remain convinced of the "objective superiority" of their prior conviction despite the exercise. This demonstrates that the inertia of one's established opinion generally trumps one's ability to evaluate other views objectively. Evangelical Regent College theologian John Stackhouse appears to share my view:

> In mission to globalizing urban populations, however, there is no way the missionary can plausibly claim that her religion is better than everyone else's, and for several reasons.

> First, no one can complete the study necessary to claim expertise on each of the other options available. Second, it is psychologically impossible to experience each of those options from the inside, as a believer, to complement the "external" knowledge of the scholarly expert. And third, there is no obvious and universally-acknowledged standard by which one could stand above all religious options and evaluate their relative worth.

> Since we cannot demonstrate that Christianity is better than all the other options, however, the happy conclusion is that we are not obliged to do so. Instead, we should follow the apostolic pattern. Do we really think that Jesus' early band undertook a comprehensive study of all of the religions available in the Roman world in the first century and then concluded that Christianity was the best option? No. "We declare to you what was from the beginning, what we have heard, what we have seen with our eyes, what we have looked at and touched with our hands, concerning the word of life" (I John 1:1).

> Jesus called us to be his witnesses, not his experts in comparative religion. We cannot prove that Jesus is the world's one Savior and Lord, or that the Bible is alone the Word of God written. Only the Holy Spirit of God can do that (Stackhouse 2007).

Despite his refreshingly candid confession of Christians' inability to make an objective comparison of various faiths, Stackhouse proceeds confidently—on the basis of personal experience—to declare the unique position of Jesus and the need to take the gospel to the ends of the earth:

> What we can and must do is what Christians can uniquely do: Testify to our experience and conviction that Jesus is indeed Savior and Lord and that the Bible is the Word of God written, and invite men and women to consider those startling propositions for themselves on the way to encountering Jesus himself. No other religion in the world places Jesus Christ where he belongs: in the center. That is our uniqueness, by the grace of God, and therefore our responsibility, by the command of God. That is all we must do—and we must do it (Stackhouse 2007).

THE NUMBERS GAME

A reigning assumption on the part of those who use the "no good alternative worldview" argument is that only major religions and philosophies deserve to be considered and eliminated before Christianity is declared the victor. The standard list may include Islam, Hinduism, Buddhism, Judaism or atheism. In my conversations I have never heard believers mention Jainism, Sikhism or Zoroastrianism, let alone any of the great number of local tribal religions or minor cults that have come and gone (or stayed) over the millennia. I wonder how many of those who subscribe to the "no good alternative" approach to validating Christianity have objectively studied these and the thousands of other religious sects to determine whether they are *all* in fact inferior to the Christian faith. Could it be that such inquirers are unwitting subscribers to the notion that a religion is to be evaluated not only by its objective merits but also by the number of its adherents? It must not be forgotten that Christianity itself was once a tiny sect in the crossroads of the Roman Empire. For those who lived in the first century CE, Christianity would not have even made it on the list of religious alternatives to consider when judging the major religions of the day. The "no good alternative" argument would have eliminated Christianity as a viable option from the outset.

Another faulty assumption associated with this line of reasoning is that one of the currently held worldviews must be correct. Perhaps no one really knows the truth, in which case agnosticism—admitting we simply do not have enough information to make a firm conclusion—is the most appropriate stance.

Certainly Christianity has very unique attributes that make it attractive to its adherents, but then so does every religion. If this were not so, there would be no differences among the religions and no loyal adherents to them. Thus we often hear, "My religion is unique (and superior) because it's the only one that has X," and "No, *my* religion is unique (and superior) because it's the only one that has *Y*." In this light, it is little wonder that Christians should consider the Incarnation and the Atonement to be unique and attractive aspects of Christianity (at least, relative to extant world religions), while Muslims consider these ideas blasphemous. And it is little wonder that Muslims should consider the communal aspects of Islamic society as prescribed by the Qur'an to be sublime, while Christians consider them to be tyrannical.

DEISM

One of the minor philosophies that typically fail to meet the cut for inclusion in the list of possible alternative worldviews is deism. It was an influential outlook during the Enlightenment in the seventeenth through nineteenth centuries, claiming such luminaries as Voltaire, George Washington, Thomas Jefferson, Thomas Paine, Benjamin Franklin, James Madison, and Abraham Lincoln.[46] It rapidly lost ground to agnosticism and atheism after the time of Darwin but has certainly not died out altogether. E. O. Wilson, Martin Gardner, and former atheist Anthony Flew are among the most prominent deists of today.

Deism, like any philosophy, has a number of variants, but is based on the premise that a force, usually referred to as God, created nature. This god may be impersonal (as E. O. Wilson holds) or personal (as many of the earlier deists seemed to have believed). In the mind of Thomas Paine, this is not the traditional god of miracles and holy books, but simply of wisdom, power, creativity, goodness, mercy, and generosity (Paine 1794, 29). His only revelation is his creation, whose authenticity cannot be forged, and not the religious books of men, whose alleged divine inspiration can never be authenticated but should be doubted on the basis of the many internal contradictions and outrageous claims they contain.

During my year or so as a deist, whenever I would explain to Christians my reservations about the Bible and Christianity, the most common response I heard was that God's ways are higher than our ways. It follows that we finite humans should expect to fail to understand certain aspects of the Christian faith and scriptures; accordingly, we must suppress our own judgment and arrogance, accepting God for who he has revealed himself to be, whether or not we're comfortable with the arrangement.

Prior to my deconversion I tended to discount deism with objections like, Why would God create us and then not reveal his will to us or provide a way for us to relate to him? or Why would he just abandon his creation and never intervene, never answer our prayers? In retrospect, these questions demonstrate a tendency on my part to dictate what the god of deism should or should not do, the very same tendency I objected to in critics of *my* god, the god of Christianity.

As a Christian who was committed to letting God be God, I ultimately came to the realization that I had to be as ready to allow him not to provide

---

[46] However, Lincoln may have warmed up to the Christian faith near the end of his life (Miller 2008a).

any sort of written revelation as to allow him to provide a holy book that contains unfathomable mysteries and difficulties.

If we *insist* that God owes us a special written revelation of himself, then how can we account for the absence of such a revelation among most peoples throughout history—for example, among the pre-Colombian Native Americans? Perhaps it's acceptable for *them* to have been in the dark, but not *us*? Surely this question deserves no response.

If we feel that God must be a god who intervenes in his creation and answers prayer, how do we account for the lack of consistent empirical evidence for such intervention? Does everything have to work together for good in the end for us (Romans 8:28) but not for a chimpanzee dying of starvation or disease in the African forest? The same question could be asked concerning heaven. If we feel God must be a god who provides an eternity of bliss to his chosen ones, why not also for the orangutans or for all the other animals in creation?

A couple of years ago I discussed these considerations with a concerned Christian, who then responded, "But what about hell? If in deism there is no provision for salvation as there is in Christianity, then we might all end up in hell." This response, which admittedly may be atypical, nevertheless reveals a profound inability to think outside one's point of reference. I countered, "Who ever said anything about hell? That's part of the Christian religion, but has no place whatsoever in deism."

To recap, many object to the deistic god because this god does not meet with certain expectations of what God should be like. Why not then offer the same latitude to deists who conclude that the Christian god does not pass muster? While I am no longer a deist, and while I sympathize with the standard Christian objections to deism, I still find the deistic god to be far more reasonable than the Christian one, for many of the reasons outlined in this book. Many of my readers may not share this evaluation, but on what grounds may it be dismissed? With reason? But reason is the very thing we short-circuit when we admit that God's ways are higher than our ways. When we judge deism, we are simply pitting *our* subjective judgment against that of deists who find the Christian god objectionable.

Though I am no longer a deist, I am still marginally open to the possibility of the deistic god's existence. After considering a great deal of arguments on both sides of the question, I find naturalism to fit best with the available evidence from a broad range of disciplines. Nevertheless, I am far from eager to argue deists out of their belief in God. Several apostates have contacted me after reading my online deconversion story, saying they have left the Bible and Christianity behind but are still convinced of God's existence. In such cases I have told my correspondents I am not interested in turning them into atheists. Instead, I have provided them this quote from Keith Parsons:

> First, I do not think it is possible to prove that belief in God is irrational. Zealous atheists may be disappointed in this, but there is no reason they should be. It is not the belief in God per se that is so offensive to the secular spirit. After all, Voltaire, Thomas Jefferson, and Tom Paine retained belief in a supreme Creator/Lawgiver. What rightly offends secular humanists is the bigotry, obscurantism, prudery, and persecuting zeal that all too often accompany theistic belief, especially in its particular institutional manifestations (Parsons 1989, 145).

I hold out deism as an alternative to agnosticism or atheism for those who have come to the conclusion that the Christian faith is untenable but who remain convinced of God's existence. I recognize that many atheists will find this concession disingenuous, but in my own experience, it would have been too great a leap for me to have transitioned straightaway from Christian theism to agnosticism or atheism. Atheists who cannot accept this concession should ask themselves whether they would prefer that everyone remain fundamentalists for fear of becoming atheists, or whether they would prefer that more fundamentalists become deists, abandoning the obscurantism, persecuting zeal, and belief in hellfire that Parson decries.

CONCLUSION

I have endeavored in this chapter to highlight the difficulties in making an objective evaluation of alternative worldviews. It is naive to think we can simply lay out a few major religions and philosophies on the table, mention a few unsatisfactory elements of each one, enumerate some positive aspects of our favorite one, and conclude it wins by default.

We may pay lip service to the reality that it is much easier for us to see the flaws in others' thinking than in our own, but we rarely take it seriously enough to consider that we—*we*—might actually be mistaken at the core of our worldview. Instead, a sense of divinely founded exceptionalism tends to come into play when it's our own position that's under scrutiny. In response to the question, "What about sincere followers of other religions? What is their fate?" one of my Christian college professors asserted, "They may be sincere, but they are sincerely mistaken." For those who speak with this sort of callous nonchalance concerning the eternal destiny of unbelievers, are they willing to consider the possibility that they, too, might be sincerely mistaken?

Chapter 8

The Foundations of Morality

In my experiences with those who seek to win me back to the faith, few other topics surface as much as the problem of how to account for and encourage moral behavior from a naturalistic perspective. Apart from perhaps the theory of evolution, I have witnessed no topic of discussion that suffers more from the "talking past each other" syndrome than this one.

A TYPICAL DISCUSSION

Debates between naturalists (N) and supernaturalists (S) on the origin of morality often take the following interminable form:

S: If you don't believe in God, why be moral?

N: There are many millions of unbelievers who manage to live moral lives. Where do you get the idea that unbelievers are more immoral than believers?

S: I didn't say there are no moral unbelievers; I simply asked what basis your materialistic worldview provides for morality.

N: It's just a matter of thinking through rationally how I want to live my life, and it happens that the moral course is the one that suits society best. It's the rational choice.

S: That may be fine for you, but if there is no Lawgiver, how can you expect everyone else to come to the same conclusion and live morally? It's just your subjective opinion.

N: No, society functions best when we live morally, and we are all a part of society. Together we come to a consensus on the broad lines of right and wrong, encouraging the socially adaptive behaviors and discouraging the maladaptive ones.

S: But if we're just a bunch of atoms aimlessly colliding together with no ultimate purpose, where do we get a sense of right and wrong, a conscience, or objective morality? Under naturalism, everything must be subjective and nothing objective. Yet you seem to have an inbuilt objective sense of morality. For example, as C. S. Lewis points out, we all experience moral indignation when someone cuts in line in front of us (Lewis 1952, 1). You cannot account for this. This objective sense of morality must come from God.

N: No, it comes from our evolutionary heritage, from the necessity of living together cooperatively as social animals.

It is not difficult to imagine how most moral expectations could have arisen in the interest of preserving harmony and cooperation in society, if for no other reason initially than for survival. Again, social morality is a balancing act between the interests of the individual and those of the society on which the individual depends. Most of us are dependent enough on others (who among us could really make it alone?) that our relationships serve to restrain our otherwise selfish tendencies.

As long as the majority of the populace wishes not to be murdered, we will have laws against murder, whether or not we have the Ten Commandments. (This is not to deny there will always be murderers.) For those of us who believe that investing time and love in our children will somehow contribute to their success and happiness, we will seek to show them love, whether or not the beautiful passage of 1 Corinthians 13 is divinely inspired. (This is not to deny there will always be bad parents.) As long as incest is harmful biologically, society at large will tend to look down on it, just as the other primates tend to do, with or without divine prohibition. (This is not to deny that some will continue to commit incest.)

There are other aspects of morality that are more difficult to make a naturalistic case for; these tend to be the areas of disagreement from one society to another. In contrast to the apes, sexual fidelity to the mother or father of one's children is esteemed in many human societies. Primatologist Frans de Waal believes (though many anthropologists do not concur) that the pervasiveness of this value suggests it is not arbitrary:

> For males, an obsession with sex may be universal, but apart from this we differ dramatically from our close relatives. We have moved sex out of the public domain and into our huts and bedrooms, to be practiced only within the family. We are by no means perfectly faithful to these restrictions, but they are a universal human ideal. The sort of societies we build and value are incompatible with a bonobo [a central African ape species related to the

chimpanzee] or chimpanzee lifestyle. Our societies are set up for what biologists call "cooperative breeding," that is, multiple individuals work together on tasks that benefit the whole. Women often jointly supervise the young while men perform collective enterprises, such as hunting and group defense. The community thus accomplishes more than each individual could ever hope to accomplish on his own, such as driving a bison herd over a cliff or hauling in heavy fishnets. And such cooperation hinges on the opportunity for every male to reproduce. Each man needs to have a personal stake in the outcome of the cooperative effort, meaning a family to bring the spoils home to. This also means that men must trust each other. Their activities often remove them for days or weeks from their mates. Only if there are guarantees that nobody will get cuckolded, will men be prepared to set out together on the warpath or a hunting trip.

The dilemma of how to engender cooperation among sexual competitors was solved in a single stroke with the establishment of the nuclear family. This arrangement offered almost every male a chance at reproduction, hence incentives to contribute to the common good. We should look at the human pair-bond, therefore, as the key to the incredible level of cooperation that marks our species. The family, and the social mores surrounding it, allow us to take male bonding to a new level, unheard of in other primates. It prepared us for large-scale collaborative enterprises that made it possible to conquer the world, from laying railroad tracks across a continent to forming armies, governments, and global corporations. In daily life we may separate the social and sexual domains, but in our species' evolution they are closely intertwined.

What makes the bonobos so appealing to us is that they have no need for any separation of these domains: they happily mix the social with the sexual. We may envy these primates for their "liberty," but our success as a species is intimately tied to the abandonment of the bonobo lifestyle and to a tighter control over sexual expressions (de Waal 2005, 124–25; see also 108–111).

It would appear that DeWaal, though by no means a conservative Christian, is as favorable toward monogamy as is James Dobson, but rather than quoting the Bible, he appeals to the success of the human species as it relates to the monogamous pair-bond that many societies value. DeWaal believes that the success of a man's offspring is enhanced by a lasting, supportive union between him and his wife or long-term partner. Under this arrangement, both society and the individual tend to benefit. An individual's reproductive success may indeed be enhanced through unfaithfulness, which explains the intense physical attraction of promiscuity, but this can be mitigated by the mother's interest in having a partner to support the children and by the father's interest in seeing his offspring succeed with his support, both physical and emotional.

S: Come on—DeWaal's perspective is not shared by the majority of human societies, where monogamy is anything but the norm. He's just making up reasons to promote his personal ideal of monogamy without God.

N: Nevertheless, despite their rampant unfaithfulness, humans on the whole value monogamy more than do the apes (apart from the gibbons). Perhaps DeWaal's explanation does not account for all the facts, and perhaps more research is required to confirm or disconfirm his hypothesis, and perhaps he illegitimately fails to proportion his confidence to the evidence for his position. But he does offer a *potential* explanation for why many of us value monogamy.

S: That sounds pretty iffy to me. On theism, our morals are based not on *potential* explanations or "just-so" stories but on the sure and unchanging foundation of God's intentions for our lives.

N: You are saying our morals are rooted in God's will and his commands. Fair enough. Are those commands arbitrary, or is there a good reason for them? In other words, are there any good reasons, *apart from* God's decrees, for us to hold monogamy as an ideal?

S: God has constituted us in such a way that monogamy benefits us and society. It creates a nurturing environment for our children and builds societal cohesion.

N: That's precisely my point: if we can recognize the benefits of monogamy for us, for our society, and for our children, then is that not a sufficient basis for us to seek the stability of a pair-bond, as deWaal calls it, whether or not God has issued such dictates?

S: It's just not the same thing without God lending weight to these commands.

N: Rather, you just cannot imagine that a naturalistic appeal to monogamy can win any hearts, because you are used to thinking morality requires a divine foundation. But even if you do not appreciate the effectiveness of an appeal to a secular, consequentialist morality, it does in fact serve as a useful guide for many of us.

S: If, as you suggest, nature instructs us to be good, then why is immorality so rampant? Think of the television show *Survivor*. An enormous audience glorifies the individualist, the cutthroat, the crafty, the winner-at-all-costs. Why be concerned about the effects of one's behavior on society when all that matters evolutionarily is passing on one's own genes to the next generation, not society's genes?

N: We do have competing interests in that regard. On the one hand, our survival often depends on our good standing in the group to which we belong, so we flaunt the rules of society to our own peril and to the peril of our genes. On the other hand, our impulse to survive and to get ahead as individuals is also adaptive in the context of competition for scarce crucial resources.

Many of the principles that underlie our values are linked by a common thread that serves our interest in the long run. The *Survivor*-style values play to the primal fantasies of the masses intrigued by the prospect of giving full reign to the evolutionarily rooted instincts for power, domination and gratification. From the perspective of our genes, these tendencies do often lead to reproductive success and thus remain strong inner urges. But, unlike most if not all other species, we have the ability to reflect on the long-term personal and social consequences of our behavior, and we can thus choose to relinquish some of our gene-driven passions in favor of strategies that promote our respect and well-being in society, ones that advance the conditions of the society in which we all take part. In sum, there is a conflict between our individual urge to survive, reproduce, and feel immediate pleasure and the more recently developed consideration of how our actions affect others' estimation of us. As for the adage that all we have is to "eat drink and be merry, for tomorrow we die," it is almost never the case that tomorrow we die, and in the meantime we have to live with the consequences of our actions and with the people whom our actions affect. If naturalism were indeed true and you could be convinced of it right now, would you run out and solicit a prostitute? Would you go and rob a bank? Is religion your only restraint? Or do you not also love your wife and fear the law?

S: You pick attention-grabbing examples like prostitution, bank robbery and murder. Sheesh. How melodramatic. Why not pick more subtle ones? If someone becomes convinced that naturalism is true, would they be more inclined to cheat on a test or on taxes or in charging a client? Would they be more inclined to lie (even tell white lies) to make life easier? Would they feel less inhibited about expressing their sexuality? Or to act with malice to badmouth others in order to get ahead on the job or in the university? For many people, there will be times when the answer to these questions would be Yes. Besides, the question is not whether we can be good without God. Of course we can (just as we can be bad without God). The real question is whether there are times when belief in God helps someone to do the morally courageous thing. Absolutely!

N: Without a doubt, religious belief can indeed push certain individuals to do the right thing. It can also impel them to do harmful or wasteful things, even (or especially) when they firmly believe they're doing the right thing. It is not at all certain whether religious belief contributes a net benefit to societal or personal morality.

But you raise a good point. If there is no god, why not take little secret shortcuts to get ahead? One good reason not to do so is that a reputation for trustworthiness is hard-won. Sooner or later, habitual violations of the rules will eventually lead to the discovery of one or more infractions. "Be sure your sins will find you out," as the Bible says. And once you are seen to be a cheat, even once, others' estimation of you will suffer a setback. If you cannot be trusted, you may be excluded from the next partnering venture.

As long as moral behavior is grounded in the relational consequences of our actions and we can ask ourselves, "What kind of society would result if everyone behaved like me?" then no holy text or divine design is necessary to explain or support morality. Certainly the tendency to take shortcuts will always remain in play, a temptation to cheat and hope everyone else but me will behave morally so I can "free load" while others do the heavy lifting. It's easier to throw my trash anonymously out the car window than to find a garbage bin, and it's easier to leave the grocery cart next to my car in the parking lot than it is to take it to the designated cart area. Many of us become upset when we find others cheating in these respects, since it might adversely affect our lives or our environment. Some of us realize that if we engage in this sort of behavior ourselves, we forfeit any basis for expecting others to do the right thing for the greater good. So to preserve our self-respect and legitimacy, we do the right thing for our society.

But there are many others who couldn't care less. Perhaps religion would do these individuals some good, in the same way (but to a greater degree) that certain children are motivated to behave if they know Santa Claus is watching them and rewarding their good behavior. There are naturalists who are happy to allow religion to flourish because of its usefulness in keeping the masses in line (while they consider themselves above the need for such props). Other naturalists prefer a more transparent tack, relying on various temporal incentives and disincentives to motivate good behavior. But this question is an intramural dispute among naturalists and does not in any way count for or against the inherent reasonableness of naturalism itself.[47]

In *The Blank Slate,* cognitive scientist Steven Pinker discusses the human temptation to harm and the opposing will to override that temptation. In doing so, he appeals not to the agency of angels, demons, and the Holy Spirit, but to regions of the brain that influence our moral decisions. From deep in our evolutionary past, we are hard-wired to survive at all costs and to trample over others in the process if necessary. We also have an enlarged (relative to other species) prefrontal cortex that allows us to foresee and consider the effect of our actions on others in our social network, thus providing the opportunity to override our instinctive antisocial tendencies:

> Damage to the frontal lobes [wherein resides the prefrontal cortex] does not only dull the person or subtract from his behavioral repertoire but can unleash aggressive attacks. That happens because the damaged lobes no longer serve as inhibitory brakes on parts of the [primitive] limbic system, particularly a circuit that links the amygdala to the hypothalamus via a pathway called the stria terminalis. Connections between the frontal lobe in each hemisphere and the limbic system provide a lever by which a person's knowledge and goals can override other mechanisms, and among those mechanisms appears to be one designed to generate behavior that harms other people (Pinker 2002, 44).

In observing what appears to be moral behavior among chimpanzees and bonobos, Frans de Waal comes to this conclusion:

> What I see, therefore, is the opposite of the traditional image of a nature "red in tooth and claw," in which the individual comes first and society is a mere afterthought. One can't reap the benefits of group life without contributing to it. Every social animal strikes its own balance between the two. Some are relatively nasty, others relatively nice. But even the harshest societies, such as those of baboons and macaques, limit internal strife (de Waal 2005, 216).

S: You're severely downplaying the positive role religion plays and kidding yourself with your mind games. Most people don't think like you and will simply act in their own selfish interests if they believe there is no god. What about the guy on the street who's teetering between sobriety and dissipation, between fidelity and adultery, between restraint and murder? Do you have no appreciation for the Salvation Army and the countless churches and religious charities that lift souls up from the depths in the

---

[47] I belong to the full transparency camp. I consider truth and honesty to be cornerstones of morality. If a little deception is needed to get morality off the ground, then it's off to a rocky start from the beginning.

name of Jesus? Doesn't it say *something* about the probable *truth* of a religion if it *works*?

N: I do not deny the power of community, Christian or otherwise, to motivate individuals to live morally. The desire to meet the moral expectations of a tight-knit community is sufficient to explain dramatic conversion stories. Yet such stories are often trumpeted in religious circles while ignoring the many who slide back into their old ways on the street, unable to fit comfortably into the church group that drew them in. Go to a local prison and ask how many of the inmates are atheists compared to those who believe in God or who claim affiliation to a church or denomination. You will not find that atheist inmates are over-represented as a proportion of the atheist population in society at large. Economic, educational, genetic, and social factors are more predictive of who will end up in prison than religious factors. Among industrialized nations, the United States ranks as one of the most religious but the least healthy according to virtually every measurable moral standard—its rates of homicide, abortion, teen pregnancy, and economic inequality surpass those of most European nations and Japan, which are considerably less religious than the United States (Paul 2005).

S: You cannot tease out cause and effect from statistics like these. It is not legitimate to hold religion accountable for the woes of American society. It would be ludicrous to assert that criminals are the most religious members of society. And there are exceptions to the generalities you provided: China has a high rate of capital punishment, Japan has a high suicide rate, and Sweden is swimming in prostitutes. Don't forget the atrocities of Hitler's Germany, Stalin's Soviet Union, or Kim Jung Il's North Korea.

N: Very true. But the overall health of less religious European and Japanese societies at least suggests that religiosity is not a *prerequisite* for a functional society. Most scientists are not religious; are they any less law-abiding on the whole than the general public, which is certainly more religious than they are? As for Hitler and other secular despots, we cannot hold naturalism responsible for their excesses any more than we can hold Christianity (a theistic religion) responsible for the excesses of radical Islam (also a theistic religion). It is impossible to say whether these tyrants were driven more by their political philosophy and personal ambition or by their metaphysical views. While Stalin was no doubt an atheist, the question is far from settled for Hitler, who stated:

> Therefore, I believe today that I am acting in the sense of the Almighty Creator: By warding off the Jews I am fighting for the Lord's work (Hitler 1939, 84).

Now, it's quite possible that Hitler was an unbeliever but was merely interested in using religious language to garner support for his programs from the German churches (Dawkins 2006, 276). Yet whether or not he believed in God (and we cannot with any evidence deny he did; his words are all we have to go by), he could not have carried out his deeds without the support of the German people, most of whom were not atheists.

Hitler's anti-Semitism was driven in part by a long Germanic tradition going back to before the time of Martin Luther, whose religiously motivated hatred of the Jews certainly cannot be attributed to atheism:

> If a Jew, not converted at heart, were to ask baptism at my hands, I would take him to the bridge, tie a stone round his neck, and hurl him into the river; for those wretches are wont to make a jest of our religion (Luther 1541, 355).

> I wish and I ask that our rulers who have Jewish subjects exercise a sharp mercy toward these wretched people, as suggested above, to see whether this might not help (though it is doubtful). They must act like a good physician who, when gangrene has set in, proceeds without mercy to cut, saw, and burn flesh, veins, bone, and marrow. Such a procedure must also be followed in this instance. Burn down their synagogues, forbid all that I enumerated earlier, force them to work, and deal harshly with them, as Moses did in the wilderness, slaying three thousand lest the whole people perish. They surely do not know what they are doing; moreover, as people possessed, they do not wish to know it, hear it, or learn it. There it would be wrong to be merciful and confirm them in their conduct. If this does not help we must drive them out like mad dogs, so that we do not become partakers of their abominable blasphemy and all their other vices and thus merit God's wrath and be damned with them. I have done my duty (Luther 1543, 31).

We must all acknowledge that Christians have done both exemplary and deplorable things and that unbelievers have done the same. This should be a lesson to us that we must be vigilant about our personal and corporate actions, no matter which worldview we subscribe to.

S: Yes, Christians have committed many atrocities, but in doing so they have violated their mandate from Christ. At least they have an ideal to strive for, even if they often fail. Unbelievers, on the other hand, have no such mandate and can answer to no ideal. In any case, you have no grounds for condemning others like Stalin who violate your subjective standards. It should be no wonder that atheistic political philosophies like Communism have wreaked such havoc, leading to more deaths in the twentieth century than in all the "Christian" wars of the previous centuries.

N: It's true that atheism is not a moral philosophy and cannot prescribe what we should or should not do. Just as various religions hold various perspectives on ethics and follow a variety of different holy books, so do nontheists subscribe to different approaches to ethics. Many of the nonreligious approaches to morality conclude, like their religious counterparts, that treating others as we wish to be treated is in our best interest in the long run. To paint all unbelievers with a broad brush and claim they can have no moral ideals to strive for is nonsense.

Do you believe that the Protestant-Catholic wars of the seventeenth centuries would have been any less catastrophic than the secular wars of the twentieth century if the population had been as great or their weapons as destructive in the seventeenth century as they were in the twentieth century? Fully a third of the population of Germany was destroyed in the Thirty Years War. As a proportion of the current population of Germany (82 million), that would have meant some 27 million deaths in today's Germany alone. And that was before the advent of military aircraft, automatic weapons, or gas chambers!

There is a downside to any religious or nonreligious philosophy or political system that demands unquestioned adherence to its principles. If one does not need to consider *primarily* the practical consequences of one's actions on sentient beings but can simply follow the inherited dictates of one's philosophy, and if those dictates are flawed, there exists no internal mechanism for self-correction. This can lead to needless witch hunts, the persistence of slavery, a second-rate status for women, pogroms, genocide, tyranny, neglect of the environment and other species in favor of short-term human interests, or the prohibition of certain forms of biomedical research that might benefit humanity. If God or Lenin or Marx or Mao has provided a template to follow, so what if people get caught in the crossfire? Doing one's duty for the Cause and following the all-powerful Leader are all that matter.

S: Evolution can only tell as about what motivates people and animals to do certain things. It cannot advance from "what is" to "what should be." You cannot derive "ought" from "is." In his book *Miracles,* C. S. Lewis takes head-on the fanciful notion that naturalism can tell us what we ought to do based on its consequences for our fellow man and for posterity:

> It would help only if we grant, firstly, that life is better than death and, secondly, that we ought to care for the lives of our descendants as much as, or more than, for our own. And both these are moral judgments which have, like all others, been explained away by Naturalism. Of course, having been conditioned by Nature in a certain way, we do feel thus about life and about posterity. But the Naturalists have cured us of mistaking these feelings for insights into what we once called 'real value.' Now that I know that my impulse to serve posterity is just the same kind of thing as my fondness for

cheese—now that its transcendental pretensions have been exposed for a sham—do you think I shall pay much attention to it? When it happens to be strong (and it has grown considerably weaker since you explained to me its real nature) I suppose I shall obey it. When it is weak, I shall put my money into cheese. There can be no reason for trying to whip up and encourage the one impulse rather than the other. Not now that I know what they both are. The Naturalists must not destroy all my reverence for conscience on Monday and expect to find me still venerating it on Tuesday (Lewis 1947, 47).

N: It's true that evolution cannot tell us the way things should be. Nor can it tell us whether or not we should change the oil in our car. We have to decide what's ultimately in our best interest in the long term. In the short term, neglecting an oil change saves us some time and money, and so it might be tempting to put it off, but in the end, if we put it off too long, we might end up with a functionless vehicle (Carrier 2005). Evolution does not oblige us to change the oil any more than it obliges us to treat others as we would like to be treated. But if we wish our engines to remain in good health, or if we wish to remain respected members of our society, or if we value our own self-respect, we have to make the effort to change the oil or treat others with kindness, as the case may be. It's not something we need to be told by a cosmic Lawgiver.

Lewis' forceful insistence that naturalism lacks the teeth to motivate us to look beyond our own interests or tastes is, in a sense, accurate. But if we come to understand the true extent to which our interests are tied up with others'—that no man is an island and that our actions toward others generally ripple back into our own lap—then our interest in looking out for others becomes a far less trivial affair than our taste for cheese (as opposed to yoghurt, for example). Societies that suffer loss at the hands of those who fail to gain this insight are entitled—for the sake of their own interest and well-being—to put the offenders behind bars.

As for looking out for posterity, Lewis is right: we are driven by nature to promote the welfare of our genetic descendants; we are for the most part descendants of those who cared for their progeny and we in turn have inherited that same genetic disposition. This evolutionarily indispensable impulse is stronger than a mere fancy for cheese, but is on a par with our desire for food, water, procreation, and avoidance of pain and danger. It is part of who we are, and it has contributed to the success of our species. Does Lewis imagine that, simply because an impulse might have a naturalistic explanation, we are as a consequence free from all our social obligations to our contemporaries and to our posterity? If so, this is a patent non sequitur.

S: But what about altruism? What makes humans, uniquely among the species, capable of performing sacrificial deeds for others without expectation of anything in return? Think of Mother Teresa, for example. Naturalistic evolution just can't explain her selfless acts of charity.

N: There are at least three points that can be made in response to this. First, we are without a doubt hard-wired to promote the welfare of our kin, especially our offspring, since neglecting our offspring tends to cut off our genetic progeny (Dawkins 2006). Our genes program us to preserve our genetic descendants, and so we do everything in our power to ensure the success of our children. But if the desire for success and empathy we feel toward our offspring is a part of our psyche, should it surprise us that this empathy might be transferable to other members of the wider group on which our survival depends, and if it is transferable to this wider group, why not also to society at large and indeed to all of humanity? Just as the nurturing instinct can be successfully transferred from a biological child to an adopted child, so also can it be co-opted as an impetus for societal altruism, as de Waal argues:

> But even though we and other social animals occasionally assist others without thinking of ourselves, I would still argue that these tendencies originate from mutuality and the assistance of kin. Jet the hero dog [who inserted himself between a snake and his boy owner and suffered a fatal snakebite], likely considered the boy a member of his pack. Early human societies must have been optimal breeding grounds for "survival of the kindest" aimed at family and potential reciprocators. Once this sensibility had come into existence, its range expanded. At some point, sympathy for others became a goal in itself: the centerpiece of human morality and an essential aspect of religion. Thus, Christianity urges us to love our neighbor as ourselves, clothe the naked, feed the poor, and tend the sick. It is good to realize, though, that in stressing kindness, religions are enforcing what is already part of our humanity. They are not turning human behavior around, only underlining preexisting capacities.
>
> How could it be otherwise? One cannot sow the seeds of morality on unwilling soil any more than one can train a cat to fetch the newspaper (de Waal 2005, 172–73).

Second, we are not the only species known to demonstrate sacrificial kindness outside our circle of interest. Primatologist Roger Fouts recounts the following story, set on a river island where Washoe, a female chimpanzee, was being kept:

> One morning we introduced a new female, named Penny, onto the island. That same afternoon, while playing by the shoreline, I suddenly heard Penny screaming in terror from the other side of the island. She must have panicked

at being left alone with the other chimps. The next thing I heard was a loud splash, the sound of Penny hitting the water in the moat. She had taken a running start and vaulted over the electric fence. . . . As I neared the fence I was surprised to see Washoe sprint ahead of me and leap over the two electric wires. She landed, thank heaven, on the narrow dirt ledge that dropped sharply off into the pond. After sinking like a stone, Penny had now surfaced near the island's shore and was thrashing about wildly. Then she submerged again. With one hand grasping the bottom of an electric fence post, Washoe stepped out onto the slippery mud at the water's edge. She reached out her other long arm, grabbed one of Penny's flailing arms, and pulled her to the safety of the bank. I ran to get the boat and rowed as fast as I could to where the two girls were huddled outside the fence. Penny was in shock, shivering and terror stricken. I got the two of them back onto the island, and Washoe and I sat grooming Penny for a long time. While Penny was calming down, I had time to gather my wits, and to let the enormity of what I'd just seen sink in. Washoe had risked her own life to save another chimpanzee—one she had known for only a few hours (Fouts 1997, 179–80).

The ability to empathize across species is not limited to humans:

When a bonobo named Kuni saw a starling hit the glass of her enclosure at the Twycross Zoo in Great Britain, she went to comfort it. Picking up the stunned bird, Kuni gently set it on its feet. When it failed to move, she threw it a little, but the bird just fluttered. With the starling in hand, Kuni then climbed to the top of the tallest tree, wrapping her legs around the trunk so that she had both hands free to hold the bird. She carefully unfolded its wings and spread them wide, holding one wing between the fingers of each hand, before sending the bird like a little toy airplane out toward the barrier of her enclosure. But the bird fell short of freedom and landed on the bank of the moat. Kuni climbed down and stood watch over the starling for a long time, protecting it against a curious juvenile. By the end of the day, the recovered bird had flown off safely (de Waal 2005, 2).

An experiment by Wechkin and Masserman in 1964 provides another demonstration that ours is not the only species with the capacity for self-deprivation in the interest of others.

They found that rhesus monkeys refuse to pull a chain that delivers food to themselves if doing so shocks a companion. One monkey stopped pulling for five days, and another one for twelve days after witnessing shock delivery to a companion. These monkeys were literally starving themselves to avoid inflicting pain upon another. Such sacrifice relates to the tight social system and emotional linkage among these macaques (de Waal 2006, 29).

Finally, it's rarely the case that those who engage in altruism do not benefit from their good deeds. Consider construction worker Wesley

Autrey, who in January 2007 risked his life to save an individual who had fallen onto the tracks of a New York City subway (Buckley 2007). He was celebrated as a hero across the nation and was even honored at President George W. Bush's State of the Union address. And surely Mother Teresa must have enjoyed the admiration she received. We as a society reward those who demonstrate behavior that promotes the well-being of the society or of the world in which we live. The desire for recognition is likely not the primary motivation for risking one's life to save another, but it is no doubt a contributing factor.

S: Despite your theories, the fact remains that Christians tend to be more charitable and self-sacrificing than nonbelievers.

N: Even if that's so, many unbelievers are indeed generous with their time and money and find satisfaction in being charitable. Consider also that the charity of many believers comes with spoken or unspoken strings attached. Would you rather receive charitable assistance in your time of need from a Muslim seeking your conversion to Islam or from a secularist or a government with no such ulterior motives? Often the studies that show Christians to be generous are skewed in that they include contributions of time and money to causes that merely serve to propagate their faith rather than to meet the needs of the poor or oppressed.

As technology and education have advanced and political systems have moved from oppressive conservative monarchies grounded in the divine right of kings to liberal democracies inspired by Enlightenment thinking, far more lives have been improved and lifted from poverty and disease than all the acts of charity combined. It is commendable to spend our weekends or vacations volunteering at a homeless shelter, but all our efforts to alleviate the suffering of the homeless pale in comparison to the development of political systems, antibiotics, vaccinations, telecommunications, modern transportation systems, air conditioning, entertainment, and agricultural advances that have lifted the bulk of even the lower classes of today above the lot of kings in past centuries.

Liberal Christian theologian Marcus Borg enjoins us to focus our attention not only on contributing to charity but also on pressing for reforms to bring about more just structural systems:

> Charity is always good and will always be necessary, but historically Christians have been long on [charity] and short on [structural justice]. One reason is that charity never offends; a passion for justice often does. To paraphrase Roman Catholic bishop Dom Helder Camara from Brazil: "When I gave food to the poor, they called me a saint; when I asked why there were so many poor, they called me a communist" (Borg 2003, 201).

S: But what about our conscience? Surely there can be no satisfying naturalistic explanation for the uniquely human capacity to experience guilt, shame and repentance.

N: Once again, Roger Fouts takes the edge off our imagined uniqueness in recounting this incident involving a chimp named Lucy (Fouts 1997, 156):

> Lucy was the first chimp who ever tried to put one over on me using sign language. One day she defecated in the living room when I wasn't looking.
>
> Roger: WHAT THAT?
> Lucy: WHAT THAT?
> Roger: YOU KNOW. WHAT THAT?
> Lucy: DIRTY DIRTY.
> Roger: WHOSE DIRTY DIRTY?
> Lucy: SUE (a graduate student).
> Roger: IT NOT SUE. WHOSE THAT?
> Lucy: ROGER!
> Roger: NO! NOT MINE. WHOSE?
> Lucy: LUCY DIRTY DIRTY. SORRY LUCY.

S: But all you've managed to do is to provide an example of rudimentary guilt in another species. That doesn't explain the origin of conscience, any more than the origin of consciousness or of life itself. It's all a "just-so" story that you evolutionists have concocted to take God out of the picture. You cannot prove that all this could have happened naturalistically.

N: Nor can you prove it all requires a supernatural explanation.

Though behavior is not readily fossilized, we can see clues in the artificial breeding of dogs indicating that behavior can be shaped by genetics and selection. All modern dog breeds are believed to share a common ancestry, yet we find striking differences in the typical behavior of various breeds: vicious Rottweilers and Pit Bulls on the one hand and relatively docile Golden Retrievers on the other. Just as hair length and limb size can be shaped through natural or artificial selection, so can behavioral and moral tendencies. If survival can be enhanced through the development of moral traits like cooperation, then it will be as favored as a thick coat of fur in the Arctic.

S: What do you tell your teenage children? If they are just descendants of apes and there exists no ultimate Lawgiver, why not just sleep around like the animals? It's hard enough for religious young people to remain chaste; surely if they abandon faith in God, there will be nothing left to prevent them from living out their every fantasy.

N: The best guide to our behavior should be the ultimate consequences it entails for us and for other sentient beings. That is the proper approach to take in discussing this issue with our children.

S: You're being evasive; they need more than that to navigate these treacherous waters.

N: No, by maintaining that the waters are treacherous, you acknowledge yourself that the consequences of one's actions are paramount. Teach your children the consequences of their actions, be involved in their lives, and demonstrate by your own example a model of exemplary behavior. This, and not the threat of distant imagined punishments in the hereafter, will provide the best opportunity for your children to make healthy decisions.

S: Naturalism holds that our minds are just collocations of atoms whose trajectories are predetermined by physical law. This means we do not truly have free will, even if we feel we do. And if free will is an illusion, how can we be held accountable for our actions? Why get up in the morning and strive toward any goals or deliberate over our actions if we're not responsible for what we do?

N: Certainly the prospect of not having free control over our actions is disconcerting to many of us, including this young man (Pinker 2002, 174):

> There was a young man who said Damn!
> It grieves me to think that I am
> Predestined to move
> In a circumscribed groove:
> In fact, not a bus, but a tram.

Cognitive scientists and philosophers have not yet arrived at a consensus on the question of free will. Many take the stance that our actions may not be freely chosen, but the illusion of free will is an adequate substitute for an actual free will. As the jury is still out, I will not take a position on this issue one way or the other, but let us imagine for the sake of argument that one day, after all the relevant data have come in, it is concluded that all our choices are in fact predetermined.

You worry that this will deprive us of accountability for our actions. We'll no longer be capable of outrage against those who perpetrate injustice, because, after all, they are just following the course of the tram groove laid out for them. Even so, can society not take action against evildoers in order to adjust that groove? If we deplore their actions, then let us agree together to tweak the input parameters to their brains in order to prevent a recurrence. In doing so, we send a message to others that their crimes will not pay. Depending on the situation, we can put them in prison for life or rely on a combination of punishments and rehabilitative programs.

The principle purpose of punishment is to serve as a deterrent against further crime, whether on the part of the original perpetrator or on the part of others who factor the possibility of punishment into the equation when making a deterministic "decision" concerning their own actions. Whether our will is free or not, most of us are capable of weighing the consequences of our actions, and as long as that is true, then moral outrage, accountability and various forms of punishment can indeed be effective means of steering others to do the right thing. Punishing individuals who are mentally incapable of foreseeing the effects of their actions has little or no deterrence value; this is why we do not treat them in the same way as veritable criminals. Again, Pinker:

> A third fear is the fear of determinism, or a loss of personal responsibility. It's the fear that personal responsibility will vanish if free will is shown to be an illusion. And here, too, these fearful reactions are a kind of non sequitur. Because even if there's no such thing as a soul that's separate from the brain and that somehow pushes the buttons of behavior—even if we are nothing but our brains—it's undoubtedly true that there are parts of the brain that are responsive to the potential consequences of our actions, that are responsive to social norms, to reward, punishment, credit, and blame (Pinker 2007, 50).

Perhaps our perception of free will owes itself to the very real decision-making processes we engage in every day. Shall we go to the store to buy flour for that cake we were planning to make, or shall we defer until we need other items to make the shopping trip worthwhile? Shall we cheat on our spouse, enjoying the pleasures of our dalliances, or shall we instead secure the relationship we have with our spouse, the mother of our children whom we love? We make thousands of decisions every day, some of no or little consequence to others, and some that impact others substantially. The latter we call moral decisions. But the same principles are operative in either case: we take into account what we forecast to be the results of various courses of action, and our brain settles on the course that it perceives to be in its best interest.

The "best interest" clause may be unsettling, but it is difficult to demonstrate that anyone performs any deed outside of one's perceived best interest. If you value your children or your country or your god, then laying down your life for what you value above all else is in fact in your perceived best interest. Even Jesus was said to have endured the cross, scorning its shame *for the joy set before him* (Hebrews 12:2). If we can effectively educate our children and our society that our best interest is inextricably intertwined with the interests of those around us and that we cannot ultimately be happy by making others unhappy, then we have set the stage for a well-functioning moral society, whether or not we enjoy a truly free will.

S: I follow your logic to a point, but I just don't buy it. Naturalism simply cannot fully account for our moral sense and lacks any ability to enforce an objective standard. Might makes right. There is no (upper case) Right and Wrong, only (lowercase) right and wrong as arbitrarily defined by varying human societies.

N: You may not be able to buy it, but that does not prevent me from buying it. But let us suppose you are right. Though there is no reliable statistical evidence for it, let us imagine that religion does in fact make people better than they otherwise would be and that it does give us the ability to judge ourselves and others according to an objective standard that cannot be arrived at under naturalism.

Ask yourself: would this in any sense constitute evidence against naturalism, or instead is the belief that morality depends on theism a motive for theists to reject naturalism? This distinction cannot be over-emphasized. If we desire an objective standard by which to keep society in order, and if we conclude that naturalism is less useful than theism toward that end, does our frustrated desire make theism true by default? Do our desires have anything whatever to do with establishing the truth? No. Assuming that theism has a pragmatic edge over naturalism concerning public and private morality, do we wish to argue the truth of theism on purely pragmatic grounds—that is, whatever works is true? I think not.

I do not deny the power of Christian community to motivate positive lifestyle changes. Though this positive force for morality exists in most religions, it does not establish the truthfulness of these religions, only their efficacy:

> From the perspective of evolutionary psychology, this almost mystical and seemingly irreducible sort of moral imperative is the output of a mental mechanism[48] with a straightforward adaptive function: to reckon justice and administer punishment by a calculus which ensures that violators reap no advantage from their misdeeds. The enormous volume of mystico-religious bafflegab about atonement and penance and divine justice and the like is the attribution to higher, detached authority of what is actually a mundane,

---

[48] Where did this mental mechanism come from? Where did consciousness come from? Where did life come from? Where did God come from? Over and over, these unanswered (and perhaps unanswerable) questions arise because we feel we *must* have the answers to the things that matter most to us.

pragmatic matter: discouraging self-interested competitive acts by reducing their profitability to nil (Daly and Wilson 1988, 256).

As for whether naturalism can enforce an objective moral standard, that is not the job of naturalism. It is the job of society, which is free to decide what is in its best interest. We see throughout history (both in religious or nonreligious nations) the struggle between the weak and the strong, between the haves and the have-nots. In many modern societies we have chosen to limit the abuses of the powerful by holding them accountable to the people. We have drawn up constitutions and bills of rights largely in response to lessons from the past, promoting opportunity and freedom for the greatest number of people. This is something "*we, the people*" can decide to do, whether or not God exists. In a groundbreaking move, the framers of the United States Constitution left out mention of God altogether and forbade religious tests for government officeholders. This stance garnered significant opposition to the Constitution on the part of many who wished to build the nation on an explicitly religious foundation, but in the end the Founders' position prevailed.

The progress toward freedom and respect for the good of the many in Western society is not something to be taken for granted. All societies, whatever their degree of religious observance, are forever vulnerable to those who live by the principle that might makes right. If we happen to value the freedoms of a liberal democracy, we as a people must be ever vigilant to protect the checks and balances that prevent the abuse of power common to autocracies.

THE LIMITATIONS OF FAITH-BASED MORALITY

The above conversation centers on the adequacy of naturalism to account for and promote morality. In the present section we will look more closely at the relative adequacy of religion, particularly Christianity, to fulfill the same role.

Our naturalist in the above conversation has provided the outlines of a basis for morality apart from any appeal to the supernatural. Nevertheless, those convinced that morality is the province of religion alone will not be easily convinced and will persist in appealing to our moral sense as evidence for the divine. But the supernaturalist has not proven that a supernatural explanation is *required* to explain our sense of morality. We have seen that nonbelievers not only *can* be moral but also that many *are* moral and furthermore that they have *good reason* to be moral.

What is it that typically elicits such a dogged refusal on the part of the supernaturalist to consider any arguments in favor of a nonsupernatural basis for ethics? I suspect it is due in large part to the laudable aspiration of believers to live right, coupled with the centuries-old perception that religion is the best or only guide and support for doing so, and topped off with an ongoing religious smear campaign against the morality of secularist competitors. To acknowledge that morality can be grounded outside religion is to rob religion of one of its primary reasons for existence, an acknowledgement that it can scarcely afford to make.

But there might also be a lingering sense that, despite the promise of a consequentialist-based naturalistic morality, there are too many grey areas for it to work in practice. How do we define what is best for society? What if my idea of "the greater good" is different from yours and we don't have a common standard to settle the matter? What if there are simply not enough resources to go around for everyone's survival? Who decides whether and at what age a fetus deserves the status of personhood?

I do not deny that many moral questions are difficult. However, this is a problem not only for secular ethics but also for religiously based morality. The Bible is silent or ambiguous concerning some of the most vexing moral issues of the day, leading sometimes to bitter disagreement among Christians. There are earnest believers who consider warfare immoral, while others deem it a necessary evil. In a recent nontraditional Sunday school meeting, I asserted that most Christians I know simply do not believe Jesus' teachings on violence and wealth. One responded by claiming he believed Jesus' teachings but that he fell short of practicing them. I countered that no, if he didn't practice them, he probably did not believe them. Consider Jesus' injunction:

> But I tell you, Do not resist an evil person. If someone strikes you on the right cheek, turn to him the other also (Matthew 5:39).

I recall how as a missionary in Nigeria my father kept a baseball bat at his bedside to protect the household against nighttime intruders. Though he never had occasion to use it physically (other than as a threat), he was prepared to do so. Thus, he not only did not subscribe to Jesus' clear teachings, but he violated those teachings in a deliberate, premeditated manner. Note that I am not criticizing his decision; I believe he did the right thing, as does anyone who practices self-defense when threatened. My point is to demonstrate that common sense can sometimes trump even clear biblical teachings for those who claim they subscribe to the Bible in its entirety. Thus, the claim that the Bible offers an objective standard by which to arbitrate differences of moral opinion runs counter to the reality on the ground.

If we insist that a passage such as the above has to be interpreted correctly (meaning other than at face value), then we demonstrate that we, and not the text, are the final arbiter of what is right and wrong. We decide it's unreasonable to interpret it according to its apparent meaning, so we search for other possible texts to mitigate its implications and settle on an alternative ethic we consider to be both biblical and reasonable. But in so doing, we have violated the unambiguous teachings of Jesus; we have cherry picked the texts we prefer, and we might as well have based our decision in the first place on common sense and reason like an unbeliever, since the text bears so little real weight for us in any case.

The teachings of Jesus and his followers concerning wealth are both equally clear and equally disregarded by his followers at large. Consider these passages from the Gospel of Luke:

> 3:7 John said to the crowds coming out to be baptized by him, "You brood of vipers! Who warned you to flee from the coming wrath? Produce fruit in keeping with repentance. And do not begin to say to yourselves, 'We have Abraham as our father.' For I tell you that out of these stones God can raise up children for Abraham. The axe is already at the root of the trees, and every tree that does not produce good fruit will be cut down and thrown into the fire." "What should we do then?" the crowd asked. John answered, "*The man with two tunics should share with him who has none,*[49] and the one who has food should do the same."

> 6:24 But woe to you who are rich, for you have already received your comfort. *Woe to you who are well fed now*, for you will go hungry.

> 2:32 Do not be afraid, little flock, for your Father has been pleased to give you the kingdom. *Sell your possessions and give to the poor.* Provide purses for yourselves that will not wear out, a treasure in heaven that will not be exhausted, where no thief comes near and no moth destroys. For where your treasure is, there your heart *will* be also.

---

[49] If we possess two tunics (or shirts or pairs of shoes) and give to those who have none, the most we could end up with for ourselves is one. It follows that, as long as there are those in the world who lack food or clothing, we are failing to heed John the Baptist's injunction if we have more than what we need to survive. This is a simple conclusion based on a simple instruction. Yet how many of those who insist on taking Genesis chapter 1 literally, for example, are prepared to take John the Baptist's command at face value?

16:19–26 There was a rich man who was dressed in purple and fine linen and lived in luxury every day. At his gate was laid a beggar named Lazarus, covered with sores and longing to eat what fell from the rich man's table. Even the dogs came and licked his sores. The time came when the beggar died and the angels carried him to Abraham's side. The rich man also died and was buried. In hell, where he was in torment, he looked up and saw Abraham far away, with Lazarus by his side. So he called to him, "Father Abraham, have pity on me and send Lazarus to dip the tip of his finger in water and cool my tongue, because I am in agony in this fire." But Abraham replied, "Son, remember that *in your lifetime you received your good things, while Lazarus received bad things, but now he is comforted here and you are in agony.* And besides all this, between us and you a great chasm has been fixed, so that those who want to go from here to you cannot, nor can anyone cross over from there to us."

14:33 In the same way, any of you who does not *give up everything he has* cannot be my disciple.

Or consider Paul's socialist ideals:

Our desire is not that others might be relieved while you are hard pressed, but that there might be *equality*. At the present time your plenty will supply what they [the church in Jerusalem] need, so that in turn their plenty will supply what you [the church at Corinth] need. Then there will be *equality* (1 Corinthians 8:13–14).

These are ideas that few bourgeois evangelicals rarely give the time of day; instead, they find other passages, especially from the Old Testament, to convince themselves it's not wealth *in itself* that's the culprit but simply one's *attitude* toward wealth. It's as though Jesus and Paul cannot be granted their own voice;[50] theirs must be muzzled by that of the author of Proverbs:

Through wisdom a house is built, and by understanding it is established; by knowledge the rooms are filled with all precious and pleasant riches (Proverbs 24:3–4).

The Protestant hermeneutic of "comparing scripture with scripture" here becomes a pretext for selecting the more convenient of two contradictory perspectives in scripture. When it comes to the question of wealth, many allow the New Testament to be silenced by the Old, while more commonly for other matters the Old is silenced by the New. I submit

---

[50] That is, unless their voice was applicable only to their hearers in that time and place. But this puts us on a slippery slope: Which of their many other commands were also applicable only in that context? How do we know which, if any, apply to us today?

it's a matter of common sense: most of those with an above-average share of the world's wealth (which includes almost all Americans) recognize that equality is a lofty but impractical ideal. For my part, I am in favor of generosity, even deep generosity, but the sort of radical economic egalitarianism that Jesus and Paul teach has been attempted on many occasions throughout history and has shown itself to be unsustainable; it leads to tyranny or a disincentive toward productivity or both.

Much has already been written about the objectionable ethics of parts of the Old Testament, so I need not make this the primary focus of my discussion on morality. To anyone who is convinced of the divine inspiration of the Bible on the basis of its supernatural character (for example, its ability to prophesy the future), it does not matter how morally repugnant certain passages may be to us, since it has already been established that God is the author, and by definition whatever God commands or performs is good. A deed is good by virtue only of its divine sanction, not by virtue of how it makes us feel.

I have dialogued with individuals who seem to count it an honor to point this out to anyone who expresses misgivings about, for example, God's commands to Israelite warriors to kill babies and whole families and to keep the virgins for themselves. They almost take pleasure in bursting the bubble of the prevailing God-Is-a-Nice-Guy theology by appealing to verses like Isaiah 45:7 (KJV), "I form the light, and create darkness: I make peace, and create evil: I the LORD do all these things." Their response to any emotional objection to Old Testament ethics is to imply that the objector is simply too pollyannaish and theologically wimpy to bear the revelation of a deity whom C. S. Lewis described allegorically: "He'll often drop in. Only you mustn't press him. He's wild, you know. Not like a *tame* lion" (Lewis 1950, 182; emphasis in original).

Well then, let us grant that God is not so nice after all, not as tame and squeaky clean as Victorian theology would make him out to be. Though this line of defense may take a stab at our emotional misgivings over divinely inspired atrocities, it fails to take into account the many ethical contradictions in the scriptures. For example, God informs the Israelites:

> The fathers shall not be put to death for their children, nor shall the children be put to death for their fathers; a person shall be put to death for his own sin (Deuteronomy 24:16).

Yet some four hundred years after the Amalekites refused to issue the Israelites safe passage through their territory, God commanded his people to annihilate the Amalekites, not for anything the generation then living had done, but for what their forefathers had done:

This is what the LORD Almighty says: "I will punish the Amalekites for what they did to Israel when they waylaid them as they came up from Egypt. Now go, attack the Amalekites and totally destroy everything that belongs to them. Do not spare them; put to death men and women, children and infants, cattle and sheep, camels and donkeys" (1 Samuel 15:2–3).

Though the 1 Samuel passage is objectionable to our modern sensibilities within the framework of a consequentialist ethic, for a hardened defender of Yahweh this is no cause for questioning God's prerogatives. But by juxtaposing this passage with the principle of Deuteronomy 24:16, which prohibits punishment for crimes committed by one's ancestors, I hope to convince my readers that some of Yahweh's purported commands are not simply distasteful and vengeful but also contradictory.

I will close this discussion on biblical ethics with an examination of one moral issue for which unfortunately no significant internal contradictions are apparent: the institution of slavery. I say "unfortunately" because if any part of the Bible had clearly forbidden slavery, either in the Old Testament or in the New, the passages that endorse it could have been as easily swept under the rug as the passages that endorse radical economic egalitarianism, possibly reducing the divide between the American North and South over slavery. Contrary to the standard assertion of apologists that the Bible does not endorse slavery but merely regulates it or that biblical slavery is tame and harmless, the following passage suggests it is acceptable to take foreign slaves and to treat them ruthlessly:

Because the Israelites are my servants, whom I brought out of Egypt, they must not be sold as slaves. Do not rule over them ruthlessly, but fear your God. Your male and female slaves are to come from the nations around you; from *them* you may buy slaves. You may also buy some of the temporary residents living among you and members of their clans born in your country, and they will become your *property*. You can will them to your children as inherited property and can make them slaves for life, but you must not rule over your *fellow Israelites ruthlessly* (Leviticus 25:42–46).

I suppose in a technical sense the following verse is an example of regulating rather than instituting slavery, but it provides precious little protection for slaves (whom some apologists prefer to label "servants," as if it makes any difference); they may be beaten to within an inch of their life with impunity. Indeed, if they manage to hang on a couple of days before dying (or recovering, depending on the translation), their owners are not liable, the loss of the slave's economic contribution being the master's only penalty:

If a man beats his male or female slave with a rod and the slave dies as a direct result, he must be punished, but he is not to be punished if the slave gets up after a day or two, since the slave is his property (Exodus 21:20). (KJV: "Notwithstanding, if he continue a day or two, he shall not be punished: for he is his money.")

Both the Christians and the Enlightenment thinkers who spearheaded the campaign against slavery in the eighteenth and nineteenth centuries deserve the highest praise for their compassion, justice, and courage. But even if the Christian abolitionists found general principles in the Bible to support their cause, they had no specific warrant from the text to call for the abolition of slavery *as an institution.* They sought not to reform slavery into a gentler, biblically based institution but to abolish it outright. The deist Thomas Paine did not need the inspiration of the Bible or the Holy Spirit to condemn slavery as an institution (Paine 1775, 4-9), nor did the Stoic Greek philosopher Zeno of Citium, who declared three centuries before Jesus:

> No matter whether you claim a slave by purchase or capture, the title is bad. They who claim to own their fellow-men, look down into the pit and forget the justice that should rule the world (Ingersoll 1896, 44); (Denis 1879, 346) [51]

A final danger of Christian morality is its potential for sidestepping the reality of human nature, particularly the human nature of the redeemed. In debates between Christians and secularists, the underlying assumption of the Christian is that her position, unlike that of her opponent, provides a firm foundation for making and following moral judgments, and that society would be better off morally if everyone accepted this common foundation. If all members of the community understand that they will be held accountable for their actions, and if they seek to please their creator and redeemer, and if the god of the universe enables them to produce the "fruits of the Spirit," they will look out for the interests of others rather than simply for their own interests. As a result, crime will be reduced or disappear, and harmony will reign.

However, in practice, societies that have approached 100 percent adherence to evangelical or Puritan theology, or any theology for that matter, have never enjoyed freedom from strife or undesirable excesses of

---

[51] Denis citation : « Il, y a, dit-il, tel esclavage qui vient de la conquête, et tel autre qui vient d'un achat ; à l'un et à l'autre correspond le droit du maitre, et ce droit est mauvais. »

one form or another. Somehow the underbelly of human nature always finds a way to assert itself. There will always be a certain percentage of the population for whom no theology will suppress their urges toward illicit sex, violence, authoritarianism, gossip, or a judgmental spirit. Like squeezing a water-filled balloon at one end, suppressing one vice too often produces an opposing vice. It may be that adultery in pre-Enlightenment Christendom was less pervasive than it is today (though that is not certain; it existed, but more under the surface), but few today would wish to revive its occasional inquisitions, morality police, witch trials, burnings, and internecine warfare.

Religious traditionalists commonly assert that society has taken a turn for the worse since the advent of secularism.[52] By certain measures this may be the case, but by other measures, we are far better off than were our forebears. For example, in Western societies homicide rates have declined tenfold to a hundredfold in the past millennium, from a time when religious belief was virtually unchallenged (Pinker 2002, 330). Our perception that things are "going down the tubes" is fueled in part by a barrage of media coverage that makes us aware of crimes we might have been ignorant of in previous generations. When we see reports of heinous crimes on television, we find it difficult to place them in the context of a country of three hundred million people and to think proportionally rather than anecdotally.

I accept that for a certain number of Christians who harbor no doubts about their accountability to God in the hereafter, their beliefs may prevent them from engaging in unhealthy behavior they might otherwise fall into. But in any Christian community, if there are "believers" who secretly wonder whether all the threats might just be "pie in the sky," and if the community fails to take these secret doubters into account, there will always remain a need for more earthly incentives (for example, a police force) to ensure orderly behavior. The rub is that no society has ever been free of individuals for whom even the threat of eternal punishment has been sufficient to keep them in line. In 2005 or so, I casually remarked to an outspoken Baptist acquaintance that her lifestyle seemed to be noticeably out of line with her beliefs. Without missing a beat, she responded flippantly, "Yeah, I know, I'm going to hell, but that's just who I am." Incredible!

In his book *The Blank Slate,* Steven Pinker recounts how as a youth living in Montreal he came to lose faith in the inherent goodness of

---

[52] It would seem that no group exploits this fear more than Jehovah's Witnesses, two of whom visited my home in 2008. If the world is going down the tubes, then the end must be at hand as the Bible predicted, so it is time to prepare spiritually.

humanity. As a result of the widespread mayhem, rioting and looting that ensued in the wake of the Montreal police department strike on October 17, 1969, he abandoned his idealistic anarchist political views (Pinker 2002, 331). Many of us were shocked and dismayed to witness similar behavior in New Orleans following Hurricane Katrina in August 2005. But this behavior—certainly not limited to atheists—should come as no surprise to those who understand the evolutionary underpinnings of evil in human nature and its tendency to surface in the absence of external restraint.

Christians, too, especially those in the Calvinistic tradition, recognize the inherent depravity of humanity. This is one of the few empirically justified doctrines of Christianity, yet it is rarely taken far enough. What I mean is that the doctrine of total depravity is too often applied to the unregenerate, to those outside the household of faith, without recognizing the extent to which human nature remains in effect for the redeemed. The moral fall of a pastor is almost always greeted initially with disbelief, as are allegations of child abuse on the part of missionaries or church leaders. Such abuse is by no means limited to the Catholic Church, as this article from *Christianity Today* attests concerning the evangelical Mamou Alliance Academy in Guinea, operated by the Christian and Missionary Alliance (C&MA):

> Darr and at least 30 other children at the West African boarding school suffered a more harrowing form of alienation. From 1950 to 1971, children were beaten with belts, forced to eat their own vomit, punched and slapped in the face, coerced into performing oral sex, required to sit in their own feces, fondled, and beaten with a strap to the point of bleeding.
>
> Not until 1995, after persistent complaints by a group of adults who had been Mamou students, did the C&MA impanel a commission to investigate.
>
> The panel's 95-page report, filed after 18 months of research and interviews, identifies nine offenders; four are retired, three are dead, and two are no longer affiliated with the C&MA. Two individuals who refused to cooperate with the panel have been convicted at denominational disciplinary hearings.
>
> The commission faulted the denomination for improper training, poor oversight, and negligence. The Mamou staff, rather than being loving surrogate parents, punished too frequently and affirmed too little, the report indicates.
>
> Richard W. Bailey, chair of the C&MA's board of managers, sent a letter expressing regret to Mamou alumni in January. "Please accept our heartfelt apology for our inadequate supervision and understanding of the happenings at Mamou Academy, while you were a student." (Kennedy 1998).

The above incident is only the best reported of many such heartbreaking stories of abuse in missionary boarding schools around the world. Is it possible that an incomplete acceptance of human depravity led to the lack of supervision that permitted the Mamou tragedy? Did the abusers take advantage of the trust of their fellow missionaries in the goodness of redeemed human nature, failing to implement safeguards to restrain the base impulses of their co-laborers in Christ?

Do not get me wrong. As I expressed earlier, many of the best people in world are Christians, and the majority of believers are never implicated in such crimes. The point I am trying to make is that belief in God or the Bible or a commitment to Jesus is not sufficient to prevent certain individuals from engaging in such acts. If evangelical missionaries cannot be trusted to act in the interest of others, then who can? The answer is not to despair but to recognize human nature for what it is and to set up guardrails, policies, restrictions, and penalties to prevent such abuses, whether inside or outside of the church.

In summary, in Western society we have two primary competing claims for the origin and basis of morality: naturalistic evolution and scriptural theism. Neither is without unanswered questions and difficulties; each individual must weigh for herself which alternative holds the most merit. I cannot argue you out of your position, but I hope you will be able to put yourself in my shoes and understand how I might have come to see the naturalistic position as having more explanatory value than the theistic one.

On the one hand, naturalism holds that in a world where survival is contingent on both competition and social cooperation, there is bound to be a conflict between self-serving impulses (evil, from a societal standpoint) and group-serving impulses (good, from a societal standpoint).

On the other hand, Christian theism holds that an omniscient god creates a perfect human couple (knowing they will be tempted to sin by a talking serpent), then wipes out nearly the whole of the human race in the time of Noah (knowing in advance they would all turn evil), then, with his foreknowledge, ultimately consigns the majority of the human race to an endless torment in hell (while asking us to turn the other cheek against our own enemies), requiring the murder of his own son to redeem the minority of humanity that recognizes and accepts this Grand Plan.

There is at least one more alternative—deism—for those who find the above two options implausible. For over a year I subscribed to it before transitioning to agnosticism. It was the conviction of the deist Thomas Paine that our moral sense is instilled by the creator and that the knowledge of God's existence motivates us to live justly. He judged the scriptures harshly and rejected all traditional man-made religions but paid homage to the god of nature. Any attempt to discredit naturalism on the basis of its putative failure to account for morality does not make Christianity true by default.

NOT PERFECT, JUST FORGIVEN

From time to time as a Christian I would hear the question, "Why is it that unbelievers are sometimes better behaved than Christians?" The standard response was that we are all flawed and that any misbehavior on the part of believers was more a reflection of their own failings than of the perfection of Christ, the one whose life serves as our example.

An alternative explanation was that morally deficient individuals were not really *true* believers. There is a certain degree of circularity to this: it is claimed that Christ enables his followers to lead a better life than they would if they were not his followers. However, if certain followers lead less-than-exemplary lives, then they are dismissed as not being *true* followers of Jesus, even if they say they believe. This certainly stacks the deck in favor of the hypothesis that following Christ makes one a better person: eliminate all counter examples by definition, and what do you know, all *true* believers are good people! C. S. takes a slightly different approach, maintaining that though not all Christians compare favorably with non-Christians, Christians are better off morally than they would be if they were not Christians (Lewis 1970, 59). This clever assertion is difficult to prove or disprove.

For the most part I accepted these explanations and did not allow the problem of immoral Christians to interfere with my conviction that the Holy Spirit is present and active in the lives of those who welcome him.

However, from my current vantage point I do see the failures of Christians as a problem for the New Testament teaching that believers are a "new creation" with the power of Almighty God available to cultivate in them the "fruits of the Spirit" (Galatians 5:22–23). I attended enough Bible studies and prayer meetings to know that both my fellow believers and I earnestly desired to live ever holier lives, continually inviting the Holy Spirit to transform us. Yet after having left the faith, I find it no more or less difficult to live morally than when I believed.

That a church of 14,000 members could have been duped for so long by Pastor Ted Haggard, who was exposed in October 2006 as having practiced homosexuality and drug use while preaching against it, is not only a mark against Haggard himself, but against the teaching that the Holy

Spirit provides power to overcome sin and offers the gift of discernment to his followers. As far as I am aware, none of the members of the 30-million strong National Association of Evangelicals to which he was elected president had an inkling of his double life until his escort provided answering machine messages as proof of their liaisons. In light of this and other such failures, I will go out on a secure limb and assert that there is no such thing as the Holy Spirit's gift of discernment as taught in passages like 1 Corinthians 12:10 and 1 John 4:1, 6. Nor is there any supernatural power available to straighten our paths. We must take responsibility for our own actions; there is no unseen power out there to help us or hinder us.

Ted Haggard is far from an isolated case. Consider also televangelists Jimmy Swaggart and Jim Bakker; Intervarsity president Gordon McDonald, involved in an adulterous affair; and Mel White, a pastor who ghostwrote books for Jerry Falwell, Pat Roberston and Billy Graham, but who eventually divorced his wife and came out as a homosexual. Of Billy and Ruth Graham's five children, three are divorced—one twice divorced. One of them, Ned, admitted to drug and alcohol abuse as his marriage fell apart. Especially ironic is that two of those three divorcees are authors and the third was heavily involved in Christian ministry (Bruns 2004, 143). This is not to cast aspersions or to look down on any of them—we are *all* flawed—but merely to support my contention that being "indwelt" by the Holy Spirit appears to be no more than a subjective play of the imagination.

In 1999 Christian pollster George Barna released the results of a survey of 3,854 individuals, finding that 25 percent of the interviewees had been divorced at least once. The religious group with the highest divorce rate was nondenominational evangelicals and fundamentalists (34 percent), followed by Baptists (29 percent). On the lower end of the scale were Catholics, Lutherans, atheists, and agnostics, each at 21 percent (Wicker 2000).

It may be objected that the poll does not adequately take into account the believers who take their faith more seriously than the rest—those who pray and read the Bible as a family daily, for example. It is nonetheless surprising that some of the most conservative religious groups, the ones most concerned about family values, have the highest failure rates, while atheists and agnostics enjoy among the lowest failure rates. If the Holy Spirit does not take residence in unbelievers, how is it that their marriage failure rates are lower than those of fundamentalist churchgoers, even if there are many false or lukewarm believers among them? Surely the existence of at least *some* true, Spirit-filled believers among Baptists and nondenominational evangelicals ought to lift the general marriage success rate of their churches above that of the unbelievers!

It is my conviction that every moral unbeliever and every immoral believer is a strike against the notion that the Holy Spirit exists and enables us to lead a life defined by the "fruits of the Spirit" in Galatians 5. If we believe in the role of the Holy Spirit, how do we explain the existence of millions of kind, loving, moral unbelievers in the world, many of whom are better people than the average evangelical Christian who seeks the indwelling of the Spirit? Are we to consider the love and sacrifices of an upstanding family-oriented Mormon to be nothing more than a counterfeit? Or are we to allow for the possibility that Christ's common grace takes hold even in the hearts of heretics? In either case, the reality of the situation erases any decisive evidence for the existence of a Holy Spirit who empowers us to live right.

Several years ago I watched a television documentary on addiction in which a former alcoholic testified to his failed experience with a number of self-help programs. He finally succeeded when he decided to make up his own twelve-step program: "I skipped over the first eleven steps, then made up the twelfth: just quit drinking!"

I will have more to say concerning my personal moral journey in chapter 16. For a fuller treatment of this subject, I heartily recommend Richard Carrier's *Sense and Goodness Without God* (Carrier 2005).

Chapter 9

Purpose and Meaning

O ne of the most common questions I am asked is, "If you don't believe in God, what reason do you have to get up in the morning and carry on with life?" One correspondent even suggested it was immoral for me to have brought children into the world if there is nothing more to this life than living and dying, as the popular Christian musician Steven Curtiss Chapman put it. Amy Grant sings, "I refuse to believe that we're only here to live and die." Theologian and pastor Greg Boyd captures our fear of insignificance in these terms:

> We strive to infuse our lives with some sort of significance, some sort of meaning. But if our cosmos is ultimately indifferent and purposeless, all we are, all we do, all we believe in, all we strive for is "dust in the wind." After we exist, it matters not whether anyone has ever, or ever will again, exist. Everything is ultimately meaningless (Boyd 2003, 52).

Amy Grant's refusal to believe notwithstanding, if nothing does in fact lie beyond the grave, then nothing does in fact lie beyond the grave. Reality does not bend to suit our desires. We may hold out hope that there is more to life than this, in the same way that a mother whose son has been missing in action for twenty years may hope he is alive and will return, but our hope does not change reality if there is nothing beyond the grave, any more than the mother's hope can bring her son back to life if in fact he is dead.

ANTHROPOCENTRISM

In reflecting on my experience as a believer and recalling conversations I have had with others after leaving the faith, I am convinced that the desire for eternal significance ranks near the top of most Christians' reasons for believing. There is a strong element of anthropocentrism[53] in the commonly held view that God created the universe primarily with us in mind. In this universe of trillions of galaxies, stars, and planets in an expanse of over 20 billion light years in size, we on this little speck of dust called earth would like to think we have some significance beyond the grind of mere survival. Thus we become "the apple of God's eye" (Psalm 17:8). We, unlike most if not all the animals, are to live for eternity. Everything we do on earth prepares us for eternity with God: we can have a role as the creator's instrument in directing the eternal fate of our fellow men, and our moral choices matter eternally. All things, no matter how seemingly insignificant or difficult, work together for our good (Romans 8:28). By our prayers we can influence the creator of the cosmos.

Creationist leader Ken Ham of Answers in Genesis exemplifies the fundamentalist insistence that man is the center of God's creation:

> The real world is the biblical world—a universe designed by God with the Earth at the spiritual focal point, not an evolutionary universe teeming with life. . . . Extraterrestrial life is an evolutionary concept; it does not comport with the biblical teachings of the uniqueness of the Earth and the distinct spiritual position of human beings (Ham 2008).

Is not our insistence on transcendent meaning self-focused? Chimps do not complain about the meaningless of life, perhaps only because they are not capable of mentally projecting their lives to the point of their demise. If they could do so, would they not also see life as ultimately meaningless? How many billions of microbes, fish, slugs, and cockroaches are fixated on only two things: survival and reproduction? What other purpose, from their perspective, does life serve? And why are we so insistent that our own lives, made up of the same physical substances as theirs, be ultimately any more meaningful?

I would suggest that an inflated sense of our own relative importance skews our judgment in this matter. These are not popular words, and they will not be well received by those whose "itching ears" (cf. 2 Timothy 4:3) influence their view of truth, but if truth stripped of pragmatic concerns is our objective, it is a position that must be given due consideration.

Some time ago a Christian friend of mine, whom I'll call John, recounted how, shortly before making a move across the country, he was backing out of his driveway and ran over the family dog. The dog suffered for some time before John took him to the veterinarian to have him put out

---

[53] The term *anthropocentrism* is taken from the Greek word for man (*anthropos*), making humankind the focal point of the universe.

of his misery. But incredibly, John went on to say what a blessing it was that God had arranged this, since the family was planning to move and John didn't look forward to taking the dog on this long trip and didn't know how the dog was going to fare in the new location. Do not get me wrong. John is a quality person who is friendly, leads an exemplary life, and remains a good friend of mine. Yet he is likely unaware of how narcissistic his outlook appears to those who do not share his anthropocentric worldview. It is this same outlook that leads to a greater concern for the destruction of unfeeling human embryos than for the suffering, hunting, and removal of sentient adult chimpanzees from their tight-knit social networks in the forests of Africa.

Among Christian apologists like Tim LaHaye and David Noebel (LaHaye and Noebel 2000), a favorite criticism of humanism is its inordinate focus on humankind and on personal autonomy. I find this sort of criticism deeply ironic in light of the tendency of many if not most fundamentalists to place man at the center of God's plan for the creation of this vast universe,[54] while humanists like Peter Singer are concerned for the welfare and suffering of all sentient beings, including the higher animals, and not just for humans. Humanists recognize we are transient entities doomed to extinction on this grain of sand called earth, while fundamentalists endow us with eternal, cosmic significance.

Creationists Ken Ham and Stacia Byers rely on the argument from hope in critiquing the views of evangelist-turned-agnostic Charles Templeton. According to Ham and Byers, Templeton's failure to accept the literal teachings of Genesis and a young earth sent him down a slippery slope to unbelief and its attendant hopelessness and despair, culminating in his declaration, "I believe that, in common with all living creatures, we die and cease to exist as an entity." The article sums up Templeton's journey with this assessment: "[T]he end result, the anti-gospel—the message of hopelessness for a dying world—the bottom of the 'slippery slide'" (Ham and Byers 2000).

This critique of the secular worldview holds enormous appeal to those who equate hope (defined as a blissful hereafter in the service of our redeemer) with truth. In light of our tendency toward self-deception, should we not be on our guard against arguments that appeal to our interests, to our emotions, and to our sense of how we think things ought to be? For those interested in knowing the truth concerning matters such as the age of

---

[54] C. S. Lewis, to his credit, distances himself from this fundamentalist position in his book *Miracles* (Lewis 1947).

the earth, evolution, and the hereafter, our personal feelings about the consequences of believing one way or the other should be considered not only as *unimportant*, but indeed as *obstacles to the truth*. Yet the key argument of this article, and many like it, is an appeal to the audience's fear of meaningless and hopelessness. This is a classic case of the tail wagging the dog. If we are to have any hope of arriving at the truth, we cannot allow our personal misgivings to prevent us from considering the evidence for conclusions we deplore.

MORTALITY AND MEANINGLESSNESS

The assumption that our mortality makes life meaningless too often goes unchallenged. If a coach tells his little league baseball team that the loss of their most recent game won't matter to them in ten years, does that really render their loss meaningless in the *here and now*? What if they had won a game, and he immediately indicated the same thing concerning their win—that it wouldn't matter in ten years? Would his remarks be welcome? (Stenger 2007, 251) They would be no more welcome, I submit, than the remarks of those who insist that our temporal lives are meaningless if there is no hereafter, no Grand Plan for the universe with us at its center. Most of us have enjoyed deep, meaningful friendships that eventually petered out following a move to another part of the country. Should the fear that our friendships might end in this way prevent us from making friends and enjoying them while we have the chance? Should we avoid taking household pets, knowing we are likely to outlive them and will never join up with them again? Life in the here and now can be as meaningful as we make it, and we need not depend on a sequel to savor our challenges and triumphs here on earth. I appreciate the bumper sticker that declares, "I believe in life *before* death." And I concur with Kai Nielsen: "A man who says, 'If God is dead, nothing matters,' is a spoilt child who has never looked at his fellow-man with compassion" (Nielsen 1973, 53).

For those who chafe at the prospect of our mortality, I offer this assurance from Jennifer Michael Hecht: "You will never know that you are dead, so, as far as you're concerned you will always be alive" (Hecht 2007).

Following the lead of C. S. Lewis, a number of Christian apologists have posited that our very desire for meaning and significance beyond the grave provides support for the existence of an afterlife. In other words, far from being an argument from wishful thinking, our need for significance points to something real that's bigger than us:

It is incongruous with everything else we know about the world to suppose that nature could produce creatures which have longings which nature doesn't itself fulfill. . . . If the ultimate canvas against which the cosmos is painted is not personal like we are, then we are very much like fish out of water. We desperately cry out for water, but there never was such a thing as water! But how could such a state of affairs ever come about? Where did our longing for something that never existed, and that never could exist, come from? (Boyd 2003, 56)

But is it really that difficult to account for our desire for eternal significance naturalistically? Surely one of the most fundamental of all biological instincts is the will to survive. Without it, we would scarcely have a chance of passing on our genes to the next generation. But we all inevitably die. This pits our desire for survival against the reality of death. Lewis and Boyd are right: we long for something that does not exist, but is that surprising? Nature has not endowed us with a switch that tells us, "After you've reproduced and ensured the success of your offspring, you must lose your desire to survive." Instead, we are left with an open-ended survival instinct and fear of death. Thus, the appeal of an eternal hereafter where we can continue to reap the fruits of our labor and see our loved ones beyond the grave requires no mystical explanation.

Consider for the sake of argument that there is in fact no afterlife. This is analogous to an engineering team that works several years to develop a fighter plane prototype for the government but whose contract bid is ultimately turned down. There is a sense of lost effort, frustration, meaninglessness, and disappointment. Nevertheless, the reality is that the team lost the bid. Or consider a pride of lions diligently stalking its prey. After days of going without food, they finally bring down a gazelle, only to have it stolen by a pack of hyenas. There is a sense of wasted effort, anger, and (to the extent that lions can feel it) meaninglessness. In the same way—and reasoning by extension—if our lives are to end in the grave as do those of the animals, we are horrified by the wasted effort and consider life to be ultimately meaningless. But we are no more entitled to a hereafter than are the apes, who suffer sickness, toil, hunger, broken relationships, warfare, and humiliation before their peers—in short, many of the same hardships we face—and yet who do not have the hope of eternal life, let alone an explanation from a divinely inspired book as to the meaning of it all. But we—we who can ponder our plight—cannot allow ourselves to suffer the same fate. We are special. At least it makes us feel good to think so.

Even if naturalism could offer no ready explanation for our desire for eternal significance, would that entail the existence of a hereafter? Does humanity's fascination with physical flight suggest we descended from avian ancestors or that we were divinely destined to fly? No, argument from desire does not necessarily demonstrate anything about our desire's correspondence to reality. In the case of flight, we had to make our own reality in the form of flying machines, but flight was nothing that nature could provide for us, any more than it can provide eternal significance. If we wish for our lives to be imbued with significance, we must take advantage of the opportunities available for us in this temporal life.

I freely confess it was not pleasant after my deconversion to come to terms with the finality of my life, particularly after having lived with the prior conviction that, as a missionary bringing God's word to the unreached Daza people, my every act was imbued with eternal significance. Having tasted and grown dependent on this wellspring of personal importance, it was difficult indeed to give up the addiction cold turkey. However, in the years since my initial angst over this loss of meaning, I have gradually come to terms with my mortality and no longer sense a need for my existence to have an eternal purpose.

Though there is no longer an ultimate meaning *to* life, there remain multiple meanings *in* life (Lowder and Fernandes 1999). I can still bask in the love of my wife and children; find satisfaction in my computer programming work; enjoy taking our dog on walks; watch a good movie; read intellectually stimulating books and discuss them with friends; play a game of chess with my sons; coach my daughter's soccer team; tickle my children half to death; contribute time and financial support to charitable causes; and savor a handful or two of roasted, salted sunflower seeds. I may not retain this optimistic picture of life if a crippling disaster befalls me, but I can only take one day at a time.

A legitimate criticism often leveled against us unbelievers is that our stance tends to be entirely negative. In decrying religion we offer no positive replacement. As long as there is nothing to replace the role of religion for personal meaning, morality, community, and financial security, few will consider it worthwhile to make the transition out of religion, even in the face of its many flaws. This is the argument of humanist Paul Kurtz, who calls unbelievers to stop simply debunking religion and to move on to building social structures and movements that benefit humanity at large. We can find meaning and satisfaction in making the world a freer and better place in which to live, carrying on the tradition that our Enlightenment forefathers like Thomas Jefferson and John Adams began in our country. This is the essence of humanism: to improve the lives of humans. It is not merely, as antihumanist fundamentalists suggest, to make us as humans the center of our own life, the captain of our own ship. The focus of humanism is to improve the lot of *all*, knowing that if we are to make life better for our fellow human, we cannot rely on any unseen power to make it happen; we must make it happen ourselves. It is for these reasons that I generally prefer to apply to myself the positive term *humanist* rather than the more negative term *atheist*, even if technically I could be considered an atheist.

Chapter 10

Fulfilled Prophecies

Prediction is very hard, especially when it's about the future
—Yogi Berra

My conviction that the messianic prophecies of the Old Testament were supernaturally fulfilled in Jesus was for me one of the most compelling reasons for accepting the authority of the Bible. Accordingly, I will examine the matter of supernatural prophecy at some length in this chapter. In so doing I hope to convince my readers that not only do biblical predictions fail to provide support for the Christian faith, but that they instead cast doubt on the methods and conclusions of the biblical authors.

PROPHETIC PRESUPPOSITIONS

Much of the debate over prophecies centers on our presuppositions. Before we can claim that any of the predictions of the Old Testament were supernaturally fulfilled, we must establish valid criteria for evaluating our claims.

I remain in principle open to the possibility that God exists and reveals his intentions through prophecy, but before drawing any conclusions we must examine each claim (for example, the contents of the Bible, the Qur'an, or the Book of Mormon) on a case-by-case basis to determine whether in fact God has revealed himself through supernatural prophecies.

The same principles apply to miracle claims in general: they are theoretically possible but must be examined on a case-by-case basis to establish their legitimacy. Since fantastic stories abound in premodern cultures, no report of miracles from any source should be accepted without evidence. It is difficult to go back two or three millennia to verify whether a stick turned into a snake, a child was born of a virgin, or water turned to wine. According to apologists, however, there are some special cases that offer us an opportunity even at this distance to investigate possible instances of supernatural intervention. The two principle cases are messianic prophecies, which I treat in the present chapter, and the resurrection of Jesus, which I will explore in chapter 11.

I will not be examining a large number of prophecies in this section, my aim being to discuss representative ones as they relate to the criteria below. For a more extensive analysis of individual cases, I recommend Thomas Paine's treatise, *An Examination of the Passages in the New Testament, Quoted from the Old, and Called Prophecies of the Coming of Jesus Christ* (Paine 1807).

What is a supernatural prophecy? Here are some of the conditions that would have to be in place before I could acknowledge that any given prophecy (whether biblical or extrabiblical) requires a supernatural explanation. Any one condition not met by a given prophecy would disqualify it from consideration as a miracle.

Criterion 1: It can be proven that the event happened after the prophecy.

We have ample evidence that all the purported messianic prophecies of the Old Testament were written well before the time of Jesus. There are other prophecies, however, that bear marks of having been written after the "fulfilled" events.

In his best-selling volume *The Case for Christ* (Strobel 1998), former journalist turned Christian apologist Lee Strobel interviewed the late Princeton New Testament Greek scholar Bruce Metzger, who affirmed the reliability of the Gospels. However, Metzger apparently accepted the mainstream scholarly position that the prophecies of Daniel were written sometime in the second century BCE rather than in the sixth century BCE as traditionally claimed and that all the intricately detailed prophecies of Daniel 11 were written after those events occurred. The following is taken from *The Oxford Companion to the Bible,* edited by Metzger and Coogan:

> The book of Daniel is one of the few books of the Bible that can be dated with precision. . . . The lengthy apocalypse of Daniel 10–12 provides the best evidence for date and authorship. This great review of the political maelstrom of ancient Near Eastern politics swirling around the tiny Judean community accurately portrays history from the rise of the Persian empire down to a time somewhat after the desecration of the Jerusalem Temple and the erection

there of the "abomination that makes desolate" (Dan. 11.31) in the late autumn of 167 BCE by the Greco-Syrian king Antiochus IV Epiphanies. . . . The portrayal is expressed as prophecy about the future course of events, given by a seer in Babylonia captivity; however, the prevailing scholarly opinion is that this is mostly prophecy after the fact. Only from 11.39 onward does the historical survey cease accurately to reproduce the events known to have taken place in the latter years of the reign of Antiochus IV. The most obvious explanation for this shift is that the point of the writer's own lifetime had been reached. Had the writer known, for example, about the success of the Jewish freedom fighters led by Judas Maccabees in driving the garrison of the hated Antiochus from the temple precincts (an event that occurred on 25 Kislev, 164 BCE, according to 1 Macc. 4.34–31), the fact would surely have been mentioned. But evidently it had not yet happened. . . .

One of the best pieces of evidence available for the rapid acceptance of the book of Daniel as scripture is the inclusion of Daniel and his three friends in the list of the heroes of the Jewish faith in 1 Maccabees 2.59–60, thought to have been written in Hebrew about 100 BCE. In contrast, in Ben Sira's similar list (Sir. 44–49), written about 180 BCE, Daniel figures not at all (Metzger and Coogan 1993, 151).

Those who wish to defend the traditional dating of the book of Daniel might object that absence of evidence is not evidence of absence. This goes only so far. If I claim that an elephant is in the room, but others object they cannot see the elephant, I would not be taken seriously if I used the "absence of evidence is not evidence of absence" card. The traditionalist should pause to consider (a) that we have no evidence of these prophetic manuscripts prior to 167 BCE and (b) that the prophecies correspond in minute detail to events leading up to 167 BCE but not afterward.

Moderate and liberal scholars propose that the detailed prophecies of Daniel chapter 11 were written shortly after their fulfillment around 167 BCE. A common objection to such a proposition is that these scholars simply don't believe God is up to the task of making predictions. But if a scholar like John Goldingay, author of the book of Daniel volume of the evangelical *Word Biblical Commentary*, believes in God's power to raise Jesus from the dead, why should he hesitate to pronounce Daniel 11 as a marvelous prophecy uttered four centuries in advance of its fulfillment? It is not because of prior lack of faith in God's ability to do whatever he pleases; rather, it is a result of examining the text and identifying linguistic and historical anachronisms that place its composition in the second rather than in the sixth century BCE (comments in brackets are mine).

What assumptions should we bring to it [a study of the book of Daniel] regarding the nature of the stories and the origin of the visions? Critical scholarship has sometimes overtly, sometimes covertly approached the visions with the *a priori* conviction that they cannot be actual prophecies of events to take place long after the seer's day, because prophecy of that kind is impossible. Conversely, conservative scholarship has sometimes overtly, sometimes covertly approached these visions with the *a priori* conviction that they must be actual prophecies because quasi prophecies [those made after the fact] issued pseudonymously [written by someone other than the claimed author] could not have been inspired by God; it has also approached the stories with the *a priori* conviction that they must be pure history, because fiction or a mixture of fact and fiction could not have been inspired by God.

All these convictions seem to me mistaken. I believe that the God of Israel who is also the God and Father of our Lord Jesus Christ is capable of knowing future events and thus of revealing them, and is capable of inspiring people to write both history and fiction, both actual prophecy and quasi prophecy, in their own name, anonymously, or—in certain circumstances—pseudonymously. It was excusable for Pusey to think that pseudonymity makes the author a liar and must be incompatible with being divinely inspired. It is less excusable now we know that in the ancient world, and in the Hellenistic age in particular, pseudonymity was a common practice used for a variety of reasons—some unethical, some unobjectionable—for poetry, letters, testaments, philosophy, and oracles, and by no means confined to apocalypses. That pseudonymity is a rarer literary device in our culture, especially in religious contexts, should not allow us to infer that God could not use it in another culture. Whether he has actually chosen to do so is to be determined not *a priori* but from actual study of the text of Scripture (Goldingay 1989, xxxix–xl).

The practice of "quasi prophesying" was common in the Near East during that era; indeed, Goldingay's rationale for maintaining the integrity and inspiration of the book of Daniel is that its readers would have understood that it was written in the genre of "quasi prophecy" as a means of encouraging its readers in the midst of their present trials and tribulations, and thus it would not have been viewed as a deception. If "quasi prophesying" was a common practice at the time, on what grounds should we isolate the book of Daniel as an exception? Is it merely because it happens to be found in the biblical canon? Is there any concrete evidence that the book was in fact written before the events it prophesies? No, there is nothing substantive on which to build such a case.

In addition to the quasi prophecies of the book of Daniel, at least one other precise biblical prophecy is worthy of singling out as an after-the-fact prediction. The following passage from 1 Kings (which, along with its companion 2 Kings, records the history of kings prior to and after Josiah, and so must have been written after Josiah) ostensibly reveals some three centuries beforehand the name of a king who will wreak havoc on the lineage of King Jeroboam:

> By the word of the LORD a man of God came from Judah to Bethel, as Jeroboam was standing by the altar to make an offering. He cried out against the altar by the word of the LORD : "O altar, altar! This is what the LORD says: 'A son *named Josiah* will be born to the house of David. On you he will sacrifice the priests of the high places who now make offerings here, and human bones will be burned on you'" (1 Kings 13:1–2).

Biblical archeologists Finkelstein and Silberman are not convinced the prophecy is genuine:

> This is an unparalleled prophecy, because the "man of God" revealed the name of a specific king of Judah who would, three centuries later, order the destruction of that very shrine, killing its priests and defiling its alter with their remains. It is something like reading a history of slavery written in seventeenth century colonial America in which there is a passage predicting the birth of Martin Luther King. . . . The precision of the earlier prophecy of the "man of God" gives away the era when it was written. The Davidic king Josiah, who conquered and destroyed the altar at Bethel, lived at the end of the seventh century BCE. Why does a story that takes place in the late tenth century BCE need to bring in a figure from such a distant future? What is the reason for describing what a righteous king named Josiah will do? The answer is much the same as we suggested in explaining why the stories of the patriarchs, the Exodus, and the conquest of Canaan are overflowing with seventh century allusions. The inescapable fact is that the books of Kings are as much a passionate religious argument—written in the seventh century BCE—as they are works of history (Finkelstein and Silberman 2001, 166–67).

Similar after-the-fact prophecies were commonplace in Egyptian literature and can also be found in the writings of Joseph Smith, among others. Consider a "prophecy" from the Book of Mormon concerning the colonization of North America and the Colonies' war of independence from Britain. The following passage is taken from Nephi 13:12–20, said to have been written around 600 BCE:

> And I looked and beheld a man among the Gentiles, who was separated from the seed of my brethren by the many waters; and I beheld the Spirit of God, that it came down and wrought upon the man; and he went forth upon the many waters, even unto the seed of my brethren, who were in the promised land.

> And it came to pass that I beheld the Spirit of God, that it wrought upon other Gentiles; and they went forth out of captivity, upon the many waters.

And it came to pass that I beheld many multitudes of the Gentiles upon the land of promise; and I beheld the wrath of God, that it was upon the seed of my brethren; and they were scattered before the Gentiles and were smitten.

And I beheld the Spirit of the Lord, that it was upon the Gentiles, and they did prosper and obtain the land for their inheritance; and I beheld that they were white, and exceedingly fair and beautiful, like unto my people before they were slain.

And it came to pass that I, Nephi, beheld that the Gentiles who had gone forth out of captivity did humble themselves before the Lord; and the power of the Lord was with them.

And I beheld that their mother Gentiles were gathered together upon the waters, and upon the land also, to battle against them.

And I beheld that the power of God was with them, and also that the wrath of God was upon all those that were gathered together against them to battle.

And I, Nephi, beheld that the Gentiles that had gone out of captivity were delivered by the power of God out of the hands of all other nations.

And it came to pass that I, Nephi, beheld that they did prosper in the land; and I beheld a book, and it was carried forth among them.

Virtually all non-Mormons agree that the above passage was not composed before the European discovery of the New World. Why? First, it describes in some detail the events that followed the discovery of the New World, events that an author writing in 600 BCE would not have been able to foresee. Second, the corpus of text in which this prophecy is found (that is, the Book of Mormon) does not go on to make detailed and accurate prophecies of any events following the publication of the Book of Mormon (for example, World War II).

It is a common complaint among Christian apologists that skeptics are too quick to dismiss supernatural biblical prophecies simply because the skeptics nurse an incurable bias against the supernatural. That is a red herring, one that I am weary of hearing. Those who instinctively dismiss the prophecies of the Mormon scriptures but are inclined to accept the Josiah prophecy as bona fide run the risk of operating under a double standard. There is no more proof that the man of God uttered his prophecy before Josiah's time than that the prophecies in the Mormon scriptures were written before the life of Joseph Smith.

If the scriptures were truly inspired by an all-knowing god, it would not have been any more difficult for the book of Kings to have mentioned George W. Bush by name than to have singled out Josiah. If the author of Kings had stated that in the year to be known as 2003, troops commissioned by George W. Bush from the other side of the world would cross the Euphrates, overthrowing an evil despot named Saddam Hussein, and if this prophecy had been circulated widely in texts for over two and a half millennia, there would have been no doubt upon its fulfillment that this prophecy was legitimate, issued well in advance of the events it foretold. But when the only reference to the Josiah prophecy is contained in a book that also documents its fulfillment, it is a smokescreen to complain of skeptics' bias against the supernatural. Those who will not entertain the possibility of a natural explanation for the purported prophecy in the book of Kings, simply because the story finds itself in their holy book, may fairly be charged with bias against the natural. Fabrication is a well-attested capacity of human nature. Predicting the distant future accurately is not.

Criterion 2: It can be proven that the event that was said to have been fulfilled actually happened.

None of the events of Jesus' life have any contemporary historical corroboration outside the Gospels (external corroboration of Jesus' existence and death, which I am not here disputing, appear many decades after Jesus' death). So without an a priori acceptance of the gospel record, there can be no historical certainty that every event in the Gospels happened as depicted.

Among the many gospel stories whose historicity critics question, none receive more attention than the birth narratives of Jesus in Matthew and Luke.

The two stories share very little in common other than that the birth occurred in Bethlehem of Judea (see map in this section[55]). Matthew and Luke understood on the basis of Micah 5 that the messiah was to be born in Bethlehem, but they also understood he grew up in Galilee. Given these parameters, they were faced with the problem of accounting for the difference in location between his birth in Bethlehem and his later home in Galilee.

These authors apparently did not have a common source for the birth narratives, since the earlier gospel Mark makes no mention of the circumstances of Jesus' birth. It is also apparent that Matthew and Luke did not consult each other. An independent reading of Matthew strongly suggests that Mary and Joseph were living in Bethlehem of Judea at the time of Jesus' birth. The challenge for Matthew, then, is to explain how the family ended up in Galilee. This he pulls off by having them take a detour to Egypt to avoid Herod's "slaughter of the innocents," then thwarting their return to Bethlehem by means of a warning in a dream:

> After Herod died, an angel of the Lord appeared in a dream to Joseph in Egypt and said, "Get up, take the child and his mother and go to the land of Israel, for those who were trying to take the child's life are dead."

> So he got up, took the child and his mother and went to the land of Israel. But when he heard that Archelaus was reigning in Judea in place of his father Herod, he was afraid to go there. Having been warned in a dream, he withdrew to the district of Galilee, and he went and lived *in a town called Nazareth* (Matthew 2:19–23a).

No mention is made of Nazareth or Galilee prior to this point in Matthew. The most natural reading is that Mary and Joseph were living in Bethlehem of Judea at the time of Jesus' birth and that they migrated to Nazareth only out of fear of Herod's dynasty.

Luke, on the other hand, has Mary and Joseph living initially in Galilee, so his challenge is to explain how the birth could have taken place in Bethlehem. This he accomplishes through the famous story of the census. Much has been written about the historical corroboration and plausibility of such an unprecedented census requiring individuals to return to their place of ancestral origin. I will not dwell on that here but will draw attention to the discrepancy between Matthew and Luke's accounts with regard to the date of Jesus' birth. Matthew places it in the time of Herod, who died in 4 BCE, while Luke favors the reign of Quirinius beginning in 8 CE. Apologists have provided many ingenious attempts to reconcile this

---

[55] Map from http://en.wikipedia.org/wiki/Image:First_century_palestine.gif.

discrepancy, but all fall short. Those who have studied this issue and are convinced they have a solution to the problem are encouraged to submit their solution to Richard Carrier, who has written extensively on this subject in his document, "The Date of the Nativity in Luke" (Carrier 2006).

In a Christmas Sunday school lesson I attended in 2006, one of the participants expressed how remarkable it was that the census took place just at the right time to ensure that Jesus would be born in Bethlehem as prophesied. I consider it remarkable instead, in light of the extensive lack of agreement between the Matthew and Luke stories, that so few believers fail even to consider the possibility that the two accounts are fabricated to place Jesus' birth in Bethlehem as a fulfillment of prophecy.

Another fulfilled event of suspicious historicity is Matthew's apparently simultaneous placement of Jesus on a donkey and on a colt, inspired by the following Old Testament passage:

> Rejoice greatly, O Daughter of Zion! Shout, Daughter of Jerusalem! See, your king comes to you, righteous and having salvation, gentle and riding on a donkey, on a colt, the foal of a donkey (Zechariah 9:9).

Matthew interprets the prophecy as follows:

> This took place to fulfill what was spoken through the prophet: "Say to the Daughter of Zion, 'See, your king comes to you, gentle and riding on a donkey, on a colt, the foal of a donkey.'" The disciples went and did as Jesus had instructed them. They brought the donkey and the colt, placed their cloaks on them, and Jesus sat on them (Matthew 21:4–7).

Matthew is the only gospel writer to place Jesus on both the donkey and the colt ("Jesus sat on *them*"); the others have him simply on the donkey, as would be expected. Is it not plausible that Matthew, failing to recognize Hebrew poetic parallelism (the common practice of repeating the same idea using different terms) in the Zechariah passage, interpreted the prophecy literally to mean that the king would sit on *both* a donkey *and* its foal, leading to the awkward arrangement found in Matthew 21:6?

The primary objection I have heard to this analysis is that the Gospel of Matthew is the most Jewish-oriented of the Gospels, and it would be unthinkable that Matthew should have been unaware of Hebrew poetic parallelism, so his dual-donkey fulfillment must have some other explanation. Bear in mind, however, that the Gospel of Matthew was anonymous and was written by a Greek speaker about whom we know very little.[56] Perhaps the author was a member of the Jewish Diaspora and did not even know Hebrew. That he drew from the Greek Septuagint when quoting the Old Testament is not disputed. That the book of Matthew is known for its focus on Jewish concerns does not guarantee that the author would have recognized poetic parallelism in the particular passage at hand.

Criterion 3: The prophecy must be presented explicitly as a prophecy, not simply as a historical event that has some incidental parallels with a later historical event.

There is no limit to the scope of "fulfilled" prophecies or "types" that can be imagined or chosen from a large corpus of text. I am reminded of Arthur Pink's insight that the three stories of Noah's Ark represent our threefold salvation in Christ (body, soul and spirit):

> The ark had three stories in it, "with lower, second, and third stories shalt thou make it" (Gen. 6:16). Why are we told this? What difference does it make to God's saints living four thousand years afterwards how many stories the ark had, whether it had one or a dozen? Every devout student of the Word has learned that everything in the Holy Scriptures has some significance and spiritual value. Necessarily so, for *every* word of God is pure. When the Holy Spirit "moved" Moses to write the book of Genesis, He knew that a book was being written which should be read by the Lord's people thousands of years later, therefore, what He caused to be written must have in every instance, something more than a merely local application. "*Whatsoever* was written aforetime was written for our learning." What then are we to "learn" from the fact that in the ark there were *three* stories, no less and no more?
>
> We have already seen that the ark itself unmistakably foreshadowed the Lord Jesus. Passing through the waters of judgment, being itself submerged by them; grounding on the seventeenth day of the month—as we shall see, the day of our Lord's Resurrection; and affording a shelter to all who were within it, the ark was a very clear type of Christ. Therefore *the inside* of the ark must speak to us of what we have *in Christ.* Is it not clear then that the ark divided into three stories more than hints as our *threefold salvation in Christ?* The salvation which we have in Christ *is* a threefold one, and that in a double sense. It is salvation which embraces each part of our threefold constitution,

---

[56] Though some fundamentalists dispute the claim that the Gospels are anonymous, most evangelical scholars concur that the authors' names were not included in the earliest manuscripts. Evangelical apologist Greg Boyd states, "While the canonical Gospels themselves are *anonymous* texts, according to early Christian tradition each was written either by an eyewitness of Jesus' ministry (Matthew and John) or a close associate of a first-generation apostle (John Mark and Luke). . . ." (Boyd 2007, 391). (Emphasis mine.)

making provision for the redemption of our spirit, and soul, and body (1 Thess. 5:23); and further, our salvation is a *three tense* salvation—we *have been* saved from the penalty of sin, *are being* saved from the power of sin, we *shall yet be* saved from the presence of sin (Pink 1922, 106–07; emphasis in original).

Who could not, given a little ingenuity and effort, draw similar parallels between, say, Moby Dick and the Mormon prophet Joseph Smith? Or between the Qur'an and Elvis Presley? It is a tragedy when the minds of intelligent individuals such as Arthur Pink are sidetracked in service to the church, while they could be applying their energies to more practical endeavors.

The Mormons cite a number of prophecies in the Bible that correspond to the ministry of Joseph Smith the Restorer. See the previously mentioned *A Marvelous Work and a Wonder* (Richards 1950) for an introduction. Why do evangelicals not find these parallels convincing?

Because only relatively few of the prophecies that are now claimed to be messianic were originally presented as such, it struck me as preposterous when I heard nationally televised pastor D. James Kennedy claim in 2000 that 100 percent of the messianic prophecies were fulfilled. If one matches up after the fact a few dozen events (let's say 100) in Jesus' life with some of the thousands of events (let's say 10,000) in the Old Testament, calling all the parallel events prophecies, then of course 100 percent of them were fulfilled. But if we're going to call parallel Old Testament-New Testament historical events fulfilled prophecies, then we need to consider all the other historical Old Testament events as unfulfilled prophecies, in which case the rate of fulfillment is much lower than 100 percent (let's say hypothetically 100/10,000 or 1 percent; others may be more generous than I, but in any case it would be hard to arrive at 100 percent). Looking at it any other way is like having your cake and eating it too. To find parallels between Old Testament events and Jesus' life may be profitable as a spiritual exercise to believers, but it's a mistake to go beyond that and claim that this is objective proof of supernatural prophecy.

The following from Matthew's nativity story serves as an example of cherry-picking ancient texts to establish a "fulfilled" prophecy:

When they had gone, an angel of the Lord appeared to Joseph in a dream. "Get up," he said, "take the child and his mother and escape to Egypt. Stay there until I tell you, for Herod is going to search for the child to kill him." So he got up, took the child and his mother during the night and left for Egypt, where he stayed until the death of Herod. And so was fulfilled what the Lord had said through the prophet: "Out of Egypt I called my son" (Matthew 2:13–15).

Even granting that Jesus' sojourn in Egypt was historical (although Matthew provides the only account we have of the story; no corroborating evidence exists for it), can it be claimed legitimately that the following "prophecy" (which Matthew cites above) was fulfilled in any sense whatsoever?

> When Israel was a child, I loved him, and out of Egypt I called my son. But the more I called Israel, the further they went from me. They sacrificed to the Baals and they burned incense to images (Hosea 11:1–2).

Note that the original Old Testament passage is not presented as a prophecy and was referring to a nation, not to an individual. It occurs in the past tense as a reference to the Exodus. But even more damning for the establishment of any parallel between "my son" in Hosea and "my son" in Matthew is the unflattering attributions to "my son" Israel in the original passage. Did Jesus flee from God? Did he sacrifice to the Baals and burn incense to images? Matthew was clearly grasping at straws. His credibility, not to mention his status as a divinely inspired author, should be roundly challenged. Let's call a spade a spade. Is it likely that anyone not having a prior commitment to the divine inspiration of the Bible should be won over by such hand waving? What reason do we have to give Matthew the benefit of the doubt or to consider his narrative historical?

Criterion 4: The object and circumstances of the prophecy must be clearly identified in such a way that there can be no mistake as to its precise fulfillment.

Christians reprove the Jews for not recognizing that Jesus had to be the messiah, but even Jesus' disciples who knew him best did not comprehend the connection between the prophecies and the events in Jesus' life. They expected a restoration of the Davidic monarchy and triumph over their enemies (rightly so, according to the explicit messianic prophecies) but, according to Christians, failed to see that the messiah would be a "suffering servant" as announced in Isaiah. But can we blame them for not thinking of all the servant/anointed/shepherd narratives as messianic?

Perhaps the most famous of these passages, Isaiah 53, was not presented primarily as a prophecy but as a series of past events. Isaiah 44:28–45:3 would sound messianic if the name had not been made explicit: Cyrus, emperor of Persia. There are many references to "servant" in Isaiah, the most common being to Jacob/Israel (a simple computer text search can be used to confirm this), but also to Eliakim (22:20–25, which also has a messianic ring to it) and others. The problem is that most of the prophecies Christians consider to be messianic were not labeled as such when written. In order simply to perceive the parallels, it took special explanations from Luke, who reported them in a conversation between the risen Christ and two disciples on the road to Emmaus (Luke 24:13–35). The right texts have to be selected and viewed from the right angle, pulled from their context and divided up into thin slices and applied to multiple events, each separated by hundreds or even thousands of years (in the case of dual or multiple fulfillments) in order to see the picture.

While believers may able to appreciate and discern these kinds of prophecies and rebuke unbelievers for their inability to see them through the eyes of faith, our concern here is whether the fulfillments *require* a supernatural explanation. I hold that an unmistakably true prophecy must be specific and unambiguous without requiring special instruction and faith to see the connection. The role of faith is so paramount in Christianity that even the ostensibly faith-building prophecies require faith and special discernment in order to see them correctly as proofs of their divine origin. But for those who do not have faith to begin with, how can they be convinced the ambiguous prophecies are supernatural?

If I predicted in an official, dated, and widely disseminated document that an earthquake was going to destroy the city of Dallas exactly one year from today and that the president of the United States was going to die in the earthquake, and if it were fulfilled to the letter, that would be an objective, readily evident supernatural prophecy. Without the eyes of faith, all the messianic prophecies fall far short of this kind of specificity. Maybe God does indeed want us to believe more on the basis of faith than on evidence, but if that is the case, then let us not pretend that the messianic prophecies are irrefutably supernatural.

Criterion 5: Every part of the prophecy must be fulfilled.

It is well documented that in 1832, Joseph Smith issued the following prophecy in section 87 of the Latter Day Saints' (Mormons') *Doctrine and Covenants*:

> VERILY, thus saith the Lord concerning the wars that will shortly come to pass, beginning at the rebellion of South Carolina, which will eventually terminate in the death and misery of many souls;

> And the time will come that war will be poured out upon all nations, beginning at this place.

For behold, the Southern States shall be divided against the Northern States, and the Southern States will call on other nations, even the nation of Great Britain, as it is called, and they shall also call upon other nations, in order to defend themselves against other nations; and then war shall be poured out upon all nations.

And it shall come to pass, after many days, slaves shall rise up against their masters, who shall be marshaled and disciplined for war.

And it shall come to pass also that the remnants who are left of the land will marshal themselves, and shall become exceedingly angry, and shall vex the Gentiles with a sore vexation.

And thus, with the sword and by bloodshed the inhabitants of the earth shall mourn; and with famine, and plague, and earthquake, and the thunder of heaven, and the fierce and vivid lightning also, shall the inhabitants of the earth be made to feel the wrath, and indignation, and chastening hand of an Almighty God, until the consumption decreed hath made a full end of all nations;

That the cry of the saints, and of the blood of the saints, shall cease to come up into the ears of the Lord of Sabaoth, from the earth, to be avenged of their enemies.

Wherefore, stand ye in holy places, and be not moved, until the day of the Lord come; for behold, it cometh quickly, saith the Lord. Amen.

This is an interesting prophecy in that the American Civil War actually did break out in South Carolina almost 30 years later, and slaves were involved in the fighting. Evangelicals are nonetheless unimpressed. Why not? It's one thing to be lucky and predict one isolated event (e.g., the start of the Civil War in South Carolina), but it's far more difficult to succeed in predicting *multiple* events successfully. The more line items in the prophecy, the more spectacular the fulfillment, provided that *all* the line items are fulfilled.

In the case of this so-called "Prophecy of Wars," at least two of the line items were fulfilled, but several of the others never happened. That does not stop the Latter Day Saints from positing a yet future fulfillment of the remaining line items. According to the *Doctrine and Covenants Student Manual,* "The war that started with the rebellion of South Carolina marked the beginning of the era of war that will last until the Savior returns to establish peace" (Church Educational System 2001, sec. 87).

An appeal to an as yet future fulfillment of certain line items in a multifaceted prophecy is a tacit acknowledgment that the prophecy was not fulfilled in its entirety, i.e., that it failed. Note that it is always *after the failure of the prophetic package as a whole* that proponents of a multifaceted prophecy posit that the remaining line items are to be fulfilled *at a later date*. This is in fact what we should expect to hear from such partisans if it is not possible naturalistically for detailed, multifaceted prophecies to be fulfilled all at once. One can almost always slice up prophecies finely enough so that their constituent pieces can be applied to various events throughout history. A fulfilled prophecy is impressive only when it contains multiple components, *all* of which are clearly fulfilled together *as a package*.

We are thus justified in questioning whether the Micah 5:2 prophecy predicting that a "ruler" will be born in Bethlehem can be applied legitimately to Jesus, even if we grant that Jesus was in fact born in Bethlehem. The entire context of the Micah 5 prophecy has little to do with Bethlehem in the time of Jesus: it discusses an Assyrian invasion; the role of the "ruler" in delivering the Israelites from the Assyrians; and the destruction of horses, chariots, and Asherah poles, none of which took place in Jesus' lifetime.

Criterion 6: The prophecy must have a literal fulfillment, not just an imagined spiritual fulfillment.

The Jehovah's Witnesses prophesied the return of Jesus in 1874 and again in 1914. When his return failed to materialize on these dates, the Witnesses saved face by claiming he returned only "spiritually." The "prophecy" of the suffering servant in Isaiah 53 seems amazing for those who accept the Christian assumptions about the purpose of Jesus' death, but most of what it refers to is spiritual in nature, so it was possible to apply it to Jesus or to any other righteous person who was unjustly executed. There are a few physical references in the passage, most notably to the servant's being pierced (which could mean on a cross or with a sword or spear; being pierced has been a common enough method of execution throughout history) but also to his being "crushed." It is not legitimate to focus literally on "pierced" as a miraculous prophecy of Jesus' crucifixion while viewing "crushed" in a more figurative sense. Those who wish to employ the literal meaning of the first to posit a fulfilled prophecy must, in order to be consistent, accept the second as a failed prophecy, since John 20:36 testifies that "not one of his bones was broken."

These six criteria are not exhaustive or canonical; they are simply common-sense reflections on the conditions most reasonable people would place on any claim to prophecy outside one's own religious system. They can be used without discrimination to discount the prophecies of Jeanne

Dixon, the Jehovah's Witnesses, Joseph Smith, Nostradamus, Jesus, and Isaiah alike. For those who feel that the six criteria laid out above are unreasonable, the challenge is to determine how to relax them in such a way as to preserve the supernatural nature of the biblical prophecies while filtering out the spurious ones from other traditions. A less problematic alternative is to acknowledge that none of them are in fact supernatural.

I could go through many of the remaining messianic prophecies and find one or more conditions they fail to meet, but Thomas Paine (Paine 1807) has already demonstrated the spuriousness of a great number of them. Furthermore, the onus is on the believer to demonstrate that they pass all the tests, not on the unbeliever to demonstrate that they fail.

THE "SEVENTY WEEKS" OF DANIEL 9

One prophecy that does not fit neatly into my six criteria above is the "seventy sevens" or "seventy weeks" of years in Daniel 9. Since it served as an important corroboration of my faith as a believer, I will spend some time on this question, but if it is not important for your faith, then you are welcome to skip to the next section.

Josh McDowell and other apologists claim that Daniel 9 pinpoints the actual date of Jesus the messiah's crucifixion. However, the assumed starting point, duration, and continuity of the seventy weeks have shown themselves so fluid and adaptable as to be applicable to virtually any event since the prophecy was made. Prophetic endpoints from the book of Daniel have been linked to milestones such as Oliver Cromwell's Puritan Revolution; the scandalous acts of the pope during the Reformation period; and the abomination of Antiochus Epiphanes during the second century BCE at the time that critical scholars believe the book of Daniel was written. Again, evangelical scholar John Goldingay:

> Ancient and modern interpreters have commonly taken vv 24–27 as designed to convey firm chronological information, which as such can be tested by chronological facts available to us. It may then be vindicated, for instance, by noting that the period from Jeremiah's prophecy (605 B.C.) to that of Cyrus's accession (556) was 49 years and the period from Jeremiah's prophecy to the death of the high priest Onias III (171) was 434 years so that the sum of these periods is 483 years, the final seven years taking events to the rededication of the temple in 164. Or it may be vindicated by noting that according to some computations the period from Nehemiah (445 or 444 B.C.) to Jesus' death at Passover in A.D. 32 or 33 was exactly 483 years, the seventieth seven being postponed. Both these understandings of the seventy sevens may be faulted on the grounds of their arbitrariness. In the case of the first, it is not obvious why two partly concurrent figures should be added together. In the case of

the second, it is not obvious why the word about building a restored Jerusalem should be connected with Artaxerxes' commission of Nehemiah to rebuild the walls of Jerusalem; nor why we should separate off the seventieth seven, as the theory requires; nor why we should date Nehemiah's commission in 444 B.C. or Jesus' crucifixion in A.D. 32—the computation requires one or the other, but the usually preferred dates are 445 and A.D. 30 or 33. . . . Further, it is striking that the NT itself does not refer to the seventy sevens in this connection; Luke 1–2 applies v 24 in a quite different way (Goldingay 1989, 257).

At the start of Daniel 9, the main character is pondering the meaning of Jeremiah's prophecy of a seventy-year Babylonian exile, said to have resulted from Israel's failure to let their land lie fallow once every seven years as required by law. According to Leviticus 26:28, God would multiply his afflictions sevenfold if his people continued to resist him. The seventy-times-seven theme was full of symbolism and was never intended to be taken literally (any more than we are to take literally Jesus' injunction to forgive 490 times rather than, say, 491 times):

Jeremiah had spoken of seventy-years' desolation for Jerusalem, but it was actually to last centuries longer than that. God is free to exact whatever chastisement he chooses. But the message's good news is that it is not chastisement without end. The number 490 is not an arithmetical calculation to be pressed to yield chronological information. It is a figure that puts together two symbolic figures, the seventy years (a lifetime) of Jer 25:11/29:10 and the sevenfold chastisement of Lev 26:28. The result is a doubly symbolic figure extending from the beginning of chastisement in the exile to whenever it is seen as ending. . . . The climax to which chap. 8 looks lies in the crisis in the second century B.C., when God delivered his people and his sanctuary from the combined threat of Antiochus Epiphanes and reformist Judaism (Goldingay 1989, 266–67).

In an interesting twist, Goldingay goes on to argue that if we understand the seventy weeks of years (490 years) as having a predetermined outcome, we run the risk of accepting a deistic notion of God. This is because God would be seen as winding up the clock at the beginning of the 490 years so that even he himself would not be free to intervene in the subsequent course of events, in much the same way as deists believe God wound up the clock of the universe at the beginning of creation without further intervention.

This final excerpt from Goldingay effectively sums up the question of Daniel 9:

In Jewish and Christian tradition, Gabriel's promise has been applied to rather later events: the birth of the messiah, Jesus' death and resurrection, the fall of Jerusalem, various subsequent historical events, and the still-future manifesting of the messiah. Exegetically such views are mistaken. The detail of vv 24–27 fits the second-century B.C. crisis and agrees with allusions to this crisis elsewhere in Daniel. The verses do not indicate that they are looking centuries or millennia beyond the period to which chaps. 8 and 10–12 refer. They do not suggest that the cleansing and renewal of which v 24 speaks is the cleansing and renewal of the world: it is the cleansing and renewal of Jerusalem. The passage refers to the Antiochene crisis. Yet its allusiveness justifies reapplication of the passage, as is the case with previous chapters, in the following sense. It does not refer specifically to concrete persons and events in the way of historical narrative such as 1 Maccabees, but refers in terms of symbols to what those persons and events embodied, symbols such as sin, justice, an anointed prince, a flood, an abomination. Concrete events and persons are understood in the light of such symbols, but the symbols transcend them. They are not limited in their reference to these particular concrete realities. They have other embodiments. What these other embodiments are is a matter of theological, not exegetical, judgment—a matter of faith, not of science. But if I am justified in believing that Jesus is God's anointed, and that his birth, ministry, death, resurrection, and appearing are God's ultimate means of revealing himself and achieving his purpose in the world, they are also his means of ultimately achieving what the symbols in vv 24–27 speak of (Goldingay 1989, 267–68).

In the Christmas Sunday school class I attended in 2006, Josh McDowell's views on Daniel 9 were presented as ironclad evidence of the supernaturally prophesied passion of Jesus. The only possible naturalistic explanation, it was stated, was that the prophecy was made after Jesus' crucifixion (and we know that is not the case). Given the myriad endpoints of the original prophecy that have been put forward throughout history, I would call for more circumspection, more humility, and less confidence when making claims of this nature.

JESUS' FAILED PROPHECY

A final prophecy meriting closer examination is Jesus' prediction of his return during the generation in which he lived:

> For the Son of Man is going to come in his Father's glory with his angels, and then he will reward each person according to what he has done. I tell you the truth, some who are standing here will not taste death before they see the Son of Man coming in his kingdom (Matthew 16:27–28).

At that time the sign of the Son of Man will appear in the sky, and all the nations of the earth will mourn. They will see the Son of Man coming on the clouds of the sky, with power and great glory. And he will send his angels with a loud trumpet call, and they will gather his elect from the four winds, from one end of the heavens to the other. . . . Even so, when you see all these things, you know that it is near, right at the door. I tell you the truth, this generation will certainly not pass away until all these things have happened. Heaven and earth will pass away, but my words will never pass away (Matthew 24:30–34).

There will be signs in the sun, moon and stars. On the earth, nations will be in anguish and perplexity at the roaring and tossing of the sea. Men will faint from terror, apprehensive of what is coming on the world, for the heavenly bodies will be shaken. At that time they will see the Son of Man coming in a cloud with power and great glory. When these things begin to take place, stand up and lift up your heads, because your redemption is drawing near. . . . Even so, when you see these things happening, you know that the kingdom of God is near. I tell you the truth, this generation will certainly not pass away until all these things have happened. Heaven and earth will pass away, but my words will never pass away (Luke 21:25–33).

When we compare these three passages together in the context of the whole New Testament, in which Jesus' return was expected in the generation then living, a strong case can be made that this is really what Jesus meant (or that this is what the writers who reported Jesus' words intended to convey). The problem is so acute that C. S. Lewis, arguably the greatest Christian apologist of the twentieth century, acknowledged this is what Jesus meant, but that he in his humanity was limited in his foreknowledge, so he did not in fact return in that generation as predicted:

The facts, then, are these: that Jesus professed himself (in some sense) ignorant, and within a moment showed that he really was so. To believe in the Incarnation, to believe that he is God, makes it hard to understand how he could be ignorant; but also makes it certain that, if he said he could be ignorant, then ignorant he could really be. For a God who can be ignorant is less baffling than a God who falsely professes ignorance (Lewis 1960, 99).

Lewis' solution, which mistakes false prophecy for mere ignorance (why prophesy concerning matters about which one is ignorant?), cannot be entertained by those who hold to Jesus' authority in all he said. The following Old Testament passage shuts out this possibility:

You may say to yourselves, "How can we know when a message has not been spoken by the LORD?" If what a prophet proclaims in the name of the LORD does not take place or come true, that is a message the LORD has not spoken. That prophet has spoken presumptuously. Do not be afraid of him (Deut. 18:21–22).

As a believer I had often heard evangelicals making fun of Jehovah's Witnesses for their failed prophecies of Jesus' return, yet I was for many years effectively oblivious to the same problem in the New Testament.

In an alternative attempt to address the problem of Jesus' predicted early return, a significant minority of evangelicals holds to a Preterist view of prophecy, maintaining that Jesus did in fact return in the first century:

> If Jesus meant what He said, said what He meant, and was an infallible Prophet, all the components of his prophecy must stand or fall together. These certainly include his coming on the clouds with power and glory. The failure of any one component to occur within that existing generation would disqualify Jesus as a prophet and call into question the truth of Scripture. If He did not return when He said He would, we have a dilemma of huge proportions (Noē 1996).

It is doubtless the lack of evidence for Jesus' return in the first century that allows most evangelicals to dismiss this view without serious consideration. But for Preterists, the lack of evidence for Jesus' past return is less of a problem than is any attempt to twist the face value of Jesus' prophecies to allow for his return in a later generation. Likewise, for Lewis it was less problematic to believe that Jesus was mistaken than to reinterpret his words in the manner that most evangelicals tend to do in order to get around the first-generation problem. This is a dilemma for which there is apparently no good solution; I cannot believe that Jesus has returned in the past or will ever return in the future.

Some have argued that Jesus' use of the word *generation* (*genea* in Greek) does not necessarily signify a generation as commonly understood, but that a secondary meaning of *genea,* namely, *race* (that is, the Jewish race), may have been intended. This suggests the unlikely possibility that all the scholars who produced the major English translations of the Bible (KJV, NIV, NASB, and others) were incompetent in their ability to discern the true meaning of the word, despite their mastery of Greek and the textual context. In addition, consider what such an interpretation would mean:

> Jesus told his disciples, living in the first century, this parable: "Look at the fig tree and all the trees. When they sprout leaves, *you* [meaning his hearers, disciples of the first century] can see for yourselves and know that summer is near. Even so, when *you* see these things happening, *you* know that the kingdom of God is near. "I tell *you* the truth, *this* race [that is, the Jewish race, of which *you* disciples are a part] will certainly not pass away until all these things have happened. Heaven and earth will pass away, but my words will never pass away (Luke 21:25–33).

The term *race* simply makes no sense in this context. There is no expectation anywhere in scripture that the Jewish race will ever cease to exist. Introducing such a timeframe in a prophecy clearly intended to place parameters on the timing of his return would be meaningless, on a par with, "I'm going to return before the human race ceases to exist." Would it have been of any comfort or significance to the disciples to know that their race would last until Jesus' return, not having any prior reason to think otherwise? No, this passage only means anything to its recipients if taken at face value: members of *this* generation, that is, Jesus' generation, not the Jewish race, and not some future generation (the Greek has a word for "that" in opposition to "this," so if Jesus meant "that generation," he could easily have made it explicit) will still be alive when Jesus returns. This is all the more evident when we consider that Jesus directs his comments to his disciples in the second person, making inescapable the conclusion that his disciples were expected to witness "these things."

Tangentially, it would seem odd for members of a particular race to refer to that race as "this race." Imagine you are a Caucasian speaking to your fellow Caucasian friends in the United States, and you have a hunch that the Caucasian race will last at least until the Boston Red Sox repeat their win of the World Series. Would you say, "This race won't come to an end before the Boston Red Sox win the World Series again," not having provided any clue as to the nature of the race? Even if there were not multiple meanings of the word *race* in English (for example, a one-mile race or an ethnicity), your friends would likely be confused if you meant an ethnicity. Only by adding a qualifier such as, "The Caucasion race won't come to end" would your statement communicate anything.

But let us imagine for the sake of argument that "this generation" might refer to "that [future] generation" or that *generation* might mean *race.* It is a cornerstone of Protestant hermeneutics to compare scripture with scripture when the meaning of one passage is in doubt. The intent of this approach is to enable us to grasp more clearly the meaning of the ambiguous passage (assuming it is truly ambiguous and not merely inconvenient; in the present case, "inconvenient" would be more appropriate than "ambiguous"). Do other passages give comfort to those who would interpret this passage contrary to its face value in order to excuse what appears to be a failed prophecy? No.

Let us revisit these verses:

> For the Son of Man is going to come in his Father's glory with his angels, and then he will reward each person according to what he has done. I tell you

the truth, some who are standing here will not taste death before they see the Son of Man coming in his kingdom (Matthew 16:27–28).

There is no ambiguity here concerning the meaning of "generation"; the terms are explicitly laid out. There is no clearer way to say "this generation will not pass away" than to say, "There are some of those who are standing here who shall not taste death until. . . ." Since denying the meaning of this timeframe is not an option, the only recourse (other than admitting Jesus' fallibility *à la* C. S. Lewis) is to interpret the phrase "see the Son of Man coming in his kingdom" as something other than Jesus' literal return. Accordingly, many apologists suggest that the story of the Transfiguration, which immediately follows Jesus' speech in the narrative, represents the fulfillment. Or perhaps it referred to some other event in Jesus' first advent—for example, the resurrection. This may seem plausible at first, until all the details are taken into account.

First, if the Transfiguration followed on the heels of Jesus' prediction, what could have been the purpose of including the clause, "there are some of those who are standing here who shall not taste death until. . . ."? Though there is wiggle room for interpreting Jesus' meaning, this is not language ordinarily used to describe an event that is to take place in short order. If Jesus knew that the transfiguration was right around the corner (or that the resurrection was to occur within a year, this being the final year of Jesus' ministry), it seems strange for him to have placed the event merely within his disciples' lifetime rather than "soon," "within a week," or "within a year," as the case may have been.

Perhaps he knew that saying "within a week" would have deprived the future depraved Ken Daniels of an opportunity to trump up a charge of false prophecy against Jesus. He knew in advance that Ken's heart would be a heart of stone and that he would be unable to believe merely on faith, so he gave Ken some fodder to harden his heart further, much like Yahweh's hardening of Pharaoh's heart in the time of the Exodus. You may chuckle, but such a suggestion has actually been made to me when discussing this passage with a believer.

More importantly, none of the events in Jesus' subsequent ministry—certainly not his transfiguration or resurrection—fulfill the terms Jesus laid out in his prophecy. In context, he states, "For the Son of Man is going to come in his Father's glory with his angels, and then he will reward each person according to what he has done." The Transfiguration story mentions no angels, and though the resurrection account includes angels, in no way can Jesus be said to have "come in the glory of his Father with His angels." And in neither case did he "recompense every man according to his deeds." This language, along with the mention of the Son of Man coming in his kingdom, is unmistakably apocalyptic, referring to the end of the age; to interpret it as an event occurring during the first century is to rationalize it in much the same way as Jehovah's Witnesses did when it became apparent that Jesus' expected return failed to materialize physically.

The above passages are not isolated suggestions that Jesus would return in the lifetime of his disciples; that expectation is expressed repeatedly throughout the New Testament. An extensive list of these passages is available from Edward Babinski's article, "The Lowdown on God's Showdown" (Babinski 2006); I will mention only a small subset here. (Comments in brackets in the following sets of verses are Babinski's.)

> The world and its desires pass away ["This world, as it is now, will not last much longer" - Today's English Version], but the man who does the will of God lives forever. Dear children, this is the last hour; and as you have heard that the antichrist is coming, even now many antichrists have come. This is how we know it is the last hour (1 John 2:17–18).

By what legitimate hermeneutic can "the last hour" be transmuted to two millennia? Such a stretch renders language meaningless, as does the statement in 2 Peter 3:8 that "With the Lord a day is like a thousand years, and a thousand years are like a day," used to excuse Jesus' failure to return up to the point of its writing. It goes without saying that the writer of 1 John did not mean "the last 60 minutes," but it is clear that a sense of urgency is being expressed to individuals who lived in his day, not to those who have lived in the subsequent nineteen centuries.

Paul certainly expected to be counted among those still living at the end of the age (comments again are Babinski's):

> According to the Lord's own word, we tell you that *we* who are still alive, who are left till the coming of the Lord, will certainly not precede those who have fallen asleep. For the Lord himself will come down from heaven, with a loud command, with the voice of the archangel and with the trumpet call of God, and the dead in Christ will rise first. After that, *we* who are still alive and are left will be caught up together with them in the clouds to meet the Lord in the air. And so we will be with the Lord forever. Therefore encourage each other with these words (1 Thessalonians 4:15–17).

> The time has been shortened so that from now on both those who have wives should be as though they had none [i.e., Paul preached that the time was so "short" that married Christian couples "from now on" ought to abstain from having sex!]; and those who weep, as though they did not weep; and those who rejoice, as though they did not rejoice; and those who buy, as though they did not possess; and those who use the world, as though they did not make full use of it [i.e., there was no time for marriage or buying or selling—

only in a state of holy celibacy could the Elect remain pure while awaiting the soon return of Christ]; for the form of this world is passing away ["This world, as it is now, will not last much longer"—Today's English Version]. ... These things were written for *our* instruction, upon whom the *ends of the ages have come*. ... Proclaim the Lord's death until he comes [i.e., Paul did not say, "Proclaim the Lord's death until the day you die," but rather, "until he comes," which means that he considered Christ's coming to be nearer than the time when the believers he was writing to would all be dead] (1 Corinthians 7:29–31; 10:11; 11:26).

The New Testament repeatedly warns its first-century readers that their time is short and that they are to conduct themselves with the knowledge of his imminent return. Yet dozens of generations have come and gone since the time of Jesus, so we are confronted in this generation with the question, Are we more likely to meet God through the return of Jesus or through death? For generation after generation the answer has been death. If this is the case, then it would have made far more sense for the New Testament writers to have been more concerned with their readers' readiness for death than with their readiness for Jesus' return.

It is ironic that some who most ardently defend the authority of scripture and object to loose interpretations that justify homosexuality, for example, tend to reverse course when presented with passages that clearly teach the return of Jesus in the first century. If it is a matter of defending the moral high ground against sexual impurity, the Bible must be taken at face value, but if it comes to defending the authority of the Bible itself, reinterpreting what it appears to say is not only permissible but mandatory and laudable.[57] Apologists who present alternate interpretations to get the Bible off the hook are placed on a pedestal of high honor, having vindicated the Bible against the infidels who dare to bring against the Exalted Savior the charge of false prophecy. But infidels who insist on taking these passages at face value are demonized, branded as polemicists, or castigated for refusing to accept the creative thinking of apologists, who, after all, are every bit as human and subject to error as infidels. And if apologists are subject to error, then so were the New Testament authors, who were no less human themselves than the rest of us.

It was painful during my deconversion process to admit this level playing field, but I came to recognize that my instinct for placing the redeemed—including apologists, the New Testament authors, and Jesus

---

[57] Note that I am not accusing such believers of deliberate hypocrisy. In their heart they are no doubt taking the high ground, but from an outsider's perspective there appears to be an unintentional double standard at play.

himself—in a special untouchable category was a fatal impediment to an honest search for the truth. Only after this realization could I come to terms what should otherwise have been plain: Jesus did not return when he promised he would.

A skeptic could hardly ask for a more objective falsification of any religion: the religion's leader prophesies a globally identifiable series of events within a specified time period, but the events do not take place within that time period. Yet Christianity did not fail after the first generation; there were already too many believers with too much at stake, and when the fuzzy boundary of one generation was passed, reason was not going to stand in the way of the movement, since reason was not the primary impetus for Christians to believe in the first place. Instead, various explanations arose to account for what appeared on the surface to be a failed set of prophecies, just as the Mormons and Jehovah's Witnesses later came up with explanations for their failed prophecies.

Those who expect Jesus to return and take them to glory appear to be resting in a false hope. It is very unlikely to happen. We should expect no judgment day before Jesus for those who deny the promise of his return, any more than we should expect a judgment day before Allah for those who deny the teachings of Muhammad.

Some may respond with anger to what they perceive as an overly confident and strident analysis of these passages. This is understandable for those who are resolved under no circumstances to abandon their faith. But instead of directing their anger at me, the messenger, why should believers not consider the simple possibility that they have been led down the wrong path? After all, considering the wide range of intransigently held erroneous beliefs in the world today, is it not possible or even probable that Christians are mistaken, despite their very good intentions? Why not do the right thing and show the world that it is in fact possible to change one's mind in the face of evidence that invalidates one's position? Why continue striving to excuse a faith that is, by all appearances, demonstrably false? Why delay coming to terms with reason one for more generation, only to have the same battles fought in the next? While Muslim extremists sow terror in the name of their faith around the world, we in the West must show by example that maintaining our ideologies at all costs against the best available evidence is not the way forward. How can we call on Muslims to abandon their unsupported faith if we are unwilling to give up our own?

Chapter 11

The Resurrection of Jesus

Though I no longer regularly attend church, I continue doing so on special holidays for the sake of family solidarity. During the 2005 or 2006 Easter service, the pastor explained some of the historical factors that in his view lead to the conclusion that Jesus arose supernaturally. He proceeded to lament the "sinfulness of the human heart that denies the evidence for the resurrection." This kind of rhetoric is common in evangelical and fundamentalist circles, but I am not sure the pastor understood how inflammatory it is. By using the word *sinfulness*, he is not merely claiming that we unbelievers are honestly mistaken, but that we are *willfully* mistaken and are therefore subject to divine judgment for our decision. I am sympathetic to believers who complain about Dawkins' insensitivity and ridicule, but a posture that attributes willful, eternally punishable sinfulness to the majority of the world's population is in my estimation far more provocative. All the much more so in light of the likelihood that few who make such statements have studied in any depth the arguments against their position.

What is the source of apologists' confidence in the resurrection? William Lane Craig, perhaps the foremost living defender of Jesus' resurrection, relies on four events he says are acknowledged by the majority of biblical scholars. These events support the claim that Jesus must have physically risen from the dead (Craig and Ehrman 2006):

1. Jesus' burial
2. The discovery of his empty tomb
3. His postmortem appearances
4. The origin of the disciples' belief in his resurrection

If the majority of biblical scholars do subscribe to Craig's four facts, it should be no more surprising or conclusive than that the majority of Qur'anic scholars believe an angel visited Muhammad in a cave and dictated to him the teachings of the Qur'an. It is saying nothing more than that the majority of those who study religious texts subscribe at least to the basic tenets of those texts.

Craig maintains that these four facts are established by five independent sources, all of which testify to the same basic conclusion. However, it is difficult from our present vantage point to ascertain that all five sources are truly independent, at least up through Mark's empty tomb story.[58] There is a near consensus among biblical scholars that the authors of the later Gospels drew from earlier Gospels and from other lost sources. There is no evidence that any of the authors of these five sources witnessed the events they described.[59] Thus, it is probable that the five allegedly independent sources drew at least to some extent upon the core of an oral tradition that had developed within a few years after Jesus' death. This makes them no more independent than five documents reciting the tales of Paul Bunyan during the American colonial period.

There is a general failure among evangelical apologists to appreciate the power of hearsay to generate firmly held beliefs in a very short time. This is accompanied by a failure to appreciate the intransigency of such beliefs even in the face of insufficient or disconfirming evidence. For example, in the seventeenth century CE a Jewish messianic movement grew up around Rabbi Sabbatai Sevi, whose followers attributed to him all manner of miraculous signs within days or weeks of his appearances, continuing in their devotion to him even after his defection to Islam! (Scholem 1973); (Price 1993) It is estimated there are still over 100,000 followers of this movement today.

Was there not an abundance of other sources outside the New Testament canon that acknowledged the existence, death, burial, and resurrection of Jesus? No, not for at least 60 years from the time these

---

[58] Craig does not spell out in the debate with Ehrman his reasons for maintaining that the gospel burial accounts, for example, were all independent. Even if it could be shown (to my knowledge, it has not) that there is no literary dependency, this does not rule out a dependence on a common oral tradition.

[59] The authorial attributions of the Gospels were suggested first in the second century CE by Papias, bishop of Hierapolis in Asia Minor. For the authorship of Mark and Matthew, see Papias, Fragment 3:15-16 (cf. Fragment 21); for the authorship of John, see Fragment 19, as arranged in *The Apostolic Fathers: Greek Texts and English Translations of Their Writings* (Lightfoot and Harmer 1992, 307-330).

events allegedly occurred. I recall attending a seminary class in which one of the students asked the professor about extrabiblical sources confirming Jesus' life and deeds. The whole class expected the professor to launch into a litany of citations. To our chagrin, however, the professor somewhat apologetically confessed there are no known first-century references to Jesus prior to a text by the Jewish historian Josephus dating to at least CE 90, or some 60 years after Jesus' death (Josephus ca. 94 CE, 20.9.2=20:200). [60]

A seldom-questioned practice of resurrection apologists is the tendency to take the details of biblical accounts at face value. The presence of a large stone that could not have been easily moved by Jesus' followers is one example of a detail whose veracity is simply assumed because it appears in the Gospel texts. Josh McDowell quotes Frank Morrison:

> Let us begin by considering first its size and probable character. . . . [N]o doubt . . . the stone was large and consequently very heavy. This fact is asserted or implied by all the writers who refer to it. St. Mark says it was "exceeding great." St. Matthew speaks of it as "a great stone." Peter says, "for the stone was great." Additional testimony on this point is furnished by the reported anxiety of the women as to how they should move it. If the stone had not been of considerable weight the combined strength of the three women should have been capable of moving it. We receive, therefore, a very definite impression that it was at least too weighty for the women to remove unaided. All this has a very definite bearing upon the case. . . ." (McDowell 1979, 208–09).

But why would a gospel writer invent a detail like the large stone? [61] Whether or not there was such a stone, the inclusion of this element in the narrative would certainly be useful for helping "seal off" theft as one of the proposed naturalistic alternatives to the resurrection story.

The entire edifice of the traditional case for Jesus' resurrection is built on the assumption that we are justified in taking the biblical accounts at face value. If there is reason to doubt the historicity of the texts, however,

---

[60] Josephus speaks of "the brother of Jesus, who was called Christ, whose name was James. . . ."

[61] The answer to this question is more obvious than the answer to the question of why the gospel writers may have arranged to have women be the first eyewitness of the Resurrection. See Ehrman's remarks in (Craig & Ehrman 2006) for one possibility. Another is that a source of inspiration for the accounts was the prior resurrection of the Egyptian god Osiris, of which women were the primary witnesses (Boyd and Price 2003).

our confidence in any proposed reconstruction of the events based on the accounts is compromised (Price 1993, ch. 6). In his debate with Bart Ehrman (Craig and Ehrman 2006), William Lane Craig does not refute Ehrman's contention that the accounts vary in a great number of details, but he insists that the differences lie only at the periphery of the narrative, not at its core. My approach in this chapter will be to examine just one of the many well-known discrepancies in the gospel accounts, contending that it is a central element of the story and that its variants reveal an intentional textual manipulation on the part of at least one of the authors.

PRESUPPOSITIONS

Before examining this discrepancy I will address what I consider to be the core of the controversy over Jesus' resurrection. It is plain from even a cursory glance at the Ehrman-Craig debate that both participants came to the table with very entrenched presuppositions. Craig is convinced that any naturalistic explanation for the resurrection accounts is less plausible than the traditional supernatural explanation, while Ehrman is convinced, like Sherlock Holmes, that "when you have eliminated the impossible, whatever remains, *however improbable*, must be the truth."

I do not subscribe to all four of Craig's facts, but let us grant them here for the sake of argument. Clearly any one naturalistic scenario we could imagine to explain these facts is inherently unlikely. But there are perhaps dozens of such scenarios that have been proposed by the skeptical community, some more plausible than others. We are interested not in the probability of any single one of these scenarios (many of which have been laughed to scorn individually by apologists), but in the statistical sum of the probabilities of all the dozens of scenarios that have been proposed, plus any that have not yet been imagined. It is somewhat as if you had a die with 100 unevenly weighted sides, each one representing a naturalistic resurrection scenario with an average 1-in-100 likelihood of being true. If you roll the die, one of the 100 sides will be obtained, even if the probability of that particular side's coming out on top is inherently low.

The reason naturalists cannot reconstruct a consensus scenario to account for the events of Easter morning is that we have such a narrow and opaque window into the days surrounding Jesus' death. The gospel writers had a religious agenda; they drew from earlier sources and previous Gospels; their accounts were written decades after the events;[62] and there

---

[62] Some fundamentalists claim the Gospels were written very early based on colophons (endnotes) dating from the third century CE, in which the Gospel of Matthew was

were no surveillance cameras monitoring the tomb or grave in which Jesus' body was laid. There are simply too many variables and too many unknowns to come to a definitive conclusion. Fortunately for Watson and Sherlock, they were able to find a hole in the roof through which the intruder apparently passed, but if no hole had been found, what then? Should they have concluded that the intruder magically passed through the wall? No, the most reasonable approach is to continue making hypotheses until the pieces fit. But what if the pieces never fit due to insufficient information? I, along with Ehrman, but contra Craig, consider it more reasonable to say, "I don't know," than to throw up our hands and say it was a miracle. I make no apologies for my position; if Craig wishes to accuse me of being biased against the possibility of divine intervention, so be it, but he cannot rule out all possible naturalistic scenarios any more conclusively than I can rule out a miracle.

In their debate, Craig and Ehrman discuss at length the probability of divine intervention versus that of naturalistic scenarios. The debate will never end: how can one possibly assign a probability to something as inaccessible and untestable as divine intervention? We do not have all the relevant details at our disposal, so we cannot even calculate the odds of nonsupernatural scenarios, let alone supernatural ones. From my perspective, if the odds of all the naturalistic hypotheses put together are greater than zero (and we know that the possibility of human fabrication

---

"published eight years after the ascension of Christ" (Carlton 2008, xv). Nonetheless, most evangelical scholars place the writing of the Gospels no earlier than 50 CE. *The NIV Study Bible* (Barker 1985, 1437), for example, considers Mark, the earliest Gospel, to have been composed after 50 CE.

Irenaeus (Bishop of Lugdunum), one of the earliest writers to attest to the traditional authorship of the four Gospels, wrote the following around 180 CE:

Matthew for his part published also a written Gospel among the Hebrews in their own language, whilst Peter and Paul were at Rome, preaching, and laying the foundation of the Church. And after their departure, Mark, Peter's disciple and interpreter, did himself also publish unto us in writing the things which were preached by Peter (Irenaeus ca. 180 CE, Book III Preface, 204).

If Peter and Paul's "departure" refers to their death, which occurred around 64-67 CE, then (according to Irenaeus) Mark must have been composed in the mid 60's CE at the earliest. Though "departure" could refer to something other than their death, it is believed (based on Acts) that Paul lived out at least the last two years of his life in Rome and died in Rome. Even if we grant that "departure" means something other than his death, certainly Peter and Paul were not both in Rome prior to AD 50, which would entail that Mark was indeed written decades after Jesus' death.

and legendary development is far greater than zero), there is no need to look to the supernatural. When we short-circuit the search for natural explanations and appeal to miracles, we violate the law of parsimony, also known as Occam's Razor, by introducing more entities than needed to explain any given phenomenon. For example, if we can explain planetary motion through the laws of gravitation, angular momentum, and so forth, then throwing in occasional angelic or divine course corrections becomes superfluous. And even if we cannot initially explain certain orbits with our model, this should serve as an impetus to refine our model, not to give up and invoke tweaking on the part of angels.

Ehrman never came out in the debate and admitted he was not open to the possibility of divine intervention, and Craig never come out and admitted he was not open to the possibility of a naturalistic explanation for the events. Without such admissions, the dialogue dances in circles around the edges of what one's opponent is prepared to accept, and no further ground can be made. For my part, I freely confess that as long as the probability of any imaginable naturalistic scenario is greater than zero, I am reluctant to invoke the miraculous. I am more interested in applying Sherlock's Principle *consistently* than in applying it arbitrarily in mundane aspects of life but short-circuiting it to support a given theological agenda.

THE LOCATION OF JESUS' POST-RESURRECTION APPEARANCES

The authors of Mark and Matthew (hereafter referred to as Mark and Matthew) placed Jesus' first appearance in Galilee in northern Israel, while the authors of Luke and John (hereafter referred to as Luke and John) indicated it took place in the environs of Jerusalem, some 70–80 miles to the south of Galilee in Judea (see map on page 209). John was explicit in numbering the appearances, the first two apparently occurring a week apart in Jerusalem (if "that first day of the week" of John 20:19 corresponds to Resurrection Sunday) or no more than a day's walk from the city (Luke 24:13, 33 reports that the first appearance was in Jerusalem or on the road to nearby Emmaus) and the third by the Sea of Galilee some time later (John 21:1, 14). Given this timeline, then if Jesus did indeed appear to the disciples on a mountain in Galilee, he must have done so after the third appearance mentioned by John.

However, a straightforward reading of Matthew demands that Jesus first appeared to the disciples in Galilee. Even before his death, Jesus prophesied at the Last Supper in Matthew 26:32, "But after I have risen, I will go ahead of you into Galilee." After the resurrection, Jesus tells the women, "Then go quickly and tell his disciples: 'He has risen from the dead and is going ahead of you into Galilee'" (28:7). As they were running along to carry out his instructions, Jesus met them again, underscoring the same point: "Do not be afraid. Go and tell my brothers to go to Galilee; there they will see me" (28:10). If it was Jesus' intention to appear to the disciples in Jerusalem, why did he instruct them three times before appearing to them that they were to meet him in Galilee? Since he sent word to the disciples through the women, it is warranted to conclude he did not intend to see them first in Jerusalem, where he could have simply instructed them face-to-face to meet him in Galilee. Matthew's account of Jesus' first post-resurrection appearance, set in Galilee, reads, "When the Eleven saw him, they worshiped him; but some doubted" (Matthew 28:17), further suggesting that Jesus had not previously appeared to them— certainly not two or three times as the Gospel of John requires. In the second appearance in John, Thomas had already seen Jesus and had overcome his doubts: "My Lord and my God!" (John 20:28). For those who are here tempted to consult creative apologetic solutions to this problem, I ask whether it is likely, given Matthew's repeated emphasis on Galilee, that Matthew himself would accept any harmonization that places Jesus' first appearance in Jerusalem.

This is all troubling enough, but it gets worse. Not only does Luke not mention a Galilee appearance, but on the day of the resurrection in the environs of Jerusalem, Jesus tells his disciples, "I am going to send you what my Father has promised; but *stay in the city* **until** you have been clothed with power from on high" (Luke 24:49). There can be little doubt that Jesus is referring to the promise of the Holy Spirit, poured out at Pentecost after Jesus' Ascension in Acts 2. If this is so, then Jesus is in effect prohibiting the disciples from going to Galilee, directly contradicting his multiple instructions in Mark and Matthew.

Furthermore, there is evidence that Luke has tampered with his source account (Mark) to place the first appearance in Jerusalem rather than in Galilee. Consider the following parallel accounts of the events immediately following the resurrection:

Mt 26:32 "But after I have risen, I will go ahead of you into Galilee."

Mk 16:5 As they entered the tomb, they saw a young man dressed in a white robe sitting on the right side, and they were alarmed. 6"Don't be alarmed," he said. "You are looking for Jesus the Nazarene, who was crucified. *He has risen! He is not here.* See the place where they laid him. 7But go, tell his disciples and Peter, 'He is *going ahead of you into Galilee.* There you will see him, just as he told you.'"

Mt 28:2 There was a violent earthquake, for an angel of the Lord came down from heaven and, going to the tomb, rolled back the stone and sat on it. [3]His appearance was like lightning, and his clothes were white as snow. [4]The guards were so afraid of him that they shook and became like dead men. [5]The angel said to the women, "Do not be afraid, for I know that you are looking for Jesus, who was crucified. [6]*He is not here; he has risen,* just as he said. Come and see the place where he lay. [7]Then go quickly and tell his disciples: 'He has risen from the dead and is *going ahead of you into Galilee.* There you will see him.' Now I have told you."

Lk 24:4 While they were wondering about this, suddenly two men in clothes that gleamed like lightning stood beside them. [5]In their fright the women bowed down with their faces to the ground, but the men said to them, "Why do you look for the living among the dead? [6]*He is not here; he has risen!* Remember how he told you, *while he was still with you in Galilee:* [7]'The Son of Man must be delivered into the hands of sinful men, be crucified and on the third day be raised again.'" [8]Then they remembered his words.

Mt 28:10 Do not be afraid. Go and tell my brothers to *go to Galilee*; there they will see me.

Lk 24:49 "I am going to send you what my Father has promised; but *stay in the city [Jerusalem]* **until** you have been clothed with power from on high."

Jn 20:19 On the evening of that *first* day of the week, when the disciples were together, with the doors locked for fear of the Jews, Jesus came and stood among them and said, "Peace be with you!"[20]After he said this, he showed them his hands and side. The disciples were overjoyed when they saw the Lord.

Mt 28:16 Then the eleven disciples went to Galilee, to the mountain where Jesus had told them to go. [17]When they saw him, they worshiped him; but some doubted.

Acts 1:3 After his suffering, he showed himself to these men and gave many convincing proofs that he was alive. He appeared to them over a period of forty days and spoke about the kingdom of God. [4]On one occasion, while he was eating with them, he gave them this command: "*Do not leave Jerusalem,* but wait for the gift my Father promised, which you have heard me speak about.

Jn 20:26 *A week later* his disciples were in the house again, and Thomas was with them. Though the doors were locked, Jesus came and stood among them and said, "Peace be with you!" [27]Then he said to Thomas, "Put your finger here; see my hands. Reach out your hand and put it into my side. Stop doubting and believe." [28]Thomas said to him, "My Lord and my God!"

Jn 21:12 Jesus said to them, "Come and have breakfast." None of the disciples dared ask him, "Who are you?" They knew it was the Lord. [13]Jesus came. . . . [14]This was now the *third* time Jesus appeared to his disciples after he was raised from the dead.

Note how the (first three) synoptic accounts are tightly bound in virtually every detail until Luke changes Mark's wording (Mark is generally agreed to be a source for the other two synoptic Gospels) from

"He is going ahead of you into Galilee" to "Remember how he told you, while he was still with you in Galilee . . ." What is Luke's purpose for mentioning Galilee? Standing alone, it is a very incidental detail. It hardly seems to matter whether Jesus told them these things in Galilee or Judea. But if Luke was using Mark as a source, and if he preferred Jesus' first appearance to be in Jerusalem rather than in Galilee, then he could have arranged this while preserving the original mention of Galilee by transforming Jesus' instructions to go to Galilee into a historical speech that happened to be located in Galilee.

I have already noted the lengths to which Matthew goes to place the first appearance in Galilee and the lengths to which Luke goes to insist on an initial Jerusalem appearance to the exclusion of any other appearance, so it should not be surprising that Luke would purposefully manipulate his source text in this case to put aside the idea of a Galilean appearance. I want to underscore again the correspondence in detail in this passage among the synoptic Gospels, suggesting that they are drawing from a common source (likely from Mark), except in this case, where a specific geographical location is mentioned. It would be difficult to pass this off as a coincidence. Though it cannot be proven with any certainty, it appears that Luke may be deliberately bending the narrative to some end and that the historicity of this account is suspect.

When viewed from a historical-critical perspective, there are numerous other examples of such apparent alterations in the gospel, reflecting the particular motives of the authors within the context of the early church. This is likely the case in the very next verse:

> Trembling and bewildered, the women went out and fled from the tomb. *They said nothing to anyone*, because they were afraid (Mark 16:8).

> So the women hurried away from the tomb, afraid *yet* filled with joy, and *ran to tell his disciples* (Matthew 24:8).

It is generally recognized (even by the conservative translators of the New International Version) that the second half of Mark 16 (after verse 8) constitutes a much later scribal addition to the original text. So "They said nothing to anyone, because they were afraid" is how it all ends according to Mark, who may have been explaining why no one had yet heard of the empty tomb up until the time of Mark's writing. Notice how Matthew skips on from the word *afraid* in Mark, fleshing it out into a positive account that is at odds with Mark's: "afraid *yet* filled with joy, and ran to tell his disciples." Matthew, writing later than Mark, after the story has had more time to spread and progress, turns Mark's abrupt ending into a full-fledged resurrection account.

Some might take exception to this analysis, figuring my heart is already bent against belief and prone to look for the negatives, unwilling to consider any possible harmonization. Even if this is so, could it not also be that those who try to force Matthew to allow for an initial Jerusalem appearance are not reading according to Matthew's intentions but are feeding their prior judgments into the text? Anyone unfamiliar with the story and reading it for the first time would most certainly conclude on the basis of Matthew that Jesus first appeared to the disciples in Galilee.

If a man claimed to have run a one-minute mile (with or without God's help), we would demand precise, irrefutable evidence of the feat before accepting his claim. We would demand to see him do it with our own eyes, we would use two stopwatches, we would record it on camera, we would look at it from every angle to preclude the possibility of foul play, and only then would we be willing to accept it. Does this make us into pitiable Doubting Thomases? I don't think so. If a man claimed to have run a four-minute mile, I would require less proof than for the one-minute mile, because I know a four-minute mile, while an exploit in itself, is within the realm of natural possibility. But in the case of Jesus' resurrection, we do not have the ability to go back and verify the details beyond a shadow of a doubt; all we have are anonymous accounts which at times draw from each other and at other times diverge so completely that they cannot agree whether Jesus first appeared to his disciples at the northern or southern end of Palestine.

ARGUMENTS FOR THE RESURRECTION

I will round out this brief examination of the resurrection by addressing three common arguments made in its favor. First, it is often claimed that the disciples' willingness to die for their faith in Jesus' resurrection proves that they actually saw the risen Jesus. People are never willing to die for what they *know* to be untrue (McDowell 1979, 246). But the assertion that Jesus' disciples died for their faith has no historical foundation; it is mere hearsay, as Bart Ehrman informs us:

> And an earlier point that Bill made was that the disciples were all willing to die for their faith. I didn't hear one piece of evidence for that. I hear that claim a lot, but having read every Christian source from the first five hundred years of Christianity, I'd like him to tell us what the piece of evidence is that the disciples died for their belief in the resurrection (Craig and Ehrman 2006, 28–29).

What Erhman is saying is that we have no historical grounding for the martyrdom of even one of Jesus' disciples. All details regarding their manner of dying emerge years later in accounts that are far removed from the actual events. Even if it could be proven historically that some of the earliest disciples were martyred, we would still be unable to look into their minds and know they died *specifically* for their belief in Jesus' resurrection.

Joseph Smith was murdered by a mob in 1844 in Nauvoo, Illinois. Latter Day Saints believe he was martyred for his unwavering conviction that God revealed himself through golden tablets that Smith had discovered in 1830. Many non-Mormons believe he was killed because he was a criminal. If the facts are so readily disputed for a relatively recent and well-documented event like Joseph Smith's death, how can we say with any confidence how or why Jesus' disciples perished, let alone what was in their minds when they died?

Second, it is claimed that Jesus' disciples could not have experienced a mass hallucination to convince them of Jesus' resurrection. Apologist Gary Habermas makes the argument as follows:

> Hallucinations are individual occurrences. By their very nature only one person can see a given hallucination at a time. They certainly are not something which can be seen by a group of people. . . . Since an hallucination exists only in this subjective, personal sense, it is obvious that others cannot witness it (Habermas 2001).

This may be obvious to Habermas, but in fact such occurrences are historically well documented. Mass sightings of the Virgin Mary are common, and as a Protestant, Habermas is unlikely to attribute all of them to actual manifestations of Mary. For example, on June 24, 1981, six children reported an appearance of the Virgin at a hilltop near the town of Medjugorje in Bosnia-Hercegovina. She has continued appearing regularly to these individuals since that time, and millions of others have made their pilgrimages to the site to experience visions, healings, and other supernatural events. Could it be that the power of suggestion is at play? (Sullivan 2004, 18-22); ("Overview of Medjugorje" 2006); (Horner and Barker 1996)

Note that I am not here arguing that Jesus' followers *necessarily* experienced a mass hallucination, but I am merely establishing its *possibility,* contrary to the assertions of resurrection apologists.

Third, it is claimed that if the anti-Christian Jewish authorities had wished to disprove Jesus' resurrection, they could have simply exhumed Jesus' body and paraded him through the streets of Jerusalem for all to see

(McDowell 1979, 246–47). However, the New Testament mentions no public proclamation of Jesus' resurrection until seven "short weeks"[63] (McDowell 1979, 246) after Jesus' alleged resurrection. If there was concern about the deterioration of Lazarus' body just four days after his death (John 11:39), then Jesus' body must have been unrecognizable after seven weeks. Parading such a decomposed body through the streets of Jerusalem would have proven nothing (Price and Lowder 2005, 427).

Apologists have advanced a number of other arguments in favor of Jesus' resurrection: 1 Corinthians 15:3 preserves an early tradition of the resurrection; there were no competing burial traditions other than the one presented in the Gospels; there was no early tomb veneration site; no one making up a story at that time would make women into the first eyewitnesses; there was no precedent in Jewish thinking for such an event as Jesus' resurrection (and therefore it must not have been made up); and so on. Robert Price takes apart each of these arguments in his provocative collection of essays entitled *Jesus is Dead* (Price 2007).

For those who have read only one perspective on the resurrection (for example, C. S. Lewis, Frank Morrison, Josh McDowell, N. T. Wright, William Lane Craig, Gary Habermas, Lee Strobel, and Mike Licona) and who feel confident that all skeptics willfully ignore the facts to their eternal detriment, I would recommend some alternate readings as a counterbalance. A good start would be the collection of essays in *The Empty Tomb: Jesus Beyond the Grave* (Price and Lowder 2005), or, for a ready online resource, chapter 6 of *Beyond Born Again: Towards Evangelical Maturity* (Price 1993). I also recommend the online video debate "Licona vs. Carrier: On the Resurrection of Jesus Christ" (Licona and Carrier 2004).

---

[63] See Acts 2:1, 24. Pentecost, the Feast of Weeks, fell on the fiftieth day after Passover (Deuteronomy 16:1-12).

Chapter 12

The Reliability of the Bible

In addition to the wonder of fulfilled prophecies, when I was a believer there were several other factors that contributed to my considering the Bible divinely inspired. These included the sublime teachings of Jesus, the beauty and truth of the gospel, the apparent trustworthiness of the scriptural authors, and the unity and historical reliability of the Bible. In this chapter I examine each of these oft-cited reasons for believing.

The Bible is a big book (or collection of books), about which more has been written than any other book. I cannot hope to address every relevant aspect of the scriptures in this single chapter, so I will have to limit myself to a few highlights. Each section of this chapter will address a different argument in favor of the reliability and divine inspiration of the Bible.

THE UNITY OF THE BIBLE

As a Christian I often heard one variant or another of the following argument in favor of biblical inspiration:

> By any standards, the Bible is a remarkable document. It was written over the course of many years by dozens of men from diverse walks of life—men in different countries and educated at various levels. Yet, despite all these differences, the Bible presents a consistent message from beginning to end. Why? Christians believe it is because the authors wrote the Bible as they were led by God. This amazing consistency is evidence the Bible is of a supernatural nature (Howse 2005, 191).

However, given the long, convoluted, and nonunanimous process by which the scriptural canon was selected, any unity to be found among its composite books does not demand a supernatural explanation. Despite evangelical scholar F. F. Bruce's insistence to the contrary ("There is a unity that binds the whole together. An anthology is compiled by an anthologist, but no anthologist compiled the Bible" (Howse 2005, 191)), the Bible as we currently know it was in fact compiled by men.

It was not compiled by a single person on a single occasion. In fact, no one denies that its individual books were carefully considered for inclusion in the canon by various groups of men who debated the matter over a period of several hundred years. Nor does anyone deny that there were disagreements among various Christian scholars about which books to include or exclude. The books that now constitute our Protestant Bible were successively weeded out from a much larger corpus of religious material. Books that had not reached a certain level of prominence within the religious community or whose teachings diverged significantly from established theology were simply ignored. Others that were only marginally at odds with the orthodoxy of the day were hotly debated, some becoming part of the deuterocanonical or apocryphal literature.

The claim that the Bible displays supernatural unity fails for the following reasons: (a) the sixty-six books of the Protestant Bible were not the only Jewish books written in their time; (b) each successive writer generally drew from earlier accepted writings and traditions; and (c) a human selection process existed to guarantee some degree of unity among the selected texts. (The differing canons of the Catholic, Protestant and Orthodox churches alone should give pause to those who hold to the perfect unity of the Bible. Which Bible is the truly unified one?)

What is more, the level of unity of the biblical text assumed in this claim cannot be taken for granted; indeed, it appears to depend on the eye of the beholder. Muslims will tell us it is not a unified book, as will liberal Christians, atheists, and Hindus—virtually anyone who is not a conservative Christian. Even the latter will acknowledge there are differences in the teachings of various books of the Bible but will insist they are a unified whole when understood using the correct hermeneutic.

For example, the Old Testament enjoins its readers to stone to death those who would entice us to worship anyone but Yahweh, or any son who rebels against his parents, or anyone who gathers wood on the Sabbath. The New Testament takes a softer line (at least on the question of Sabbath breaking, though it nowhere abrogates the teaching against stoning heretics). The Torah of the Old Testament contains a litany of over 600 laws governing every imaginable detail of everyday life—leprosy, menstrual cycles, mold, excrement, warfare, livestock, clothing material, and diet, to name a few—many of which are set aside or ignored by the

New Testament or by later Christian theologians. This is true even of decrees that were declared to be eternal:

> "This shall be a *permanent* statute [NIV: 'lasting ordinance'] for you: in the seventh month, on the tenth day of the month, you shall humble your souls and not do any work, whether the native, or the alien who sojourns among you; for it is on this day that atonement shall be made for you to cleanse you; you will be clean from all your sins before the LORD. . . . Now you shall have this as a *permanent* statute, to make atonement for the sons of Israel for all their sins once every year." And just as the LORD had commanded Moses, so he did (Leviticus 16:29–30, 34, NASB).

> By calling this covenant "new," he has made the first one obsolete; and what is obsolete and aging will soon disappear (Hebrews 8:13).[64]

Whether the New Testament authors or later theologians were justified in setting aside the Old Covenant is not my focus here; the scriptural and theological rationale for replacing it with the New Covenant is beside the point. I simply wish to challenge the claim that the Bible presents a unified front and that its teachings are consistent across the hundreds of years of its composition process. Those who personally consider it a cohesive book tied together by the story of redemption and who offer a hermeneutic by which to explain the contrasts found in its teachings ought not, in the face of its many discrepancies, expect the wider world to grant their assertion that the Bible is a unified whole.

---

[64] The author of Hebrews is here referring to the new covenant in Jeremiah 31:31-34, which Christians believe applies to Christianity itself. This is a questionable reading, as the larger context of Jeremiah makes it clear he was referring to a renewed commitment to Yahweh on the part of the exiles ("remnant") returning to Israel from Babylon, not to a new covenant ushered in through the Messiah's death:

A nation from the north will attack her and lay waste her land. No one will live in it; both men and animals will flee away. "In those days, at that time," declares the LORD, "the people of Israel and the people of Judah together will go in tears to seek the LORD their God. They will ask the way to Zion and turn their faces toward it. They will come and bind themselves to the LORD in an *everlasting covenant* that will not be forgotten." . . . Therefore this is what the LORD Almighty, the God of Israel, says: ". . . I will bring Israel back to his own pasture and he will graze on Carmel and Bashan; his appetite will be satisfied on the hills of Ephraim and Gilead. In those days, at that time," declares the LORD, "search will be made for Israel's guilt, but there will be none, and for the sins of Judah, but none will be found, for I will forgive the remnant I spare" (Jeremiah 50:3–5, 18a, 19–20). See Sandoval 2008.

There are many other well-known biblical contradictions (referred to by inerrantists as alleged or apparent discrepancies), and I do not wish to tire my readers with a large number, so I will present only a small sampling here.

Before discussing these passages I wish to head off some common reactions I anticipate to encounter. The first is, "How dare you second guess God!" I have previously addressed this objection, but will say again that this improperly assumes from the outset that the Bible, though written by men, is or contains the very words of God.

Second, "These apparent discrepancies have already been addressed adequately a thousand times. Why are you hell bent on not accepting these perfectly good explanations?" The reason I do not uncritically accept these explanations is that they have been developed by *human* apologists attempting to defend their a priori conviction that the Bible contains no errors or contradictions. Why, indeed, does God need ambassadors to explain how apparent contradictions are really nothing of the sort? There is no a priori reason to think that Christian apologists like J. P. Holding or John Haley should be right simply by virtue of their Christianity, while skeptics like Farrell Till or Robert Price should be wrong simply by virtue of their skepticism. Moreover, why is it more laudable to accept the sometimes convoluted attempts of human inerrantists to harmonize *apparent* contradictions than to accept that what is "apparent" is, in fact, real? Why insist on solving the apparent contradictions of the Bible rather than those of the Qur'an? On what grounds are we to give the Bible the benefit of the doubt?

In short, why should we prefer to listen to the apologists, who propose a third unstated way of seeing two contradictory texts (an approach that Robertson McQuilken, former president of Columbia Bible College, termed "finding the center of biblical tension," which I take as an unwitting acknowledgement of biblical disunity), than to acknowledge the face value of the divergent teachings of the different authors? By accepting the apologists' nonbiblical work-arounds, we undermine the teachings of the individual authors, showing disregard for their intentions in favor of apologetic harmonizations foreign to the text—all under the guise of upholding the authority of the text. (I am indebted to Robert Price for some of these observations.)

Third, "These passages are taken out of context." In response, I would gladly include more context, but I do not have room in this book to include it all. Instead, I provide references for those who wish to read the verses in context, but I do not believe it will in any way help the case for inerrancy.

I compiled most of the following sets of passages during my college crisis but somehow managed to explain them away for over a decade, until they and many others caught my attention while later rereading through the Bible in Africa. I have included my rejoinder to some of the common resolutions put forward by inerrantist apologists for these discrepancies. As Gleason Archer's *Encyclopedia of Bible Difficulties* (Archer 1982) is perhaps the best-known reference of the biblical inerrancy movement, I engage his explanations where applicable.

Are children to be punished for their parents' sins?

> You show love to thousands but bring the punishment for the fathers' sins into the laps of their children after them. O great and powerful God, whose name is the LORD Almighty (Jeremiah 32:18).

> The soul who sins is the one who will die. The son will not share the guilt of the father, nor will the father share the guilt of the son. The righteousness of the righteous man will be credited to him, and the wickedness of the wicked will be charged against him (Ezekiel 18:20).

Archer maintains that not inflicting punishment for the sins of one's forebears is a general principle of human governance, but that God himself reserves the right to override this principle in specific instances as he sees fit. Despite the several Old Testament incidents in which God commanded his servants to kill individuals or groups because of the sins of their fathers, Archer attempts to exonerate God and his servants by appealing to God's prerogative to abrogate the general principle stated in Ezekiel 18 and Deuteronomy 24. But read all of Ezekiel 18: this is a long argument detailing precisely why it is unjust to kill a man for the sins of his fathers. It is rooted in a general moral principle that a man is responsible for his own actions and not for those of others. Certainly Archer is free to maintain that the Sovereign God has the right to do as he pleases, but then I am also free to maintain that in doing so, God violates his own moral principles laid out in Ezekiel 18. (Note: When I refer to "God" here, I am not in my mind referring to any actual god who really commanded these things, but to the biblical writers' *conception* of their god and his actions and commandments.)

In most of the Old Testament incidents in which children were killed for the sins of their parents (for example, Achan's family in Joshua 7), it was not God himself who inflicted the punishment, but instead God's delegates. What Archer wants us to believe is that an immoral action can become moral if God commands his servants to perform it. Let's say a Christian leader today felt God was telling him to commit adultery. Few evangelicals would believe it was really God's voice since God has prohibited adultery. But if he can make exceptions to the rule against killing sons for the sins of their fathers, why not also for the rule against adultery? Is adultery worse than murder? Whenever I have heard a sermon about how to discern God's will for our lives, the pastor has *always* exhorted us, "God will never tell you to do anything contrary to what is written in the Bible, the Word of God." But Archer would like us to accept the opposite: that God can say one thing in one passage and then ask his servants to violate his commandment in another.

Did God command child sacrifice?

> You must give me [the LORD] the firstborn of your sons. Do the same with your cattle and your sheep. Let them stay with their mothers for seven days, but give them to me on the eighth day (Exodus 22:29b–30).

> Then God said, "Take your son, your only son, Isaac, whom you love, and go to the region of Moriah. Sacrifice him there as a burnt offering on one of the mountains I will tell you about" (Genesis 22:2).

> Also I swore to them in the wilderness that I would scatter them among the nations and disperse them among the lands, because they had not observed My ordinances, but had rejected My statutes and had profaned My sabbaths, and their eyes were on the idols of their fathers. I also *gave them statutes that were not good* and ordinances by which they could not live; and I pronounced them unclean because of their gifts, in that *they caused all their firstborn to pass through the fire so that I might make them desolate*, in order that they might know that I am the LORD (Ezekiel 20:23–26, NASB).

> They have built the high places of Baal to burn their sons in the fire as offerings to Baal—*something I did not command or mention, nor did it enter my mind.* So beware, the days are coming, declares the LORD, when people will no longer call this place Topheth or the Valley of Ben Hinnom, but the Valley of Slaughter (Jeremiah 19:5-6).

Though child sacrifice has been considered an abomination in Jewish and Christian tradition since the time of the biblical prophets, the question was not as clear cut in earlier times. We instinctively recoil in horror against the very thought of it in our era, but offering one's child to God was apparently a live option in the days of Abraham (Genesis 21) and Jephthah (Judges 11). Indeed, God required the offering of every firstborn son (Exodus 22:29), even if elsewhere he provided a way out of the child sacrifice requirement, benefiting the priests who received substitute offerings of animal meat or silver (Exodus 13:13; Numbers 3:40-41). Jeremiah's assertion that it did not even enter God's mind to command child sacrifice stands in contrast to (a) the Abraham and Isaac narrative, (b)

God's law to offer all firstborn sons, and (c) Ezekiel's view that God's statutes that were "not good."

Biblical inerrantist Evans Criswell attempts to absolve God of any responsibility for unjust child sacrifice laws by appealing to alternate modern translations of Ezekiel 20:25 (Criswell 2001). Though the KJV and the RSV are in agreement with the NASB cited above, the NIV reads as follows:

> I also gave them over to statutes that were not good and laws they could not live by.

If this translation is correct, then God did not directly give them these statutes; he merely "gave them over" to these heinous acts as punishment for their own rebellion. Criswell maintains this is analogous to desperate parents of rebellious children leaving them to their own devices. Yet the NIV has God playing a decidedly more active role in the Israelites' deeds than an exasperated parent who lets go of the reins: *he deliberately hands them over to these statutes.*

But the NIV translation is not correct, so Criswell's argument, even if valid, is moot. Liberal Christian Thom Stark examines the original Hebrew, rather than the modern translations, offering this analysis:

> The NIV intentionally mistranslates the verb here, rendering the clause, "I gave them over to statues that were not good." This is a deceitful attempt to protect Yahweh's character from the implications of Yahweh's "inspired" scriptures. The verb in the Hebrew is *natan*, "to give." In the Hebrew, the indirect object is "them" and the object of the verb is "statutes." The NIV makes "them" the object of the verb and makes the statutes the receivers of the action. The NIV does this with absolutely ZERO exegetical warrant. It's a purely theologically motivated distortion of the text. Shame (Stark 2009; emphasis in original).

For a more complete discussion of child sacrifice in Israel, see John Joseph Collins' *Encounters with Biblical Theology*, whose text is available online through Google Books (Collins 2005, 50–58). For another helpful introduction to this topic, see John Loftus' *Why I Became an Atheist* (Loftus 2008, 136).

Does God tempt anyone, or are we tempted by our own desires?

> Finally, a spirit came forward, stood before the LORD and said, "I will entice him [King Ahab]." "By what means?" the LORD asked. "I will go out and be a lying spirit in the mouths of all his prophets," he said. "You will succeed in enticing him," said the LORD. "Go and do it" (1 Kings 22:21–22).

When tempted, no one should say, "God is tempting me." For God cannot be tempted by evil, nor does he tempt anyone; but each one is tempted when, by his own evil desire, he is dragged away and enticed (James 1:13–14).

Some assert it wasn't God who tempted or lied to King Ahab directly in 1 Kings 22; therefore, this passage does not directly contradict James 1:14. But if I were to hire a hit man to kill my enemy and then claimed, "I didn't kill the guy directly," my plea would stand little chance of vindicating myself in a court of law. Whether I killed him directly or by proxy, I was to blame for the crime. Those who attempt to explain away 1 Kings 22:21–22 in this way should ask themselves whether they are more interested in salvaging the doctrine of inerrancy than in coming to terms with the truth.

Did God or Satan incite David to take a census?

Again the anger of the LORD burned against Israel, and he incited David against them, saying, "Go and take a census of Israel and Judah" (2 Samuel 24:1).

Satan rose up against Israel and incited David to take a census of Israel (1 Chronicles 21:1).

Archer (Archer 1982, 186–188) explains away this discrepancy by proposing that both God and Satan were involved in inciting David to take the census. For example, just as God and Satan participated together in Job's testings—God intending them ultimately for good and Satan for evil—so both God and Satan were involved in David's decision to take the census. But if Archer wishes to implicate God in these affairs, he must acknowledge that God is involved in tempting his children, contrary to James 1:14, which states that God does not tempt anyone. Some may prefer to use the word *testing* rather than *tempting*, but given the context of David's census (which was considered a sin), is there any practical difference between the two words? Whether we choose to say "test," "incite," or "tempt," it's all the same. What comfort is James 1:14 to us if God can in fact "incite" or "test" us, and we, like David, can end up failing the test?

Are iron chariots an impediment to God's power?

On the plains of Moab by the Jordan across from Jericho the LORD said to Moses, "Speak to the Israelites and say to them: 'When you cross the Jordan into Canaan, drive out *all* the inhabitants of the land before you. Destroy all their carved images and their cast idols, and demolish all their high places.

Take possession of the land and settle in it, for I *have given you* the land to possess.'" (Numbers 33:50–53).

But Joshua said to the house of Joseph—to Ephraim and Manasseh—"You are numerous and very powerful. You will have not only one allotment but the forested hill country as well. Clear it, and its farthest limits will be yours; though the Canaanites have iron chariots and though they are strong, you can drive them out" (Joshua 17:17–18).

The LORD was with the men of Judah. They took possession of the hill country, but they were unable to drive the people from the plains, because they had iron chariots (Judges 1:19).

Apologist George Konig concludes that God intended for the men of Judah to take the hill country but not the plains at that time (Konig 2001–2008). However, God had earlier commanded them to drive out *all* the inhabitants of the land, and later chastised them for not completing the job and sparing a remnant of Canaanites. If God did not intend for them to take the plains at that time, why does the text omit that fact, and why does it instead focus on the proximate cause, the inability of the Judahites to contend with iron chariots? Why is it more praiseworthy to seek out or invent a dubious, unstated premise (that God did not want the men to take the plains at that time) than to perceive a contradiction among the statements in Numbers, Joshua and Judges?

Did God approve of Jehu's massacre at Jezreel?

The LORD said to Jehu, "Because you have done well in accomplishing what is right in my eyes and have done to the house of Ahab [Jehu massacred them all in Jezreel; see 2 Kings 10:11] all I had in mind to do, your descendants will sit on the throne of Israel to the fourth generation" (2 Kings 10:30).

Then the LORD said to Hosea, "Call him Jezreel, because I will soon punish the house of Jehu for the massacre at Jezreel, and I will put an end to the kingdom of Israel" (Hosea 1:4).

Archer maintains God approved of Jehu's actions but not his motives: "Although Jehu had only done what God had commanded, he did so out of a carnal zeal that was tainted with protective self-interest" (Archer 1982, 207–09). This, Archer supposes, explains why God approves of Jehu's actions in 2 Kings but not in Hosea 1:4. But does Hosea offer any hint of such an explanation? No. Taken at face value, Hosea is referring to the act of the massacre, not to Jehu's disposition in carrying it out. This is a typical example of the tendency of apologists to invent elements foreign to the text merely to preserve the doctrine of inerrancy. What if (as it would appear to those without a prior theological agenda) Hosea truly saw the massacre in a different light from the author of 2 Kings? If so, this fact would be lost to Archer as a result of his attempt to make all the parallel accounts agree. In so doing, Archer tramples on Hosea's clearly expressed opinion.

Is it possible for true believers to lose their salvation, and will they as a result be swiftly destroyed?

> And you also were included in Christ when you heard the word of truth, the gospel of your salvation. Having believed, you were marked in him with a *seal*, the promised Holy Spirit, who is a deposit *guaranteeing* our inheritance until the redemption of those who are God's possession—to the praise of his glory (Ephesians 1:13–14).

> Now, *brothers*, I want to remind you of the gospel I preached to you, which you received and on which you have taken your stand. By this gospel you are saved, *if* you hold firmly to the word I preached to you. Otherwise, you have *believed in vain* (1 Corinthians 15:1–2).

> But there were also false prophets among the people, just as there will be false teachers among you. They will secretly introduce destructive heresies, even denying the sovereign Lord who *bought* them—bringing swift destruction on themselves (2 Peter 2:1).

There is a long history of debate between earnest, pious Calvinists (for example, Presbyterians) and Arminians (for example, Methodists) over the question of "eternal security." If God purchased his elect through the blood of Christ, can they then turn around and deny him, as 2 Peter suggests, or are those who trust him guaranteed an inheritance with Christ, as Ephesians suggests? These two passages are but a representative sample of the many verses that both camps use to support their position. If the Bible had spoken with one voice on this question, it would not have been possible for these two opposing camps to arise. One of my seminary professors, a Calvinist, admitted the 2 Peter 2 passage was "a problem for the Calvinist position," one for which he had no answer.

Semi-Calvinists who accept eternal security but not predestination or limited atonement might conclude that Christ "bought" these apostates in a general sense, in that he died for the whole world, and that these false prophets never were truly saved. But it becomes trickier to get around Paul's teaching in 1 Corinthians 15:1–2. The implication of this passage is that you cannot know whether your belief is efficacious until you take your last breath, having successfully held firm until the end. If you give up your faith before your earthly journey is up, heaven is not your destiny.

Does God condone wealth?

> I walk in the way of righteousness, along the paths of justice, bestowing wealth on those who love me and making their treasuries full (Proverbs 8:20–21).

> In the same way, any of you who does not give up everything he has cannot be my disciple (Luke 14:33).

The most common harmonization of this discrepancy is to assert it isn't wealth in itself that Jesus opposes, but one's improper attitude toward wealth. But go back and read the selection of teachings on wealth in the book of Luke cited in my chapter 8. Jesus was unequivocal in Luke, requiring his followers to abandon their possessions and give to the poor; he was not merely talking about a state of mind. This was a reasonable stance under the expectation of Jesus' imminent return, but is not practical over multiple generations.

Is there a conscious afterlife?

> No one remembers you when he is dead. Who praises you from the grave (Psalm 6:5)?

> It is not the dead who praise the LORD, those who go down to silence (Psalm 115:17).

> After this I heard what sounded like the roar of a great multitude in heaven shouting: "Hallelujah! Salvation and glory and power belong to our God, for true and just are his judgments (Revelation 19:1–2).

Has anyone seen God and lived?

> "But," he said, "you cannot see my face, for no one may see me and live." Then the LORD said, "There is a place near me where you may stand on a rock. When my glory passes by, I will put you in a cleft in the rock and cover you with my hand until I have passed by. Then I will remove my hand and you will see my back; but my face must not be seen" (Exodus 20:20–23).

> So Jacob called the place Peniel, saying, "It is because I saw God face to face, and yet my life was spared" (Genesis 32:30).

> In the year that King Uzziah died, I [Isaiah] saw the Lord sitting on a throne, high and lifted up, and the train of His robe filled the temple (Isaiah 6:1).

> No one has seen God at any time; the only begotten God who is in the bosom of the Father, He has explained Him (John 1:18 NASB).

Apologist Clay Willis (Willis n.d.) contends that the several instances of human-divine contact in the Old Testament were in actual fact incarnations of Jesus (the Second Person of the Trinity), and not of God the Father (the First Person of the Trinity). Many humans have seen Jesus, but not God the Father. But this explanation is strained. If, as the doctrine of the Trinity supposes, Jesus is God, then the assertion of John 1:18 that no one has seen God is untrue. Later in John (14:9), Jesus informs Philip, "Anyone who has seen me has seen the Father." Also, the word Elohim is used for God in Genesis 32:30 and in other visitations, providing no indication that this was someone other than the Almighty, whom the early Jews believed to have a body. For example, he walked in the Garden of Eden (Genesis 3); bore sons (Genesis 6); visited and ate with Abraham (Genesis 18); and possessed a face, hand and back (Exodus 20:23).

There is no indication in the text that this was a pre-incarnation of the Second Person of the Trinity; this is simply an apologetic invention to circumvent two uncomfortable facts: (a) the early Jews believed God had a body, and (b) there are contradictory statements in the Bible concerning whether anyone has seen God.

Are we to make vows?

Make vows to the LORD your God and fulfill them; let all the neighboring lands bring gifts to the One to be feared (Psalm 76:11).

But I tell you, Do not swear at all. . . . Simply let your "Yes" be "Yes," and your "No," "No"; anything beyond this comes from the evil one. (Matthew 5:34, 37).

Was Jesus divine?

As Jesus started on his way, a man ran up to him and fell on his knees before him. "Good teacher," he asked, "what must I do to inherit eternal life?" "Why do you call me good?" Jesus answered. "No one is good—except God alone" (Mark 10:17–18).

In the beginning was the Word, and the Word was with God, and the Word was God (John 1:1).

Anyone who has seen me has seen the Father (John 14:9).

The most common Trinitarian explanation of the Mark passage is that Jesus is in fact claiming to be God when he declares that no one is good but God. Yet nowhere else in the book of Mark is Jesus said to be divine, so the context supports the most natural reading, namely, that Jesus was denying his perfection out of modesty. In contrast to the Gospel of John, Mark makes no attempt to explain why John the Baptist should need to baptize Jesus (baptism being seen as a symbol of repentance for sins). Matthew understood the embarrassing implications of Mark 10:18 and deliberately reworded the dialogue to avoid any indication that Jesus might not be absolutely perfect. Robert Price analyzes this Christological progression as follows:

> In 3:1, introducing [John the] Baptist, he [Matthew] omits from his Markan text the description of the rite as a baptism of repentance for the forgiveness of sins [Mark 1:4], as if there might possibly be some other reason for showing up. . . .

> Matthew alters this interchange [of Mark 10:17–18] so that it reads, "Teacher, what *good* deed [not, 'Good Teacher'] must I do to have eternal life?" "Why do you ask me concerning what is *good*? [In Mark, the interrogator only asked about eternal life, not about what is good.] One there is who is good" (Matt. 19:16–17). So Jesus is not flattered and need not repudiate it. Nor does he deny his own goodness, which is for Matthew the operative concern. The trend here is evident (Price 2003, 118–19; emphasis and comments added).

Are works necessary for salvation?

> For it is by grace you have been saved, through faith—and this not from yourselves, it is the gift of God—not by works, so that no one can boast (Ephesians 2:8, 9).

> You see that a person is justified by what he does and not by faith alone (James 2:24).

Archer (Archer 1982, 395) offers the standard Protestant harmonization of the tension between Paul and James:

> Those who are truly saved receive Christ Himself (John 1:12) as Savior and Lord (Rom. 10:9–10); and from the dynamic of His indwelling Spirit (Col. 3:1–4), will produce works of righteousness and goodness that will manifest the life of Christ within us. . . . Nevertheless it remains true that man contributes nothing substantive toward his salvation (Archer 1982, 394).

But the Reformation cry of "Faith alone!" did not square well with James' insistence on justification through both faith *and* works, as evidenced by Martin Luther's calling into question the canonicity of James, "an epistle of straw." To pretend there is no conflict between Paul and James is to trivialize the struggle that led Luther to this conclusion. James was apparently responding to a notion in circulation that justification was to be had only through faith. There can be little doubt that this notion came from Paul's teachings and that James was directly responding to Paul. But there are larger questions at stake: Do our works flow from our faith as a matter of course, or do we have to expend our own effort to produce works? If our works flow from our faith, why does the New Testament exhort us to produce good works? How will these works come about if *we* do not produce them through *our* efforts? Good works are never automatic, even for those whose faith never wavers: if you don't make the effort to do anything, nothing happens. But if we must expend our effort to produce good works, and if, as James insists, good works are necessary for our justification, then our justification is based at least in part on our efforts, which is anathema to Protestant theology. C. S. Lewis, in a 1950 letter to his friend Sheldon Vanauken, supplied perhaps the most hopeful way out of this dilemma:

> The contradiction "we must have faith to believe and must believe to have faith" belongs to the same class as those by which the Eleatic philosophers proved that all motion was impossible. And there are many others. You can't swim unless you can support yourself in water & you can't support yourself in the water unless you can swim. Or again, in an act of volition (e.g., getting up in the morning) is the very beginning of the act itself voluntary or involuntary? If voluntary then you must have willed it, therefore you were willing already, therefore it was not really the beginning. If involuntary, then the continuation of the act (being determined by the first moment) is involuntary too. But in spite of this we *do* swim, & we *do* get out of bed (Lindskoog 2001, 394).

In this light the diverging teachings of Paul and James do not constitute an irrefutable contradiction on an esoteric theoretical level, but on a practical level, if I must expend effort to produce works to show I have faith (because the works don't simply happen on their own, even if I have faith), then in what sense can it be said that my salvation is free? "Here, child, take this candy—it's completely free! Oh, but there's a small catch: if you're truly grateful for my free gift, you'll show your gratitude by working in my field for an hour; otherwise, your refusal to work in my field will show you're not grateful, and I don't give free gifts to ungrateful children, so the candy won't be yours." C. S. Lewis effectively punted on this question when he stated, "It looks as if in one sense we do nothing, and in another case we do a damned lot" (Lewis 1970, 55).

Is divorce permissible for any reason?

> If a man happens to meet a virgin who is not pledged to be married and rapes her and they are discovered, he shall pay the girl's father fifty shekels of silver. He must marry the girl, for he has violated her. He can never divorce her as long as he lives (Deuteronomy 22:28–29).

> When you go to war against your enemies and the LORD your God delivers them into your hands and you take captives, if you notice among the captives a beautiful woman and are attracted to her, you may take her as your wife.... If you are not pleased with her, let her go wherever she wishes [NKJV: "set her free"] (Deuteronomy 21:10–11, 14).

> Then Shecaniah son of Jehiel, one of the descendants of Elam, said to Ezra, "We have been unfaithful to our God by marrying foreign women from the peoples around us. But in spite of this, there is still hope for Israel. Now let us make a covenant before our God to send away all these women and their children, in accordance with the counsel of my lord and of those who fear the commands of our God. Let it be done according to the Law" (Ezra 10:2–3).

> "I hate divorce," says the LORD God of Israel (Malachi 2:16).

> He answered, "Anyone who divorces his wife and marries another woman commits adultery against her. And if she divorces her husband and marries another man, she commits adultery" (Mark 10:11–12).

> I tell you that anyone who divorces his wife, *except for marital unfaithfulness*, and marries another woman commits adultery (Matthew 19:9).

Archer (Archer 1982, 151–52) discusses the more commonly quoted Deuteronomy 24:16 passage and concludes that divorce was permitted only as a concession to the hardness of the Israelites' hearts (Matthew 19:1–9), but that in the New Covenant, God sanctions divorce only in the wake of marital infidelity. But in Deuteronomy 21:10–14, divorce is not only permitted but almost encouraged if the husband (notice it's never the wife who can make the decision) no longer finds her to his suiting. And in Ezra 10, divorce is outright *required* for mixed marriages (whether or not the foreign wives were converts to Judaism, presumably). Yet Paul commands believers married to unbelievers to remain married if possible, thus sanctifying their unbelieving spouse (1 Corinthians 7:12–14). See my discussion on divorce in the context of progressive revelation later in this chapter.

Can God change his mind?

> But Moses sought the favor of the LORD his God. "O LORD," he said, "...Turn from your fierce anger; relent and do not bring disaster on your people...." Then the LORD relented and did not bring on his people the disaster he had threatened (Exodus 32:11, 12, 14).

> God is not a man, that he should lie, nor a son of man, that he should change his mind (Numbers 23:18).

Does God determine in advance those who will be saved?

> Therefore God has mercy on whom he wants to have mercy, and he hardens whom he wants to harden. One of you will say to me: "Then why does God still blame us? For who resists his will?" But who are you, O man, to talk back to God? Shall what is formed say to him who formed it, "Why did you make me like this?" Does not the potter have the right to make out of the same lump of clay some pottery for noble purposes and some for common use? What if God, choosing to show his wrath and make his power known, bore with great patience the objects of his wrath—prepared for destruction? What if he did this to make the riches of his glory known to the objects of his mercy, whom he prepared in advance for glory—even us, whom he also called, not only from the Jews but also from the Gentiles (Romans 9:18–24)?

> For there is one God and one mediator between God and men, the man Christ Jesus, who gave himself as a ransom for *all* men—the testimony given in its proper time (1 Timothy 2:5–6).

> For the grace of God that brings salvation has appeared to *all* men (Titus 2:11).

> He is patient with you, not wanting anyone to perish, but *everyone* to come to repentance (2 Peter 3:9).

Archer's discussion of the problem of human free will versus divine predestination does little to clarify the relationship between the two:

> Whoever rejects the Lord Jesus must bear all the blame for remaining condemned and lost, but whoever is saved must give to God all the glory and honor for his salvation and his new life in Christ. . . . To sum up, then, God chooses from all eternity those who will be saved; and the sole basis of His choice is His mere good pleasure. . . . Yet God never chooses those who do not and will not believe in Christ. . . . But what it is that causes a sinner to open his heart to God's truth and become willing to believe is not really spelled out in Scripture. All we can be sure of is that God, "who is not willing that any should perish, but that all should come to repentance" (2 Peter 3:9), has not made their choice for them (Archer 1982, 390–95).

What? Has God made the choice for us, or has he not? It doesn't appear that Archer really answers the question, and for good reason: the scriptural authors do not speak with one voice. But do not take the word of an outsider like me on this; witness the deep divisions among fervent believers who insist, based on scripture, that the choice is God's alone or that the choice is up to us or that it's a combination of the two.

The progressive revelation solution

While some of these contradictory passages are relatively inconsequential for Christian living and theology today (for example, whether or not God approved of Jehu's massacre at Jezreel), many of them contribute to deep, persistent divisions in Christendom. Believers disagree sharply over questions concerning divorce and remarriage, the way to salvation, predestination, eternal security, wealth, warfare, the role of women, Sabbath keeping, and the applicability of Old Testament law, to name a few. These divisions, I maintain, are not all due to the shortcomings of Jesus' followers but to the real differences in the biblical texts themselves.

Many are already familiar with the above challenges to biblical harmony yet have settled upon what they consider to be satisfactory avenues to preserve the overall unity of the Bible. In my own journey, I found in the doctrine of "progressive revelation" a temporarily helpful framework for reconciling the contrast between Old Testament and New Testament ethics. On the heels of an earlier crisis of faith at the age of 21, I wrote the following for my 1991 seminary apologetics class:

> Several writers of the past century offered in the principle of progressive revelation a much more fitting though not all-encompassing solution to many of the puzzles of Old Testament morality. This argument suggests that the Scriptures constitute a living organism (Bruce 1909, 274) whose precepts cannot be examined in isolation but with an understanding of the progressive development of its parts to form a coherent whole. "Let the critic be content to glance at only portions of it, and he will blunder over the incompleteness of its ethics, its rudimentary legislation, and its defective sense of individual rights" (Bruce 1909, 274).
>
> The theory assumes that the people of Israel, after having spent over four hundred years in pagan Egypt, were with respect to ethical standards essentially barbarians. Slavery was a universally accepted practice in their world, as was the disregard for women's rights, the shunning of ethics in times of war (Jarrel 1882, 219), and various other behaviors which appear grievous from the contemporary standpoint. It was in this context that God began to reveal his law and gradually to cultivate for himself a people who would be prepared eventually to receive his incarnation.
>
> However, to have suddenly foisted upon such a people the most lofty mores of Christian virtue would have been no more reasonable than to require that an infant not cry. A responsible teacher recognizes the necessity of laying out only those rules that function best at the stage of development in which s/he finds his/her pupils (Bruce 1909, 275; cf Gal 3:24). If rules from elementary school were to be integrated into a university classroom setting, they would

appear at once both overly restrictive and approbative, just as the OT law appears to our modern ethical sensibilities. While the laws which God introduced to the Israelites were of great utility in those circumstances, they were perfect not in an absolute sense but in a relative sense, since they were perfectly adapted to that stage of the nation's progress (Bruce 1909, 274).

One who doubts the progressive development of the Scriptures would do well to trace the gradual development in the theology of the afterlife, the distinction between the physical and spiritual dimensions of the human frame, the existence and work of devils, the inclusion of the Gentiles in God's covenant family, and a host of other intimations concerning the nature of the Messiah and the Kingdom of God. The NT speaks of our seeing through a glass dimly now, indicating that revelation must be adjusted according to how its recipients can bear it (John 16:12, "more than you can bear"; 1 Cor 3:2, "milk rather than solid food"; Heb 5:11, "much more to say," "slow to learn"). Indeed, the inheritors of the eternal estate of perfection will look back with incredulity at all that God tolerated during the enlightened age of the Church, just as we look back in wonder at all God permitted in the era of the OT.

Though the concept of progressive revelation helped keep my doubts at bay for a decade, I subsequently came to view it as a rationalization for why the Bible's teachings are not consistent, much as the concept of "prophetic dual fulfillment" is used after the fact to explain why Old Testament prophecies were not fulfilled in their entirety. I had to be honest with myself: these are the types of things an apologist would *have* to come up with to rescue divine inspiration from what otherwise appear to be incompletely fulfilled prophecies or discordant teachings across the canon.

A particularly unsatisfying apologetic that often accompanies the principle of progressive revelation is that in the Old Testament, the Holy Spirit had not yet been poured out on his people, and therefore God maintained lower expectations of his children (for example, with regards to divorce) than after Pentecost. But this did not prevent God from pouring out his Spirit on Samson, who took personal revenge on his enemies, killing 1,000 of them with the jawbone of a donkey.[65] If God was willing to

---

[65] Incidentally, we are told in Judges 16:30 that Samson brought "many" more people to their death in his final act of pulling down a temple on pagan worshipers and on himself than he had killed previously in all his life. It is likely this murder-suicide resulted in more deaths than did the attacks on the World Trade Center on September 11, 2001. Why, then are the 9/11 attackers, who acted on behalf of their god, any worse than Samson, who acted on behalf of his god? It would seem our evaluation of these incidents depends merely on which god we consider to be the true god: Yahweh or Allah.

pour out his Spirit for that purpose, why not also for the purpose of keeping marriages intact?

Upon close examination, a number of the issues progressive revelation is supposed to address remain problematic. The Old Testament teaching on divorce does not seem to converge on any one standard over time. Within the Torah, a rapist is required to marry the victim with no possibility of divorce (Deuteronomy 22:8: imagine, if you are a woman, being forced to marry the one who has violently stripped you of your virginity, and of having no way out of this arrangement for life; imagine also what a diabolical opportunity this law presents to a young man who cannot otherwise obtain the object of his passion—raping her will make her his for life!), while in Deuteronomy 24, divorce for normal marriages is permitted. Micah states God hates divorce, but in the same era, Ezra and Nehemiah demand their fellow Jews to put away their foreign wives and children. In the New Testament, Paul enjoins believing husbands and wives not to put away their unbelieving spouses, while at the same time telling believers to let their unbelieving spouses go if they want a divorce, thus putting the decision to stay or go in the hands of the unbeliever. In Mark, Jesus does not permit divorce for any reason at all, while in Matthew he adds an exception for unfaithfulness. It is difficult to see any sort of progression in all of this.

My purpose in listing the contradictory passages above is to respond to the common apologetic that the Bible was written over a period of 1500 years by more than 40 authors from all walks of life but is in perfect agreement throughout. Certainly a concept like progressive revelation may be useful for propping up the unity of the scriptures, but I am merely pointing out that *on its face*, the Bible is not in such perfect agreement as the party line suggests. It will not do to *say* the Bible is unified because that is what we like for it to be. Its unity or lack thereof is independent of what we might like to think; it can be evaluated only on the basis of its content. I have shown here that its content, taken at face value, demonstrates deep divisions among different authors over different times, undermining the oft-repeated claim of its perfect unity.

THE INTEGRITY AND TRUSTWORTHINESS OF THE BIBLICAL AUTHORS

By nature we as humans generally prefer to give others the benefit of the doubt, particularly those who endorse admirable moral values. Though we know hypocrisy is always a possibility, we tend to refrain from attributing it to others without good reason. If someone promotes honesty or kindness, we normally assume the person is not a liar or a sadist. If a biblical writer enjoins us not to bear false witness or admonishes us to speak the truth to one another, we are inclined to believe he is speaking the truth to us about whatever else he says.

This was my default assumption concerning the authors of the Bible in my youth, an assumption that has been challenged through my subsequent observation of human nature and through my ongoing study of the biblical text.

Is it safe to presume that the faith of esteemed religious leaders prevents them from deceit? Martin Luther, a pillar of the Protestant Church, asked,

> What harm would it do if a man told a good strong lie for the sake of the good and for the Christian Church? . . . a useful lie, a helpful lie. Such lies would not be against God; he would accept them (Lenz 1891).[66]

Shocking as this sounds today, the unapologetic use of deception to advance religious causes has been far from uncommon throughout history. In our culture deception and hypocrisy are rarely owned up to until they are incontrovertibly exposed, as in the fall of Pastor Ted Haggard (see chapter 8 for details) and of many prominent televangelists and conservative politicians. So prevalent are the failings of prominent Christian leaders that Billy Graham is held out as one of only a very few who have managed to escape the corruption of the spotlight.

There is no reliable way to discern who is genuine and who is not. If this were not the case, hypocrites could have no chance of thriving, but in fact they do thrive and continue to do so unless they happen to be exposed. And it is safe to say that many manage to live out their lives forever unexposed. *Shock* would be the most appropriate word to describe the reaction of most of Haggard's congregation after his outing. They simply could not believe that one who had led them so capably, who seemed to have the genuine authority and earnestness and teaching of the Spirit, could have been living such an outrageous lie.

Pseudepigraphy, the act of attributing one's writings to another, more famous figure, was a common practice in ancient times, used to gain a wider hearing than would have otherwise been possible for an unknown author. There is a large corpus of pseudepigraphal works from roughly 200 BCE to 200 CE, when many of the books of the Bible were written or

---

[66] I lack access to the context of this quotation, so, to be charitable, I acknowledge the possibility that Luther could have been mocking others who used deception, rather than advocating its use himself.

canonized (Teeple 1994, 23). Perhaps the most famous example is that of 1 and 2 Enoch, books penned in the name of Noah's great-grandfather and referenced by the canonical book of Jude. Others were written in the names of Adam, Abraham and various biblical prophets.

The Testaments of the Twelve Patriarchs is a particularly interesting collection of pseudepigraphal works, likely written by a Pharisee in the second century BCE. It purports to convey the last words of each of Jacob's twelve sons. H. F. D. Sparks summarizes the pattern of each testament as follows:

> First, the patriarch gives his immediate family, assembled round his death-bed, details about his own early life and experiences: next he discourses at some length either on a particular virtue they should cultivate or on a particular vice they should avoid, charging them meanwhile to keep "the law of the Lord" and live in obedience to "the commands of the Most High": then he warns them (not infrequently on the basis of what he has read in "the writing of Enoch") of the evils that will come upon them as a result of their moral deterioration, though he can usually assure them that "in the last times" God will bring "salvation," not only to Israel, but also to the Gentiles; and then finally he asks to be buried, not in Egypt, but in Canaan, at the family burial-place in Hebron. . . .

> The author was a Pharisee, who combined loyalty to the best traditions of his party with unbounded admiration for Hyrcanus, in whom the Pharisaic party had come to recognize the actual Messiah.

> Having dated the Testaments thus exactly, [Oxford professor R. H.] Charles[67] went on to stress that their permanent value lies, not so much in the light they shed on movements within Judaism in the late second century BCE, as in the influence they exercised on the authors of the New Testament. "The main, the overwhelming value of the book," he wrote, "lies . . . in its ethical teaching, which has achieved a real immortality by influencing the thought and diction of the writers of the New Testament, and even those of our Lord" (Sparks 1984, 505, 508).

Given the widespread phenomenon of pseudepigraphal and apocryphal writing during the time in which the Old and New Testaments were being formed, we can make no a priori assumption that the canon itself is immune from the inclusion of such invented material, even if it contains lofty ethical injunctions and words of great encouragement. If we grant the spurious authorship of *The Testaments of the Twelve Patriarchs* or of *The*

---

[67] Sparks here transitions from his writing his own thoughts on the Testaments to quoting R. H. Charles.

Gospel of Thomas but are disdainful of mainstream critical scholarship discounting the Pauline authorship of 1 and 2 Timothy simply because we are committed to the integrity and historical reliability of the books between the covers of the Bible, rather than because of sufficient counterarguments in favor of our view, then we are driven more by our loyalty than by the evidence.

Unfortunately we cannot go back and examine the lives of those who penned the Bible. Indeed, we do not even know with any real certainty who wrote most of the books of the Bible or anything concerning their character. They are more hidden to us than the lives of any of the televangelists; we can evaluate them only by their words.

We have already seen in chapter 10 that there existed a cottage industry of religious *quasi prophecy* (pseudoprophecy might be a more appropriate term) in the time that the book of Daniel was composed. These authors were convinced that a little deception was fair game in the service of a greater Cause. We have seen how Matthew alone awkwardly placed Jesus simultaneously on two donkeys to accord with the Hebrew parallelism of the Old Testament source. We have seen in chapter 11 how Luke and Mark take their own divergent routes for locating Jesus' appearances to his disciples, Luke's divergence apparently having been deliberate.

In his book *The Incredible Shrinking Son of Man,* Robert Price goes beyond simply listing discrepancies in the text (as I have done above) and seeks to uncover the reasons for the variants and the processes by which they arose. In taking this approach, we gain glimpses into the theological agenda of the authors and of the communities in which they wrote. These fascinating glimpses are unfortunately off the table for conservative scholarship because of an unwillingness to countenance any personal human agenda or evolving theology on the part of the authors. Take, for example:

> Similarly, when the later gospel has a seemingly more theologically sophisticated version of a saying or story than its source and predecessor, we may conclude that the later version is the creation of the evangelist. . . . Take the important story of Peter's confession of Jesus' messianic identity at Caesarea Philippi. Our earliest version has Jesus solicit Peter's opinion, "You are the Christ" (Mark 8:29). Luke modifies the title accorded Jesus: "You are the Christ of God" (9:20), a simple clarification: the anointed of God. Matthew wants a beefier Christology, so his Peter says a mouthful: "You are the Christ, the Son of the living God" (16:16). Merely "the Christ" is no longer good enough. Matthew piles on the theology: Jesus is also Son of God, and not just of some pagan Gentile god but "the living God," the God of Israel. . . . Whatever is going on here, we can be sure of one thing: in the

original circumstance, Peter did not say something like, "You are the Christ, the Holy One and Son of the Living God," with each evangelist picking and choosing whatever verbal fragments he liked best. . . . There is a clear development from a "lower" Christology to a "higher" one. Thus, if any version is most likely to be historical, it is surely the earliest and simplest, the least theologized (Price 2003, 12–13).

The principle that stories generally grow in the telling is not one that Price or his critical allies invented for the purpose of casting doubt on the objectivity of the biblical authors. It is a well-established phenomenon that we can observe time and again throughout history and in contemporary experience. A story that is a little more adorned than the original, all else being equal, stands a better chance of being noticed and propagated than one that reports the bare facts. And traditions are more likely to acquire new features over time than to lose them. How did we end up with such a dizzying array of Christmas traditions, with trees, Santas, reindeer, gifts, carols, Yule logs, mistletoe, lights, and cards, for example? Many of the matter-of-fact contradictions I presented early in this chapter reflect a fascinating and complex evolutionary development of ideas, some original and some borrowed from surrounding cultures. It is difficult not to conclude, for instance, that the Chronicler reporting David's census was embarrassed by the thought that God should have tempted David, so instead availed himself of the more recently introduced figure of Satan (likely from exilic contact with the Persian Zoroastrians), a concept presumably not readily available to the author of the original story.[68] A similar evolutionary process led to the origin of the doctrines of heaven and hell in later Judaism and early Christianity. This accounts for the Psalmist's bleak view of "the grave" and for the Old Testament's focus on rewards and punishments in this earthly life, in contrast to the New Testament's emphasis on rewards in the hereafter.[69]

---

[68] The date of writing of the book of Job, which refers to Satan as "the Adversary," is quite uncertain, so it cannot be taken as evidence for an early reference to Satan. There is no textual justification for considering the serpent in Genesis 3 to be Satan, despite the Christian tradition of importing the New Testament concept of Satan into the reading of Genesis.

[69] This is not merely the conclusion of liberal scholars bent on humanizing the development of theology. One of my Old Testament professors at conservative, missions-minded Columbia Biblical Seminary readily acknowledged that no clear teachings on the afterlife are to be found in the Old Testament until the Book of Daniel. He also acknowledged a similar development in the doctrine of Satan.

Those who are committed to a traditional vision of the scriptures are likely to find such analyses full of subjective or faulty assumptions, grounded in human hubris and wishful thinking. Yet in my own journey I came to suspect that at least some of the biblical authors were driven by a personal agenda rather than by a commitment to objective truth even before reading any critical challenges to verbal plenary inspiration like Price's above. When a friend asked me if there was a particular "straw that broke the camel's back," I reflected and recalled a particular day when I was reading through the Old Testament in a sweltering missionary guest room in the country of Burkina Faso. I told my friend he would think my "straw" to be trivial (I was not mistaken on this count), but that it came on the heels of struggling with a great many other questionable passages during my devotional readings.

This passage from Numbers chapter 3 looks tame enough on the surface, but a little digging raised some troubling questions for me:

> [39]The total number of Levites counted at the LORD's command by Moses and Aaron according to their clans, including every male a month old or more, was 22,000.

> [40]The LORD said to Moses, "Count all the firstborn Israelite males who are a month old or more and make a list of their names. Take the Levites for me in place of all the firstborn of the Israelites, and the livestock of the Levites in place of all the firstborn of the livestock of the Israelites. I am the LORD."

> [42]So Moses counted all the firstborn of the Israelites, as the LORD commanded him. The total number of firstborn males a month old or more, listed by name, was 22,273.

> [44]The LORD also said to Moses, "Take the Levites in place of all the firstborn of Israel, and the livestock of the Levites in place of their livestock. The Levites are to be mine. I am the LORD. To redeem the 273 firstborn Israelites who exceed the number of the Levites, collect five shekels for each one, according to the sanctuary shekel, which weighs twenty gerahs. Give the money for the redemption of the additional Israelites to Aaron and his sons."

> [49]So Moses collected the redemption money from those who exceeded the number redeemed by the Levites. From the firstborn of the Israelites he collected silver weighing 1,365 shekels, according to the sanctuary shekel. Moses gave the redemption money to Aaron and his sons, as he was commanded by the word of the LORD (Numbers 3:39–49).

First, verse 39 lists Levites as numbering 22,000, while the sum of the three Levite groups (7,500 Gershonites + 8,600 Kohathites + 6,200 Merarites) in verses 21–37 of the same chapter is instead 22,300. No big deal; there could have been a scribal copyist error somewhere along the way, leading to this discrepancy of 300 Levites. I figured initially that as long as the error was in the manuscript copies and not in the original, the conviction that God inspired the original version could be safeguarded. (In retrospect, however, this "inspired original" reasoning fails to satisfy; what, after all, is the point of insisting that God inspired the original texts without error if he was not interested in preserving them from subsequent copyist errors, especially if we no longer have access to the originals?)

Second, the numerical discrepancy in verse 39 likely would not have caught my attention if the number were of little consequence, but the reasoning in the remainder of the chapter depends entirely not only on its accuracy but also on its precision. Let us grant that it (that is, the number in verse 39, rather than the sum of those in 21 through 33) is accurate; the question remains whether it is precise, down to a man, or whether it is rounded to the nearest hundred. The same question pertains to each of its constituent numbers (7,500, 8,600 and 6,200) in verses 21 through 33. Census numbers are prevalent throughout the book of Numbers (that is how it got its name), yet in virtually every case, they appear to be rounded to the nearest 100 or 50. (I know of no one, especially with any sense of statistical probability, who would maintain there was no rounding going on, and that there were, for example, exactly 35,400 Benjamites in Numbers 2:22; not 35,407, not 34,399, but 35,400 on the money.) Yet the whole of Numbers chapter 3 turns on the assumption that there were precisely 7,500 Gershonites (not a man more or less—but maybe 300 fewer due to a scribal error), precisely 8,600 Kohathites (not a man more or less—but maybe 300 fewer due to a scribal error), and precisely 6,200 Kohathites (not a man more or less—but maybe 300 fewer due to a scribal error), for a total of (after adjusting for the off-by-300 scribal error) precisely 22,000.

The necessity of this numerical precision appears in verses 42 and following, in which a precise count of all firstborn Israelite males a month old or more is reported to be 22,273. It is the difference between 22,273 and 22,000 that determines the number of leftover firstborn Israelites (22,273 − 22,000 = 273) for whom the LORD requires monetary compensation, to be given to his high priestly family at the rate of 5 shekels of gold per leftover firstborn, for a total of 1,365 shekels.

It is mathematically unwarranted to combine precise and rounded numbers in calculations such as these. "But," you say, "the Bible is not a book of mathematics, and is not required to pander to our modern notions of mathematical propriety." But I say if God himself inspired this passage, he certainly knew better than to stake its conclusion on calculations involving numbers of mixed precision, even if the original recipients failed to detect such a fundamental, common-sense mathematical *faux pas*. Let us consider the range of possible values if we subtract 300 from one of the Levitical figures to correct for the apparent scribal or addition error. If the individual clan counts are rounded to the nearest 50, the total could be anywhere from 21,925 to 22,072; if to the nearest 100, the range would be from 21,850 to 22,147, for a variance of up to 297.[70] It does not require a modern mathematician to understand that this does not make a sound basis for computing the difference of 273 between a rough total of 22,200 and the apparently precise count of 22,273 firstborn males.

Third, the rationale behind counting Levites and firstborn males to arrive at a sum for priestly compensation appears positively arcane and self-serving, bearing the marks not of the divine wisdom of the creator of the universe[71] but of human interest and clever, numerological priestcraft to bilk the credulous, mathematically naive flock.

Fourth, the count of Israelite firstborns is precise, but is it accurate or reasonable? There were only 22,273 firstborn Israelite sons (and therefore approximately the same number of families), but according to Numbers 2:32 there were 603,550 Israelite men 20 years of age or older, likely entailing a total of over two million men, women and children. This would suggest an average of about 45 children per mother,[72] stretching the limits of credulity. The footnote for Numbers 3:43 in the evangelical *NIV Study*

---

[70] Let us start with the apparently rounded figures of 7,500, 8,600 and 6,200, which total 22,300. To arrive at the biblical figure of 22,000 we will assume that 7,200 was the original figure instead of 7,500 before an off-by-300 copyist error occurred. Thus 7,200 + 8,600 + 6,200 = 22,000. If these figures were rounded to the nearest 100, the lowest constituent values (with each having 50 fewer than the rounded values) would have been 7,150 + 8,550 + 6,150 = 21,850. The highest constituent values (with each having 49 more than the rounded values) would have been 7,249 + 8,649 + 6,249 = 22,147. Thus the maximum variance due to rounding would have been 297, or roughly 300.

[71] This creator is also said to have fine-tuned the cosmological constant to a staggering, unimaginable precision of 1 part in 10 to the fifty-third power. See chapter six.

[72] 2,000,000 people/22,273 families (about half of whom had firstborn sons and half firstborn daughters) ≈ 45 children/family. This is only an approximation that does not take into account childless women. Some have suggested that a high incidence of polygamy may solve the problem if only the firstborn son of each father is counted. However, elsewhere in scripture a firstborn is defined as the first offspring of every womb (i.e., of every woman; see Exodus 13:2 and Luke 2:23), ruling out the polygamy solution. See *The Pentateuch and Book of Joshua Critically Examined* (Colenso 1865, pp. 49-50, sec. 88) for a more detailed critique of several other solutions that have been suggested for this problem.

Bible (Barker 1985, 195) responsibly acknowledges this problem without offering a solution it considers satisfactory.[73]

In sum, we are confronted with a passage that uses improperly copied or added numbers, improperly rounded numbers, and unreasonable numbers (entailing several dozen children per mother) to determine with great precision just how much money was to enrich the coffers of Aaron (the brother of Moses) and his sons. This is the same Aaron who had earlier (Exodus 32) made the famous golden calf, the worship of which had led to the divinely sanctioned slaughter of 3,000 Israelites, excluding Aaron himself. Does this passage represent the height of divine wisdom or rather the machinations of avaricious men associated with the priesthood? Do we wish to expend our creative powers to explain and defend this and countless other passages like it throughout the Bible, merely to avoid confronting the dreadful but very real possibility that it was written by mere men—flawed men without a pipeline to God—like every other book?

I lack space to include a number of other passages that appear innocent enough on the surface but which reveal a nest of contradictions and implausibilities upon closer inspection. I urge my readers to examine critically the parallel accounts of David's census or the story of the many who were raised following Jesus' resurrection (Babinski 2005b) to gain a sense of the difficulties involved in accepting these texts as divinely inspired in any sense whatsoever.

THE ARCHAEOLOGICAL CONFIRMATION OF THE SCRIPTURES

There is a widespread conception on the part of apologists and lay believers that archaeological findings confirm most of the major biblical stories. The following statement is representative of such optimism:

> It is not too much to say that it was the rise of the science of archaeology that broke the deadlock between the historians and the ... Christian. Little by little, one city after another, one civilization after another, one culture after another whose memories were enshrined only in the Bible, were restored to their proper places in ancient history by the studies of archaeologists. ... Contemporary records of biblical events have been unearthed and the uniqueness of the biblical revelation has been emphasized by contrast and

---

[73] A correspondent suggested to me an interesting solution: all firstborn sons just prior to the Exodus had been killed at Pharoah's command, thereby reducing the firstborn census totals. However, this runs counter to the narrative in Exodus 11:7, which states that the Israelite firstborn sons were spared; not even an Israelite dog barked. No mention is made of any other massacre of Israelite firstborn sons.

comparison to newly discovered religions of ancient peoples. Nowhere has archaeological discovery refuted the Bible as history" (Elder 1960, 18).

While it is true that the existence of a number of the Israelite kings mentioned in the second half of the Old Testament has been corroborated archaeologically or through historical records, the situation is different for the events recorded in the Pentateuch, the first five books of the Bible, said to have been written by Moses. For example, there is no physical or extrabiblical historical evidence for a large number of Israelites (at least 600,000 fighting men and their families, according to the book of Numbers) having sojourned in Egypt or wandered in the desert for forty years thereafter:

> Even if the number of fleeing Israelites (given in the text as six hundred thousand) is wildly exaggerated or can be interpreted as representing smaller units of people, the text describes the survival of a great number of people under the most challenging conditions. Some archaeological traces of their generation-long wandering in the Sinai should be apparent. However, except for the Egyptian forts along the northern coast, not a single campsite or sign of occupation from the time of Ramesses II and his immediate predecessors and successors has ever been identified in Sinai. And it has not been for lack of trying. Repeated archaeological surveys in all regions of the peninsula, including the mountainous area around the traditional site of Mount Sinai, near Saint Catherine's Monastery, have yielded only negative evidence: not even a single sherd, no structure, not a single house, no trace of an ancient encampment. One may argue that a relatively small band of wandering Israelites cannot be expected to leave material remains behind. But modern archaeological techniques are quite capable of tracing even the very meager remains of hunter-gatherers and pastoral nomads all over the world. Indeed, the archaeological record from the Sinai Peninsula discloses evidence for pastoral activity in such eras as the third millennium BCE and the Hellenistic and Byzantine periods. There is simply no such evidence at the supposed time of the Exodus in the thirteenth century BCE.

> The conclusion—that the Exodus did not happen at the time and in the manner described in the Bible—seems irrefutable when we examine the evidence at specific sites where the children of Israel were said to have camped for extended periods during their wandering in the desert (Numbers 33) and where some archaeological indication—if present—would almost certainly be found. According to the biblical narrative, the children of Israel camped at Kadesh-barnea for thirty-eight of the forty years of the wanderings. The general location of this place is clear from the description of the southern border of the land of Israel in Numbers 34. It has been identified by archaeologists with the large and well-watered oasis of Ein el-Qudeirat in eastern Sinai, on the border between modern Israel and Egypt. The name Kadesh was probably preserved over the centuries in the name of a nearby

smaller spring called Ein Qadis. A small mound with the remains of a Late Iron Age fort stands at the center of this oasis. Yet repeated excavations and surveys throughout the entire area have not provided even the slightest evidence for activity in the Late Bronze Age, not even a single sherd left by a tiny fleeing band of frightened refugees (Finkelstein and Silberman 2001, 62–63).

For those whose faith is anchored in the historicity of the Bible, these are fighting words, bound to be met with character assassination of the authors or with the aphorism, "Absence of evidence is not evidence of absence"—an objection the authors took pains to address.

In 2001 National Public Radio's Michael Sullivan interviewed Professor D. N. Jha concerning his book *Holy Cow: Beef in Indian Dietary Traditions,* which discusses the origins of the Hindu ban on eating beef (Jha 2001). His research concluded it was introduced by the Brahmans of the fifth and sixth centuries BCE, prior to which there had been no such restriction. He did not anticipate the uproar his claim would provoke among conservative Hindus, who believe the ban on beef to be as old as Hinduism itself. He received a number of death threats and calls for imprisonment on the part of Hindu fundamentalists. Similarly, in an earlier interview on NPR, an Egyptian journalist suggested the Hajj (pilgrimage to Mecca) predated Mohammed and had pagan roots. As a result, she was forced to divorce her husband and lose her job.

Surely most evangelicals would have no problem accepting evidence that the beef ban was a late addition to Hinduism or that the Hajj predated Mohammed. This is because for them there is nothing to lose. But when it comes to the historicity of Bible, there is much at stake in conservative Christian and Jewish communities, and it will be difficult to view Finkelstein and Silberman as anything like objective archaeologists. Some might wish to warn me against accepting their conclusions uncritically, and they would be right to do so, but I would ask the same in reverse—do not accept the authors of the biblical stories uncritically, keeping in mind their possible political and religious agenda.[74]

Not long after our return from the mission field, I found in our mission's library the book *Introduction to the Pentateuch* by Old Testament scholar R. N. Whybray, published by the traditionally evangelical publishing house Wm B Eerdmans (Whybray 1995). I was

---

[74] The truth may lie between Finkelstein and Silberman's position and that of Kenneth Kitchen, a respected Egyptologist who defends the historicity of the biblical stories based largely on circumstantial evidence.

surprised to read Whybray's conclusion that the Moses of the Bible is far from the Moses of history, if there ever was such a person:

> Whatever historical reality may lie behind this figure, there has been a legendary development, perhaps of tremendous proportions. Every aspect of greatness and virtue has been piled on Moses at some later time, making him an ideal person, the fount and origin of all subsequent nobility and greatness—a development comparable with that concerning David, and to a lesser extent Samuel and Solomon.

> That the story of Moses as recounted in the Pentateuch is a late literary construction is supported by a recent and increasingly accepted hypothesis put forward on other grounds, that there was no mass immigration of Israel into Canaan from outside at all! . . . [This] view has been supported on both archaeological and sociological grounds. These scholars and those who have followed them maintain that there was no occupation of the land from outside. Rather, the later Israelites were actually descendants of part of the Canaanite population. . . . There was no "conquest" of Canaan by immigrants, nor was there a gradual infiltration by nomads. . . . Modern archaeological research has revealed that there was neither a cultural nor a linguistic break which would suggest the arrival of a new population (Whybray 1995, 65–67).

While reading Whybray I reflected on the well-known tendency of institutions (for example, Harvard and Yale) and individuals that start out with a conservative view of the Bible to drift toward theological and biblical liberalism, making one concession after another until little is left worth salvaging.

The conventional fundamentalist wisdom—an axiom that virtually always accompanies this discussion and preempts the consideration of any other factors—is that we are all in danger of losing our "first love" (Revelation 2:4), of allowing our initial fervor for God to dissipate, of letting down our guard and giving into the wiles of the Enemy. This perspective places the blame squarely on those who drift from God's original standard. It might start with a simple concession that Moses could not have written the account of his own death in the final chapter of Deuteronomy, followed by an admission that the mention of Israelite kings in Genesis 36:31 may have been a later editorial insertion. Sliding farther down this slippery slope, the incipient apostate concedes Numbers 22:1 was written from the perspective of the western side of the Jordan River and so could not have been penned by Moses.

These and many other observations culminate in the realization that the Pentateuch was written centuries later by someone other than Moses.[75] Once the door is open to considering nontraditional conclusions on the authorship of the Torah, more interesting questions arise, and the temptation grows to read more widely on other critical and historical research, and before long the snowball has grown until it appears fairly certain that much of what is in the first five books of the Bible is unhistorical, just as Whybray has concluded.

Why was Moses' existence or the historicity of the Exodus or the Mosaic authorship of the Pentateuch virtually unquestioned within Christendom prior to modern times? Put another way, why does the burden of resisting the temptation to water down the historical integrity of the Bible fall so heavily on the shoulders of those who have lived in the past two centuries or so, and not on those who lived in prior centuries? Did God select those who lived prior to the eighteenth century to be more blessed and more immune from this temptation, while exposing more recent believers to this greater test of faith, perhaps because there was insufficient faith-testing fodder in the days of yore?

The tendency to place the entire blame for this state of affairs on skeptics is exemplified by this typical analysis:

> Still, some people work tirelessly to discredit the Bible as a God-inspired record of critically important history. Some have stubbornly overlooked overwhelming evidence. Others have purposely misinterpreted the facts to hold on to pet theories. Are we surprised? Not really. Why?

> The Bible has the answer. No man of himself can accept or submit to the authoritative Word of God. Paul wrote: "Because the carnal mind is enmity against God: for it is not subject to the law of God, neither indeed can [it] be" (Romans 8:7). Men have been successful in getting rid of God and His great authority (though in reality, God is very much present). They don't want Him back! To admit that the Bible is accurate historically would mean accepting that God does exist[76]—and that His Word holds authority over the lives of all men.

---

[75] The conclusion that Moses did not write the Pentateuch is independent of the validity of the Wellhausian Documentary Hypothesis; the two do not stand or fall together. While a number of mainstream scholars like Whybray dispute the Documentary Hypothesis, few if any today accept Mosaic authorship of the Pentateuch.

[76] Not so. If evidence had been found for a mass exodus from Egypt to Palestine, it would have proven neither that God exists nor that the Bible is divinely inspired. Does

The brightest minds know that if the Bible is exact in its history, then its commands are in full force. You cannot separate Bible history from Bible law! The entire Bible is true, or it is false. It cannot be both (Leap 2005).

It would seem Leap imagines all skeptical scholars setting out with an agenda to disprove the Bible in order to get God off their backs. But why not consider another possibility, a possibility that places the blame not on those who come to the realization that the traditional views are untenable, but that places the blame on the traditional views themselves? Responsible scholars who come to these conclusions have done so after patiently sifting through the available, relevant evidence. Human knowledge is indeed cumulative, even if it grows in fits and starts. Just as our knowledge of the natural world has grown immensely in the past half millennium with the advent of modern science, so has our knowledge of the world in which the Bible was composed. This is one of the most significant factors driving so many young seminarians away from the conservative faith of their youth.

Should we be surprised at the vilification of mainstream scholarship on the part of apologists like Leap? Not any more than that we should be surprised at the reaction of traditional Hindus and Muslims against researchers who challenge their understanding of sacred history.

Though I could say a great deal more concerning the Bible and archaeology, I refer interested readers to *The Bible Unearthed* (Finkelstein and Silberman 2001).

THE BEAUTY AND WISDOM OF THE GOSPEL

I have presented thus far a one-sided perspective of the Bible, stemming from my admitted objective of leading my readers closer to the conclusion I have become convinced of—that the Bible is not the product of divine inspiration; it is the product of human composition, just like all other books. But I am not so jaded that I cannot recognize beauty and wisdom wherever they are to be found, be it in the Bible or any other source. One of my favorite passages in all of literature is 1 Corinthians 13, even if I fall far short of its ideals. Would that I could learn to love my wife, my children, my friends and needy individuals the world over in this way!

---

divine inspiration follow from the accurate reporting of historical events? If so, then all historians are divinely inspired. In the present case, it would have proven only that a mass exodus occurred, not that God caused it. Finding evidence for an exodus would do no harm to the skeptical position; it would simply mean acknowledging that the Bible mentioned events that really did happen or that certain references such as those to the Hittite people were valid. On the other hand, scouring the field and not finding evidence for it does in fact cast a shadow of doubt on the traditional position.

If I speak in the tongues of men and of angels, but have not love, I am only a resounding gong or a clanging cymbal. If I have the gift of prophecy and can fathom all mysteries and all knowledge, and if I have a faith that can move mountains, but have not love, I am nothing. If I give all I possess to the poor and surrender my body to the flames, but have not love, I gain nothing.

Love is patient, love is kind. It does not envy, it does not boast, it is not proud. It is not rude, it is not self-seeking, it is not easily angered, it keeps no record of wrongs. Love does not delight in evil but rejoices with the truth. It always protects, always trusts, always hopes, always perseveres.

Love never fails. But where there are prophecies, they will cease; where there are tongues, they will be stilled; where there is knowledge, it will pass away. For we know in part and we prophesy in part, but when perfection comes, the imperfect disappears. When I was a child, I talked like a child, I thought like a child, I reasoned like a child. When I became a man, I put childish ways behind me. Now we see but a poor reflection as in a mirror; then we shall see face to face. Now I know in part; then I shall know fully, even as I am fully known.

And now these three remain: faith, hope and love. But the greatest of these is love.

Who can fail to be inspired by Jesus' call to love our neighbors as ourselves, to do to others what we would have them do to us, to forgive others, and to be generous to the needy? The Bible contains many pearls of wisdom and beauty, as do many other religious and secular writings throughout history, yet we are not obligated to consider them all as divinely inspired in order to appreciate them.

Historian and ethicist Howard Teeple examines the principle ethical teachings of Jesus and relates them to extrabiblical teachings of the same or previous era. Among them are, in alphabetical order, admonitions on Anger (Matthew 5:22; the *Testament of Dan* chapters 1–4); Charity (Luke 12:33; Tobit 4:9–10: by giving alms "you will be laying up a good treasure for yourself against the day of necessity"); Divorce (Mark 10:1–12; *Damascus Document* 4:20–21); the Golden Rule (Matthew 7:12; *Shabbat* 31a; Herodotus, fifth century BCE); Humility; Hypocrisy; Judging others; Love of enemies (Matthew 5:44, "Love your enemies, and pray for those who persecute you"; *Testament of Joseph* 18:2: "If anyone wishes to do you harm, you should pray for him, along with doing [him] good"; *Testament of Benjamin* 4:3: The good man "loves those who wrong him as he loves his own life"); Love of neighbor (Mark 12:28–31; Jubilees 36:4; *Testament of Dan* 5:3; *Testament of Issachar* 5:2); and so on through the alphabet (Teeple 1994, 90–99).

To recognize parallels between the teachings of Jesus and of others who came before him (whether inside or outside the Judeo-Christian tradition) does not diminish the value of the teachings; they stand, if at all, not on who pronounced them, but on their own merits, on whether they make the world a better place in which to live were everyone to follow them, as I discussed in chapter 8.

In conclusion, I readily acknowledge that the Bible contains a good deal of admirable moral teachings, fascinating stories, and reliable history. But I am not bound by a prior commitment to inerrancy to overlook its many flaws, pretending that they, by virtue of their provenance, are immune from criticism. I can contemplate the sublime beauty of 1 Corinthians 13 without ideologically glossing over the ugly side of the Bible, insisting there had to be a good reason for the law requiring rapists to marry and never divorce their victims (Deuteronomy 22); or for the command to kill all one's enemies, including children, but to keep the virgins as spoils of war (Numbers 31); or for the injunction to stone heretics and rebellious sons (Deuteronomy 21); or for the biblical endorsement of slavery (Leviticus 25); or for the call to test a woman's faithfulness to her husband by forcing her to drink bitter water mixed with dust and the words of curses written on a scroll (Numbers 5); or for the numerous passages that pronounce damnation on the unfaithful.

Most believers are not prepared to travel as far as I have from my former position as a fundamentalist believer. I implore such readers to consider a middle ground, one that acknowledges both the virtues and vices of the scriptures, as millions of moderate and liberal believers already do. While it is unrealistic to expect a large percentage of Muslims to abandon their faith, most of us can agree that the world would be a better place if Muslim fundamentalists moderated their rigid commitment to every precept of the Qur'an as the divine word of Allah, especially those that call for the destruction of infidels and apostates. Likewise, the world would be a better place if fundamentalist Christians could frankly acknowledge the good, the bad, and the ugly in their own scriptural tradition, whether or not they end up abandoning their faith outright.

Chapter 13

Miracles and Answered Prayer

MIRACLES

B
ecause I do not categorically deny the hypothetical possibility of God's existence, I cannot exclude the attendant possibility that a supreme being might intervene supernaturally in human events. In my initial doubts as a Christian, I had never considered the existence of miracles in the Bible as a stumbling block to faith. Later, however, as I became more aware of the pervasiveness of miracle and myth in the traditional thinking of all cultures, I grew increasingly hesitant to accept their genuineness without good evidence. Before living in Africa I had no idea how naive a premodern society could be.

Shortly before we left Africa I recounted to our guard how a friend lost $1500 after setting it on a pharmacy counter during a purchase transaction. The guard insisted there are sorcerers who are able to tele-transport money away from hapless individuals who remove cash from their pockets. He also mentioned having heard on the radio that when a special soap was rubbed on a woman in neighboring Nigeria, the woman turned into money! I assured him in the strongest terms that this account was impossible and that he should insist on seeing it with his eyes before believing it. I heard this story repeated (and believed) from one end of the country to the other. But if I were to take the Bible literally, I could not so confidently assert this kind of thing to be impossible.

In his book *Miracles*, C. S. Lewis concerns himself with the appropriateness of miracles in the context of salvation history. He examines the miracles of Jesus and contends they are all paralleled by actions God carries out in nature on a larger scale or over a longer period of time. In other words, they are more plausible than the far-fetched miracles of other mythologies. For example, when Jesus turned the water into wine, he was acting out the natural process by which grape plants convert water and energy (sunlight) into grapes, which then ferment to become wine. Lewis sees many of the miracles of the Old Testament as more fantastic or mythological, not adhering to the pattern he sees in Jesus' miracles:

> My present view ... would be that just as, on the factual side, a long preparation culminates in God's becoming incarnate as Man, so, on the documentary side, the truth first appears in *mythical* form and then by a long process of condensing or focussing finally becomes incarnate as History.... Whether we can ever say with certainty where, in this process of crystalisation, any particular Old Testament story falls, is another matter. I take it that the memoirs of David's court come at one end of the scale and are scarcely less historical than *St. Mark* or *Acts*; and that the *Book of Jonah* is at the opposite end (Lewis 1947, 161).

Presumably Lewis would have included the following incident at the book of Jonah (that is, mythological) end of the spectrum:

> Aaron threw his staff down in front of Pharaoh and his officials, and it became a snake. Pharaoh then summoned wise men and sorcerers, and the Egyptian magicians also did the same things by their secret arts: Each one threw down his staff and it became a snake. But Aaron's staff swallowed up their staffs (Exodus 7:10–12).

If this really happened, then how can I exclude the possibility that a woman was turned into money in Africa in the year 2000? This Exodus account appears to be part of an epic contest of the gods. The assumption is that the Egyptian gods truly could turn staffs into snakes, but Yahweh's snakes were more powerful and swallowed them up: "My god is better than your god" (similar to our childhood taunts, "My daddy is stronger than your daddy").

Some would argue that Satan indeed does have such powers (though of course the Exodus text does not mention Satan, since the belief in Satan's existence appears not yet to have been developed, nor had the belief in the existence of other gods been excluded). But such a view runs perilously close to dualism. Where does Satan's power end? No less seriously, how do we distinguish between God's miracles and Satan's? Admitting that Satan can perform such acts invalidates the gospel's argument from miracle. If we cannot determine whether a miracle is from God or from Satan, we cannot determine whether the miracle worker is from God or Satan, unless we have already predetermined in our minds whose side the miracle worker is on, in which case we no longer need the miracle to validate the miracle worker. According to the Gospel of John, the purpose of Jesus' miracles was to demonstrate that he was from God:

> Jesus did many other miraculous signs in the presence of his disciples, which are not recorded in this book. But these are written *that* you may believe that Jesus is the Christ, the Son of God, and that by believing you may have life in his name (John 20:30–31).

This teaching is absent from the synoptic Gospels. To the contrary, they downplay the role of signs as a means of leading one to believe:

> The Pharisees came and began to question Jesus. To test him, they asked him for a sign from heaven. He sighed deeply and said, "Why does this generation ask for a miraculous sign? I tell you the truth, no sign will be given to it" (Mark 8:11–12).

> But he said to him, "If they do not listen to Moses and the Prophets, neither will they be persuaded if someone rises from the dead" (Luke 16:31).

So there appear to be two contrasting opinions in the Bible: one that recognizes the value of signs and another that minimizes it. Some may attempt to resolve the problem by arguing that signs serve to confirm the belief of those who are already willing to believe but are ineffective for those who refuse to believe. If this is so, why appeal to miracles as a reason for skeptics to believe? The inclusion of both perspectives in scripture may serve as a convenient situational response to skeptics, but these approaches are mutually exclusive; it is having one's cake and eating it too. "You don't believe? Well, what about all these miracles in the Bible and in the modern church? Oh, so you doubt those accounts and you insist on seeing evidence they really happened? You want to see a demonstration with your own eyes? Well, you of little faith, only a wicked and adulterous generation demands a sign! Blessed are those who have not seen and yet have believed." With that logic, all bases are covered (whether or not verifiable miracles happen), and the skeptic is the cretin who either demands a sign or doesn't believe it when informed of it. Yet also by this logic, any supernatural claim from any religious perspective, Christian or otherwise, should be counted in support of that tradition.

C. S. Lewis reluctantly recognizes he cannot shut out the possibility of miracles in other faiths without dismissing those of the Christian tradition:

> If, as Tacitus, Suetonius, and Dion Casius relate, Vespasian performed two cures, and if modern doctors tell me that they could not have been performed without miracle, I have no objection. . . . If it can be shown that one particular Roman emperor—and let us admit, a fairly good emperor as emperors go—once was empowered to do a miracle, we must of course put up with that fact.

But it would remain a quite isolated and anomalous fact. Nothing comes of it, nothing leads up to it, it establishes no body of doctrine. . . . What raises infinite difficulties and solves none will be believed by a rational man only under absolute compulsion. Sometimes the credibility of the miracles is in an inverse ratio to the credibility of the religion (Lewis 1947, 160).

Indeed. Lewis acknowledges that our evaluation of miracle claims should take into account their religious context. But if we find that the religion itself is fraught with logical, historical, and ethical difficulties, we are not bound to accept the claims except under absolute compulsion. To believers, this smacks of "bias against the supernatural." Sometimes, however, biases can be warranted, as even Lewis admits.

During one of our final road trips in Africa, we clipped the leg of a teenage boy who ran in front of our pickup truck on a rural highway. His leg was badly broken and needed surgical intervention to align the bones, according the hospital surgeon. Unfortunately the boy's relatives wanted him instead to undergo traditional medicine (which consists of citing verses from the Qur'an), to which the surgeon did not object. I protested and asked why the surgeon did not even attempt to reason with the family. His response was, "The traditional healers have powers." I wanted to ask why he was even in the surgical profession—why he had bothered to train in medical science for perhaps a dozen years—if he believed that. Another nurse said that these traditional powers work as long as the fracture is closed, but it is not as effective for open (compound) fractures. That figures. When I told the story to another missionary, she responded by saying, "Well, Satan does have powers." So that's how we tell whether a miracle is from God or from Satan: if the miracle is done in the Bible or in the name of *our* religion, we know it's from God; otherwise, it's from Satan or maybe (but not likely) a hoax. This kind of reasoning removes all apologetic value from miracle.

It is remarkable how much power some evangelicals ascribe to Satan, an invisible malevolent being who flits about, prompting us to commit a range of dastardly deeds, all the way from breaking our diets ("Go ahead, eat that extra piece of cake") to mass murder. Does he also prompt animals to be cruel to each other or to steal each other's food or mates, or are these behaviors simply built into their nature? If built into their nature, why not also built into our nature? And if built into our nature, what is the explanatory need for the ongoing activity of Satan and his minions?

When I consider how thoroughly and incurably credulous premodern people can be, to the point that a whole society believes a woman was turned into money by the application of soap, I do not think it unwarranted to take all their other claims of magic and supernatural occurrences with a large grain of salt. The miraculous can be seen to be virtually as routine and unsurprising as the natural. This is true not only of contemporary African society, but also of most traditional societies throughout history. The literature of the Ancient Near East is rife with myth and the supernatural, often with parallels in the Bible. One example will suffice as a representative of many such stories:

> One of the tales of wonder that the Egyptians told about the magicians was the case of the lector-priest Djadja-em-ankh who saved the day on the occasion of a royal yachting party. When one of the princesses lost her pendant, which fell into the water, the day was almost ruined. But the hero said his say of magic, parted the waters, recovered the lost pendant on dry land, returned it to the princess, and then brought the waters back together again so that the party could continue (Gordon and Rendsburg 1997, 148).

What reason do we have to believe that the above account was not historical but that the parting of the waters in the time of Moses or Joshua or Elijah or Elisha was genuine history? Far from serving as an impetus to belief, most of the biblical miracles confirm my suspicion that the scriptures are merely a human product of their times. What possible purpose does it serve for me in the twenty-first century to read about miracles that happened in an age of credulity when I cannot go back in time to verify them? How does hearing that a staff turned into a snake help me believe that God is all-powerful or that I should worship him alone or that I should love my neighbor? Again, I am not denying that these things could have happened, but is it not more reasonable to see them as embellished history in keeping with the times? With this perspective I find it difficult to swallow stories about a snake that spoke to people who lived to be over 900 years of age (the Sumerians record antediluvian kings who lived up to 24,000 years; African friends informed me that their relatively young-looking uncle was 140 years old); a talking donkey; the stopping of the sun's movement; the hero Samson's slaying of a thousand men with the jawbone of a donkey while taking personal revenge on enemies; the turning of water into wine; healings effected by the proxy of handkerchiefs and aprons that had touched Paul; or Philip's being tele-transported across the desert.

The inclusion of Jacob's sheep experiment in the Bible made it difficult for me as a missionary to argue against superstitions and charms in an African context. Jacob had made an agreement that he would own the spotted sheep while his uncle Laban would have the unspotted ones. Jacob stacked the deck in his favor using sympathetic magic as follows:

Then he placed the peeled branches in all the watering troughs, so that they would be directly in front of the flocks when they came to drink. When the flocks were in heat and came to drink, they mated in front of the branches. And they bore young that were streaked or speckled or spotted. Jacob set apart the young of the flock by themselves, but made the rest face the streaked and dark-colored animals that belonged to Laban. . . . So the weak animals went to Laban and the strong ones to Jacob (Genesis 30:38–43).

I can readily accept that the very human patriarchs were prone to such superstition, but must we accept the writer's perspective that this superstition was rewarded, presumably by God? Is this the sort of activity that we believe God would or should reward today? If not, why should he have done so in the time of Jacob? In teaching this passage to Africans, all I would have been able to say is, "That was then; this is now. We don't encourage such practices today." But I would have had no basis for maintaining this position.

Though I had never witnessed a bona fide miracle as a believer, it was fashionable to use the term *miracle* rather liberally in my Christian milieu, and I myself employed it from time to time. But I couldn't help thinking that our prayers for healing were a charade: in corporate prayer groups we petitioned God to heal our colds, knowing there would be no difference between believers and unbelievers in the rate of our recovery. We never prayed for an amputee's leg to grow back or for a woman with a hysterectomy to have a child; we didn't have enough faith for that sort of miracle. We prayed only for the possible, and those who prayed for the truly impossible and claimed it happened appeared disingenuous like the televangelists. James' promise of healing upon offering a prayer of faith and anointing oil seemed hollow after witnessing the slow, painful death of several who had followed James' directives. Elijah's floating ax head (2 Kings 6:6) was a capricious joke in comparison. I came to believe that God, while able to intervene, expressly constrains himself from intervening in the world. This did not fully answer the problem of suffering, but it did for me vindicate God from the charge of arbitrary intervention by which he solves a trivial problem here but not a holocaust there. In taking this position I became a deist, believing in the existence of a personal god but not in his ongoing intrusion into the natural course of events.

So what are we to make of miracle reports made by credible, educated individuals in our day, some of them first-hand witnesses? I cannot prove there are no miracles since it is impossible to investigate every reported case; I can only go off impressions and inferences based on how the world appears. To prove there are miracles should be easy; one undisputed case would suffice. It is much more difficult to prove that none of the miracle claims are valid.

Consider the example of a woman (whom I'll call Jeanine) who attended my church while I was still a believer. She was bound to a wheelchair for over a year and a half, unable even to stand up. One day as she was listening to inspirational music and praying for God to heal her, she felt a wave of God's presence over her and was then able to stand up and walk about on her own. I am told that anyone who remains bound to a wheelchair for an extended period of time would not subsequently be able to walk without therapy, due to muscle atrophy alone. This provided additional corroboration that God had intervened on her behalf.

Stories like this are fairly commonplace in faith healing circles, but third-party investigations of such incidents have consistently exposed the emptiness of their claims. In this case, however, the church I attended was a non-Charismatic Bible church with little or no emphasis on present-day miracles or supernatural manifestations of the Spirit. Furthermore, I knew the woman, had seen her every Sunday in her wheelchair, and had no reason to doubt her.

Later, after my deconversion, an acquaintance (I'll call him Doug) asked me what I thought of this incident and how I could account for it under my new worldview. I asked him whether he thought all miracle claims were bona fide, and he said that no, probably over 99 percent are spurious, but the 1 percent that are legitimate demonstrate that God is still alive and active in the world today.

Based on Doug's admission that most miracle claims are not genuine, it should follow that it is unwise to give the benefit of the doubt to a miracle claim until it has been thoroughly investigated and proven to be genuine. Yet when Doug mentioned the healing of Jeanine, he immediately chastised me when I paused and said, "Well, . . .", instead of admitting up front it was a supernatural event. Our guard in Niger likewise could not understand why I didn't accept his claim (and the claim of many others) that a woman turned into money after a certain kind of soap was applied to her. I am not equating Jeanine's experience to that of the African woman who turned into money, but it is premature to consider her experience a supernatural event without further investigation. Minimally we would need to know her diagnosis and whether it is reversible in the medical literature. To some, this all may sound like fancy excuse-making—"Why can't he just accept it?"—but again, given that most miracle claims turn out not to be genuine, I believe it is not only warranted but also wise to greet claims like this with at least some degree of skepticism.

We do know that people *want* miracles to be true and will tend to call something a miracle even if it is not clear that it is one. Unusual things happen, and it's often tempting to attribute them to a divine cause. Some time ago I was carpooling to work and listening to the news while reading an issue of *Discover* magazine. At the very moment I read the word *meningitis* in the magazine, I heard the same word on the radio in a completely unrelated story! As the magician Penn Jillette put it (unscientifically, of course), given New York City's eight million inhabitants, "Million to one odds happen eight times a day in New York" (Kida 2006, 85).

Jeanine's experience is even more unusual than my meningitis coincidence, but what if I had the ability to look through medical records and find cases of unbelievers who had experienced spontaneous rehabilitations like Jeanine's? The way the story was recounted made it sound as though she had never before prayed to be healed or listened to Christian music, but then when she was listening to Christian music and praying, begging God for healing, she was suddenly healed. If I were a betting man, I would wager a significant sum that she had prayed about this on a great many occasions prior to her recovery. I do not know what her medical diagnosis was or whether it was reversible, so it is premature for me to join in on the spot and say, "Yes, this is undeniably a miracle and can be explained in no other way."

Why is it that we never witness an amputated human limb growing back in front of our eyes? Why is it that ascertaining the authenticity of miracles is always just beyond certainty, like proving that the Loch Ness monster exists based on grainy photos and sporadic eyewitness accounts? There is enough tantalizing evidence to believe for those who are inclined to accept miracles, but not enough for those of us who think a 99 percent false miracle record may be just 1 percent off. If I received 99 letters assuring me that I had won a million dollars (for example, from Publisher's Clearinghouse), and each of them turned out to be nothing more than come-ons, I think I would be justified in greeting the hundredth such letter with similar skepticism, no matter how authentic it looked. Not until they placed the million dollars cash in my hands (and it was verified the bills were not counterfeit) or I saw the money in my own bank account would my doubts be erased.

Most would say that skepticism in this domain is a virtue. But then why is skepticism in the miracle domain not considered a virtue? Why is the skeptic of incredible claims so routinely vilified not only in the church but also throughout the popular media? If the majority of the American populace considers Doubting Thomas a villain rather than a hero for requiring evidence of Jesus' resurrection, should we be surprised at the lack of scrutiny given to alternative quack medicine like homeopathy?

It is not that I refuse to believe against the evidence; it's simply that the evidence is inconclusive against the backdrop of all the claims that have turned out to have a naturalistic explanation upon closer examination. But show me a person with an amputated limb that grows back before my eyes, and I will believe. Or bring my resurrected mother before me and let me ask questions about my childhood that only she could answer. I can hear some readers saying, "Ken, don't kid yourself; you would find some excuse to deny it." Would those who make this assertion pretend to know me better than I know myself? I assure you, if I saw such a thing transpire right in front of me (not on a stage), I would believe. And if God exists and is omnipotent, this would be no harder for him to pull off than to heal Jeanine of a condition about which I know so little.

What should be our approach to claims of the miraculous? It should be the approach of detective and paranormal investigator Joe Nickell, who advocates withholding judgment until being granted the opportunity to *investigate* the claim (Nickell 2007). Nickell never pronounces his judgment on a reported paranormal phenomenon, be it a weeping statue or a haunted house, until he has been given the chance to examine the claim. If he must place a stethoscope on a statue purported to have a heartbeat, that is what he will do. So far, no claim of the paranormal has given him pause, no reason to think a supernatural explanation was required, but he will examine each claim on a case-by-case basis. Unfortunately, most of the claims we hear in the present day, not to mention those found in the Bible, are not amenable to this sort of controlled investigation. This being the case, we are under no compulsion to accept them as authentic.

There are at least two kinds of false miracle reports: misperceptions and intentional deceptions. I did not know Jeanine very well at all, but I know that a lot of trustworthy people consider her trustworthy, so I am disinclined to think she was pulling a deception by sitting in her chair and pretending to be disabled (though it is a possibility that should be kept open). I know too little of her condition to make a call: was she diagnosed? If so, are there any statistics on recovery rates from her condition? Have any physicians evaluated her healing? It is not unfair to ask these questions before coming to the conclusion that it had to be supernatural. After all, a certain percentage of people recover spontaneously from even the most deadly of cancers, on the order of 1 in 100,000.

As for the second category of false miracle reports, I concur with Thomas Paine:

If we are to suppose a miracle to be something so entirely out of the course of what is called nature, that she must go out of that course to accomplish it, and we see an account given of such miracle by the person who said he saw it, it raises a question in the mind very easily decided, which is, is it more probable that nature should go out of her course, or that a man should tell a lie? We have never seen, in our time, nature go out of her course; but we have good reason to believe that millions of lies have been told in the same time; it is therefore, at least millions to one, that the reporter of a miracle tells a lie (Paine 1794, 60).

The weak link in all miracle claims is that they rely on fallible human testimony and cannot be reproduced on demand before a skeptical audience. "But," some say, "God doesn't work like that; he does not provide miracles on tap for those who demand to see a demonstration of his power." Or, "God no longer routinely performs miracles since the time of the Bible." But to this I say that these are *precisely* the sorts of excuses one would *have* to give to salvage a belief in miracles, if in fact they do not occur. If Elijah was able to call on Yahweh to bring fire down from heaven before his adversaries (taunting the priests of Baal for their failure to do the same), why has no one been able to come forward to skeptic James Randi, perform a bona fide miracle, and claim his one million dollar reward for doing so (Wagg 2008)? Perhaps those who believe in miracles should do as Elijah advised the priests of Baal: "Shout louder! Surely he is a god! Perhaps he is deep in thought, or busy, or traveling. Maybe he is sleeping and must be awakened" (1 Kings 18:27).

Let's assume God exists and has the power to perform miracles, an assumption I do not categorically deny, but about which I am very skeptical. If, in addition to these assumptions, we also assume the Bible is true, then God causes an ax head to float in the Old Testament to preserve a prophet's investment, and God causes the Jordan to part so a prophet can cross it on foot without having to use a boat like most mortals, but he doesn't prevent an infant from starving at its mother's dried-up breast in an African drought, nor does he orchestrate the early demise of Hitler to prevent the many millions of deaths of World War II.

Does it not more readily comport with experience that, if God exists, he has purposefully restricted himself from all supernatural intervention in the world, rather than that he sometimes intervenes off and on again in ways that appear so whimsical to us? It seems a mockery to the agony of my mother (though, faithful as she was, she never expressed it) that God would cause an ax head to float but not relieve her suffering as she slowly died of cancer. If we assume that God as a matter of principle does not intervene in the course of nature, then the arbitrariness vanishes. Of course the question remains, How could he choose to stand by and not intervene? This is a problem for deism, I grant, and one of the reasons for which I have come to doubt the existence of God. But I leave the question of God's existence marginally open, since I do admit that I as a human am limited in my understanding. In summary, if God exists, it is more reasonable to believe in a god who chooses never to intervene than in one who intervenes in ways that bear the stamp of capricious whim, indistinguishable from random good and bad fortune.[77]

ANSWERED PRAYER

Life is filled with millions of events, some pleasant, some difficult, and others neutral. Out of this multitude of happenings some will, on a purely statistical basis, appear to be very unusual or nearly impossible. If something unusually favorable happens to us, and if we have asked God for such a blessing prior to its occurrence, we become convinced it is an answer to prayer, the result of divine intervention. If our requests are not granted, it must not have been God's will, and we more readily allow these experiences to slip from our minds than the positive ones. This approach allows us to "count the hits" and "discount the misses," so to speak. Such a selective memory will lead to the conviction that God is active in our life and that he responds to our prayers.

The human mind is a story-seeking mechanism that bases many of its conclusions on anecdotes and personal experiences. We tend to place more stock in personal anecdotes than in statistical findings. For example, say you read in several independent consumer magazines that car model X is the most reliable vehicle on the market, based on a systematic battery of long-term tests. But your best friend has a model X and has had nothing but bad experiences with it. It will be natural on the basis of this one lemon to question the results of the statistically based study and to avoid purchasing this model. Though this reaction is wholly irrational, we all regularly fall victim to this fallacious thinking (Kida 2006).

---

[77] One category of miracles I do not have space to address here concerns reports of Near-Death Experiences (NDE) and Out-of-Body Experiences (OBE). Some have indicated that the evidence for these experiences has convinced them there's more to life than the physical world. David Lester's *Is There Life After Death? An Examination of the Empirical Evidence* (Lester 2005) thoroughly examines the evidence and demonstrates how it has been misconstrued. Additionally, Keith Augustine's "Hallucinatory Near-Death Experiences" provides a well-documented online exploration of these claims (Augustine 2003).

How is it that astrology has been able to maintain its hold on the imagination of millions over the millennia despite its scientifically demonstrated failure to yield fruit? It is because the hits are counted and the misses ignored and because extraordinary anecdotes are preferred over statistical patterns. Belief in the efficacy of prayer retains its hold for largely the same reasons.

In recent years there has been a spate of interest in the results of experiments suggesting that praying for hospital patients increases their chances of recovery. Even though liberal scholar Marcus Borg of *The Jesus Seminar* refuses to believe in an interventionist God, he confesses:

> Moreover, I think prayers for healing sometimes have an effect, and perhaps other kinds of prayer do as well. The statistical data about the effect of prayers for healing are very interesting, even though not conclusive. . . . And this leads to my final reason for continuing to do prayers of petition and intercession. To refuse to do them because I can't imagine how prayer works would be an act of intellectual pride: if I can't imagine how something works, then it can't work (Borg 2003).

A 2001 study associated with Columbia University claims to have demonstrated a 50 percent pregnancy rate for women who received prayers versus a rate of 26 percent for those who did not. Irregularities were later found in the study, and of the three authors, one was imprisoned for the fraudulent use of deceased individuals for financial gain, and the primary "author" maintained he was unaware of the study until after it was complete, and he subsequently withdrew his name. Other studies purporting to demonstrate the power of prayer for coronary patients have also been severely flawed (Stenger 2007, 96–99).

The most extensive and carefully controlled study to date is the STEP project (Study of the Therapeutic Effects of Intercessory Prayer), a ten-year, $2.5 million study of coronary artery bypass graft surgery patients, published in 2006. It was funded by the profaith Templeton Foundation. Of the 1,802 patients studied, 52 percent of prayed-for patients experienced complications, versus 51 percent of those who were not prayed for. Of those who knew they were being prayed for, 59 percent experienced complications, versus the 52 percent complication rate of those who were unaware of having been prayed for (Benson et al. 2006, abstract; Stenger 2007, 101–102).

These results demonstrate that intercessory prayer produces no statistically significant effects (other than perhaps heightened nervousness on the part of those who knew they were being prayed for). Fair enough; maybe God is simply not in the business of granting signs to those who demand them under scientifically controlled conditions. Yet who can maintain that if the studies had shown a statistically significant positive effect, believers would not have used the results to argue the case for the efficacy of prayer (as they have in fact done when the outcome has appeared to be in their favor)? If we are willing to use positive scientific evidence to promote our position, we must also be willing by the same token to accept scientific evidence that disconfirms it.

I wonder how many believers take comfort in the possibility that God, the almighty creator of the universe, should reveal himself in slight statistical differentials between patients who receive prayers and those who do not. Does it inspire awe to think that the same god who designed the laws of physics and flung the stars in space, who engineered the marvels of the bacterial flagellum and the human brain, is now relegated to statistical anomalies? Let's be done with this sort of dabbling. If we're going to put God to the test, why not do it with some flair like Elijah did when he called down fire from heaven? Why not recruit an army of prayer warriors to request that God restore the legs of an amputee? A positive, well-documented result would be more in line with the capacities of the god most Christians worship and would provide solid support for those seeking evidence of an active higher power (Gaudia 2007).

Even when I still firmly believed in God's existence as a deist, I was troubled by certain questions about the nature of intercessory prayer. In the summer of 2001, as my wife and children were taking a trip from Texas to California, I found myself praying for their safety on the road, somewhat out of habit. I began to ask myself, "What if I don't pray for them? Is God going to take note and say, 'Aha! Ken hasn't offered his full prayer quotient for his family's safety; maybe I'll give their guardian angel a little break today, and we'll see what happens to them.'" Is God so capricious that he would withhold what he knows we need, simply because we have not asked him sufficiently for it? Would we neglect to tend to the safety or nourishment of our children because of their failure to ask us every morning and throughout the day to keep them safe and well fed? What kind of monster do we think he is? Jesus himself taught that God knows our needs before we ask, yet he did not take this insight to its final conclusion: if God knows our needs, and if he is all-good, all-wise, and all-knowing, then what is the point of asking him for anything, as if we somehow knew better than he what is best for us and for those around us?

A common response to such critiques is to maintain that the primary purpose of prayer is communion with God, and that prayers of petition are merely a secondary outgrowth of one's relationship with God. I can appreciate this outlook, yet a heavy emphasis is placed on intercessory prayer in the Bible, both by example and through injunction. And in responding to those who appeal to answered prayer as evidence for their faith, it is the efficacy and legitimacy of *intercessory* prayer that we are obliged to examine.

Appealing to the gods to manipulate one's fortunes is a nearly universal cultural phenomenon. Such appeals can take many forms, ranging from silent prayer to rituals like penance, animal sacrifice, and (when all lesser measures fail to obtain the intended outcome) human sacrifice. Life has always been replete with hardships, many of them beyond human control. Crops fail due to drought, locusts, and pests. Armies invade. Infants and mothers die in childbirth. Diseases stalk us. Storms wreak havoc. These unpredictable events can seem to be the work of unseen powers or gods with capricious personalities. If we can somehow gain an inside track to these powers through prayer or personal sacrifice or confession or ritual, things might go better for us. The god who controls the rain might then provide it when our crops need it. The Old Testament consistently associates worship of Yahweh with good fortune, and unfaithfulness to him with disaster (though secular history provides a more nuanced picture, in which Israel enjoyed some of its most prosperous years under the "wicked" Omride kings; see Finkelstien 2001).

In the Old Testament, intercessory prayer is but one of a panoply of methods used for currying God's favor or seeking his guidance. For example, priests were to seek God's guidance by means of divination tools (possibly stones used in the same way as a coin toss) known as the Urim and Thummim (Exodus 28:30; Numbers 27:21). Joshua cast lots before the Lord to determine how to partition the Promised Land among the tribes (Joshua 18:6). Gideon divined the Lord's will for his war plans on the basis of the dampness of wool fleece (Judges 6). Joseph claimed to use his trusty silver cup for divination (Genesis 44:3).

Animal sacrifices were considered to be "food" for the Lord (Leviticus 21:6, 7, 16, 21, 22), suggesting that by giving up something valuable that God needed or wanted, his favor might thereby be won. The hero Jephthah vowed to offer as a burnt sacrifice whoever or whatever came out of his house first if the Lord would give him victory over the Ammonites. The text states that the Lord granted Jephthah's request, whereupon Jephthah was obliged to sacrifice his virgin daughter to the Lord (Judges 11:29–39). Shaving one's head, fasting, and abstaining from the fruit of the vine were other attempts to capture God's attention.

Any woman suspected of adultery was to drink holy water mixed with dust from the tabernacle floor along with curses washed from a scroll, and if her thigh wasted away and her abdomen swelled, her guilt was established, presumably by divine intervention (Numbers 5:11–31). As previously mentioned, Jacob bested his uncle Laban through sympathetic magic (Genesis 30:35–43). According to Acts 19:11–12, "God did extraordinary miracles through Paul, so that even handkerchiefs and aprons that had touched him were taken to the sick, and their illnesses were cured and the evil spirits left them."

The varieties of means by which believers sought and received divine favor or guidance are too numerous to mention here, but the above examples should provide a taste. Modern believers may consider themselves more sophisticated than those of yore who cast lots or shared "hot" handkerchiefs, but at bottom, are they not performing the functional equivalent of these rituals when they pray to God for forgiveness, healing, success, and guidance? Or when they discern "signs" in the everyday events of their lives?

My mother's death from cancer was certainly not due to lack of prayer or faith, nor to any failure to follow the prescriptions outlined in James 5:14–15:

> Is any one of you sick? He should call the elders of the church to pray over him and anoint him with oil in the name of the Lord. And the prayer offered in faith will make the sick person well; the Lord will raise him up.

The only conditions laid out in this passage are anointing, prayer, and faith. Did Jeanine have more faith than the hundreds of people who prayed for my mother? What of the millions of mothers whose children succumbed to smallpox or other diseases despite desperate and faithful prayers to God? And what of atheists who are spontaneously healed of their cancer or other conditions without ever praying?

Should not these verses in the Epistle of James be enough to discredit any notion of its divine inspiration altogether? Believers are often so accustomed to accepting paradoxes in their faith that this hardly fazes them, even though it simply does not line up with experience. Despite the instances when James' prescription has the appearance of being effective, it fails because the passage states unequivocally that the sick person *will* be made well, and we know this does not always happen, even when offered in faith. I suppose the blame could be placed on our lack of faith to get the Bible off the hook, but talk about a guilt trip! How must it feel to know that our loved ones might suffer and die because we lack sufficient faith!

Dispensationalists may object that the James passage is no longer applicable today but only during the initial apostolic period. Yet James makes no more than three conditions for healing, with no mention of whether the healing is God's will or whether it is limited to a particular era.

I'm reading James for what James says. I'm not reading into it an external theology that was not his own. These words were written for people to take and read at face value, not rationalized by comparison with other scriptures that have since been interpreted to mean that supernatural signs were to cease after the apostolic period.

Chapter 14

A Personal Relationship with a Loving, Almighty God

For many if not most evangelicals, a "personal relationship with Christ" is the primary shibboleth by which others' inclusion in the Christian faith is evaluated. If you are a former evangelical, you have no doubt been confronted with the charge that you were never a true believer to begin with, by which it is meant you did not have this personal relationship with Jesus. Otherwise, given the benefits of this relationship, you could not possibly have turned your back on him, nor would God have let you go.

In an online forum discussing my journey away from faith, one participant provided this analysis of my situation:

> There is a lesson here for Christians. Apparently this person [Ken] had head knowledge and not a personal relationship with Jesus. There are lots of people that are church goers but not really Christians. They may call themselves Christians because they go to a Christian church, but more likely they will identify themselves as Baptist, Catholic, Pentecostal, or other denomination rather than Christian. It is the personal relationship with the risen Christ that matters (2ndAmendment 2005).

As an aside, I predict that not long after the publication of this book, one of the most common responses will be, "This guy never had a personal relationship with Christ. He was a follower of Christianity (the religion) but not of Christ." This conclusion will not be based on any real familiarity with my background but on a theological conviction that does not allow for the redeemed to be unredeemed. To illustrate this point, in 2004 I received a book entitled *Don't Waste Your Life* (Piper 2004) from a Christian friend who wrote to me on the first page, "I believe you are still a brother in Christ." After I read the book and responded indicating clearly where I stood, she wrote back and confessed she now believed I had never been a true Christian in the first place. What changed her assessment? Was it something new she learned about my life as believer?

No. It was a result of her preconceived theology, not an evaluation of the evidence.

It was *entirely* a result of her realization that I had indeed rejected Christ as the Son of God. In other words, her conclusion was based on her adherence to the theological doctrine that true believers cannot lose their faith, and not on any objective evaluation of my prior relationship with Christ. The upshot is that I could attempt to demonstrate the authenticity of my former faith until I am blue, but for many believers, my claims will fall on deaf ears—their theology bars any conclusion other than that I was only going through the motions and was a believer in name only.

I do not object to those who hold this doctrine, as long as they freely acknowledge that this and this *alone* is what is driving their conclusion that I was never a true believer. However, if they cannot let it rest at that, but insist on determining precisely what was deficient about my former relationship with Jesus, they are in danger of drawing successively smaller circles around the household of faith, to the point that they might find themselves nearly alone in their privileged circle. When they finally get to the bottom of what separates my former counterfeit faith from their bona fide faith, they are likely to have left out the vast majority of believers, including the most earnest of evangelicals and fundamentalists whose identity is built on their relationship with Jesus. Could it be that this circle-drawing tendency is driven by a fear of being vulnerable to apostasy? Perhaps such believers need the assurance that *something* distinguishes their secure present faith from my insecure former faith so they can rest easy in the *guarantee* that they will persevere in their faith until death. They do not wish to acknowledge that someone who showed every indication of having experienced the same kind of rich, intimate relationship with Jesus as theirs could have given it up. No one in his right mind could even consider abandoning such a treasure for the empty philosophy of the world.

There is an unavoidable danger in considering oneself a member of an elite club that enjoys a "true" relationship with Jesus. It is a danger to which I sometimes—perhaps often—succumbed, despite my earnest desire to avoid it. To this day I vividly recall looking around at the other students in my high school chemistry lab, wondering how many of them were "practicing the presence of God" as I was doing—or thinking I was doing—at that moment. It was my desire to spend every waking moment of my day in communication with the Holy Spirit, thanking him for every blessing; praising him for his nature: asking him to show himself to my friends; seeking his indwelling in the furtherance of a life pleasing to him; and sharing with him every hope, frustration and longing of my life. As I engaged in this moment-by-moment *tête-à-tête* with God, it was difficult to suppress the thought that very few, if any, of those around me were similarly engaged in such a relationship. I was tempted to think that I was somehow a notch above the others. But as soon as that notion cropped up, I immediately recognized it was a diabolical thought that, left unchecked, would lead to runaway pride. I then asked God to grant me humility, whereupon I felt good about the way I had handled my incipient pride, which led to another opportunity for pride, and another opportunity for confession and a plea for humility, and so on without end. Many of my readers will identify with this kind of experience. I wish them the best in coming to terms with it, but it is a battle they will never stop fighting, so long as they consider that (a) the kind of relationship they have with Jesus to be the mark of a true believer and that (b) this kind of relationship remains relatively rare in the world at large, and even in the wider church.

I think back on a night during my high school years when I lay in bed, conversing with God about my Mormon friend, confessing my struggles over the whole "enterprise" of religion. As I continued pouring out my heart to God, I started experiencing the most wonderful sense of peace, slowly at first, but then working up to a flood of emotion rushing through my soul for what seemed like an hour. I was as certain as I could be certain of anything that God was invading my life, assuring me of his presence and favor. The experience was so real and so exhilarating that I vowed I would never doubt God's ways again. This, alas, was not to be.

Few evangelicals conclude that a Hindu or a humanist who becomes a Christian was never a "true Hindu" or a "true humanist" in the first place. Christians generally welcome the news when true members of other worldviews convert to Christ, but they (especially Calvinists) often cannot acknowledge that true members of the Christian faith abandon it.

MARRIAGE TO JESUS

I have no personal commitment to my current convictions. I came to my present perspective initially against my will, and I persevere in it only because I genuinely believe it is where the evidence leads. If I thought the evidence led to Jesus, I would immediately submit my life to him.

My reluctance to leave the faith was mirrored in reverse by author and apologist C. S. Lewis, who came to faith while struggling against God:

> You must picture me alone in that room in Magdalen, night after night, feeling, whenever my mind lifted even for a second from my work, the steady, unrelenting approach of Him whom I so earnestly desired not to meet. That which I greatly feared had at last come upon me. In the Trinity Term of 1929 I gave in, and admitted that God was God, and knelt and prayed: perhaps, that night, the most dejected and reluctant convert in all England. . . . But who can adore the Love which will open the high gates to a prodigal who is brought in kicking, struggling, resentful, and darting his eyes in every direction for a chance of escape? (Lewis 1955, 226)

Yet despite our similar reluctance to abandon our original positions, our commitments to our respective beliefs are not of the same nature. Unlike skepticism or naturalism, Christian faith is not simply an assent to propositional truths; it is a commitment to the person of Jesus. The New Testament paints Jesus as the groom and the church as the bride. This commitment is even weightier than an earthly marriage vow "'till death do us part"; marriage to Jesus is for all eternity.

In light of this matrimonial backdrop, it should not have come as a surprise to me when a friend insisted his relationship with Jesus is literally more real to him than his relationship with his wife. This was the same friend who maintained he would *never* deny Jesus. He is loyally committed to a Person: "Here I stand, come hell or high water." Given such a stance, no amount of evidence will sway my friend to abandon Jesus. He is locked in for life.

This outlook works to the advantage of the Christian faith, whether or not a living Jesus exists. If a religion can manage to convince its adherents to think in terms of personal commitments rather than following the evidence wherever it leads, then the battle is won. No longer is there room for an ongoing critical search for truth, because the Truth is living and is in my heart, and I am committed to Him. There is no longer a need to pay heed to empirical, scientific, archeological, or scholarly findings that challenge the Truth; these findings must henceforth be dismissed or reinterpreted to submit to the Truth. If that entails believing in a young earth against all the evidence, then so much for the evidence.

By its very definition, the term *commitment* precludes genuine consideration of any competing views. It is antithetical to a spirit of open inquiry, to science and truth. By contrast, the freethinker maintains no a priori commitment to any particular view, other than the commitment to follow the evidence.

THE BIBLE AND JESUS AS PERSONAL SAVIOR

Despite the evangelical emphasis on a "personal relationship" with Jesus, our "personal savior," these terms are nowhere to be found in the Bible. I quote the late Christian evangelist and musician Keith Green:

> **The Term and Concept of "Personal Savior."** I find it very disturbing when something unnecessary is added to the Gospel. The use of the term "Personal Savior" isn't very harmful in itself, but it shows a kind of mind-set that is willing to "invent" terms, and then allow these terms to be preached as if they were actually found in the Bible.
>
> But why must we do this? Why must we add needless, almost meaningless things to the Gospel? It is because we've taken so much out that we have to replace it with "spiritual double talk."
>
> That's right, **double talk!** Would you ever introduce your sister like this: "This is Sheila, my **personal** sister"?! Or would you point to your navel and say, "This is my personal bellybutton"? Ridiculous! But nevertheless, people solemnly speak of Christ as their **personal** Savior, as if they've got Him right there in their shirt pocket—and as if when He returns, He will not have two, but **three** titles written across His thigh: **King of kings, Lord of lords, and PERSONAL SAVIOR!** (See *Rev. 19:16*.) This is only one example of how a nonbiblical term can be elevated to reverence by the Church, as if to say, "Well even if it isn't in the Bible—it should be!" (Green n.d.; emphasis in original)

In his *The Reason-Driven Life,* a rejoinder to Pastor Rick Warren's bestseller *The Purpose-Driven Life*, Robert Price takes Keith Green's observation further and demonstrates not only that the words "personal savior" are absent from the New Testament, but also that the very concept of a personal relationship with Jesus is nonexistent in scripture. I quote Price at length:

> The greatest irony of the whole thing is that the "personal savior" piety to which Warren reduces the whole of Christian worship, indeed the whole of Christianity itself, is never so much as intimated in the New Testament. Where do you propose to find it? Granted, you can find all manner of passages requiring the sinner to repent and sin no more, to believe that God raised Jesus from the dead, that you must come to the Father through Jesus, and so on. But where does Jesus or anybody else say a single word about having a personal relationship with a personal savior? Does John 15:1–11,

the True Vine discourse, discuss it? "Abide in me, and I will abide in you"? No one is denying Christianity involves some sort of spiritual union with Christ, but the crucial element of personal, back-and-forth communication is conspicuous by its absence here. Surely the passage deals with the Eucharist, the Lord's Supper, Holy Communion, given the Dionysian imagery of the fruitful vine and its grapes.

[Price then discusses John 10:1–15 (The Good Shepherd Discourse) and compares it with other passages, concluding as follows:]   There is simply nothing implicit or explicit in such texts suggesting that the believer has an ongoing personal acquaintance with Jesus.

Revelation 3:20 ("Behold, I stand at the door and knock; if anyone hears my voice and opens the door, I will come in to him and eat with him, and he with me." RSV) is perhaps the last resort, but I'm afraid it is irrelevant to the "personal savior" business, too. If you look at the context of the verse, you will see that it appears in the letters of John to the seven churches. [Price goes on to discuss the promises made to each of the seven churches.] When the Risen One says that he stands at the door, calling on those within, hoping for their sake that they hear his voice, we are, on the one hand back with the Good Shepherd who calls his flock to salvation's pasture (see also John 5:25 and 18:37). And, on the other hand, we find ourselves on the very verge of the Second Coming, as in Mark 13:29 ("When you see these things taking place, you know that he is near, at the very gates." RSV) and James 5:9 ("Behold, the judge is standing at the doors." RSV). In all these cases "standing at the door" language denotes the imminence of the Second Coming and the Final Judgment; it has nothing to do with devotionalism or an evangelistic appeal. The supper he promises them (Revelation 3:20) is no cozy, devotional klatch such as Robert Boyd Munger envisions in *My Heart, Christ's Home*, but rather the Marriage Supper of the Lamb at the end of the age (Revelation 19:6–7) (Price 2006, 97–99).

THE REALITY OF A PERSONAL RELATIONSHIP

Earlier I mentioned the claim of a friend that his relationship with Jesus is more real, more tangible than that with his wife. Given the evangelical emphasis on a personal relationship with God, it should be no more surprising to hear such claims than to hear that the Bible is a unified whole, whether or not the Bible in fact demonstrates such unity, and whether or not any relationship with an invisible, incorporeal god is in fact as tangible as that with one's visible spouse. In short, I take both claims with a grain of salt, not because I doubt the goodness, sincerity, or integrity of those making these claims, but because these claims are widely circulated assertions propagated in the service of the faith without having any real, verifiable basis in fact.

What sort of evidence or experience would constitute a real basis in fact for a tangible personal relationship? Since my friend introduced the comparison of his relationship with his wife, let us evaluate the two relationships to determine which is more tangible. My relationship with my wife (the same holds true for marriage relationships in general) is far more tangible than any relationship with God that I have heard described by anyone. For starters, Charlene responds to me in English when I address her. We kiss before I leave for work and when I return. She'll call me to tell me to pick up an extra loaf of bread when I'm at the store. I might propose an idea that she disagrees with and vice versa, but we talk it out and come to an agreement, using language with nouns, verbs, pronouns, and so forth, that we can both clearly hear and understand. We take walks, hand in hand (with real physical hands, not metaphorical ones). We make love, and we respond to each other's promptings to make the experience better. We make meals and eat them together. We laugh, we hug, we grieve together. In short, we have a tangible personal relationship.

None of this applies to anyone's relationship with an invisible God, except perhaps in a metaphorical sense. So even for those who feel, as I once did, that God floods their soul with his presence, this does not constitute any sort of direct, bidirectional cognitive communication like that between my wife and me. You might claim you sensed God telling you to buy an extra loaf of bread while at the store the other day, but how do you know it was not just your own inner voice, based on a hunch that the extra loaf might come in handy? (In a world full of coincidences, it proves nothing if you ended up having surprise guests for supper and needed that extra loaf.) Many evangelicals (and Mormons) consider that God speaks to them personally through the Bible (and the Book of Mormon), but what indication is there that the scriptures are any more than the words of men written thousands of years ago? Is it not possible that such believers are reading their personal desires between the lines and calling them God's voice? If my wife wrote me a series of letters before passing away, I might find great comfort in reading her letters, but I could not claim to have an ongoing relationship with her in any real sense.

If God is powerful enough to create quarks and quasars, black holes and galaxies, the Grand Canyon, the mighty Sequoia trees, great white sharks, army ants, and tigers—if he can create human beings with personality, communication skills, and a desire for a relationship with the divine—then why does he not fulfill that desire he has implanted in us? Why does he not just come right out and talk to us? Is he not capable? If humankind has created the telegraph, telephone, radio, television, the

World Wide Web, satellite communications, and the like, cannot the god who made us communicate with us? Why must he resort to speaking indirectly through dreams, visions, prophets, and books? Or is it that he is simply not interested in communicating with us or is not present at all? When our children are traumatized by events they must endure but do not understand, we hold them in our arms and reassure them *tangibly* of our love, even if we cannot adequately explain to them what is happening. By contrast, many strong believers freely confess to experiencing often a "dark night of the soul" when no comfort or sense of God's presence is to be found. This is not how a loving parent relates to her child.

Determining whether the voices we hear in our head are from God is tricky business. While I was attending a nondenominational church from 2000 to 2004, the pastor at one point announced God had told him to move the Sunday church services to the high school across the street, providing more room without the need for an expensive building project. The church followed his lead, worshiping in the high school auditorium for several months, after which time the pastor announced it was not working out. He confessed he was not sure why God had led them to the high school, but he assured us it was all in God's plan. The church summarily moved back across the street to the original location. Did God truly speak to the pastor, or did the pastor simply hear his own internal voice and mistake it for God's? It is most reasonable to assume the latter. In this situation, little or no harm came from mistaking the pastor's internal voice for God's, but there are many other situations for which the consequences can be devastating.

Richard Dawkins offers this analysis of believers' claims to hearing God's voice:

> You say you have experienced God directly? Well, some people have experienced a pink elephant, but that probably doesn't impress you. Peter Sutcliffe, the Yorkshire Ripper, distinctly heard the voice of Jesus telling him to kill women, and he was locked up for life. George W. Bush says that God told him to invade Iraq (a pity God didn't vouchsafe him a revelation that there were no weapons of mass destruction). Individuals in asylums think they are Napoleon or Charlie Chaplin, or that the entire world is conspiring against them, or that they can broadcast their thoughts into other people's heads. We humour them but don't take their internally revealed beliefs seriously, mostly because not many people share them. Religious experiences are different only in that the people who claim them are numerous (Dawkins 2006, 88).

GOD'S POWER AND LOVE

There are two primary sources for the conviction that God is love or that he is all-powerful, all-knowing, and all-present. The first is the Bible itself; the other is personal experience.

Without a doubt the Bible does in various places proclaim the love, sovereignty, omniscience, omnipotence, and omnipresence of God.[78] In addition, believers often experience fortuitous events they consider to be divine blessings in their lives, confirming God's goodness to them. Even in the difficult times, they are often able to discern a silver lining that shapes their character or leads to unexpected subsequent benefits. Whatever the circumstances, they are convinced, on the basis of Romans 8:28, that God works all things together for their good.

Whether or not God exists, and whether or not he is love, it is (from the perspective of a religion whose goal is self-propagation) a good public relations move for believers to proclaim his goodness and love. Believing him to be all-powerful, it would be foolish, like sawing off the branch you're sitting on, to call him evil or even indifferent, just as it would have been suicide to taunt Saddam Hussein to his face while he was in power.

Given these considerations, believers are obliged to proclaim God's goodness and love, whatever the evidence might show. Indeed, evidence is beside the point, except for supporting evidence. If we experience good fortune, that is evidence of God's love, but if we experience great trials, it is only evidence that God is refining us or that Satan is attacking us. No matter what happens, it is evidence for the firmly held conclusion decided in advance. It is simply too troubling to come to any other conclusion or to acknowledge any evidence that we live in an indifferent universe.

When using evidence to weigh a proposition, it is important to lay out ground rules for what might constitute evidence both for and against the proposition. We cannot cite evidence *for* a proposition unless we are willing to state what might constitute evidence *against* the same

---

[78] The god of certain portions of the Bible, however, does not correspond to later theological developments. He is seen to change his mind (Jeremiah 18:5-10), to be unaware of the future (Genesis 22:12), to walk physically in the Garden of Eden (Genesis 3:8), to have physical offspring (Genesis 6:1-2), to have a visible back and face (Exodus 33:23), to be unable to drive out Israel's chariot-equipped enemies (Judges 1:19), to be territorial (2 Kings 5:17-19), to be one (albeit the most important) of many gods among the nations of the Middle East (Psalm 82:1), to create evil or disaster (Isaiah 45:7), and to condemn his enemies to eternal hellfire.

proposition.[79] Otherwise, our positive evidence has no "teeth." But I have never heard a Christian state, "If such and such were to happen, that would count as evidence against God's love." No, this kind of statement is off the table, since God is love by definition, whatever the evidence.

Is it merely a humanistic idea to expect that there should be some measure, some standard by which to determine whether God is good? No, the Bible itself sets expectations for what it means for God to be good, but experience dashes these expectations:

> The eyes of all look to you, and you give them their food at the proper time. You open your hand and satisfy the desires of every living thing. The LORD is righteous in all his ways and loving toward all he has made (Psalm 145:15–17).

In what way is God demonstrating love to, providing food for, or satisfying the desires of a gorilla as it slowly starves to death? If we cannot see a contradiction in this, then religion is simply unfalsifiable.

In our human-to-human interactions, we generally know what constitutes love and goodness, and we can readily enumerate criteria for deciding whether a particular individual manifests them. My wife would be clearly justified in concluding I do not love her if I stood and watched while she was raped by a man weaker than me. The same would hold true if I did not provide for her but spent all my earnings on myself, if I never spoke to her, if I slept with other women, or if I regularly beat her. But no matter what happens to us in this life—even if God allows us to suffer horrifically without intervening or speaking to us—we can be sure, as the praise chorus goes, that "God is good all the time." Certainly theists may hold to this as a matter of faith, but they cannot legitimately claim it is based on any evidence whatsoever unless they are willing to accept evidence that counters their premise.

We routinely hear what counts for evidence of God's goodness and love: "He spared my life in a traffic accident; he gave me a beautiful wife and family; he healed me of a chronic disease; he gives me peace and comfort; he met my pressing financial needs in the nick of time; he unexpectedly brought an old friend back into my life to encourage me; he provided rain just in time to save the harvest; or he prepared a beautiful sunset." But how often do we hear the converse counted as evidence for God's indifference or malice? "Though he spared me in the car accident, I

---

[79] This is referred to as the criterion of falsifiability. I cited a couple of examples earlier: If trilobite and dolphin fossils were found together in the same strata, that would falsify evolution. Likewise, if I witnessed an amputee growing a new leg before my eyes, that would falsify naturalism in my view.

am disfigured and in chronic pain, and my daughter was not spared; he has not calmed my anxieties and fears (even though I have given them over to him repeatedly); he allowed my business to fail due to market shifts beyond my control; he prolonged the drought that led to our crop failure; he permitted the death of my best friend due to leukemia; he created a tsunami that snuffed out 230,000 lives—men, women and children—in one day; or he carefully designed the Candirú fish of the Amazon to enter the penis or anus of a bather, causing a slow and painful death due to the backward-pointing spines that prevent its removal" (Bush 2001, 306–07).

Note that I am not attempting in this section to disprove God's existence, nor even his goodness, as long as we do not have in mind the normal definition of "goodness." I fully understand the argument that God is not subject to our scrutiny, does not have to answer to our notions of right and wrong, and may have higher purposes we cannot grasp. The "God is not there because he's not fair" argument does not work; he might indeed be "there" and (to us) "unfair," or even malevolent. But if God exists and instills in us reason and a conscience, how can unbelievers be blamed for using reason and conscience to come to the conclusion that there is no benevolent force guiding our lives or that the Bible displays the earmarks of human authorship, self-interest, and superstition common to the written works of other peoples? I grant that God could have authored the scriptural commands to kill infants; to take virgins; and to stone infidels, Sabbath-breakers and rebellious children, but applying the word *good* to this god would be devoid of all comprehensible meaning.

We could adopt the word *godgood* to describe the nature of this god, but it would bear no relation to the normal meaning of *good*. I would not object to the statement, "God is *godgood*," as long as *godgood* can be defined to mean anything that in some way accrues to God's glory, bearing no relation to the normal meaning of *good*, which for most humans entails a regard for the well-being of others. What I object to is attributing these acts of the Old Testament and the damnation of the New Testament to God while using the word *good* (in the conventional sense) to describe him.

In the collection of essays included in the book *The Evidential Argument from Evil,* atheist philosopher William Rowe introduces the problem of evil with an example of natural suffering he finds incompatible with an all-good, all-powerful God:

> Suppose in some distant forest lightning strikes a dead tree, resulting in a forest fire. In the fire a fawn is trapped, horribly burned, and lies in terrible agony for several days before death relieves its suffering. So far as we can see, the fawn's intense suffering is pointless. For there does not appear to be

any greater good such that the prevention of the fawn's suffering would require either the loss of the good or the occurrence of an evil equally bad or worse (Howard-Snyder 1996, 4).

The remainder of the essays in the book (including contributions by leading Christian philosophers Richard Swinburne and Alvin Plantinga) argue alternatively in favor of or against Rowe's central thesis. None, however, succeeds in making a case that a world in which innocent animals suffer horribly for no apparent reason is what we should *expect* on theism. At best, they make a case that such woes are merely *compatible* with the existence of a loving God whose ultimate purposes are hidden from us. Other theologians would argue that such tragedies are a result of the Fall. Yet can it be said that Adam and Eve were fairly warned of the far-reaching consequences of their actions on suffering fawns, and was it their intent to harm these fawns by taking the fruit? No, in this theological framework, it is *God* who decides the consequences of Adam and Eve's sin (it was his decision alone to engineer the consequences to reach to the fawn), and as such, he is (assuming the story of the Fall is true) no less responsible for the suffering of the fawn than if Adam and Eve had never sinned.

As an exercise, we ought ask ourselves in precisely what ways the world, once established (whether through natural processes or by divine creation), would be different from this world if God never intervened in it or if he did not exist at all. As we watch the news and hear the sole survivor of an airplane crash thanking God for sparing her (but not the others), do we have objective grounds for concluding God was lovingly involved, rather than for concluding that these events just happened? Is the proclamation of God's goodness not skewed when only the living—those who narrowly survive tragedy—remain with us to praise him for his deliverance? As we go about our day, do more fortuitous circumstances happen to us than inconveniences, or are we simply counting the good and ignoring the bad?[80] For every favor is there a corresponding irritation? Are the favors Christians receive more frequent than those of the average nonbeliever?

How many of the good things we enjoy in life stem from the goodness, friendship, and effort of others, as opposed to the goodness of an invisible, undetectable deity? If we take antibiotics to treat an ailment, do we give thanks to the scientists who made available the cure through their diligence,

---

[80] I am all in favor of focusing on the positive, of relishing the good that comes into our lives, but not for the purpose of propping up an ideology that runs counter to reality.

and do we give thanks to our employer or clients who provided the income that allowed us to purchase the antibiotics, or do we rather give the credit to God? An omnipotent god need not have expended any effort to provide a cure for a disease that he could just as well have prevented from befalling us in the first place. Diseases that are treatable today struck down millions in previous generations when the benefits of modern science were not available; often the only recourse was to pray fervently in vain. By thanking God for these medical advances we now enjoy, are we not implicitly indicting him for failing to provide the same benefits to others from a bygone era?

I close this chapter with a thought from biblical scholar and former evangelical Bart Ehrman:

> Some authors—such as the one who wrote the powerful poetic dialogues of Job—maintained that suffering is a mystery. I resonate with this view, but I do not think highly of its corollary—that we have no right to ask about the answer to the mystery, since we are, after all, mere peons and God is the ALMIGHTY, and we have no grounds for calling him to task for what he has done. If God made us (assuming the theistic view for a moment), then presumably our sense of right and wrong comes from him. If that's the case, there is no other true sense of right and wrong but his. If he does something wrong, then he is culpable by the very standards of judgment that he has given us as sentient human beings. And murdering babies, starving masses, and allowing—or causing—genocides are wrong (Ehrman 2008, 275–76).

Chapter 15

Fear of Eternal Loss

Rarely does much time pass in a conversation with a concerned believer before I am presented with one or another version of Pascal's Wager (Pascal 1670, sec. 233), articulated in the seventeenth century by Christian philosopher Blaise Pascal. The gist of this argument is this: "If I as a believer am mistaken, any loss I incur as a result is limited to this life. But if you as an unbeliever are mistaken, your loss will be felt across an infinite number of lifetimes."

Let me first say that if you use this line of reasoning on an apostate, chances are the apostate has already grappled with this issue and has decided it is without merit. How could anyone steeped in fundamentalism *not* give serious thought to the possible consequences of being mistaken about a decision of such magnitude? That was certainly the case for me; the fear of being wrong forced me to take great pains to ascertain whether I was on the right track before taking the leap out of the fold. It is a gut-wrenching experience without parallel to weigh the risk of being wrong against living a life of hypocrisy, pretending to believe in that which appears untrue.

Second, betting on Pascal's Wager does not offer immunity from danger. It may be that Islam is the One True Religion rather than Christianity, and Christians will end up in Muslim hell for believing that God is three or that he can father a son. In the course of my journey I came to see the hellfire religions as finely tuned machines determined to claim and retain the allegiance of as many souls as possible by any means possible. I consider it no coincidence that the two most successful world religions, Christianity and Islam, are the ones that feature most prominently the doctrine hell. As E. O. Wilson observed, "Every major religion today is a winner in the Darwinian struggle waged among cultures, and none ever flourished by tolerating its rivals" (Wilson 1998, 267).

Third, as I concluded in my deconversion story, belief is not something over which we have conscious control. An idea or worldview either makes sense to us or it does not. No amount of arm-twisting will change that. For example, although Galileo was forced on pain of death to recant his view that the earth rotates about the sun, no one thinks his public recantation reflected any change of inward conviction, a conviction rooted in his unwavering understanding of the facts.

I confess I abhor the use of Pascal's wager as an argument for faith. It is not an argument, but a pusillanimous threat used to compensate for the lack of good arguments for the Christian faith. And it is an idle threat, because there is no evidence whatsoever for a place of eternal torment. It is akin to walking into a crowded theater and crying, "Fire!" Of course, those who value their skin will seek the nearest exit, and chaos will ensue. But it is irresponsible to make such threats without any solid evidence for danger. Anyone can invent a threat to induce adherence to a particular cause; fear, after all, is among the most primal of our instincts. In politics, this tactic goes by the name of fear mongering. Thomas Paine had no patience for the religious version of this practice:

> Of all the tyrannies that affect mankind, tyranny in religion is the worst; every other species of tyranny is limited to the world we live in; but this attempts to stride beyond the grave, and seeks to pursue us into eternity (Paine 1797, 211).

If I knew nothing about the tenets or history of a religion except that it claims its adherents are destined for eternal bliss while nonadherents are destined for eternal torment, I would expect upon further examination to find that the religion has some very, very good—indeed, irrefutable—supporting evidence. Otherwise I would conclude that the inducements of heaven and the threats of hellfire serve merely as mechanisms to gain and keep adherents, the religion not being able otherwise to stand on the evidence. I reject Pascal's Wager as mental enslavement. If a belief is true, it is true regardless of the possible consequences of believing or not believing it. If I am fully convinced that Christianity is untrue, based on much observation, reading, prayer, and reflection, then no threats, even eternal threats, can or should have any influence *whatsoever* on my decision. Let me underscore the *whatsoever* part of it. It should be completely removed from any discussion about the truth of any religion.

I ask my readers to consider a thought experiment to determine to what extent they are influenced by the threat of hell. It is by no means a realistic thought, but imagine a world in which the penalty for subscribing to *any* false worldview is eternal torment. This would mean that if Christianity turned out to be false and deism or atheism (or any other worldview) turned out to be true, then some natural or divine law would ensure that Christian believers face damnation. If we believed that the Almighty called for rapists to marry their victims, or asked Abraham to sacrifice his son, or killed all the firstborn babes of Egypt for the hardness of Pharaoh's heart, or physically impregnated a virgin, or required his own innocent son to be tortured and killed to atone for the sins of a humanity that he had endowed with a sinful nature—if we believed any of these things that in the end turned out to be untrue, then under this thought experiment, our fate would be irrevocably sealed at the end of our lives.

Let us go even further and completely reverse Pascal's Wager. Let us imagine that Christianity did not call for the damnation of unbelievers, while every other worldview maintained that believers in Christianity were subject to damnation in the event that they were mistaken. Would Christians be as eager to embrace their particular faith as they now are? This is a question not to be brushed over lightly but to be pondered soberly. Is your confidence in the truth of the Christian faith so strong that you would be willing to submit yourself to eternal hellfire if you were misguided? If it makes any difference to you, however slight, this suggests that your decision to embrace Christianity is based at least partly on fear and not entirely on the inherit merits of Christianity.

Can we imagine the effect on our justice system if the jury were offered millions of dollars for making one decision and were threatened with death for making the opposite decision? "Oh, you're not convinced that Christianity is true after all the evidence I've presented in support of it? Well, let me throw this in for your consideration, then: if I'm right and you're wrong, then here's what's in store for you. . ." If such cajoling is required to get an individual across the threshold of faith, can we say the new convert is truly inwardly convinced?

Indeed, were it not for the insidious doctrine of hell, it is not likely I would have undertaken to write this book or to oppose Christianity in any public way. If you have sensed any passion in my previous chapters, it pales in comparison with my passion against this one human teaching, this assertion that so effectively paralyzes millions and ensures they never give a fleeting thought to an alternative worldview. I sympathize with the sentiments of Robert Ingersoll:

The orthodox God, when clothed in human flesh, told his disciples not to resist evil, to love their enemies, and when smitten on one cheek to turn the other, and yet we are told that this same God, with the same loving lips, uttered these heartless, these fiendish words; "Depart ye cursed into everlasting fire, prepared for the devil and his angels."

These are the words of "eternal love."

No human being has imagination enough to conceive of this infinite horror.

All that the human race has suffered in war and want, in pestilence and famine, in fire and flood—all the pangs and pains of every disease and every death—all this is as nothing compared with the agonies to be endured by one lost soul.

This is the consolation of the Christian religion. This is the justice of God—the mercy of Christ.

This frightful dogma, this infinite lie, made me the implacable enemy of Christianity. The truth is that this belief in eternal pain has been the real persecutor. It founded the Inquisition, forged the chains, and furnished the fagots. It has darkened the lives of many millions. It made the cradle as terrible as the coffin. It enslaved nations and shed the blood of countless thousands. It sacrificed the wisest, the bravest and the best. It subverted the idea of justice, drove mercy from the heart, changed men to fiends and banished reason from the brain.

Like a venomous serpent it crawls and coils and hisses in every orthodox creed.

It makes man an eternal victim and God an eternal fiend. It is the one infinite horror. Every church in which it is taught is a public curse. Every preacher who teaches it is an enemy of mankind. Below this Christian dogma, savagery cannot go. It is the infinite of malice, hatred, and revenge.

Nothing could add to the horror of hell, except the presence of its creator, God.

While I have life, as long as I draw breath, I shall deny with all my strength, and hate with every drop of my blood, this infinite lie (Ingersoll 1896, 21–23).

I do not include this severe Ingersoll tirade merely out of the impatience I feel toward those who persist in subscribing to the doctrine of eternal damnation; my hope is that it will bring them to a stark realization of the awful horror of what they believe, thereby effecting *change* in their outlook, or repentance.

At this point some might be tempted to respond in the way I often did as a believer when confronted with the unreasonableness of hell. I recall discussing the subject with a Spanish Catholic priest during our year of French study in Belgium in 1995. He was considerably more liberal than I was, attempting to make a case that people from every religion would ultimately be saved. My rejoinder: I personally do not find pleasure in the idea that the majority of the world's population will spend an eternity in hell, but I am obliged by the teaching of my Master Jesus to subscribe to this doctrine. It was he who said, "Enter through the narrow gate. For wide is the gate and broad is the road that leads to destruction, and many enter through it" (Matthew 7:13).

In retrospect I now see I was using Jesus' authority as a cover to justify my subscription to the most horrendous of all imaginable beliefs. It only slowly dawned on me that *I* had been responsible for subscribing to the entire package that included this inexcusable doctrine. This being the case, it was *I,* not merely Jesus, who was responsible for believing in it. Imagine I were to adopt a worldview—call it Jagarianism—that promoted every virtue but which taught that all babies were to be tortured. If non-Jagarians challenged my conviction that babies should be tortured, would they be convinced if I were to respond, "I can't help it. I don't find it agreeable myself, but I'm obligated to follow the teachings of the Great Jagar"? If not, then I beg fundamentalists not to hide behind Jesus' authority to excuse their belief in hell.

During the year or so that I retained my belief in God after my departure from Christianity, I continued to seek God, imploring him to open my eyes and to help me know the truth. In a dialogue with a Christian pastor and theologian in 2001, I sent him these thoughts concerning eternal punishment (the names have been changed):

> My son Sam has a friend named Fred. Imagine I were to go to Fred and tell him some things I want Sam to believe and practice. Some of those things seem reasonable, while others are bizarre and don't appear to correspond to reality. I tell Fred to communicate these messages to Sam, and Fred does so.
>
> Sam isn't sure the messages originated from me, so he asks me each day whether I did in fact author them, but I do not respond. He lives according to the parts of the messages that seem reasonable, which he would have done even if he hadn't heard the messages. However, he does not believe that the messages as a whole came from me, because much of their content does not fit with my character, which he believes to be benevolent, and because I never confirm directly to him that I gave the messages to Fred. Though Sam tries to be responsible, he makes mistakes. He faces hardships, but often there is no direct link between his mistakes and his hardships. When he does wrong, I do not punish him in such a way that he links the punishment directly to the offense.

All along I am hurt and angered by his disregard for the messages I sought to communicate to him through Fred. When he reaches 20 years of age, I finally open the veil and tell him that I did indeed try to speak to him through Fred, and that because he refused to listen, I must banish him forever from my family. "But wait, Dad, I asked you almost every day if those messages were from you, and you never said a word. How was I supposed to know?" "How dare you talk back to me, insolent son! Away with you forever!"

Though the meaning of the parable is plain, I want to highlight one particularly troubling aspect. A good parent does not save up punishment for a later date; the punishment is meted out as soon as possible after the infraction occurs in order to prevent further infractions. The problem with hell is that it is delayed and final. Some would say that God indeed does discipline us as we go along, but often it is impossible to discern whether a negative experience is the result of our sin, someone else's sin, God's testing, Satan's obstruction, or simple bad luck. During the past couple of years of doubting, I have experienced some anguish, but it seems to stem more from the social consequences of disbelief than from a stricken conscience. I've asked God to do something, anything to stop me if I'm headed in the wrong direction. Maybe (as one individual suggested to me) an accident I had in 2000 was the answer, or my recent bout with pneumonia. These were not tragic, but even if they had been, what does it all mean? There are no labels to go along with our experiences.

What possible purpose can hell serve but to satisfy God's vindictiveness? In the traditional Protestant view, there is no chance for reprieve on the part of those who end up in hell, so it cannot serve to reform us. Perhaps it can serve to keep us away from the righteous so as not to spoil their bliss, or to keep us from the holy presence of a god who cannot tolerate sin. But if so, simple annihilation (perhaps after a few decades or lifetimes of punishment) would do; there is no point in dragging it out forever and ever. Perhaps it can serve as an impediment for those on earth who still have a decision to make. But it cannot legitimately serve this purpose if we on earth are given no evidence of its existence, if we cannot in this life witness a taste of the torments of the damned. I can only conclude that hell exists merely as a concept, one that effectively serves the purpose of the religions that gave it birth.

As a child of missionary parents and later as a missionary myself, I attended a number of church missions conferences in the USA in which a paramount concern was for the souls of the unreached millions destined for a "Christless eternity." This belief in hell serves as a powerful impetus to evangelical missionary endeavors. Often I have heard stories of missionaries who were persecuted, blamed for village misfortune, or chased out of town. Yet rarely do we hear the other side of the story. How do we expect we would react if someone came from afar and told us our deceased relatives were now roasting in hell for eternity, then sought to convince us to adopt their point of view and escape this same fate? Would we take kindly to their proposition? How is it "good news" that we can avoid eternal torment if it is too late for our parents who were so dear to us? Is it good news to hear that most of those who have ever existed have gone into a Christless eternity, even if those of us still living have a chance of reprieve? No, it is far greater news to know that there is no such thing as hell in the first place, and that none of us will be aware of or give the least thought to our nonexistence once it arrives.

Have you ever been to a funeral in which the pastor said of the deceased, "This woman rejected our Savior to her dying day and is therefore now consigned to an eternity of torment"? Or, "This man professed to believe, but by his fruits we know he was not among the redeemed (Titus 1:16), and is therefore now in hell"? How about, "He went out from us, but he did not really belong to us. For if he had belonged to us, he would have remained with us" (1 John 2:19)? Or, "She denied Jesus; therefore, Jesus will deny her" (2 Timothy 2:12)? Very few if any pastors dare make such pronouncements, no doubt for fear of offending friends and relatives in attendance. Yet for pastors who truly believe God teaches these things, it is difficult to imagine a worse disservice to those in attendance than to lull them falsely into thinking they can follow the worldliness or unbelief of the deceased and still escape the flames of hell. Whatever happened to having the courage of one's convictions? Do pastors really believe what they say they do? Then they ought either to show some backbone in funeral services or simply to declare their disavowal of belief in hell altogether. Few religious leaders today have as much courage to express the implications of their purported belief in hell as has the conservative Catholic actor Mel Gibson, who had this to say when asked about the fate of Protestants:

> "There is no salvation for those outside the [Roman Catholic] Church," Gibson replied. "I believe it." He explained: "Put it this way. My wife is a saint. She's a much better person than I am. Honestly. She's, like, Episcopalian, Church of England. She prays, she believes in God, she knows Jesus, she believes in that stuff. And it's just not fair if she doesn't make it, she's better than I am. But that is a pronouncement from the chair. I go with it" (Dennett 2006, 289).

I recall as a sixth-grade student at my missionary boarding school a devotional time in which our "dorm parent" read us the biblical story of the bronze serpent:

Then the LORD sent venomous snakes among them; they bit the people and many Israelites died. The people came to Moses and said, "We sinned when we spoke against the LORD and against you. Pray that the LORD will take the snakes away from us." So Moses prayed for the people. The LORD said to Moses, "Make a snake and put it up on a pole; anyone who is bitten can look at it and live." So Moses made a bronze snake and put it up on a pole. Then when anyone was bitten by a snake and looked at the bronze snake, he lived (Deuteronomy 21:6–8).

It occurred to me to ask the dorm parent whether all who were bitten chose to look at the serpent, and if not, whether they died. She surmised that some refused to look and perished as a result, at which point I complained, "Why didn't they *just look* at the serpent and live? How hard is *that*? How foolish of them!" Our dorm parent agreed and proceeded to use this as an object lesson, admonishing everyone of their need to look to Jesus to save them from eternal death.

The problem with this reasoning is that there are myriads of "cures" on the market, both physical and spiritual, which people in desperate straights are willing to accept as true. To sample all the scientifically untested infomercial products in the hope of addressing this or that ailment would be not only a waste of time and money but might also be a safety hazard; what's more, it would serve as encouragement for more and more outrageous quackery to thrive until someone—an unwelcome skeptic, perhaps—had the courage to test (and likely debunk) their claims. If a magnetic mattress or powdered shark cartilage is touted as a cure for cancer but double-blind scientific tests have not borne it out, it is folly to open one's wallet to grasp these wispy straws, no matter how desperate the situation. It is more than folly—it is an open-ended endorsement and enabling of those who prey on the gullible for a living.

APPEASING THE LIVING

We have all heard stories of those who lived a life of profligacy or apostasy but, to the great relief of their believing kin, uttered a prayer of repentance and belief on their deathbed. Perhaps some such conversions are genuine, while others are calculated to relieve the unbearable pain of relatives who might otherwise consider them to be destined for hell. I have given some thought concerning my own situation, for there is a distinct possibility that I might not see eye to eye with my family for the rest of my life. Will I, out of fear for my own skin or out of consideration for the pain of my relatives, declare my allegiance to Jesus on my deathbed? I cannot predict the future even of my own thinking, but it is my considered decision at present that, if

I remain genuinely convinced that the Christian gospel is untrue, I will not bow to whatever pressure is exerted upon me to lend legitimacy casually to a system of beliefs I find untenable. It will be painful to my loved ones, but I trust the pain will serve for them only to come to terms with the inhumanity of what they (in apparent good faith) believe, helping to chase the last vestiges of hellfire out of their compassionate hearts.

Why is there such great interest in the alleged deathbed conversions of skeptics? Certainly compassion is a factor, especially for relatives; few today relish the thought of a loved one's spending eternity in hell. But I am convinced there is far more to it than mere compassion. Those who continue to spread the false rumor that Charles Darwin recanted his theory of evolution and embraced Christ on his deathbed are probably less concerned about his post-terrestrial welfare than they are about the vindication of their creationist and theistic convictions. Those of us who persist in good conscience to deny the gospel until the end constitute a threat to those who believe that Christianity is an inherently compelling worldview to fair-minded, honest, informed seekers. But this threat can be attenuated if we unbelievers repent on our deathbed, recanting a lifetime of objections against the gospel. It shows in the end that we didn't *really* believe our skepticism was as warranted as we had claimed.

It is for this reason that it is important for those of us who take a principled stand against fundamentalism and the doctrine of hell to persist in that stand until we draw our final breath. If enough individuals stand up with courage to this madness, this stranglehold, and say, "Enough!" then perhaps the next generation will take courage and liberate itself from this curse, ending forever the paralyzing fear and tyranny of the hereafter and freeing humanity to focus on *this* life, the only one we know we have. The scourge of hell can only be broken if we have the backbone to declare that the emperor has no clothes. But why should I care about all this if it won't matter when I die? It is because it matters to me *in this life* how my damnation-believing family, friends and society perceive the majority of us on earth that do not embrace the Christian faith.

I do not wish to give false comfort to my loved ones that I will one day join them in heaven. If we are to believe the author of 2 Timothy 2:12, who stated, "If we deny him, he will also deny us" (KJV), and if we are to believe Jesus when he declared, "If anyone is ashamed of me and my words, the Son of Man will be ashamed of him when he comes in his glory and in the glory of the Father and of the holy angels" (Luke 9:26), then I will not be counted among the redeemed. If we are to believe the author of the book of Hebrews, I will surely face God's judgment:

If we deliberately keep on sinning after we have received the knowledge of the truth, no sacrifice for sins is left, but only a fearful expectation of judgment and of raging fire that will consume the enemies of God. Anyone who rejected the law of Moses died without mercy on the testimony of two or three witnesses. How much more severely do you think a man deserves to be punished who has trampled the Son of God under foot, who has treated as an unholy thing the blood of the covenant that sanctified him, and who has insulted the Spirit of grace? For we know him who said, "It is mine to avenge; I will repay," and again, "The Lord will judge his people." It is a dreadful thing to fall into the hands of the living God (Hebrews 10:26–31).

But why, you ask, must I be so brazen? Why not allow a glimmer of hope for those whom I hold dear, encouraging them to suppose that by virtue of my former faith or by virtue of my future openness to the gospel (even if not my present acceptance of it), I will ultimately be saved? It is because the most effective weapon at my disposal to combat hellfire-induced fear-mongering is my example of fearless defiance in the face of it. We skeptics must demonstrate we are not bluffing in our contention that the hellfire threats of fundamentalists are empty, baseless, and rotten to the core. My aim is to bring my readers to terms with the starkness and horror of what they believe, if they continue to cling to the idea that the majority of humankind, including me, will suffer eternally while they themselves enjoy a get-out-of-hell-free card. My hope is not that others should fret over my fate but that they will relinquish their grip on hell and rest in the assurance that no one will ever go there, because such a place does not exist.

If the author of the Hebrews and the other New Testament writers were alive today, this is what I would say to them: "How dare you cry, 'Fire!' in a crowded theater of billions of souls over two millennia, holding them captive to doctrines for which there is no evidence for fear they will roast eternally at the hands of a vengeful God! How dare you make my wife and children agonize over the possibility that a horrendous fate might await me in the hereafter! How dare you divide brother against brother, wife against husband, father against children, friend against friend! How dare you prevent countless souls from being honest about their very real doubts out of fear they might be destined to the hell you prescribe for apostates!"

DEFENSES OF THE DOCTRINE OF HELL

In response to my charge that hell is an invention to coerce people into faith or to retain their allegiance, some have responded that neither they nor anyone they know of is a Christian out of a fear of hell. Though it is not currently fashionable to admit that the fear of damnation is a motivating factor for believing, it was indeed quite commonly used in past centuries (and in many fundamentalist circles still today) to shake people up and to lead them to a faith commitment. One need only visit an independent fundamental Baptist church or a Southern Baptist revival to verify my claim. If stoking the fear of hell is not an effective tool for garnering belief and commitment, why was it such a key component of renowned theologian Jonathan Edwards' revivals and his essay, "Sinners in the Hands of an Angry God" (Edwards 1741)? In that 7,200-word sermon, I count 51 instances of the word *hell*, 17 of *fire*, 14 of *destruction*, nine of *torment*, six variants of *damnation*, five of *eternal*, four of *worm*, three of *curse*, two of *brimstone*, and two of *pain*.

Even if the doctrine of eternal damnation is not preached weekly from every evangelical pulpit, it can nonetheless serve its purpose quietly in the minds of those who might otherwise consider defection. As Robert Ingersoll observed, "Orthodoxy cannot afford to put out the fires of hell" (Ingersoll 1884, 405).

In 2005 my precious but concerned six-year-old daughter told me, "You're the best daddy in the whole world, except for one thing: you don't believe in God." I asked her why she believed the Bible. She told me she wasn't sure but that she didn't want to go to hell if she didn't believe it. And how could I be sure there's no such thing as hell? Now, I know that my wife and the church she goes to do not make a regular habit of drumming the fear of hell into her, but a child's mind is very impressionable, and even an occasional suggestion of hell can have a profound and lasting impact. I take issue with anyone who attempts to dismiss the usefulness of hell as an evangelistic tool. Granted, it was no doubt more effective in the past when faith reigned supreme, and it has increasingly become a liability in modern and postmodern times as people have questioned the very premises on which the doctrine of hell was built. But on balance, the doctrine of hell has served very well the interests of the religions (for example, Christianity and Islam) that have preached it.

Some have sought to defend belief in hell by asserting that it is simply a matter of justice. How calloused! This rationalization is normally based on an appeal to the infinite nature of the god against whom our offenses are committed. But as theologian and Nazi resistance leader Dietrich Bonhoeffer admonished,

The church must stop trying to act as a kind of "spiritual pharmacist"— working to produce acute guilt, and then in effect saying: "We just happen to have the remedy for your guilt here in our pocket" (Babinski 1995, 99).[81]

Think for a moment about the human condition: We were born into this world, uninvited, with a propensity to selfishness, without our having had a say in what kind of nature we would be given. We struggle to make a living, raise a family, battle disease, and endure hardship of all sorts. We inevitably make mistakes along the way (because of both our nature and our choices), and then we are told that our condition is infinitely abominable to God. Christians have the right to accept that view of God, but they should not expect the rest of us to think it reasonable.

We all make many mistakes, and we should not make ourselves out to be more righteous than we are. But as Paul warns us not to think of ourselves more highly than we ought (Romans 12:3), should we not also avoid thinking of ourselves more lowly than we ought? Or as Paul goes on to say, to think of ourselves "with sober judgment?" I understand the tendency to lower ourselves infinitely in the face of an infinitely perfect God, but after all, if God exists, are we not then his handiwork? In this light, is it not an insult to God to think of ourselves as worms, unable to reason on our own, inherently deplorable in God's sight? Even the crimes of Hitler were not sufficient to merit *eternal* punishment; he committed his evil acts during only a finite lifetime. To assert that our sin is infinite because it's against an infinite God stacks the deck against a humanity that had no say in the arrangement and that in any case is largely unaware of the alleged infinitude of its sin while groping through life.

In his interview with Christian journalist-apologist Lee Strobel, evangelical philosopher J. P. Morland seeks to vindicate God's decision to create hell by insisting God had no choice: "Hell is something God was forced to make because people chose to rebel against him and turn against what was best for them and the purpose for which they were created" (Strobel 2000, 175). Whatever happened to God's sovereignty? How can the words "God was forced" be used by anyone who believes God is free to do whatever he wishes? No, God was not *forced* to do anything, as if his creatures' rebellion had taken him by surprise: he could just as easily have let them die and be remembered no more, or he could have wooed them or cajoled them into repentance, or he could have taken any other course of action that we in our finite wisdom might not even be capable of imagining. If God's sovereignty means anything, then for those who

---

[81] I was unable to trace this quotation to its original source. The argument to be made, however, is independent of whether or not Bonhoeffer himself penned these words.

believe in hell, *he freely and unapologetically chose* to create hell and confine his unrepentant subjects to that place of torment forever, and *he planned this outcome from "before" the beginning of time.* It will not do to sugarcoat this reality and to absolve the Christian god of all responsibility in his decision to make hell.

In response to those who wonder why God could not have simply annihilated his rebellious subjects, Moreland offers the following logic:

> Believe it or not, everlasting separation from God is morally superior to annihilation. Why would God be morally justified in annihilating somebody? The only way that's a good thing would be the end result, which would be to keep people from experiencing the conscious separation from God forever. Well, then you're treating people as a means to an end. . . . What hell does is recognize that people have intrinsic value. If God loves intrinsic value, then he has got to be a sustainer of persons, because that means he is a sustainer of intrinsic value. He refuses to snuff out a creature that was made in his own image. So in the final analysis, hell is the only morally legitimate option (Strobel 2000, 183).

How can Moreland ignore Paul's explicit teaching that God has indeed created certain individuals as a means to an end, namely, that of making known his power and wrath?

> Does not the potter have the right to make out of the same lump of clay some pottery for noble purposes and some for common use? What if God, *choosing to show his wrath and make his power known*, bore with great patience the objects of his wrath—prepared for destruction? (Romans 9:21, 22).

Moreland's conjecture that God should avoid annihilating us for fear it would be a means to an end is based not on biblical teaching but on a philosophical agenda that seeks to justify the orthodox doctrine of eternal damnation. To his credit, Moreland recognizes more intrinsic value in the existence of the damned than did Paul, who compared us with common-use pottery. We recognize intrinsic value in a horse, but we don't hesitate to put the animal out of its misery if it is suffering and wounded beyond recovery. Does God have any moral compulsion to preserve the horse's existence throughout eternity? If I ended up in hell, whether in mild discomfort or in supreme agony, and I begged God to end my existence, would it be immoral for him to do so, simply for fear that he would be treating me as a means to an end, even if I desired that end? If this is the case—if he gives me the choice to reject him in this life but not to end my existence in the next—then his respect for my free will extends only as far as is necessary for apologists to feel justified in believing in hell. It's pick-and-choose apologetics: appeal to free will when convenient; discard it when not.

While some believers seem eager to justify the traditional view of hell, others tend to recognize it as an uncomfortable liability, an albatross preventing general acceptance of the Christian faith in a pluralistic society. Their approach might be to reinterpret or mitigate the horrors of hell as commonly understood. Rather than a place of endless involuntary torment where souls roast in literal flames, perhaps hell is simply a metaphor for separation from God. J. P. Moreland insists, "Hell is not a torture chamber," and "God will have absolutely no choice but to give us what we've asked for all along in our lives, which is separation from him. And that is hell" (Strobel 2000, 175).

Others go farther and suggest that individuals who end up in hell will ultimately be given a chance to reconsider their decision, repent and be welcomed back into the gates of heaven. For example, C. S. Lewis in his books *The Problem of Pain* (Lewis 1940) and *The Great Divorce* (Lewis 1946) proposes that hell is locked from the inside (Lewis 1940, 130). In other words, souls that end up in hell remain there only by their own choice, and most (though perhaps not all) choose to stay as a result of their pride. Lewis suggests a Hell Lite that's dreary and lonely but certainly not agonizing like the Hell Supreme that Jonathan Edwards and Dante envisioned.

While this softer view of hell or purgatory is far less objectionable than the traditional Calvinist view, it is neither biblical nor especially coherent. None of the biblical texts suggest a willingness on the part of hell-goers to accept their fate; instead, they are thrown against their will into the fire, where there is weeping and gnashing of teeth (Matt. 13:42). The rich man in Luke 16 certainly did not relish his consignment to hell and even desired to warn his brothers to avoid the same fate. But even if this view were biblical, how could anyone whose mental faculties are intact—no matter how stubborn or proud—*choose* to remain *forever* in even a mildly uncomfortable situation when the bliss of paradise or the nothingness of annihilation remains an option for them? And if their mental faculties are not intact, how can they be held responsible for their decision? (Talbott 1999, 195–196)

Others go even farther than C. S. Lewis and deny the eternality or existence of hell altogether in favor of some form of universalism. For instance, quasi-evangelical Thomas Talbott systematically examines every New Testament text on the subject of hell and concludes that hell is not eternal after all, but that everyone will ultimately be saved, though for unbelievers this will entail a stint of finite duration in a refining hell before repenting (Talbott 1999). While some of his hermeneutic practices used to reach this conclusion may be somewhat strained, and traditionalists like

William Lane Craig are quick to identify his weaknesses, Talbott does make a valiant and (mostly) effective effort to rescue the gospel from the pit of eternal damnation.

We should note that no single position is fully supported by all the scriptural passages that bear on this topic: some biblical authors speak of the final destruction or annihilation of sinners, while others speak of an eternal lake of fire. It is not as though the traditional Protestant position is *the* biblical stance; it is just as easy for Talbott to marshal passages against an eternal hell as it is for traditional Protestants to catalogue passages in its favor. The Bible simply lacks unity on this subject, as on so many others.

Whether or not Talbott's position is scripturally defensible,[82] I can only hope that more and more Christians will embrace his perspective, thus rendering the gospel infinitely more humane, tolerant, and unifying. Those who are convinced that the New Testament offers only one perspective on this matter are challenged to read Talbott's *The Inescapable Love of God*.

It could be that I am fundamentally mistaken in my evaluation of God's existence or the truth of Christianity. Perhaps (though I highly doubt it) the Christian faith is in some sense true after all, or perhaps there exists a creator with no attachment to any human religion. But in that case, I am wagering that he (or she or it) is less interested in the particulars of my beliefs than in how I treat my fellow humans, and that he is not such a fiend as to consign even a single soul to eternal torment. I close this chapter with these reflections from Robert Ingersoll:

> I had rather think of those I have loved, and lost, as having returned to earth, as having become a part of the elemental wealth of the world—I would rather think of them as unconscious dust, I would rather dream of them as gurgling in the streams, floating in the clouds, bursting in the foam of light upon the shores of worlds, I would rather think of them as the lost visions of a forgotten night, than to have even the faintest fear that their naked souls have been clutched by an orthodox god. I will leave my dead where nature leaves them. Whatever flower of hope springs up in my heart I will cherish, I will give it breath of sighs and rain of tears. But I can not believe that there is any being in this universe who has created a human soul for eternal pain. I would rather that every god would destroy himself; I would rather that we all should go to eternal chaos, to black and starless night, than that just one soul should suffer eternal agony.

---

[82] I believe Talbot's biblical case for dismissing the eternality of hell is stronger than any biblical case for abolishing slavery.

I have made up my mind that if there is a God, he will be merciful to the merciful.

Upon that rock I stand. –

That he will not torture the forgiving. –

Upon that rock I stand. –

That every man should be true to himself, and that there is no world, no star, in which honesty is a crime.

Upon that rock I stand. –

The honest man, the good woman, the happy child, have nothing to fear, either in this world or the world to come.

Upon that rock I stand (Ingersoll 1880, 524-25).

And I wager that Ingersoll—the late implacable enemy of Christianity—is not now roasting in God's torture chamber. Nor will anyone. That is the good news, the gospel of naturalism.

Chapter 16

Questions, Answers, and Final Thoughts

Following my deconversion and the posting of my story on the Web, a number of individuals have contacted me with questions and comments. These have come from staunch fundamentalists, from confirmed atheists, and from people of every shade in between. In this chapter I will address some of the most common questions I been asked by e-mail or in person.

ARE YOU HAPPIER NOW THAN BEFORE?

As happiness is a subjective, multifaceted quality, it is difficult to provide an unequivocal "Yes" or "No" in response to this question. What's more, I must respond carefully: If I say I'm happier as a result of my liberation from religion, I might be accused of having left Christ merely out of a desire for personal liberty. If I say I'm miserable without God, it might be taken as an indication that I truly need God. Either way, I can't win.

On the one hand, I do feel the pain of no longer being able to see eye to eye with many of my friends and family. I live in a degree of tension with my friends stemming from our philosophical differences; it is sometimes difficult for us to accept each other for who we are rather than for what we'd like each other to become. And, like a former smoker craving another cigarette, I still do occasionally—though far less often than in the early stages of my deconversion—feel the sting of knowing my life lacks the cosmic significance I once thought it had.

On the other hand, hardly a day goes by without my feeling a sense of *relief* over no longer having to defend the indefensible. There are certainly many things I do not know and that I may never know, and though I am always driven to learn more, I have come to accept that I don't have to know more than that which is knowable. Virtually every day I look forward to learning more, taking in the mystery of the world and of the process by which it came to be what it is. I feel a great sense of freedom in uncovering truth from a wide variety of sources, without feeling constrained to relate every finding to an orthodox biblical framework whose old wineskins have burst with the wine of science, reason, archaeology, and common sense.

I can experience the wonder of studying the strata of the earth, fossils, the evolutionary tree, the coalescing of interstellar dust into stars and planets, and human and animal psychology. I can delight in how the pieces of the puzzle fit together, rather than attributing it all to a magical creation event, which, in its attempt to explain everything, explains only what God did in his inscrutable ways, not how or why he might have done it. It's fascinating and gratifying to explore why we are plagued with parasites, why men are more eager to have sex than women, why men are more prone to violence than women, why babies have a grasping instinct, why we have toenails, why we crave sweet and fatty foods and become obese, why we gossip, why trees bear fruit, why attractive and fragrant flowers exist, why birds sing, and why there are so many human languages. Pondering the evolutionary underpinnings of these phenomena is far more satisfying than reading about a talking serpent in a garden or about the Tower of Babel or hearing, "That's just the way God made it." Perhaps it's due to my inquisitive nature, but I've always been more fascinated by "why" and "how" questions than "what" questions.

Earlier I mentioned a closet deist missionary physician with whom I have been corresponding. Here is his description of the relief he experienced after letting go of the quandaries of his Christian faith:

> One of the advantages of losing one's faith … is that I can look on some of the controversial topics within Christianity with dispassion (or perhaps "indifference" would be a better word). The role of women in the church, homosexuality, divorce and remarriage, God's ability to change or remain the same ("openness theology"), predestination, Sabbath keeping, tithes, etc. all become nonissues...and I must say that this is refreshing to not have to go through the intellectual castigation of trying to work out all the thorny matters as filtered through one's personal theology. You can just...let it go... because again, these things are non-issues... And just like Pilgrim in "Pilgrim's Progress" who let go of his burden and watched it roll down the hill, so I feel with so many previously troubling theological issues (including the problem of pain and the problem of evil, in addition to the ones I mentioned previously) as I've watched that intellectual/theological burden go rolling down the hill and I feel the weight lifted off my shoulders … (and how heavy it was I didn't realize until it was gone....)

Additionally, I no longer feel any compulsion whatsoever to try to make sense out of the things that happen to me, as though there were some cosmic lesson God were trying to teach me. If I am involved in a car accident, the lesson for me to learn is what to do next time to avoid it, insofar as possible—not to try to figure out why God arranged or permitted it. If my flight is cancelled due to a snowstorm when traveling to my grandfather's funeral (as happened to me in 2004), I accept it and move on, without wondering what God's plan was or why I wasn't "supposed" to go the funeral. Nothing was "supposed" to happen; it just happened! This is tremendously freeing, and I believe it would be for you also if you are held captive by futile efforts to understand what God is doing in your life or to figure out God's will for your future. Though I was never particularly drawn into the practice of discerning signs as a believer (a practice Robert Price terms "evangelical divination"), I, along with most of my fellow evangelicals, often reflected on good and bad events, wondering what God was trying to teach us. In the end I came to see this as hit and miss, being no more reliable than tealeaves, astrology, or entrails. There are no labels to go with our experiences, no handwriting on the wall, no voice from the sky to tell us what it means. We have no reliable standard for distinguishing between God's voice and our own.

Finally, I can now look at all humans as fellow journeyers along the road of life and appreciate them for who they are, not for how they stand in relation to an exclusive theology that divides us into the damned and the redeemed. While flying to India on a business trip in 2004, I observed my fellow passengers and reflected on how I would have seen them if I had still been a believer. Most on board were not Christians and, under traditional evangelical theology, likely would have been doomed to an eternity of hell if the plane had crashed. How freeing it was to think of them all as simply members of my species, some better behaved than others, some whose beliefs correspond better to reality than others, but most traveling through life like me, facing trials and triumphs, tears and joy, toil and leisure! Until you have been released from the weight of believing that others around you might be bound for hell, you can never appreciate what a great relief it is to live as a nonbeliever. I have a new lightness in my step as I go about my life, a freedom to take things a little less seriously than before. No one is going to hell!

So the short answer to the question is that I am in some ways less happy and in other ways happier than I was as a believer, but overall I would have to say I am more content now that I am free to pursue the evidence wherever it leads.

HAVE YOUR MORALS CHANGED?

Very little. I do not expect others to live just as I do, but I have found no reason to change my lifestyle in any significant way since my deconversion. I live the way I do simply because I believe it's the way that works best for me, not so I can find favor with God or his representatives.

Though I no longer believe in an objective body of laws handed down from a transcendent Lawgiver, I do accept that some behaviors are healthier than others for the well-being of society. I want other people to trust what I say, so I refrain from lying. I want other people to be kind to me, so I strive to be kind to others. I want my marriage to be happy, so I strive to please my wife, even if I have much room for growth. I love my wife and want my family to remain intact, so I remain faithful to my marriage. I want my children to flourish, so I spend time with them and love them. I gain satisfaction from supporting the poor and sick, and I would like other people to support me should I fall into poverty myself (cf. 2 Cor. 8:14), so I contribute financially to their cause. I am not bound by a higher authority to do these things, but I find them desirable. I do not judge others for having different perspectives unless their behavior results in harm to society, especially to those whom I love.

When a Christian friend asked, "Is it more difficult to live morally now than when you were a believer?" he was somewhat surprised when I said no. I am still the same person with the same weaknesses and strengths as I ever was, and it is neither harder nor easier to refrain from temptation now than it was before. I still struggle with procrastination, a battle I fight (and often lose) daily. At times I become angry and yell at my children, though no more now than when I was a believer. I can be argumentative and arrogant when presenting my views to others; this may indeed be one temptation I have fallen prey to more often as an unbeliever as the opportunities for confrontation have grown. While a Christian, I often prayed to avoid sexual temptation, but I no longer do so now, and the temptations are no greater. When pornographic spam e-mail finds its way into my inbox, I simply think, "If I look at this, how will it affect my relationship with my wife and family?" At that moment I simply resolve not to look at it, then delete it and go on. I do not think of Satan or the Holy Spirit or any eternal reward or punishment during these times; it's just a matter of resolving to do what I believe is in my best interest.

Several years ago, when looking for a lost dog leash, I announced to my children, "Whoever finds the leash first gets a candy." My then six-year-old son asked, "What if *you* find it first, Dad? Do *you* get to have a candy?" My eight-year-old son responded, "He's an adult; he can have as many candies as he wants." Some Christians believe that, in the absence of divine restraints, we would all fall into debauchery, eating as many candies as we want, so to speak. But this ignores the natural reality that, in general, living morally benefits us *in this life,* and there are many good reasons to behave ourselves other than the fear of future punishment or the desire to please our maker.

I no longer spend any significant time in prayer, devotional Bible study, or church attendance, but I do not consider these to be moral issues—they are religious. I held back from listening to popular secular music for a year or two after leaving the faith, continuing to listen to a mixture of contemporary Christian and classical music. But over time I have also become interested in classic pop and rock music in the genre of the Beatles and Creedence Clearwater Revival.

Though I'll occasionally enjoy a glass or two of wine, I have never been drunk. This is a personal decision; I have no problem with those who overdo it now and then, as long as they don't get out on the road inebriated or cause harm to others.

Nor has my language changed. Though I don't take offense at the colorful speech of others, I have chosen to avoid expletives, again purely as a personal decision. I don't deny this is due at least in part to my upbringing; in this respect I am like a former Orthodox Jew who finds it difficult to eat pork after leaving the Jewish faith.

Contributing my time and money to the needs of those in unfortunate situations is still a value I espouse and practice, though I have always had room for improvement, both pre- and postdeconversion.

My political views have moderated somewhat—I now vote Democratic or Republican depending on my view of the candidates, rather than voting straight Republican as in the past. I do not oppose stem cell research on unfeeling embryos. If in my old age I come to live in chronic pain, or if heroic and costly measures are required to keep me alive and out of misery, I would like to have the option to end my life humanely and with dignity. I would prefer to take this step without the meddling of politicians or acquaintances who object to my decision on religious grounds. These views reflect a change from my former position, a change to which my evangelical friends will object. I am willing to dialogue with those who differ, but I will be more responsive to arguments based on practical consequences than on the Bible, religion, authority, or tradition.

DO YOU EVER DOUBT YOUR DOUBTS?

I certainly vacillated in my earlier crises of faith and during the months following my watershed crisis in March 2000. I did not begin seriously doubting God's existence until the summer of 2001. Starting at some point between those two dates, I have lost not so much as a moment's sleep over the truth of Christianity. Some have asked me how I can be so confident in my position. Most believers who read this book will not make the transition I have made; until you cross that bridge, you can never understand or appreciate the interlocking web of evidence that confirms unbelief. But whether or not you can personally appreciate it, you can take my word that I have no doubts about my doubts concerning the divine inspiration of the Bible, the Trinity, hell, and all other exclusively Christian doctrines.

Though I have not shut out the possibility of God's existence, with each passing year I have become more convinced that no personal being or supernatural force exists outside the natural world. I can respect those who believe in God—I fully appreciate the mysteries of the universe that drive most of humanity to the conclusion that there is a mind behind it all. Contrary to my conclusions concerning Christianity, there are occasional moments when I wonder whether I may be mistaken in my belief that there is no god. However, if someone who really knew the answer to the question approached me with a billion dollars, saying the prize would be mine if I answered correctly, I would say God does not exist, and I think (even if I'm not certain) I would be a billion dollars richer. In the absence of any social pressure, pretense, or threat of punishment, and with the offer of a potential jackpot if you can correctly answer a "Yes" or "No" question, what would you say? What would you say if a similar prize were offered concerning the truth of biblical Christianity?

DO YOU EVER FEEL GUILTY ABOUT YOUR DECISION?

Do I regret some of the consequences of my deconversion, consequences like the difficult situation I have put my wife and family into? Certainly. Through no fault of their own, they happen to have a husband, father, son, and brother who has mysteriously turned his back on what they cherish above all else. I and I alone take responsibility for this unexpected turn of events. No one drove me to it; I came to this conclusion on my own.

Do I feel guilt over my decision? Not in the least. It would be like asking Galileo whether he felt guilty for believing the earth revolves about the sun, even in the wake of all the turmoil it caused the church and those who believed they had the world figured out, with God's beloved humankind in the center of it. Surely Galileo felt no guilt for following what he understood to be the truth, even if he regretted the fallout his heretical ideas incurred. Similarly, I feel no shame for my decision to go where I believe the preponderance of the evidence leads.

If the gospel is true, and if God will hold me eternally accountable for my decision, why has he not plagued me with an acute sense of guilt? Would you not do everything in your power to prevent your child from going down a path you knew would end in her self-destruction? Or would you wait until it's too late and pronounce, "You should have known better!" at her demise?

HOW DO YOU RELATE TO YOUR WIFE AND FAMILY?

As you might imagine, my journey away from faith has introduced into our marriage a set of difficult challenges we did not previously face. Charlene has asked God, "Why me? Why did this have to happen to me?" She has also felt a sense of loss in not being able to fulfill her call to missions. She feels like a single mother when she takes our children to church, and she can no longer pray with me, read the Bible with me, or join me in meaningful conversations about spiritual matters. We simply no longer see eye to eye about God, the Bible, Jesus, or anything else I've discussed in this book. For her, it must be in some sense like being married to a spouse affected by Alzheimer's Disease: the person she is now married to is not the same person she first married, and she feels a real sense of loss.

Yet for all these challenges, we have managed to feel each other out, to know where our tender points are, to avoid provoking each other, and to continue respecting and loving each other for who we are. In the first couple of years following my deconversion, we engaged in some relatively spirited conversations that led to hurt feelings, but we have learned with time to avoid pressing our views on each other. As in any marriage, neither of us is without our faults, our blind spots, our selfish and judgmental tendencies. But I love Charlene—I love you, Charlene—and have no desire to change the way I feel about you, whether or not you ever come to see things the way I do, and whether or not I ever see things the way you do. I believe we have a stronger marriage than many who never face the kinds of challenges we are confronted with, and I look forward to spending the rest of my life with you.

I can relate to the pain of Charles Darwin, who remained faithful all his life to his believing wife Emma and to their ten children. He never succeeded in changing Emma's mind, nor she his. Darwin's autobiography includes the following excerpt from a letter Emma wrote Charles to persuade him to reconsider his freethinking views (Darwin, Darwin, and Barlow 1958, 236):

> Your mind and time are full of the most interesting subjects and thoughts of the most absorbing kind. . . . May not the habit in scientific pursuits of believing nothing till it is proved, influence your mind too much in other things which cannot be proved in the same way, and which if true are likely to be above our comprehension.

Darwin's pain over the impasse with his wife is apparent from the note he wrote at the bottom of Emma's letter (Darwin, Darwin and Barlow 1958, 237):

> When I am dead, know
> that many times, I
> have kissed and cryed
> over this. C.D.

These few lines are among the most trenchant and heart-wrenching I have ever read.

Concerning a few practical matters: Though I no longer pray at mealtimes, I do join hands with the family and bow my head respectfully when the others pray. I have not prevented Charlene from taking our children to any church functions, but I have also let them know where I stand, and to a certain extent, why I have come to believe what I do. It is my aim to instill in them the need to think these matters through for themselves when they come of age and not to feel pressured—either by Charlene or by me—to make a permanent decision one way or the other as children. And of course, I will always love them whether or not they ultimately side with me on the question of the Christian faith.

PARTING THOUGHTS

Why do Christians believe? Why did I believe? There is no single answer to the question, but I am convinced it has to do with desire—the desire for the promises in the song "Heaven Came Down":

> Heaven came down and glory filled my soul
> When at the cross the Savior made me whole
> My sins were washed away
> And my night was turned to day
> Heaven came down and glory filled my soul
>
> O what a wonderful, wonderful day, day I will never forget;
> After I'd wandered in darkness away, Jesus my Savior I met.

O what a tender, compassionate friend, He met the need of my heart;
Shadows dispelling, with joy I am telling, He made all the darkness depart.

Born of the Spirit with life from above into God's family divine,
Justified fully thru Calvary's love, O what a standing is mine!
And the transaction so quickly was made, when as a sinner I came,
Took of the offer, of grace He did proffer, He saved me, O praise His dear
name!

Now I've a hope that will surely endure after the passing of time;
I have a future in heaven for sure there in those mansions sublime.
And it's because of that wonderful day, when at the cross I believed;
Riches eternal and blessings supernal, from His precious hand I received.

We would like to think that for all the suffering and the massive injustice we see on a daily basis, there is someone who is in charge, someone who can right all the wrongs some day (if not in this life, then in the life to come). We want the existence of cosmic justice. Following is a list of desires my closet deist missionary physician friend passed along to me. I believe his list captures the essence of the desires that fuel Christian religious belief.

1. We don't want to die.
2. We want to be free from disease, aging, and suffering.
3. We want some being to be in control of everything, i.e., we want security and the overcoming of evil.
4. We want cosmic justice (if not in this life, then in the next).
5. We want to see deceased friends and relatives again.
6. We want to be forgiven for the wrongs and mistakes we commit.
7. (Corollary to #3 and #5) We want all the bad actions in this life to be *redeemed* some day, to be made right; i.e., we want all bad things to be reversed.
8. We want a life free of conflict and full of love (if not in this life, then in the next).
9. We want a permanent friend, Someone who is always available to hear our thoughts, Someone to whom we can unburden ourselves, and who always understands us.
10. We want Someone who is always available to help us.

If the gospel lacks correspondence to reality, why is it that the majority of believers never comes to terms with this? As I expressed in my opening chapter, I am convinced it is not due to a lack of intelligence. Nor is it due to a lack of goodness or noble intentions on the part of most believers. Rather, from the perspective of one who has escaped the finely tuned clutches of the Christian machinery designed to keep me in the fold, I see it primarily as a lack of courage, at least for those who have encountered good reasons for doubting. I, like most believers, experienced serious doubts as a young Christian, but I lacked the courage to pit my reservations against the authority of the church and against its fallible, humanly authored scriptures, finding it safer to submit to the supremely well-crafted, guilt-inducing tactics of apologists who assured me that all the fault lay with me and not with the divinely inspired Bible. I capitulated and managed to hold my doubts at bay for over a decade longer while serving God on the mission field.

Many if not most of you have faced similar questions and misgivings about the Bible and the Christian faith, even if not to the same extent. You might be like me during my initial short-lived crises of faith: I could not bring myself to face with courage the possibility that life might not have any cosmic Meaning; that there might be no higher power to guide, protect, and provide for me; that justice might not prevail in the long run; that I might no longer be able to hold sinners accountable with the words, "Thus says the Lord"; that life ends at the grave; or that I might have followed and lead others to follow a grand mistake. I lacked the courage to face my church, family, and friends whom I feared would look upon me as a reprobate. I lacked the courage to think for myself—to accept that the virtues of humility and meekness must not be used as an excuse for failing to challenge entrenched ideas that lack sufficient evidence.

In short, I preferred to squelch the seed of doubt and label it as sin rather than as healthy, critical thinking, lest it flower and make life unbearable. That I viewed my incipient doubt and disbelief as sin was no accident: the church has a powerful vested interest in keeping believers in the fold, and it *will not* let them go without a fight. My courage-squelching guilt or angst was the result of a concerted effort developed over the centuries to make me feel like a depraved worm, a proud and willful rebel, a traitor, a God-hater, and an enemy of all that is good. I was programmed to consider that I would be better off if I were to commit adultery or murder than if I were to abandon the one who created me and redeemed me. Without Christ I would be worse than a good-for-nothing, and, like the traitor Judas, it would have been better for me had I never been born. No wonder most believers never muster the courage to break free from this cage!

Note that it wasn't as though I was only pretending to believe during the decade that I continued in the faith after my initial doubts. I truly did believe, but only because I desperately wanted to believe, so I focused my attention on things that bolstered my faith. This approach worked for many years, but ultimately I could not sustain it.

If you have reservations about your faith but lack confidence to act on your doubts, I would encourage you to start by placing your toe in what from the outside looks like an icy pool of disbelief. Ask yourself, "What if the Christian gospel is untrue? What would the world be like?" Start a checklist like the following and surprise yourself with how many items you can check off. I found all of these things to be true during my deconversion process, helping to confirm I was onto something. As you stick your toe in that icy water, see whether these hold true for you as well; you might find the water to be strangely warmer than expected. If the Christian faith is untrue, then:

- It will make no difference whether or not I pray to be healthy, to be safe, or to find a lost item, despite Jesus' unconditional promise to grant me what I ask when I pray in his name (John 14:13–14). If I stop praying, good and bad things will happen to me on average at the same rate as when I prayed.

- If I renounce my faith, I will not be subject to "swift destruction" as 2 Peter 2:1 threatens. (Note: if this biblical threat is baseless *in this life* for millions of apostates like me, we ought have no fear of the biblical threats of hellfire *in the next life*!)

- I will find it no more difficult to control my passions as a skeptic than as a believer.

- I will begin to notice a similar mix of goodness and depravity in unbelievers as I observe in Christians. Believers and unbelievers will appear to have the same basic nature, with no apparent supernatural ability to be good conferred to the faithful.

- I will observe no appreciable difference between the fortune and misfortune that befall Christians and non-Christians having a similar culture, work ethic, and lifestyle. Evangelicals will experience no better health or safety on the road than Mormons, even though evangelicals believe Mormons pray to a false god.

- I will come to recognize that if Christianity is not divinely ordained, the following *must* hold true (note: this is not to say that these prove Christianity *untrue*, but only that they must be true if Christianity is untrue, which should at least temper our faith):
  - No miracles would be publicly or scientifically verifiable or reproducible on demand when calling on Jesus. (And believers would make up excuses as to why this should be the case, while placing the blame on the skeptics who call attention to this.)

o   The books of the Bible would have to have been written, selected and compiled by men, not written in the stars, for example, where they would have been immune from forgery. (And believers would offer arbitrary reasons for this situation, like, "God works through humans to accomplish his will"; or "God doesn't want to be too pushy or hit us over the head.")

o   The biblical manuscripts would have been subject to copyist errors like all other handwritten human manuscripts and would not have been kept from alteration over time. There would be multiple divergent copies, and it would be difficult to determine which ones are most faithful to the original. (Note: what is the point of making inerrant originals if they are not to be kept inerrant for later recipients?)

o   There would be significant differences of opinion on various topics among the biblical authors (whether or not they could be made by later apologists to agree).

o   There would be no unmistakable signs of supernatural inspiration in the Bible: no clear or detailed prophecies whose fulfillment can be positively ascertained to have happened without fabrication or whose fulfillment we can witness in our time, and no scientific insight ahead of its time (for example, that germs, rather than demons, cause disease; or that the earth revolves around the sun, which is an ordinary star; or that the earth is approximately 4.5 billion years old).

o   Believers who rely on guidance for their future based on the Bible or the Holy Spirit would be no less prone to making mistakes as nonbelievers who carefully but humanely weigh their options before making decisions.

o   Believers would be no less likely to perish in an airplane crash than their fellow unbelieving passengers, despite the many promises of protection in the Psalms, and despite the New Testament doctrine of guardian angels.

o   Those who curse God would be no more likely to face a premature death than those who don't, contrary to the supposition of Job's wife, who enjoined her suffering husband to "curse God and die" (Job 2:9).

- I would come to understand that in a natural universe, the following facts would have to be true, and the evidence would confirm each fact:
    o The universe would have to be enormous enough and contain enough stars and planets to allow at least one planet (the earth, and possibly many others) to have the right conditions to support conscious life. If ours were the only planet, and it just happened to have all the right conditions to support life, this would demand an explanation. As it is, the fortuitous placement of the earth at just the right distance from our star (the sun), for example, requires no explanation other than that there are billions of other planets in the universe, boosting the chances that at least one (the earth) should find itself if the right position. Note that until the 1990's it was an open question whether there existed other planets outside our solar system. This was a naturalistic presumption that has been recently borne out by the evidence; under theism, there was no reason to presume that other solar systems and planets should exist. (Using this as an analogy, could the same be true of multiple universes to explain the fine-tuning of our physical laws? It's difficult to say, but it certainly has not been ruled out.)
    o The universe would have to be old enough to have allowed life to evolve, not over thousands of years, but over billions of years. As it is, evidence from the IMAP satellite has pegged the age of the universe at about 13.7 billion years. We have witnessed supernova explosions up to 10 billion light years away, meaning they occurred some 10 billion years ago.
    o If conscious life developed naturalistically, it would have to be bound to a physical frame and a physical brain following physical laws. This could be true under theism, but we could also just as well be spirits without the need to eat and eliminate waste. Our minds could be spiritual, but as it is, all our mental faculties are traceable to particular regions of our physical brain, just as naturalism would demand.

In short, ask yourself the following questions as you place your toe in the water (which should be getting increasingly warm and comfortable): Is there *any* empirically verifiable difference between the world we observe and the world we would expect if the Christian god did not exist? And is there any satisfactory apologetic rejoinder to this state of affairs other than the suggestion that God doesn't want the evidence to be too obvious for fear that we would forfeit the free will he wishes us to enjoy (an approach that could at the same time validate all other religions, no matter how far removed from reality)? Does the apologist not have a better strategy than to heap blame and guilt on the doubter for failing to appreciate the evidence that the apologist finds satisfactory (but which looks for all the world like empty salesmanship to the doubter)?

As your entire foot enters the water, followed by your legs, consider taking a little swim in the waters of unbelief. You won't be struck by lightning (or, at least your chances will be no greater than for anyone else), and, if your experience is like mine, you'll find nothing—from sunrise to sundown, from sundown to sunup, from north to south and east to west, from the past to the present—nothing that will invalidate your new perspective that the Christian god resides only in the imagination of those who accept him. If your experience differs from mine, I will be eager to hear from you, but it won't do to hear anecdotes about the way the Lord has blessed you unless the blessings lie outside the realm of natural possibility, or unless you can demonstrate supernatural wonders for all to investigate publicly.

It's time for me to bring this book to a close. I find myself continually wanting to add more to it, but I realize no one will pick up a book that says everything I'd like to say—it would be significantly longer than this already beefy volume. But if this book has raised questions in your mind and you'd like to explore further, there are a great many helpful resources available for you, several of which I have indicated in earlier chapters.

The Secular Web (Secular Web 2009) boasts perhaps the most comprehensive set of skeptical resources available on the Internet. You might also enjoy listening to the weekly podcasts published from a skeptical standpoint by the Center for Inquiry (Grothe 2009).

Whether or not you ultimately agree with my perspective, I wish to express my appreciation for your having taken the time to consider my thoughts in this book. It is my hope that you will leave with at least some inkling of the intellectual and emotional struggle endured by the millions of us who have left the faith of our youth, and that you will come to consider it a virtue rather than a vice to examine your faith critically.

If you are in the process of deconversion, and if I have influenced you in any way to take this direction, perhaps you can identify with the character Jane in Agatha Christie's *Death in the Air* after the private investigator Hercule Poirot revealed her boyfriend to be a murderer:

"I ought to hate you, Monsieur Poirot." She looked pale and fine-drawn with dark circles round her eyes. Poirot said gently, "Hate me a little if you will. But I think you are one of those who would rather look truth in the face than live in a fool's paradise" (Christie 1974, 600).

My apostasy can hardly be said to be unique, even if the path I traveled was particular to me. From the many references made to apostasy in the New Testament—including Jesus' allusions to it in the parable of the sower and the seeds in Luke 8—to the many testimonies of former Christians published in books and on the Internet, it is clear that apostasy is neither a recent phenomenon nor a rare one. Biologist E. O. Wilson, Billy Graham's fellow traveling evangelist Charles Templeton, astronomer Chet Raymo, social scientist and science writer Michael Shermer, NBA basketball coach Phil Jackson, and New Testament scholar Bart Ehrman are some of the more notable genuine believers who eventually left the Christian faith. These famous examples are but the tip of the iceberg.

I dream of a world in which individuals are not evaluated on the basis of their metaphysical beliefs, where brother is not divided against brother, husband against wife, father against daughter, neighbor against neighbor, nation against nation. This will be a very different world from the one Jesus imagined:

> Do not suppose that I have come to bring peace to the earth. I did not come to bring peace, but a sword. For I have come to turn a man against his father, a daughter against her mother, a daughter-in-law against her mother-in-law—a man's enemies will be the members of his own household (Matthew 10:34–36).

I dream of a world where all the brightest minds are devoted to solving the challenges we are presented with in *this* world, not in any hoped-for world to come. No longer will bright, promising young people be diverted to the professions of pastor, priest, theologian, or proselytizing missionary. Instead, some of these same minds might be free to devote their energies to discovering cures for the scourges that still plague humanity, or to developing technologies that improve agricultural production, transportation, and communication for those who need it most. To be sure, not all will take a path that benefits society, but I can at least dream that a world free of religious divisions and diversions will be, on balance, better than one that is not.

I dream of a world not only where charity is practiced without ideological strings attached, but one in which the need for charity is reduced as pervasively unjust systems are supplanted by just political structures (we have, at least in the West, already come a long way since the time of the European monarchs), and one in which widespread technology and education improve the lot of those who might otherwise suffer deprivation.

I dream of a world where individuals are guided in their moral decisions only—and I do mean *only*—by the consequences of their actions on other sentient beings, not by the dictates of tradition or holy books. I am not a utopian; the dark side of human nature will always assert itself, regardless of which religious or nonreligious philosophy reigns. But there is no place in my dreams for a world in which we are judged more for our religious allegiances than for the tangible effects of our actions on others.

I dream of a world where young people can grow up without the need to take seriously the empty hellfire threats of believers. I dream this world will include you: my wife, my children, my friends and former friends, my country, and all nations. Yes, I'm a dreamer, and I know that many of my dreams will remain unfulfilled, but if you cannot take the path I have taken, then I dream you will at least come to accept your fellow members of the human family for who they are, rather than for their potential to leave the ranks of the damned and join the ranks of the eternally redeemed.

References

*Indicates references accessed through Google Books at http://books.google.com.
†Indicates references accessed through Amazon.com's "Look Inside the Book®" feature at http://www.amazon.com/books/.

2ndAmendment. 2005. "From Missionary Bible Translator to Agnostic." Southern Maryland Online. http://forums.somd.com/religion/62342-missionary-bible-translator-agnostic.html or http://tinyurl.com/czg3lx (accessed March 22, 2009).

Abdallah, Osama. n.d. "My rebuttal to Sam Shamoun's 'The Bible on Camels' Hooves' response." Answering Christianity. http://www.answering-christianity.com/camel_hooves_rebuttal.htm or http://tinyurl.com/5ofn7d (accessed March 1, 2009).

American Historical Association. 1888. *Papers of the American Historical Association.* New York: G. P. Putnam's Sons.*

Archer, Gleason. 1982. *Encyclopedia of Bible Difficulties.* Grand Rapids, MI: Zondervan.

Attar, Farid al-Din. 1177. *The Conference of the Birds.* Trans. Afkham Darbandi and Dick Davis. Repr., London: Penguin Classics, 1984.*

Augustine. 408 CE. *The Literal Meaning of Genesis (De Genesi ad litteram libri duodecim).* Trans. J. H. Taylor. Repr., Westminster, MD: Newman, 1982.*

Augustine, Keith. 2003. "Hallucinatory Near-Death Experiences." The Secular Web. http://www.freethought.org/library/modern/keith_augustine/HNDEs.html or http://tinyurl.com/2khl2b (accessed April 18, 2009).

Babinski, Edward T. 1995. *Leaving the Fold: Testimonies of Former Fundamentalists.* Amherst, NY: Prometheus.

———. 2005a. "Answers in Genesis' Response on Evidence for Whale Evolution." Edward T. Babinski's official website. http://www.edwardtbabinski.us/evolution/aig_response.html or http://tinyurl.com/2mljyl (accessed April 28, 2009).

———. 2005b. "What Happened to the Resurrected Saints?" Edward T. Babinski's official website. http://www.edwardtbabinski.us/religion/resurrected_saints.html or http://tinyurl.com/bx3l8n (accessed March 1, 2009).

———. 2005c. "Hell's Final Enigma." Edward T. Babinski's official website. http://www.edwardtbabinski.us/history/hell_final_enigma.html or http://tinyurl.com/yqoh23 (accessed May 18, 2009).

———. 2006. "The Lowdown on God's Showdown." Edward T. Babinski's official website. http://www.edwardtbabinski.us/religion/christ_return.html or http://tinyurl.com/39wy4o (accessed April 28, 2009).

Bacon, Francis. 1620. *The New Organon.* Bk. 1, *Selected Philosophical Works,* ed. Rose-Mary Sargent. Repr., Indianapolis: Hackett, 1999.* Quoted in Shermer 2006.

Baldwin, J. F. 1998. *The Deadliest Monster.* New Braunfels, TX: Fishermen.

Barker, Kenneth, ed. 1985. *The NIV Study Bible..* Grand Rapids, MI: Zondervan.

Behe, Michael J. 1996. *Darwin's Black Box: The Biochemical Challenge to Evolution.* New York: Free Press.

———. 2007. *The Edge of Evolution: The Search for the Limits of Darwinism.* New York: Free Press.

Benson, Herbert, MD et al. 2006. "Study of the Therapeutic Effects of Intercessory Prayer (STEP) in cardiac bypass patients: A multicenter randomized trial of uncertainty and certainty of receiving intercessory prayer." *American Heart Journal* 151, no. 4 (April): 934–942. doi:10.1016/j.ahj.2005.05.028 or http://tinyurl.com/9mwf2o (accessed March 16, 2009).

Biello, David. 2006. "Mutant Chicken Grows Alligatorlike Teeth." *Scientific American*, February 22. http://www.sciam.com/article.cfm?articleID=000E9965-99A6-13FB-99A683414B7F0000 or http://tinyurl.com/fyyd3 (accessed April 28, 2009).

Bierce, Ambrose and Bufe, Chaz. 2004. *The Devil's Dictionaries: The Best of the Devil's Dictionary and the American Heretic's Dictionary.* Tucson, AZ: See Sharp.*

Borg, Marcus J. 2003. *The Heart of Christianity: Rediscovering a Life of Faith.* San Francisco: HarperSanFrancisco.

Bottaro, Andrea, Matt A. Inlay, and Nicholas J. Matzke 2006. Supplementary material from "Immunology in the spotlight at the Dover 'Intelligent Design' trial." National Center for Science Education. http://www2.ncseweb.org/kvd/exhibits/immune/index.html or http://tinyurl.com/2vy48r (accessed March 16, 2009).

Boyd, Gregory A. 2003. *Letters From a Skeptic.* Colorado Springs, CO: Cook Communications.

———. 2007. *The Jesus Legend: A Case for the Historical Reliability of the Synoptic Jesus Tradition.* Grand Rapids, MI: Baker Academic.†

Boyd, Gregory and Robert M. Price. 2003. "Jesus: Legend, Teacher, Critic, or Son of God." Santa Barbara, CA: University of California at Santa Barbara. http://webcast.ucsd.edu:8080/ramgen/UCSD_TV/7816.rm or http://tinyurl.com/367xts with introduction at http://www.uctv.ucsb.edu/more/light/3816boyd.html or http://tinyurl.com/2xhr6l (accessed March 16, 2009).

Brooks, Arthur C. 2006. *Who Really Cares: The Surprising Truth about Compassionate Conservatism.* New York: Basic.*

Bruce, William Stratton. 1909. *The Ethics of the Old Testament.* Edinburgh: T & T Clark.

Bruns, Roger. 2004. *Billy Graham: A Biography.* Westport, CN: Greenwood.*

Buckley, Cara. 2007. "Man Is Rescued by Stranger on Subway Tracks." *The New York Times,* January 3. http://www.nytimes.com/2007/01/03/nyregion/03life.html or http://tinyurl.com/c9kroe (accessed March 16, 2009).

Bush, Albert O. 2001. *Parasitism: The Diversity and Ecology of Animal Parasites.* Cambridge, UK: Cambridge University.*

Calvin, John. 1578. *Commentaries on the First Book of Moses Called Genesis.* Trans. John King. Repr., Grand Rapids, MI: Baker, 1996. Also available at Christian Classics Ethereal Library. http://www.ccel.org/ccel/calvin/calcom01.vi.html or http://tinyurl.com/2xwdl5 (accessed January 7, 2009).

Carlton, Matthew. 2008. *The Translator's Reference Translation of the Gospel of Luke.* Dallas, TX: SIL International.

Carrier, Richard. 2005. *Sense and Goodness without God.* Bloomington, IN: AuthorHouse.

Carrier, Richard. 2006. "The Date of the Nativity in Luke," 5th ed. The Secular Web. http://www.freethought.org/library/modern/richard_carrier/quirinius.html or http://tinyurl.com/2v42r7 (accessed March 16, 2009).

Carville, James. 2003. *Had Enough? A Handbook for Fighting Back.* New York: Simon & Schuster.*

Christianity Today. 2007. "The New Intolerance." February.

Christie, Agatha. 1974. *Death in the Air.* In *Murder on Board: Including The Mystery of the Blue Train, What Mrs. McGillicuddy Saw, and Death in the Air.* New York: Dodd, Mead.*

Church Educational System. 2001. "War in the Last Days." In *The Doctrine and Covenants Student Manual: Religion 324–325.* Salt Lake City: Church of Jesus Christ of Latter Day Saints. http://www.ldsces.org/inst_manuals/dc-in/dc-in-081.htm#87 or http://tinyurl.com/a2ksnl (accessed April 29, 2009).

Churchill, Winston. 1947. (Speech to House of Commons.) In Keyes, Ralph. 2006. *The Quote Verifier: Who Said What, Where, and When.* New York: Macmillan.*

Coffee, Lane. 2008. "Notable Christians Open to an Old-universe, Old-earth Perspective." Reasons to Believe. http://www.reasons.org/resources/apologetics/notable_leaders/index.shtml or http://tinyurl.com/7lfe5z (accessed January 10, 2009).

Colenso, John William. 1865. *The Pentateuch and Book of Joshua Critically Examined.* London: Longman, Green, Longman, Roberts, & Green.*

Collins, John Joseph. 2005. *Encounters with Biblical Theology.* Philadelphia: Fortress.*

Collins, Francis. 2006. *The Language of God.* New York: Free Press.

Collins, Francis. 2007. Interview by D. J. Grothe. "Dr. Francis Collins – The Language of God." Point of Inquiry. Podcast. August 31, 2007. http://www.pointofinquiry.org/?p=125 (accessed May 18, 2009).

Conan Doyle, Sir Arthur. 1890. *The Sign of Four.* London: Spencer Blackett.*

Craig, William Lane. 1979. *The Kalam Cosmological Argument.* London: Macmillan. Quoted in Stenger 2007, 123.

Craig, William Lane and Ehrman, Bart. 2006. "Is There Historical Evidence for the Resurrection of Jesus? A Debate between William Lane Craig and Bart D. Ehrman." Worcester, MA: Holy Cross. http://www.holycross.edu/departments/crec/website/resurrection-debate-transcript.pdf or http://tinyurl.com/noue3 (accessed May 18, 2009).

Criswell, Evans A. 2001. "God's [*sic*] Admits His Laws Are No Good? Hogwash! (Ezekiel 20:25)." Plant Some Seeds and Watch Them Grow, Study #1 (March). http://hsvmovies.com/static_subpages/personal/seeds/s0001.html or http://tinyurl.com/nt4ss4 (accessed May 28, 2009).

Curtis, Bryan. 2002. *A Call to America: Inspiring Quotations from the Presidents of the United States.* New York: Gramercy.†

Dalrymple, Brent G. 2006. "How Old is the Earth: A Response to 'Scientific' Creationism." The TalkOrigins Archive. http://www.talkorigins.org/faqs/dalrymple/radiometric_dating.html or http://tinyurl.com/ypoawd (accessed May 18, 2009).

Daly, Martin, and Margo Wilson. 1988. *Homicide.* Hawthorne, NY: Aldine de Gruyter. Quoted in Pinker 2000, 182.

Daniels, Ken. 2003. "From Missionary Bible Translator to Agnostic." The Secular Web. http://www.freethought.org/library/modern/testimonials/daniels.html or http://tinyurl.com/36tz6o (accessed May 18, 2009).

Darwin, Charles, Francis Darwin, and Nora Barlow. 1958. *The Autobiography of Charles Darwin 1809–1882. With the original omissions restored. Edited and with appendix and notes by his granddaughter Nora Barlow.* London: Collins. http://darwin-online.org.uk/pdf/1958_autobiography_F1497.pdf, http://tinyurl.com/ckbc67, or http://tinyurl.com/37ecad (accessed May 18, 2009). Quoted in Sohail 2007.

Dawkins, Richard. 1995. "God's Utility Function." *Scientific American*, November.

———. 2006. *The God Delusion.* New York: Houghton Milton.

Debmski, William. 2004. Foreward to *What Darwin Didn't Know: A Doctor Dissects the Theory of Evolution*, by Geoffrey Simmons. Eugene, OR: Harvest House.

Dembski, William. 2008a. *Uncommon Descent.* December 3, 2008 Weblog entry entitled "Some Thanks for Professor Olofsson." http://www.uncommondescent.com/intelligent-design/some-thanks-for-professor-olofsson/#comment-299021 or http://tinyurl.com/6crutf (accessed May 18, 2009).

———. 2008b. *Uncommon Descent.* December 10, 2008 Weblog entry entitled "Reinstating the Explanatory Filter." http://www.uncommondescent.com/intelligent-design/reinstating-the-explanatory-filter/ or http://tinyurl.com/6bbk4b (accessed May 18, 2009).

Dembski, William and Wells, Jonathan. 2007. *The Design of Life: Discovering Signs of Intelligence In Biological Systems.* Richardson, TX: Foundation for Thought and Ethics.

Denis, Jacques-François. 1879. *Histoire des théories et des idées morales dans l'antiquité.* Paris : E. Thorin.*

Dennett, Daniel C. 2006. *Breaking the Spell: Religion as a Natural Phenomenon.* New York: Penguin.

de Smit, Merlijn. 2001. "Uralists Against History." http://www.geocities.com/Athens/Acropolis/3093/Uralists_Against_History.h tm or http://tinyurl.com/2ye65z (accessed May 18, 2009).

de Waal, Frans. 2005. *Our Inner Ape: A Leading Primatologist Explains Why We Are Who We Are.* New York: Penguin.

———. 2006. *Primates and Philosophers: How Morality Evolved.* Princeton, NJ: Princeton University Press.

Eagleton, Terry. 1991. *Ideology: An Introduction.* New York: Verso. Quoted in Dennett 2006.

Edgell, Penny. 2006. "Atheists identified as America's most distrusted minority, according to new U of M study." University of Minnesota Website. http://www1.umn.edu/news/news-releases/2006/UR_RELEASE_MIG_2816.html or http://tinyurl.com/r4jncj (accessed May 18, 2009).

Edwards, Jonathan. 1738. *Discourses on Various Important Subjects.* Boston: S. Kneeland and T. Green. Quoted in Babinski 2005, 59–60.

———. 1739. "The Eternity of Hell Torments." Sermon XI of *Forty Sermons on Various Subjects.* Vol. 4 of *The Works of President Edwards in Four Volumes.* Repr., New York: Leavitt, Trow & Co., 1843* Quoted in Babinski 2005c.

———. 1741. "Sinners in the Hands of an Angry God." http://www.ccel.org/ccel/edwards/sermons.sinners.html or http://tinyurl.com/2thx24 (accessed May 18, 2009).

Ehrman, Bart. 2008. *God's Problem: How the Bible Fails to Answer Our Most Important Question—Why We Suffer.* New York: HarperCollins Publishers.

Elder, John. 1960. *Prophets, Idols, and Diggers: Scientific Proof of Bible History.* Indianapolis, Indiana: Bobbs-Merrill Company.* Quoted in http://www.thetrumpet.com/index.php?page=article&id=1817 or http://tinyurl.com/27b4b6 (accessed August 28, 2007).

Eldin, Ahmed. n.d. "Is the Biblical God Able or Unable to Confront Iron Chariots?" Answering Christianity. http://www.answering-christianity.com/ahmed_eldin/is_god_able_or_not_able.htm or http://tinyurl.com/2v7mwo (accessed May 18, 2009).

Eldredge, John. 2001. *Wild at Heart: Discovering the Secret of a Man's Soul.* Nashville, TN: Thomas Nelson.

Faulkner, Danny. 1998. "The Current State of Creation Astronomy." From the *Institute for Creation Research* website. http://www.icr.org/research/index/researchp_df_r01 or http://tinyurl.com/92yxem (accessed January 11, 2009).

Feynman, Richard P. 2000. *The Pleasure of Finding Things Out: The Best Short Works of Richard P. Feynman.* Cambridge, Massachusetts: Da Capo Press.*

Finkelstein, Israel and Neil Asher Silberman. 2001. *The Bible Unearthed.* New York: Touchstone.

Forsberg, Rolf. 1972. *Peace Child.* Forsberg Associates and Gospel Films. Film.

Fouts, Roger. 1997. *Next of Kin: My Conversations with Chimpanzees.* New York: Avon.

Frost, David and Billy Graham. 1997. *Billy Graham: Personal Thoughts of a Public Man.* Colorado Springs: Cook Communications Ministries International.* Quoted in http://www.answersincreation.org/billy_graham.htm or http://tinyurl.com/7mv6we (accessed May 18, 2009).

Gaudia, Gill. 2007. "About Intercessory Prayer: A Proposal… Maybe." The Secular Web. http://www.secweb.org/index.aspx?action=viewAsset&id=749 or http://tinyurl.com/32ljct (accessed May 18, 2009).

Giberson, Karl W. 2008. "No Science Please. We're Evangelical." *Books & Culture*, September/October. http://www.christianitytoday.com/bc/2008/005/7.16.html or http://tinyurl.com/4c23ee (accessed May 18, 2009).

Goldingay, John. 1989. *Daniel.* Vol. 30 of *Word Biblical Commentary.* Nashville, TN: Word (Thomas Nelson).

Gordon, Cyrus H. and Gary A. Rendsburg. 1997. *The Bible and the Ancient Near East.* New York: W.W. Norton & Company, Inc.

Green, Keith. n.d. "What's Wrong With the Gospel? Section 2: 'The Added Parts.'" Lindale, TX: Last Days Ministries. http://www.lastdaysministries.org/articles/whatswrongwiththegospel2.html or http://tinyurl.com/2bfufy (accessed July 25, 2007). (As of May 21, 2009, no longer available at this site.)

Griffin, John Howard. 1961. *Black Like Me.* New York: Houghton Mifflin.

Gross, Neil and Solon Simmons. 2006. "How Religious Are America's College and University Professors?" http://religion.ssrc.org/reforum/Gross_Simmons.pdf or http://tinyurl.com/q24g5j (accessed May 18, 2009).

Grothe, D. J. 2009. Point of Inquiry. http://www.pointofinquiry.org (accessed March 22, 2009).

Grünbaum, Adolf. 2008. "Why Is There a Universe at All?" *Free Inquiry* 28, no. 4 (June/July).

Habermas, Gary. 2001. "Explaining Away Jesus' Resurrection: The Recent Revival of Hallucination Theories." *Christian Research Journal* 23, no. 4. http://www.garyhabermas.com/articles/crj_explainingaway/crj_explainingaway.htm#_edn36 or http://tinyurl.com/2r8dy3 (accessed May 18, 2009).

Haley, John W. 1876. *An Examination of the Alleged Discrepancies of the Bible.* Andover, MA: Warren F. Draper.

Ham, Ken and Byers, Stacia. 2000. "The Slippery Slide to Unbelief." *Creation Ex Nihilo* 22, vol. 3 (June): 8–13. http://www.answersingenesis.org/creation/v22/i3/unbelief.asp or http://tinyurl.com/2pnawq (accessed May 18, 2009).

Ham, Ken. 2008. "Speaking at the Pentagon." Answers in Genesis. http://blogs.answersingenesis.org/aroundtheworld/2008/06/18/speaking-at-the-pentagon/ or http://tinyurl.com/6c5uwn (accessed May 18, 2009).

Hamliton, William E., James Dobson, Duane Gish, and Hugh Ross. 1992. "Gish/Ross Focus on the Family Interview." http://www.skepticfiles.org/origins/gish-ros.htm or http://tinyurl.com/25azpd (accessed May 18, 2009).

Harrison, Guy P. 2008. *50 Reasons people give for believing in a god.* Amherst, NY: Prometheus.

Hartley, John E. 1992. *Leviticus 1–27.* Vol. 4 of *Word Biblical Commentary.* Nashville, TN: Word (Thomas Nelson).

Hawking, Stephen. 1998. *A Brief History of Time.* New York: Bantam.* Quoted in Stenger 2007, 126.

Hecht, Jennifer Michael. 2007. Interview by D. J. Grothe. "The Myth of Happiness." *Free Inquiry* 27, no. 5 (August/September): 8.

Herrel, Anthony et al. 2008. "Rapid large-scale evolutionary divergence in morphology and performance associated with exploitation of a different dietary resource." Abstract. *Proceedings from the National Academy of Sciences,* 105 no. 12 (March 25). doi:10.1073/pnas.0711998105, http://www.pnas.org/cgi/content/abstract/105/12/4792 or http://tinyurl.com/5cdkse (accessed May 18, 2009).

Hitler, Adolf. 1939. *Mein Kampf.* Trans. Alvin Saunders Johnson and John Chamberlain. New York: Reynal & Hitchcock.*

Holding, James Patrick. 2007. *The Impossible Faith.* Longwood, FL: Xulon Press.

Horner, Michael and Barker, Dan. 1996. "Did Jesus Really Rise From The Dead?" The Secular Web. http://www.freethought.org/library/modern/dan_barker/barker_horner.html or http://tinyurl.com/3dye7g (accessed May 18, 2009).

Howard-Snyder, Daniel, ed. 1996. *The Evidential Argument from Evil.* Bloomington, Indiana: Indiana University Press.

Howse, Brannon. 2005. *One Nation Under Man?: The Worldview War Between Christians And the Secular Left.* Nashville, TN: Boradman & Holman.

Hunter, Cornelius G. 2002. *Darwin's God: Evolution and the Problem of Evil.* Grand Rapids, MI: Brazos Press.

Huxley, Leonard and Huxley, Thomas Henry. 1901. *Life and Letters of Thomas Henry Huxley.* New York: D. Appleton and Company.

Hyles, Martin Luther. 2005a. "The Apostasy of Missionary Ken Daniels, Part 1." The Fighting Fundamental Forums. http://www.fundamentalforums.com/showthread.php?t=236 or http://tinyurl.com/6dtxrh (accessed March 22, 2009).

Hyles, Martin Luther. 2005b. "Part 2: the Apostasy of Missionary Ken Daniels." The Fighting Fundamental Forums. http://www.fundamentalforums.com/showthread.php?t=268 or http://tinyurl.com/62z5uv (accessed March 22, 2009).

Hyles, Martin Luther. 2005c. "Part 3: the Apostasy of Missionary Ken Daniels." The Fighting Fundamental Forums.

http://www.fundamentalforums.com/showthread.php?t=277 or
http://tinyurl.com/68kpo9 (accessed March 22, 2009).

Hyles, Martin Luther. 2005d. "Part 5: the Apostasy of Missionary Ken Daniels."
The Fighting Fundamental Forums.
http://www.fundamentalforums.com/showthread.php?t=410 or
http://tinyurl.com/5qrygh (accessed March 22, 2009).

Ingersoll, Robert. 1880. "What Must We Do to Be Saved?" In *Lectures*. Vol. 1 of
The Works of Robert Green Ingersoll, ed. Herman E. Kittredge. Repr., New
York: Dresden, 1902.*

———. 1884. "Orthodoxy." In *Lectures*. Vol. 2 of *The Works of Robert Green
Ingersoll*, ed. Herman E. Kittredge. Repr., New York: Dresden, 1915.*

———. 1889. "Why Am I an Agnostic?" In *Miscellany*. Vol. 11 of *The Works of
Robert Green Ingersoll*, ed. Herman E. Kittredge. Repr., New York: Dresden,
1909.*

———. 1896. "Why I Am an Agnostic." In *Lectures*. Vol. 4 of *The Works of
Robert Green Ingersoll*, ed. Herman E. Kittredge. Repr., New York: Dresden,
1915.*

Irenaeus. ca. 180 CE. *Five Books of S. Irenaeus: Bishop of Lyons, Against
Heresies*. Trans. John Keeble. Repr., Oxford: James Parker, 1872.*

Isaak, Mark. 2006. "An Index to Creationist Claims." The TalkOrigins Archive.
http://talkorigins.org/indexcc/ (accessed March 18, 2009).

Jarrel, Willis Anselm. 1882. *Old Testament Ethics Vindicated*. Greenville, TX:
W. A. Jarrel.

Jha, D. N. 2001. Interview by Michael Sullivan. "India Uproar Over Holy Cows."
RealPlayer® audio file. *National Public Radio Morning Edition*, August 10.
http://www.npr.org/templates/story/story.php?storyId=1127197 or
http://tinyurl.com/25rkqu (accessed May 19, 2009).

Johnson, Paul. 1988. *Intellectuals*. New York: Harper and Row.

Joyce, Kathryn. 2006. "Arrows for the War." *The Nation*, November 22.
http://www.thenation.com/doc/20061127/joyce/2 or http://tinyurl.com/5pe385
(accessed April 24, 2007).

Josephus. ca. 94 CE. *Jewish Antiquities* Trans. William Whiston. Repr., Ware,
Hertfordshire UK: Wordsworth, 2006.*

Kennedy, John W. 1998. "Missions: From Trauma to Truth." *Christianity Today*,
April 27. http://ctlibrary.com/1384 (accessed May 19, 2009).

Kida, Thomas. 2006. *Don't Believe Everything You Think: The 6 Basic Mistakes
We Make in Thinking*. Amherst, NY: Prometheus.

Konig, George. 2001–2008. "Is God omnipotent (all-powerful)?"
AboutBibleProphecy.com. http://www.aboutbibleprophecy.com/q16.htm
(accessed May 19, 2009).

Korthof, Gert. 2007. "Either Design or Common Descent." Towards the Third
Evolutionary Synthesis. http://home.planet.nl/~gkorthof/korthof86.htm or
http://tinyurl.com/3ehkm5 (accessed May 19, 2009).

LaHaye, Tim and David Noebel. 2000. *Mind Seige: The Battle for Truth*.
Nashville, TN: Word.

Lakoff, George. 1990. *Women, Fire, and Dangerous Things*. Chicago: University
of Chicago Press.

Leap, Dennis. 2005. "Archeology Proves Bible History Accurate." The Trumpet.com. http://www.s8int.com/page34.html (accessed May 19, 2009).

Lenski, Richard E.; Charles Ofria, Robert T. Pennock, and Christoph Adami. 2003. "The evolutionary origin of complex features." *Nature* 423 (May 8): 139-44. Abstract. doi:10.1038/nature01568 (accessed May 19, 2009). Full text available http://www.msu.edu/~pennock5/research/papers/Nature_EvoComplex.pdf or http://tinyurl.com/f98nq (accessed May 19, 2009).

Lenz, Max, ed. 1891. *Briefwechsel Landgraf Philip's des Grossmüthigen von Hessen mit Bucer.* Leipzig, Germany: S. Hirzel. Quoted in Sissela Bok, *Lying: Moral Choice in Public and Private Life* (New York: Vintage, 1999), 47.† Citation also quoted in Heinrich Denifle and Albert Maria Weiss, *Luther und Luthertum in der ersten Entwickelung: Quellenmässig dargestellt* (Mainz, Germany: F. Kirchheim, 1904), 90, 348.*

Lester, David. 2005. *Is There Life After Death? An Examination of the Empirical Evidence.* Jefferson, NC: McFarland & Company.

Lewis, C. S. 1940. *The Problem of Pain.* Repr., New York: HarperCollins, 2001.†

———. 1946. *The Great Divorce.* New York: MacMillan Publishing Company.

———. 1947. *Miracles.* London: Robert MacLehose.

———. 1950. *The Lion, the Witch and the Wardrobe* Repr., New York: HarperCollins, 1978.*

———. 1952. *Mere Christianity.* New York: HarperCollins.

———. 1954. *English Literature in the 16th Century, Excluding Drama.* Oxford: Clarendon Press.*

———. 1955. *Surprised by Joy.* Repr., New York: Houghton Mifflin Harcourt, 1995.*

———. 1960. *The World's Last Night* Repr., New York: Houghton Mifflin Harcourt, 2002.*

———. 1970. *God in the Dock: Essays on Theology and Ethics.* Repr., The Trustees of the Estate of C. S. Lewis, 2001.

Licona, Michael and Richard Carrier. 2004. "Licona vs. Carrier: On the Resurrection of Jesus Christ." Streaming or QuickTime video. The Veritas Forum. http://www.veritas.org/media/talks/396 and http://www.veritas.org/media/talks/399 (accessed May 19, 2009).

Lightfoot, J. B. and J. R. Harmer. 1992. "The Fragments of Papias." In *The Apostolic Fathers: Greek Texts and English Translations of Their Writings.* 2nd ed. Repr., Grand Rapids, MI: Baker Bytes, 1998.†

Lightner, Jean. 2008. "Life: Designed by God to Adapt." Answers in Genesis. http://www.answersingenesis.org/articles/aid/v3/n1/life-designed-to-adapt or http://tinyurl.com/opm42b (accessed May 20, 2009).

Lindskoog, Kathryn Ann. 2001. *Sleuthing C. S. Lewis: More Light in the Shadowlands.* Macon, Georgia: Mercer University Press.*

Loftus, John. 2008. *Why I Became an Atheist.* Amherst, NY: Prometheus.

Lowder, Jeffrey and Phil Fernandes. 1999. "The Lowder-Fernandes Debate: Naturalism vs. Theism: Where Does the Evidence Point?" Original VHS video no longer available.

http://video.google.com/videoplay?docid=7385355182363346492 or http://tinyurl.com/pov4bp (accessed May 19, 2009).

Luther, Martin. ca. 1540. *Conversations with Luther: Selections from Recently Published Sources of the Table Talk.* Trans. Preserved Smith and Herbert Percival Gallinger. Repr., 1915. Boston: The Pilgrim Press.*

———. 1541. Trans. William Hazlitt. *Table Talk.* Christian Classics Ethereal Library. http://www.ccel.org/ccel/luther/tabletalk.html or http://tinyurl.com/osat7m (accessed May 20, 2009).

———. 1543. "Luther the Controversialist: On the Jews and their Lies." In *Martin Luther's Basic Theological Writings.* Ed. Timothy F. Lull. Repr., Minneapolis, MN: Augsburg Fortress, 2005.†

Matson, Dave E. 2004. *How Good Are Those Young-Earth Arguments? A Close Look at Dr. Hovind's List of Young-Earth Arguments and Other Claims.* Pasadena, CA: Dave E. Matson. http://www.skeptictank.org/hs/matson-v.htm (accessed March 18, 2009).

Matzke, N. J. 2003. "Evolution in (Brownian) space: a model for the origin of the bacterial flagellum." http://www.talkdesign.org/faqs/flagellum.html or http://tinyurl.com/qugehh (accessed May 20, 2009).

Max, Edward E. 1986–2003. *Plagiarized Errors and Molecular Genetics.* http://www.talkorigins.org/faqs/molgen/ (accessed May 20, 2009).

McCabe, Tim. 2003. "Sad, sad, sad." Review of *A Marvelous Work and a Wonder*, by Legrand Richards. http://www.amazon.com/review/R24VPAJ1GNC5XU/ref=cm_cr_rdp_perm or http://tinyurl.com/lshffk (accessed May 28, 2009).

McDowell, Josh. 1979. *Evidence That Demands a Verdict.* Repr., San Bernardino, CA: Here's Life, 2004.

McDowell, Josh and Don Stewart. 1986. *Reasons Skeptics Should Consider Christianity.* Carol Stream, IL: Tyndale.

Meacham, Jon. 2007. "The God Debate." *Newsweek*, April 9.

Metzger, Bruce M. and Michael D. Coogan, eds. 1993. *The Oxford Companion to the Bible.* Oxford: Oxford University Press. (Article by J.M. Cook.)

Miller, Kenneth. 1999. *Finding Darwin's God: A Scientist's Search for Common Ground Between God and Evolution.* New York: HarperCollins.

———. 2008. *Only a Theory: Evolution and the Battle for America's Soul.* New York: Viking Adult.

Miller, Richard L. 2008a. "'I Shall Never Get to the Resting Place': The religious skepticism of Abraham Lincoln." *Free Inquiry* 29, no. 1 (December 2008/January 2009). http://www.secularhumanism.org/index.php?section=library&page=miller_29 _1 or http://tinyurl.com/9xa7ly (accessed January 10, 2009).

Moreland, J. P. 1987. *Scaling the Secular City: A Defense of Christianity.* Grand Rapids, MI: Baker Academic.

Morris, Henry M. 1974. *Scientific Creationism.* Green Forest, AR: Master.†

Musgrave, Ian. 2007. "The Open Letters File." *The Panda's Thumb.* http://pandasthumb.org/archives/2007/11/the-open-letter.html or http://tinyurl.com/2m7kyh (accessed May 21, 2009).

Nickell, Joe. 2007. Interview by D. J. Grothe. "The New Idolatry." Point of Inquiry. Podcast. September 28. http://www.pointofinquiry.org/?p=129 (accessed October 7, 2007).

Nielsen, Kai. 1973. *Ethics Without God.* Amherst, NY: Prometheus. Quoted in Stenger 2007, 252.

Noē, John. 1996. "Didn't Jesus Return When He Said He Would?" Prophecy Reformation Institute. http://www.prophecyrefi.org/excerpt4.htm or http://tinyurl.com/o69l3p (accessed May 21, 2009).

Noordtzij, Arie. 1982. *Leviticus.* Bible Student's Commentary. Grand Rapids, MI: Zondervan.

———. 1983. *Numbers.* Bible Student's Commentary. Grand Rapids, MI: Zondervan.

Numbers, Ronald. 2006. *The Creationists: From Scientific Creationism to Intelligent Design*, Expanded Edition. Harvard University Press.

Oard, Michael. 2001. "Do Greenland ice cores show over one hundred thousand years of annual layers?" Answers in Genesis. http://www.answersingenesis.org/tj/v15/i3/greenland.asp or http://tinyurl.com/5rlhdk (accessed May 21, 2009).

Olofsson, Peter. 2008. "Probability, Statistics, Evolution, and Intelligent Design." *Chance* 21, no. 3. http://ramanujan.math.trinity.edu/polofsson/research/Chance.pdf or http://tinyurl.com/5s7k5q (accessed May 21, 2009).

Orwell, George. 1946. *Animal Farm*. Repr., New York: Signet Classic, 1996.*

"Overview of Medjugorje." 2006. Medjugorje Web. http://www.medjugorje.org/overview.htm (accessed May 20, 2009).

Paine, Thomas. 1775. "African Slavery in America." In Vol. 1 of *The Writings of Thomas Paine.* Ed. Moncure Daniel Conway. Repr., New York: G. P. Putnam's Sons, 1896.

———. 1794. *The Age of Reason.* Repr., New York: Truth Seeker, 1898.*

———. 1797. "A Letter to Mr. Erskine." In Vol. 4 of *The Writings of Thomas Paine.* Repr., New York: G. P. Putnam's Sons, 1896.

———. 1807. *An Examination of the Passages in the New Testament, Quoted from the Old, and Called Prophecies of the Coming of Jesus Christ.* In *The Theological Works.* Repr., Boston: J. P. Mendum, 1859.

Panda's Thumb. 2009. http://pandasthumb.org/about.html (accessed March 18, 2009).

Parsons, Keith M. 1989. *God and the Burden of Proof: Plantinga, Swinburne, and the Analytic Defense of Theism.* Buffalo, NY: Prometheus.†

Pascal, Blaise. 1670. *Pensées.* Trans. W. F. Trotter. Repr., Minneola, NY: Dover Publications, 2003.*

Paul, Gregory. 2005. "Cross-National Correlations of Quantifiable Societal Health with Popular Religiosity and Secularism in the Prosperous Democracies." *Journal of Religion and Society* 7. http://moses.creighton.edu/JRS/2005/2005-11.html or http://tinyurl.com/dycnt (accessed May 24, 2009).

Paul, Gregory S. 2008. "The Big Religion Questions Finally Solved." *Free Inquiry* 29, no. 1 (December 2008/January 2009): 24–36.

Pennock, Robert T. 1999. *Tower of Babel: The Evidence against the New Creationism.* Cambridge, MA: Massachusetts Institute of Technology.

Pigliucci, Massimo. 2002. *Denying Evolution: Creationism, Scientism, and the Nature of Science.* Sunderland, MA: Sinauer Associates.†

Pink, Arthur W. 1922. *Gleanings in Genesis.* Chicago: Moody Bible Institute.*

Pinker, Steven. 2002. *The Blank Slate: The Modern Denial of Human Nature.* New York: Penguin.

Pinker, Steven. 2007. Interview by Marion Long. "The Discover Interview: Steven Pinker." *Discover*, September.

Piper, John. 2004. *Don't Waste Your Life.* Wheaton, IL: Good News.

Plantinga, Alvin. 2000. *Warranted Christian Belief.* Oxford: Oxford University.

———. 2007. "The Dawkins Confusion." *Books and Culture*, March/April 2007. http://www.christianitytoday.com/bc/2007/002/1.21.html or http://tinyurl.com/23cknc (accessed May 24, 2009).

Price, Robert M. 1993. *Beyond Born Again: Towards Evangelical Maturity.* http://www.freethought.org/library/modern/robert_price/beyond_born_again/index.shtml or http://tinyurl.com/68ao93 (accessed May 24, 2009).

———. 2003. *The Incredible Shrinking Son of Man.* Amherst, NY: Prometheus.

———. 2006. *The Reason Driven Life.* Amherst, NY: Prometheus.

———. 2007. *Jesus is Dead.* Cranford, NJ: American Atheist Press.

Price, Robert M. and Jeffrey Jay Lowder, eds. 2005. *The Empty Tomb: Jesus Beyond the Grave.* Amherst, NY: Prometheus.

Pride, Mary. 1985. *The Way Home: Beyond Feminism, Back to Reality.* Wheaton, IL: Good News.

Ramsden, Michael. 2001. "Is Our Future Determined or Free?" http://www.rzim.org/resources/jttran.php?seqid=79 or http://tinyurl.com/5uovs6 (accessed August 30, 2007). (As of May 24, 2009, the original essay is longer available at this location.)

Ray, Thomas. 1991. "TIERRA - Evolution Simulator Announcement." TalkOrigins Archive. http://www.talkorigins.org/faqs/tierra.html (accessed May 24, 2009).

Richards, LeGrand. 1950. *A Marvelous Work and a Wonder: Church of Jesus Christ of Latter Day Saints.* Repr., Whitefish, MT: Kessinger, 2004.*

Ross, Hugh and Samuel Conner. 1999. "The Unraveling of Starlight and Time." Reasons to Believe. http://www.reasons.org/unraveling-starlight-and-time-0 or http://tinyurl.com/pec7y9 (accessed May 24, 2009).

Russell, Bertrand. 1950. *Unpopular Essays.* New York: Simon & Schuster.

Sandoval, Craig. 2008. "Jeremiah's Covenant vs. Christianity." The Secular Web. http://secweb.org/?kiosk=articles&id=785 or http://tinyurl.com/qn3gwx (accessed May 24, 2009).

Sagan, Carl. 1996. *The Demon-Haunted World.* New York: Ballantine.

Schaeffer, Francis. 1985. *The Complete Works of Francis A. Schaeffer: A Christian Worldview.* Wheaton, IL: Crossway.

Schaff, Philip. 1892. *Modern Christianity: The Swiss Reformation.* Vol. 7 of *The History of the Reformation: History of the Christian Church.* New York: C. Scribner's Sons.*

Scholem, Gershom Gerhard. 1973. *Sabbatai Sevi: The Mystical Messiah, 1626–1676.* Princeton, NJ: Princeton University Press.*

Secular Web. 2009. http://www.freethought.org (accessed March 22, 2009).

Shapiro, Robert. 2007. "A Simpler Origin for Life." *Scientific American*, June.

Shermer, Michael. 2004. "The Enchanted Glass." *Scientific American*, May.

———. 2006. "The Political Brain: A recent brain-imaging study shows that our political predilections are a product of unconscious confirmation bias." *Scientific American*, May.

———. 2007. "Bush's Mistake and Kennedy's Error: Self-deception proves itself to be more powerful than deception." *Scientific American*, May.

Slusher, Harold. 1980. *The Age of the Cosmos.* Santee, CA: Institute for Creation Research.

Smith, Abbie. 2007. "ERV & HIV versus Behe. Behe Loses." The Panda's Thumb. http://www.pandasthumb.org/archives/2007/08/erv_hiv_versus.html or http://tinyurl.com/3xd48q (accessed May 24, 2009).

Sohail, Khalid. 2007. "Darwin's Conflict with His Wife and God." The Secular Web. http://www.secweb.org/index.aspx?action=viewAsset&id=765 or http://tinyurl.com/yr22qs (accessed February 2, 2009).

Solomon, Robert C. and Kathleen M. Higgins. 1996. *A Short History of Philosophy.* Oxford: Oxford University.

Sparks, H. F. D. 1984. *The Apocryphal Old Testament.* Oxford: Oxford University.*

Stackhouse, John G. 2007. "Christian Vision Project: A Bigger—and Smaller—View of Mission." In *Books and Culture: A Christian Review*, May/June. http://www.christianitytoday.com/bc/2007/003/11.26.html or http://tinyurl.com/3ay74h (accessed May 28, 2009).

Stark, Thom. 2009. "Prophetic Condemnations of Human Sacrifice." In "Human Sacrifice, Pt. 5." JesusPolitics.net. http://thomstark.jesuspolitics.net/?p=513 (accessed May 28, 2009).

Stenger, Victor. 2007. *God: The Failed Hypothesis.* Amherst, NY: Prometheus.

Strobel, Lee. 1998. *The Case for Christ.* Grand Rapids, MI: Zondervan.

———. 2000. *The Case for Faith.* Grand Rapids, MI: Zondervan.

———. 2004. *The Case for a Creator.* Grand Rapids, MI: Zondervan.

Sullivan, Randall. 2004. *The Miracle Detectives.* New York: Grove Press.†

Sutera, Raymond. 2001. "The Origin of Whales and the Power of Independent Evidence." The TalkOrigins Archive. http://www.talkorigins.org/features/whales (accessed May 28, 2009).

Talbott, Thomas. 1999. *The Inescapable Love of God.* Boca Raton, FL: Universal-Publishers.

TalkOrigins Archive 2006. http://www.talkorigins.org (accessed March 18, 2009).

Tavris, Carol. 2007. Interview by D. J. Grothe. "Carol Tavris - Mistakes Were Made." Point of Inquiry. Podcast. August 3, 2007. http://www.pointofinquiry.org/?p=121 (accessed May 28, 2009).

Taylor, Kevin D. 2004. "A Marvelous Book!" Review of *A Marvelous Work and a Wonder*, by Legrand Richards.

http://www.amazon.com/review/R1HNS1R1I463E8/ref=cm_cr_rdp_perm or http://tinyurl.com/nos2ep (accessed May 28, 2009).

Teeple, Howard M. 1994. *How Did Christianity Really Begin? A Historical-Archaeological Approach.* Evanston, IL: Religion and Ethics Institute.

Theobald, Douglas. 2007a. "29+ Evidences for Macroevolution." TalkOrigins Archive. http://www.talkorigins.org/faqs/comdesc/ (accessed May 28, 2009).

———. 2007b. "The Mullerian Two-Step: Add a part, make it necessary." TalkOrigins Archive. http://talkorigins.org/faqs/comdesc/ICsilly.html (accessed May 28, 2009).

Thielicke, Helmut. 1961. *How the World Began—Man in the First Chapters of the Bible.* Trans. John W. Doberstein. Philadelphia: Fortress Press.

Vinther, Bo Møllesøe. 2006. "Greenland and North Atlantic climatic conditions during the Holocene - as seen in high resolution stable isotope data from Greenland ice cores." PhD diss., University of Copenhagen. http://www.iceandclimate.nbi.ku.dk/publications/theses/PhD_Afhandling_Bo_Vinther_ny.pdf or http://tinyurl.com/8lydcp (accessed May 28, 2009).

Wagg, Jeff. 2008. "One Million Dollar Paranormal Challenge." James Randi Educational Foundation. http://www.randi.org/research/ (accessed March 22, 2009).

Whitcomb, John C. and Henry M. Morris. 1961. *The Genesis Flood: The Biblical Record and Its Scientific Implications.* Philadelphia: Presbyterian & Reformed.

Whybray, R. Norman. 1995. *Introduction to the Pentateuch.* Grand Rapids, MI: Wm B. Eerdmans.

Wicker, Christine. 2000. "Dumbfounded by Divorce: Survey inspires debate over why faith isn't a bigger factor in marriage." Adherents.com. http://www.adherents.com/largecom/baptist_divorce.html or http://tinyurl.com/gn626 (accessed May 28, 2009).

Wildman, Derek E. et al. 2003. "Implications of natural selection in shaping 99.4% nonsynonymous DNA identity between humans and chimpanzees: Enlarging genus *Homo*." *Proceedings of the National Academy of Sciences* 100, no. 12 (June 10): 7181-7188. doi:10.1073/pnas.1232172100 or http://tinyurl.com/lcd4zg (accessed May 28, 2009).

Willis, Clay. n.d. "Has Anyone Ever Seen God?" BibleStudy.org. http://www.biblestudy.org/question/has-anyone-actually-seen-god.html or http://tinyurl.com/4l6lr2 (accessed March 22, 2009).

Willis, Robert. 1877. *Servetus and Calvin: A Study of an Important Epoch in the Early History of the Reformation.* London: Henry S. King.*

Wilson, E. O. 1998. *Consilience: The Unity of Knowledge.* New York: Random House.

Wise, Kurt. P. 1995. "Towards a Creationist Understanding of Transitional Forms." Center for Origins Research (CORE). http://www.bryancore.org/anniversary/04.pdf (accessed May 28, 2009).

Yancey, Philip. 1988. *Disappointment with God.* Grand Rapids, MI: Zondervan.

Young, Davis. 1988. *Christianity and the Age of the Earth.* Muskogee, OK: Artisan Publishers.

Young, Davis A. and Ralph F. Stearley. 2008. *The Bible, Rocks and Time: Geological Evidence for the Age of the Earth.* Grand Rapids, MI: IVP Academic.

Made in the USA
Lexington, KY
19 July 2013